*I would like to dedicate this work to three
dear friends who have recently passed away
– Eric Tabarly, Gian Marco Borea d'Olmo,
and Pier Francesco Gavagnin – as well as to
my fellow skippers and the crews of vintage
yachts, and to all those who have made
organizational, technical, or financial
contributions to the revival of sailing
in the waters around Imperia.*

And, to "Her."

Flavio Serafini

Vintage Yachts
of the World

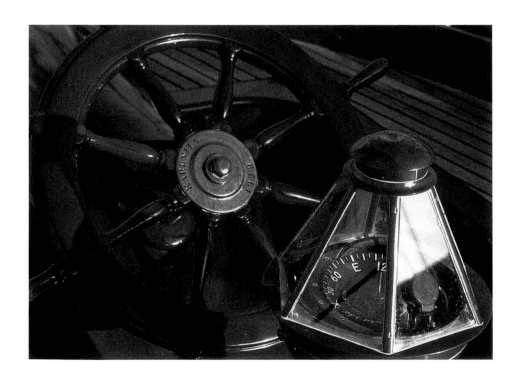

Feierabend

© 2003 Feierabend Verlag OHG
Mommsenstr. 43
D- 10629 Berlin

Translation from the Italian: Patrick Barr and Leslie Ray in association
with Cambridge Publishing Management Ltd, Cambridge, UK.
Project management: Cambridge Publishing Management Ltd.
Typesetting: Julie Crane in association with Cambridge Publishing
Management Ltd, Cambridge, UK.
Printing and Binding: Grafiche Busti – Colognola ai Colli (Vr), Italy

Printed in Italy
ISBN 3-936761-51-5
61 02020 1

Original edition © Gribaudo, Savigliano (Cn), Italy
edizioni.gribaudo@libero.it

Project manager: Stefano Delmastro, Stefano Delprete
Realization: Ufficio Tecnico Gribaudo
Design: Federico Carlo Peverada
Lithography: Gi.mac, Savigliano (Cn), Italy

Key to abbreviations:	
L.	Length
W.l.	Waterline
B.	Beam
Df.	Draft
Displ.	Displacement

Preface

onoré de Balzac once wrote, "There are three ideals of beauty: a beautiful woman dancing, a thoroughbred horse galloping, and a sailing boat with sails unfurled to the wind." Never a truer word was spoken, for Balzac's declaration manages to capture the perfect balance of movement, grace, and the ideal of beauty.

Sailing is the oldest form of human adventure, a school of life that has accompanied man throughout history, and it will always be an integral part of our concept of nature and of the challenges it offers.

The great merchant sailing-boats finally disappeared from the world's oceans after the Pamir tragedy (1957), but it was during this same period that sailing achieved a notable success with the foundation of the Sail Training Association. This organization's main aims included that of encouraging interest in sailing among young people. The training ships, which had been through rather difficult times, experienced an incredible revival as their numbers grew. This same period saw the beginnings of Operation Sail, the International Training Ship Races, and the International Sailing Festivals, all of which aimed to bring together boat-owners, skippers, and sailing enthusiasts with their shared passion for a world that was now re-emerging with increased vigor and life.

Nautical architecture is once again being appreciated and, as my dear friend Vittorio G. Rossi so rightly put it, "The architecture of sails and rigging remains the most beautiful form of architecture left in these barbaric times of ours!"

Yachting has led to the radical reevaluation of the unjustly neglected work of many boat designers and it has given a much-needed impulse to the boating world, with the transformation of the work of both old and new shipyards. Too many sailing boats of great historical value lay neglected in scattered deserted coves. Without taking into account the work of famous international architects such as Fife, Nicholson, Alden, Herreshoff, Giles, and so on, Italy alone boasts a considerable heritage of sailing-boat design – the creations of naval architects like Briasco, Oneto, Baglietto, Gotuzzo, Martinolich, Chiggiato, and Costaguta – all of which were in danger of disappearing altogether after dozens of beautiful boats had been allowed to go to ruin.

However, during the 1960s, people realized that a sailing boat was worth conserving since it symbolized its own particular historical period. It was an object of cultural value, the work of gifted designers as well as a mark of a particular lifestyle, and not simply an ostentatious status symbol or fashion item. Once again, people began to fall in love with the graceful, old "ladies" of the seas and the rare woods used to build them, and there was renewed interest in their elegant designs, the traditional values they represented, and the honest daily effort required from those who wished to enjoy the freedom of the seas.

All historical boats possess the same degree of dignity. There is no such thing as a more beautiful or less beautiful boat, but only boats that remain more or less faithful to their original design – an essential factor to be taken into account when evaluating the intrinsic worth of each vessel. I will never tire of repeating just how significant the original design is. In many European countries, thanks to the deeply rooted convictions of certain enthusiasts, a new mentality is emerging that recognizes the importance of saving those few remaining vessels defined, rather inappropriately, as vintage yachts.

To give just one example, in 1982 the Italian Vintage Yacht Association was set up with the precise aims of evaluating and classifying hulls and rigging dating from before 1950, of promoting meetings, and of bringing to light any stories and traditions pertaining to the world of sailing. The results were soon seen. Gatherings of vintage yachts blossomed, with an ever-increasing number of boats taking part and growing interest on the part of an increasingly sizeable and expert public. You only have to think of the efforts made by the town of Imperia in Liguria, Italy, with its International Naval Museum (a wonderful tribute to the history of sailing), the monument to the Cape Horn Sailor, and the biennial gathering of vintage yachts. The list could go on.

Given this remarkable reawakening of interest, national governments have been called upon, in particular through the approval of specific European regulations, to adopt an approach that recognizes the value of these historical boats and to provide tax relief to boat-owners for the management and restoration (under the supervision of a special body) of all those boats that have played a part in the history of their particular nation's navy.

After decades of neglect, there is now a real need for proper documentation to put some order into the architectural and historical archives. Restoration work should be based on the original plans and performed in a meticulous manner. To this end, specialized shipyards with proven experience should be commissioned to do the work (there are a great many such yards throughout the world). Even if this means that the boat is "landlocked" for a considerable period of time, the important thing is that the job is completed to the very highest, state-of-the-art standards.

A great number of people have already started doing just this. I personally know a variety of skippers and boat-owners who pay loving attention to their boats and, in a symbiotic relationship, spend considerable energy and money on restoration and maintenance. For example, Michele Amorosi of Derida, or the friends of Molly, capable of searching for months for a historical block; or Captain Jean Claude Lehöerff of Nocturne, who chose to conserve the bare simplicity of his boat – as a result of which he is forced to perform athletic maneuvers reminiscent of Conrad's sea-going heroes – rather than alter its original design. Then there are people like Chicco Zaccagni with his beautiful Alzavola, and Gian Marco Borea with the splendid Vistona, who in order to service and restore their boats were forced to charter them out for years. However, as well as these praiseworthy endeavors, there are also others who, for the sake of convenience, rashly decided to demolish original components with which the vessels were built.

One thing unites those skippers and owners who really love their boats – a profound belief in the fact that sailing is a combination of poetry, daring, work, fatigue, and, above all, a chosen lifestyle. This is the underlying spirit that ensures that regattas constitute a meeting of friends and of constantly renewed ideas and emotions. This transforms these occasions, which fully relive the spirit of Nelson's "Band of Brothers."

It must be a thrilling experience to see these boats, perhaps lined up anchored at the quayside. Each fairly oozes with its own past – a fascinating series of misfortunes, sacrifices, changes of ownership, and restoration work. This past often gets mixed up with idle gossip, capable of feeding often pointless, short-lived journalistic stories. At the end of the day, however, the brief moments during which these "queens of the sea" more than repay the energy spent on them are a comfort in Vittorio Rossi's "barbaric times."

What I have tried to do in this volume is make my own personal contribution towards historical research, and I hope that this may be of help as a basis for further thought on the part of all concerned – boat-owners, brokers, skippers, associations, and federations. The pages in the present volume are the result of teamwork (I can never

thank all the contributors enough for their enthusiasm and time), and there are many boats that are still to be traced. However, efforts will be made to find them and invite them to the rather unique, nostalgic gathering that lies between these pages. Historical vessels such as Milena, Islander, Yanira, Lumberjack, Carina… and what ever happened to Maverick, which I encountered one dawn way back in 1963? The search will go on until they are found.

March 2002

In this new edition, I thought it opportune to rework the previous volume, not only in order to update the details, but also to correct a number of errors and inexact details that are almost inevitable in a work of this size. Moreover, many new boats have been added to this edition, together with further information, technical specifications, and illustrations.

The book has become more technical and contains greater historical detail, while the choice of illustrations (which includes the best photographs taken by a small number of professional photographers) is designed to be more homogeneous and spectacular than the previous volume.

Where possible, the text has been updated, despite the reluctance of certain boat-owners to proffer information, and the lack of documentation by institutional bodies, who do not always do their best to look after their own archives.

The aim of my research over the years has always been to encourage greater cultural interest in the recovery and conservation of a heritage that belongs to us all and that deserves to be treated accordingly. Significant help was given by the archives departments of the Italian Association of Vintage Yachts (AIVE) and the International Naval Museum in Imperia, which at its new site offers a sizeable section completely dedicated to the world of yachting.

Flavio Serafini

Introduction

I have had increasingly close contact with Captain Flavio Serafini in recent years as a result of his taking on the difficult task of drawing up a basis for the study of so-called "vintage yachts." I have never failed to visit him at the International Naval Museum at Imperia when given the chance (for example, during the regular gatherings), as the experience of revisiting the constantly updated exhibition rooms is a truly enjoyable one for me. It also enables me to appreciate fully the extraordinary efforts he is making to conserve memoirs and curios as valuable reminders of certain traditions of our civilization.

I often find myself standing on the quayside or on board a boat during a regatta, in the company of Serafini, exchanging sailing stories and experiences. Naturally enough, over 30 years' experience has brought me that much closer to the world of vintage yachts. My views on these vessels are well known: they require a combination of love and care, both historical and technical, which has yet to materialize, but which my book Lo Yacht, together with Serafini's work, attempts to bring to the public's attention as an essential approach to boats of a certain age.

These notes offer me the opportunity, therefore, to reiterate my invitation to evaluate carefully the correct worth of certain hulls that can be considered nothing less than true works of art, and which should be allowed to remain as such. I would like to thank Captain Serafini once again for his work, which would have been much appreciated by our dear friend, the late Bruno Veronese, whom I would like to remember here with loving respect.

Carlo Sciarelli
Naval Architect and Designer
Trieste, Italy

It is a pleasure to introduce this superb book on classic sailing yachts by my friend Flavio Serafini. Apart from directing the important naval museum at Imperia, he is a prolific author and researcher, with a deep knowledge of maritime history and a passion for the sea. He is not a narrow specialist, and it is typical of him that in treating the subject of old yachts he should take a broad canvas. His aim is to record some of the most important yachts still sailing today from an international perspective. He has ranged far and wide in search of his quarry, bringing together a detailed account of the specification and history of each yacht together with superb photographs. Though this book is important as a reference work, it is also a book to be treasured and enjoyed, for it charts the story of designers and builders, owners and captains, sailors and crew, in a lively and informative text, supported by ship plans and technical data. Many of the great names in yacht design are represented here, including Laurent Giles, Colin Archer, and Charles Nicholson. The book spans traditional wooden boats from the last century to the sleek meter-class thoroughbreds of more recent times. There are famous vessels like Creole, Endeavour, and Candida alongside boats of more regional significance. For example, you will find a well-known vessel like the Altaïr rubbing shoulders with the dinghy Barbel. What is also striking is the degree of cross fertilization that has taken place in the design of yachts. Tartuga was designed by the Scandinavian Colin Archer but built by Cantieri of Viareggio. The world of sailing craft is truly international. Flavio Serafini's first edition of the book published in 1994 charted some 200 vessels. This vastly expanded second edition includes nearly 350, and presents a comprehensive picture of the yachting world of the past that is still thriving today, thanks to the enthusiasm of individual owners and captains.

Richard Ormond
former Director of the National Maritime Museum,
Greenwich, London

The "belle époque" of regatta sailing

Two images from the private collection of the author.

Vintage Yachts

The boats described in alphabetical order in the first part of this book constitute the most interesting part of a survey of sailing boats built prior to 1955. I have tried to supply as many historical and technical details as possible, notwithstanding the little or no documentary material available as a result of repeated change of ownership, which is increasingly becoming the rule with such vessels. It would be a good idea if the life of a boat were recorded in a proper "boat's register" that owners were obliged to update. A register like this could contain the dates and nature of any important restoration work that has been carried out, together with details of changes of ownership, technical specifications, inspections, and drawings. This is the only way of having a complete historical picture of the life of a boat.

This part of the book thus covers vintage yachts, called "*voiliers de tradition*" or "*vele d'epoca*" in French and Italian respectively. Of course, given the work of naval architects from different historical periods and different schools of thought, the collection of boats described in this volume is of a very heterogeneous nature, and it differs significantly from those vessels that take part in the Great Schooner Race held at Rockland on the Maine coast in the United States, where the majority of hulls are those of former working boats. At the Imperia regattas, like at those held at Porto Cervo in Sardinia and Saint Tropez in France, a harmonious blend of trysail and Bermudan rigs (which often were not originally such) has always given an impression of a lifestyle very far removed from that of the present day.

In a true forest of masts, the beauty of *Lelantina* contrasts with the grace of *Escapade* or *Joyette*, while the aristocratic *Karenita* makes headway against *Royono* and *Mariella*. The powerful *Puritan* competes with the more elegant *Altair*, the impeccable *Croce del Sud* matches the fine line of *Creole*, the slim *Elpis* complements the lines of *Cerrida* and *Four Winds*, the good looks of *Aurora* match the rapidity of *Tomahawk*, and so on. A unique sight that will remain in my mind forever.

Adria II

Rigging:	Bermudan ketch
Sail area:	480 sq. yds.
Shipyard:	Abeking & Rasmussen (Lemwerder, Germany)
Designer:	A. Tiller
Year of design:	1933
Launch:	1934
Restoration:	1986–87 Beconcini shipyards (La Spezia, Italy)
L.: 73³/₄ ft.	W.l.: 59 ft.
B.: 16³/₄ ft.	Df: 12¹/₂ ft.
Displ.: 66.14 tons	Engine: 140 Hp
Skipper:	Frederic Vergue, C. Kotterer

This boat was launched as a schooner, under the name *Swastika*, in the Abeking & Rasmussen shipyards in Germany. It seems that it was designed for the German minister Goebbels, but he never got to sail it before World War II broke out. In 1945 the Allies confiscated it and transferred it to England.

From 1952 the boat was managed by the Adria Syndicate of Teignmouth in Devon, England, who kept the boat through to 1955. During this period it appears that the boat was transformed into a Bermudan ketch, after having borne the name of *Briantais*. Its name was changed to *Adria II* in 1966 when it was rigged by Aldo Bassetti and then, from 1973 to 1992, it was owned by Jean Christophe Derain.

Built using the composite system (steel frame with mahogany planking), *Adria II* still retains its original teak deck. In 1986 the Beconcini shipyards in La Spezia, Italy, replaced 50 percent of the planking and weighted down the keel with approximately 25.35 tons of lead. *Adria II* has taken part in many vintage yacht regattas (at Saint Tropez, Porto Cervo, and Imperia), where it has always come among the first three boats in its class. It has proven to be a solidly built and reliable yacht. In a stiff breeze it has managed 17 knots, and it has shown that it can withstand gale-force winds.

TOP RIGHT: *September 2000. The ketch* Adria II, *which flew the German flag until 1945. Built by Abeking & Rasmussen, this splendid hull was restored in Italy in 1986 by Angelo Beconcini (Photo: S. Pesato).*

RIGHT: Adria II *during a regatta (Photo: S. Pesato).*

Aello

The magnificent schooner *Aello* was designed by the naval architect Max Oertz, who had already designed the famous schooner *Germania*, as well as *Meteor IV* and *Meteor V* for Kaiser Wilhelm II. Immediately after World War I, a Greek sugar magnate commissioned Oertz to design a yacht very similar to *Meteor IV* but smaller in size. The resulting vessel, *Aello*, was launched in 1921.

In 1925 the schooner was sold to an English baron, who subsequently renamed it *Xenia* ("foreigner") and used it to sail around the world for many years before re-selling it in 1953. For nearly 30 years, *Aello* was abandoned on the muddy bed of a river in southern England. This, ironically enough, turned out to be its salvation, since mud has a therapeutic effect on wood, preserving it at the right degree of humidity.

After a number of unsuccessful attempts at restoration, the schooner was finally purchased by Cameron Chisholm in 1985. The new owner was keen to restore the boat to its former splendor, and with this in mind he bought a quantity of Burmese teak that had been recovered from the sea bottom, where it had lain in the hold of a cargo ship that had sunk in 1917. This extremely valuable wood was used to rebuild the schooner, making it the only boat to have been reconstituted in Burmese teak in the last 50 years. The boat was initially taken to Bristol in

England (where restoration work took four years and cost US$6 million). The restoration project was supervised by Lloyds Register of Shipping and managed by the naval architects Ian Howlett and C.H. Temple, with the result that it was granted the top Lloyds ✠ 100 A1 Class.

The interior was restored at Southampton in 1990, after which Chisholm sailed the boat to Malta. Two years later it was purchased by an Italian who sailed it to the Caribbean and then through the Panama Canal into the Pacific. While there, *Aello* was noticed by its present owner, Tony Roumellotes, who immediately fell in love with it and decided to buy it with his business partner, Tim Britton. The schooner was further restored in the United States before sailing it back to the Mediterranean in 1998 – after its new owner had come first in his class in the 1997 Antigua Classic Yacht Regatta and Transatlantic Challenge Cup, sailing in regattas against *Mariette*, *Sumurun*, and the replica of *America*.

Today *Aello*, with its spruce masts and three booms, teak superstructures, and four spacious skylights, is one of the last remaining schooners in the world to have been designed by Max Oertz. From the sailing point of view, it is an extremely well-balanced boat that is now easier to maneuver thanks to five electric winches.

Rigging:	Trysail schooner
Sail area:	540 sq. yds.
Shipyard:	Max Oertz & Harder (Hamburg, Germany)
Designer:	Max Oertz
Year of design:	1919
Launch:	1921
Restoration:	1990 Southampton (England)
L.: 123 ft.	W.l.: 71³⁄4 ft.
B.: 13 ft.	Df. 19¹⁄2 ft.
Displ.: 165.3 tons	Engine: 235 Hp
Skipper:	Tony Roumellotes (1998)

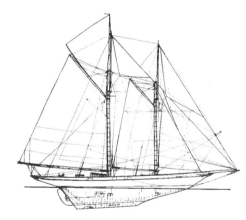

ABOVE: *A photograph of the schooner* Aello *(Photo courtesy of T. Britton).*

RIGHT: *September 1997, details of* Aello's *slender stern (Photo: P. Maccione).*

FOLLOWING PAGE: *September 1997,* Aello *as it sails towards the regatta course (Photo: P. Maccione).*

Agneta

*A*gneta is one of the most beautiful boats of its age currently in the Mediterranean. It was launched in 1951 on behalf of the architect who designed it and carries the name of his daughter to this day, despite numerous changes in ownership over the years.

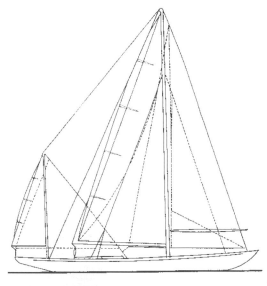

For a number of seasons, *Agneta*, with its unmistakable, natural mahogany-colored hull and ocher sails, sailed the blue waters of the Sardinian coast, displaying equine grace, marked surges, a simple shape, and a limited freeboard. The Swedish architect, Reimers, was also a keen sailor, and in 1952 had taken part in the Bermuda Race aboard the American yawl *Bolero*.

However, during the early 1950s, the elderly Reimers reluctantly had to part with the boat. He sold it to Giovanni Agnelli, knowing that the new owner would take care of his charge. In fact, Agnelli was the owner of the boat for about 25 years.

In 1982 the boat and its new owner, Luigi Donà delle Rose, took part in the first vintage yachts regatta held on the Emerald Coast of Sardinia, where *Agneta* came first in the final classification, ahead of *Skagerrak*, *Altair*, and *Mariette*. In 1987, *Agneta* was sold to the architect Giuseppe Andolina, who decided to have significant

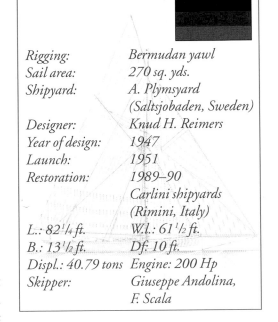

Rigging:	*Bermudan yawl*
Sail area:	*270 sq. yds.*
Shipyard:	*A. Plymsyard (Saltsjobaden, Sweden)*
Designer:	*Knud H. Reimers*
Year of design:	*1947*
Launch:	*1951*
Restoration:	*1989–90 Carlini shipyards (Rimini, Italy)*
L.: 82¼ ft.	*W.l.: 61½ ft.*
B.: 13½ ft.	*Df: 10 ft.*
Displ.: 40.79 tons	*Engine: 200 Hp*
Skipper:	*Giuseppe Andolina, F. Scala*

BELOW: *September 2000, Agneta in a fast windward stretch (Photo: J. Taylor).*

ABOVE: *Details of the interior (Photo courtesy of R. Stefani).*

BELOW: *September 2000,* Agneta *during a regatta (Photo: J. Taylor).*

interior and exterior restoration work carried out at the Carlini shipyards in Rimini, Italy, where the boat remained for 18 months (the operation took 18,000 man hours) under the loving, watchful eye of its new owner.

Giuseppe Andolina had the rigging restored to its original layout at the masthead (instead of the existing seven-eighths rig), and also had the internal spaces redistributed in accordance with a clever and elegant design. The new layout includes a "dinette" with specially designed cabin planking, cathedral windows, and a cabin with fireplace, the handiwork of one of the boatyard's artistic carpenters, Saverio Saotin.

Although the design features of *Agneta* are typical of the Swedish boat-building tradition, with its spruce masts and teak deck, the boat nevertheless features an innovative compromise between length, beam, and displacement that enables it to attain easily its maximum potential speed, even in the presence of light winds. During

his time, Reimers declared that the boat had overtaken a 18,190-ton oil tanker traveling at 13 knots.

Today the boat has regained its original splendor and combines elegance with practicality and convenience. The partial changes have not altered its original displacement, but have been designed to provide the vessel with modern equipment and navigational instruments that constitute a happy compromise with tradition – guaranteeing those on board the best of both worlds.

After its successes in 2000, at Palma di Mallorca in Spain, Imperia, and Cannes and Saint Tropez in France, *Agneta* was sold to a new German owner, who delivered the boat to the Beaulieu naval shipyard in France for major refitting (partial replacement of the planking and frame with elm, the remaking of the teak deck, and the fitting of a new spruce mizzenmast). The aluminum fittings have been replaced by bronze or stainless steel ones.

Aleph

While at Cannes during the fall of 2001, I finally came across a true gem that I had known about but had never had the good fortune to see – *Aleph*, a gaff-rigged yawl designed by Henry Rasmussen. The boat belongs to the architect Mario Pirri, also owner of *Latifa* and a true vintage boat enthusiast and expert, as well as an excellent skipper.

Aleph was launched in 1951 in the famous German shipyard of Abeking & Rasmussen, which, prior to World War II, had been one of the landmarks of world yachting. "Jimmy" Rasmussen, overwhelmed by his country's military defeat at the hands of the Allies, quickly decided to roll up his sleeves and throw himself into the business of boat-building. This was to help the yard regain a certain prestige and increase its orders once again.

The boat's original name was *Konigin*. It possesses a strong hull made from maple ribs and pine planking, and Honduran mahogany on the topside, together with galvanized iron fittings. On board, the yard's characteristic deckhouse is easily recognizable, with its raised hatchway. The mahogany interior features some engraved panels.

Little is known of the boat's early racing days until it was sold and renamed *Julla*. At the beginning of the 1960s it was noticed by Giancarlo Feltrinelli, who decided to purchase it and rename it *Eskimosa*, and fit it out for family cruising.

In the fall of 1970 the boat was sold once again, this time to its present owner, Mario Pirri, who had previously seen it moored at Porto Ercole in Italy. He renamed it *Aleph*, and this marked the beginning of a run of single-handed Atlantic crossings that proved excellent training for the new owner up until 1976, when he had the chance to acquire another splendid yawl, W. Fife's *Latifa*.

Since then, *Aleph* has been carefully conserved at the Beconcini shipyards in La Spezia, Italy. After such a lengthy period of inactivity the boat needed major restoration. This was performed between the end of 2000 and the summer of 2001 by the same shipyard, under the close supervision of its loving owner.

Despite the perfect conservation of the boat's shape, *Aleph*, which had belonged to the same owner for the previous 30 years, still required major work. The steering mechanism, with its gearing in pressed leather, needed to be fully recouped and restored. The work carried out also included the reconstruction of the sternpost and the rudder and almost complete conservation of the frame, while the frame-floor timbers connecting the ribs to the keel have been rebuilt in iroko.

The hull planking has been replaced with 1¼ inch-thick mahogany strakes, fixed to the planks using silicon bronze screws. Furthermore, all internal installations have been modernized.

Aleph's original charm has been rediscovered thanks to the special skills of the boatyard workers and to the present owner's love for his boat.

RIGHT: *VBR September 2001, close-up of* Aleph *(Photo: J. Taylor).*

BELOW: *VBR September 2001, detail of the deck (Photo: J. Taylor).*

FOLLOWING PAGE: *VBR September 2001,* Aleph *photographed as it sails close-hauled (Photo: J. Taylor).*

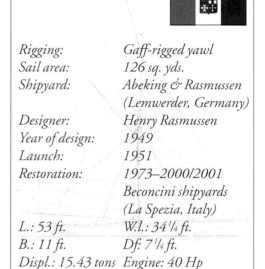

Rigging:	Gaff-rigged yawl
Sail area:	126 sq. yds.
Shipyard:	Abeking & Rasmussen (Lemwerder, Germany)
Designer:	Henry Rasmussen
Year of design:	1949
Launch:	1951
Restoration:	1973–2000/2001 Beconcini shipyards (La Spezia, Italy)
L.: 53 ft.	W.l.: 34¼ ft.
B.: 11 ft.	Df: 7¼ ft.
Displ.: 15.43 tons	Engine: 40 Hp
Skipper:	Mario Pirri

Altaïr

This truly beautiful schooner has honored the Mediterranean with its presence since 1948, when it was purchased by Señor Miguel Sans Mora.

Altair was originally commissioned by Captain Guy MacCaw from W. Fife & Son in December 1929. However, during the two years following its launch, the boat did not carry out any long-distance journeys but simply sailed around the waters off the French Atlantic coast near Saint Jean de Luz. In 1933 *Altair* was bought by Walter Runciman, whose father, Baron Runciman, rose from modest beginnings to become the founder of a shipping empire. Under the charge of Lord Runciman, the boat remained a coastal cruiser, taking part in the occasional regatta in the Solent off the south coast of England and sailing from the western coast of Scotland to the quiet Isle of Eigg in the Hebrides.

In 1938 Sir William Verdon-Smith bought *Altair*, but he managed to enjoy the boat for only two seasons before it was requisitioned by the Admiralty (together with many other beautiful yachts) to be used in World War II. After restoration work in 1948, *Altair* left Southampton and was not seen in its home waters again for 38 years.

Having sailed under the Portuguese flag for two years, the boat was sold once again, this time to Miguel Sans Mora of Barcelona. *Altair* flew the Spanish flag for all of 34 years, under the command of a Hemingway-esque character, a spirited man of considerable value, and a true sailing enthusiast. He could still be seen at 85 years of age at the helm of *Altair* at various vintage yacht regattas, with a crew made up mostly of family members. Señor Sans Mora sailed the boat for more than 100,000 miles. In 1952 it arrived in the waters around Stromboli as the volcano erupted. His last regatta was in 1960 (the Cannes–Ischia Regatta), when *Altair* managed to arrive before the jury's boat did! He successfully managed to conserve the boat and all its original components until it was resold to Blue Wave Ltd. in 1985.

Altair has always been classified with the "Master Certificate," the maximum Class index issued by Lloyds Register (Lloyds ✠ 100 A1 Class). It features Siamese teak planking (the hull section is copper-plated), oak ribs, a teak and spruce deck, Canadian red pine masts and yards, and solid mahogany furnishings and interior finishes. It has a sail area of approximately 600 square yards (not including the spinnaker). In the

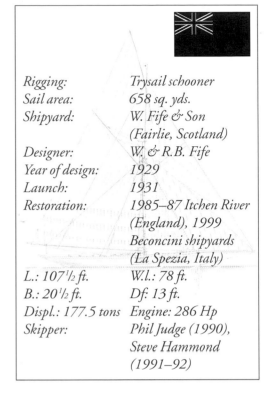

Rigging:	Trysail schooner
Sail area:	658 sq. yds.
Shipyard:	W. Fife & Son (Fairlie, Scotland)
Designer:	W. & R.B. Fife
Year of design:	1929
Launch:	1931
Restoration:	1985–87 Itchen River (England), 1999 Beconcini shipyards (La Spezia, Italy)
L.: 107½ ft.	W.l.: 78 ft.
B.: 20½ ft.	Df: 13 ft.
Displ.: 177.5 tons	Engine: 286 Hp
Skipper:	Phil Judge (1990), Steve Hammond (1991–92)

BELOW: *VBR September 2001, the schooner* Altair *with its specially-dyed sails.*

past, *Altair* has managed speeds of up to 18 knots in a fresh breeze.

Altair returned to its home waters in the spring of 1986, when it sailed into the River Itchen boatyard (in the south of England) – famous for its restoration work on historical sailing boats such as *Shamrock V* and *Puritan*. All the deckhouses and hatchways were removed before replacing the yellow pine decking with teak ply, while the panels and luxurious interior were taken out and given a new look. Next, the 55-year-old hull was carefully inspected; while the Burmese teak planking was found to be in good condition, the bolts were corroded. The job of dismantling, restoring, and rebuilding the boat at Shamrock Quay, England, took all of 1986 and the best part of 1987.

In the meantime, Ratsey & Lapthorn of Cowes, England, prepared 7,200 square yards of new sails made from a specially dyed terylene fabric that apparently offered the same shade of color as Sudanese–Egyptian cotton. Thus it was that the outside and inside of the boat were returned to their original splendor as perceived by the creative spirit of William Fife. The boom and bowsprit were refitted and restored to their original length by Harry Spencer of Cowes, England. Two months after completion of this major restoration project, *Altair* – more beautiful and efficient than ever – appeared in the Solent before sailing on to the Caribbean. To this day it continues to take part in all the vintage yacht regattas.

In 1999 *Altair* underwent further restoration work on its interior (this time at the Beconcini shipyards in La Spezia, Italy), in order to return it almost to its original state.

ABOVE: *September 1992, close-up of the deck (Photo: F. Ramella).*

BELOW: *VBR Porto Cervo 1991, close-up of the bow (Photo: J. Taylor).*

BOTTOM: *Cannes, September 2000, view of the bow of Altair (Photo: J. Taylor).*

BOTTOM RIGHT: *VBR Porto Cervo 1991, view of the sails as the boat runs free (Photo: J. Taylor).*

Alzavola

uilt in 1924 at the Philip & Sons boatyard in Dartmouth, England, and designed by Claude Worth, *Alzavola* is a splendid combination of vintage elegance, safety, and excellent performance. The same design was used by the architect, boat builder, and famous yachtsman (he was well known for a number of ocean crossings during the 1920s) on his own boat, *Thern IV*, planned at the same time as *Alzavola* (which was launched at that time with the name *Gracie III*).

Before starting building the two boats, Worth, who was a meticulous professional, spent several months in Burma looking for well-seasoned teak for the planking and went all the way to North America to choose the best Oregon pine trunks, free of knots, to make the masts. The mahogany used for the interior was purchased in Honduras, while white English oak, which

he chose already curved in the shape of the boat he was designing, was used for the framing and ribs. The bolts and screws were fashioned from gun metal.

The result was a true masterpiece of solidity, sturdiness, and speed. *Alzavola* needs some wind to pick up any speed, but once it gets going it is truly invincible.

In 1955, under the name of *Gracie III*, the boat still sailed under the English flag with its new owner, E.E. Lealock. Then, in 1967, it was bought by Gerardo Zaccagni, who kept it in perfect condition. In 1986 ownership changed hands once more, and the boat was purchased by the Astrolabio Company, of which Enrico "Chicco" Zaccagni was a director. Zaccagni had over 20 years of sailing experience, and in 1978 he established a new record for the transatlantic crossing (15 days). Chicco Zaccagni was to accomplish a number of transatlantic

Rigging:	*Bermudan ketch*
Sail area:	*263 sq. yds.*
Shipyard:	*Philip & Sons Ltd. (Dartmouth, England)*
Designer:	*Claude Worth*
Year of design:	*1922*
Launch:	*1924*
Restoration:	*1986 Beconcini shipyards (La Spezia, Italy), 1992 Esaom shipyard (Porto Ferraio, Italy), 1997 Trinidad*
L.: 60½ ft.	*W.l.: 47½ ft.*
B.: 13½ ft.	*Df: 9½ ft.*
Displ.: 55.12 tons	*Engine: 120 Hp*
Skipper:	*Enrico Zaccagni (1989–2000), Riccardo Valeriani (2002)*

BELOW: *VBR 1991, close-up of* Alzavola *(Photo: J. Taylor).*

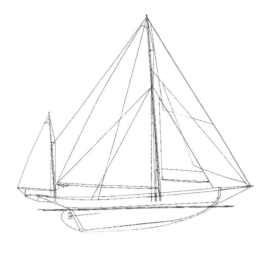

crossings with *Alzavola*, including those on behalf of the "Venturieri" Association.

The boat was moored at the Esaom boatyard at Porto Ferraio, Italy, for a thorough check-up before setting sail for the Caribbean. All the planking was checked and re-screwed in place using silicon bronze screws, and the anchor pins were replaced. *Alzavola* was also fitted with a new, powerful windlass before it reached Martinique at Christmas 1992.

In April 1993 the boat took part in the Antigua Classic Regatta and won its class and the Stormy Weather Trophy. It was to repeat this feat at Antigua in 1995. In 1997 the boat underwent routine maintenance in Trinidad after a long period in the Caribbean off the coast of Venezuela, and in particular at Los Roques where Chicco Zaccagni was interested in writing a book on the tropical meteorology of the area.

For about ten years *Alzavola* was used as a charter yacht in the Caribbean; the crew consisted of only Zaccagni (the skipper), his wife Nicole, and one other person. *Alzavola* has always managed to show its selected guests what love for the sea and sailing is really all about. I am very grateful for having had the privilege of spending time in its spacious, airy, and welcoming ward-room, the guest of a group of true friends who genuinely enjoy the freedom of the seas. Nicole, a charming, lively woman, also knew how to make her guests welcome at the dining table (another vintage item), to the extent that one witty guest had suggested that the boat be renamed "*A tavola!*" ("Dinner's ready!").

Before sailing off to Central America, *Alzavola* was a permanent feature at vintage yacht regattas. After a total of ten years away, *Alzavola* finally returned to Italy in December 1999, having been chartered in the waters around Tortuga in the Caribbean, and having performed its job as a weather station. It was taken into the Porto Ferraio boatyard for repairs after such a long period of sailing.

At present, *Alzavola* is undergoing a major overhaul at the Del Carlo boatyard in Viareggio, Italy. The refitting includes the total rebuilding of the deck, the reconstruction of the rudder, and restoration of the interior and its paneling (including the furniture). The original fittings have been replaced by new "bronzal" castings, while all the old iron frame-floors have been taken away and replaced with new stainless steel ones. The beams and ribs have only been restored, but the entire electrical and hydraulic systems have been modernized.

The most dramatic moments in the life of *Alzavola* were the eight days between November 29 and December 6, 1976, when the boat was caught in a force-ten gale in the Lion Gulf. This proved an extremely severe test for both the ten-man crew and the boat. Today, *Alzavola* has a new owner and skipper, Riccardo Valeriani.

BELOW: Alzavola *with all sails hoisted, in the waters of Nettuno, 1992 (Photo: J. Taylor).*

Avel

Avel was really the center of attraction at the 1994 vintage yacht regatta held at Imperia; rarely has such a beautiful boat ever sailed into the port before. It is the second or third boat with the same name built by Charles Nicholson at Gosport, England, for the French yachtsman Réné Calame of Nantes.

Avel is the Breton word for "wind." The boat bearing this name was launched on May 14, 1896 and was, of course, immediately noticed by the French press, who complimented the owner on the boat's elegant rig and the refinement of its interior. *Avel* took part in its first regatta at Saint Nazaire, France, on July 4, 1897, and came fifth.

The boat's original owner kept it until 1898, when he sold it to the English yachtsman E.W. Balne, who, after registering *Avel* at Southampton, England, resold it to A. Nicholson (namesake of the great naval architect), who kept it on the English east coast until 1915. It is likely that after various changes in ownership, *Avel* spent a long period at West Mersea on the same coastline.

On January 11, 1927, the British Register of Shipping was informed that the boat had had its mast removed and was being used as a houseboat by its new owner, W.W. Cocks. From 1927 through 1990, it remained the property of several local families before being purchased by a Mrs. Spurge.

The solid build of the hull, and the fact that for most of its life it had been used only as a dwelling, meant that it was conserved in a pretty good state. In October 1990 it was discovered by Dr. Gucci. The original interior had survived intact, but the hull required some repair work. The first stage of refitting consisted of the removal of the boat from the bed of mud on which it had rested since 1927. By creating a pathway of

Rigging:	Trysail cutter
Sail area:	219 sq. yds.
Shipyard:	Camper & Nicholson (Gosport, England)
Designer:	Charles E. Nicholson
Year of design:	1895
Launch:	1896
Restoration:	1993–94
L.: 62½ ft.	W.l.: 41½ ft.
B.: 12 ft.	Df.: 8 ft.
Displ.: 16.53 tons	
Skipper:	John Bardon (1994–98), D. Evans (2000)

BELOW: *Cannes 1999, a regatta in progress with* Avel *at the center (Photo: J. Taylor).*

strong wooden timbers, a crane was able to get near enough to the boat to lift it up out of the mud and onto the road, from where it was given a police escort to Harry Spencer's shipyard in Cowes, England. This shipbuilder, together with the expert American carpenter Clark Poston, managed to completely refit *Avel* over three years.

The boat was re-launched on May 28, 1994 and, after being loaded onto the cargo ship *Barok*, was taken to Palma di Mallorca. On June 19, *Avel* set sail for the first time with owner Gucci on board. Restored to its original beautiful condition, with a crew dressed in historical uniform, *Avel* was finally able to reveal its fascination and elegance. One particularly important detail is that there is no engine on board.

OPPOSITE PAGE: *1995, a fascinating shot of* Avel *(Photo: F. Ramella).*

ABOVE: *Cannes 1998, the crew performing a maneuver (Photo: J. Taylor).*

LEFT: *Imperia 1994 (Photo: F. Ramella).*

BELOW: *Imperia 2000 (Photo: F. Ramella).*

Barbel

Rigging:	Dinghy
Sail area:	9 sq. yds.
Shipyard:	V. Baglietto (Varazze, Italy)
Designer:	Vittorio Baglietto
Year of design:	1935
Launch:	1937
Restoration:	1987 Mulazzini shipyard (Italy)
L.: 10 ft.	W.l.: 9¹/₄ ft.
B.: 4 ft.	Df: 1–3 ft.
Displ.: 135 lbs.	
Skipper:	Giovanni Fumagalli

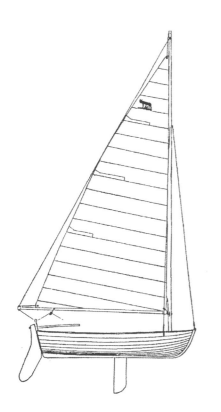

The history of this boat is well worth knowing as it is part of the history of an entire town and its shipyard, Verazze in Liguria, Italy.

A new sailing fashion began to develop along the Ligurian coast at the beginning of the 20th century, using tiny, English-style dinghies fitted with a keel, rudder, and small sail. This new pastime, especially popular with young people, attracted the attention of Vittorio Baglietto, who was always ready to pick up new developments for his ship-yard. He created a simple sailing boat for beginners, perfect for two adolescents to sail out into the sea and bring the boat back to the shore without any help, and economical enough for an average family to be able to afford one.

So it was that in the spring of 1935, the "Lupa" (dinghy) line entered the world of sailing. At the time, sailing magazines showed pictures of this small hull with its pure, graceful shape and one large mainsail, together with the announcement of the first ever national championship and the rules of tonnage to be applied.

During the Second Dinghy Champion-ships (in 1936), among other things the rules stated that: "*The Varazze Sailing Club announces the Second Dinghy Championships reserved for those boats within this category: the Championship is reserved for Avant-gardists, Young Fascists and 'Balilla'* [Fascist paramilitary youth between the ages of 8 and 14] *from the province of Savona, as well as those from other provinces who are resident in Varazze during the summer season… The Championships will consist of eight trials to be held in the waters of Varazze.*"

The general conditions of entry included a number of interesting prescriptions: "…*6) Deck – the boats must not have any kind of deck… 11) Masts – all permanently bent or intentionally curved masts or booms are prohibited… 13) Sail battens – no more than three battens may be used, and the center batten must not exceed 28 inches in length, while the two outer battens must not be any longer than 20 inches. They should divide the leech in four approximately equal parts.*" Furthermore, the boat was to: "…*have a clinker-built skin; be crewed by one or two persons; be no longer than 11 feet and no shorter than 4 feet; have a pillar of between 1¹/₂ and 1³/₄ inches; have a maximum sail area of 9 square yards, and a minimum weight of 135 pounds.*" These specifications were important – they meant that the boat had to be small, extremely light, and have a good sail. As such they started to perform even in the lightest of breezes.

This line proved incredibly successful and they could be found on lakes and in the Adriatic before World War II put paid to quiet hours of enjoyable sailing. During the post-war years, Baglietto failed to recommence production, and the only ship-yards now making these boats were small, professional yards. For obvious reasons the name of the class was changed – although the new name "Sirena" (mermaid) proved less than auspicious, and numbers dwindled despite the brave efforts of the inhabitants of Varazze to re-launch the category.

By the 1950s little or nothing more was heard of this class of vessel. The only

RIGHT: *Imperia 1989, the tiny* Barbel *takes on some of yachting's giants (Photo: G. Semeria).*

positive note during this period was a request for information regarding the sails for a "Lupa" being built in far-off Uruguay. The small hull had, it seemed, crossed the ocean! *Barbel*, built by Baglietto possibly in 1937, was bought ten years later, in perfect condition, and taken to Zoagli from Quarto where it was moored. Although it may have had a number of competitive merits, these disappeared in the archives along with its sailing number.

The boat has an oak keel, maple ribs ($^1/_2$ inch × $^3/_4$ inch flat), pine planking, and an ash washboard and dunnage. The benches are of walnut, while the transom is mahogany. The original spruce mast has been rebuilt in Douglas fir, while the fittings have been conserved as they "*go back to before they invented rust*," as Sciarelli would amusingly have put it. The hull is fastened together using copper nails only, this being the first secret to its longevity. The second lies in the careful, necessarily light construc-

tion that is both elegant and simple. The bow and transom reinforcements, for example, are limited in size so as to favor the natural tendency of the English planking to distribute stress in a flexible manner.

Barbel was rowed more than it was sailed in the subsequent 20-year period, and it was subject to mistreatment of all kinds. It was laid up in a garage for a further 20 years, where an idiot found no better use for the boat than to store his bags of cement in it. Then, finally, one day Orazio Maluzzani got his hands on the boat and restored it to its former glory. In fact, the *Barbel* succeeded in taking part in the Imperia Regatta, where it was acclaimed by the public and by its much larger sister vessels. It was a truly moving sight to see this tiny boat overlapping the immense *Raphaelo* during the course of the regatta.

Since 1999, *Barbel* has been lovingly guarded at the International Naval Museum in Imperia.

Belle Aventure

For years we had waited for the return of this splendid yacht built by W. Fife & Son of Scotland, and finally our patience has been rewarded. As it sails close-hauled, its unmistakable streamlined shape suggests considerable elegance and power.

Belle Aventure was launched in 1929 as *Eileen*, and rigged as a trysail ketch it must have been quite a spectacular sight. When the boat was first built it had 2 inch-thick

teak planking across an oak frame, and as a ketch with a sturdy, fast hull it was classified by Lloyds Register as Class ✠ 100 A1. In 1937 the boat was transformed into a Bermudan ketch, and it has remained one ever since. Over the years, *Eileen* was renamed several times, and had a number of different owners, before it was finally baptized *Belle Aventure* at the end of the 1960s. Ten years or so later, the boat was

Rigging:	Bermudan ketch
Sail area:	353 sq. yds.
Shipyard:	W. Fife & Son (Fairlie, Scotland)
Designer:	William Fife III
Year of design:	1929
Launch:	1929
Restoration:	1989 Southampton Yacht Service (England)
L.: 92 ft.	W.l.: 59$^1/_2$ ft.
B.: 17 ft.	Df.: 12$^3/_4$ ft.
Displ.: 83.78 tons	Engine: 210 Hp
Skipper:	Nigel Blackbourn (1996)

LEFT: *ACJ Cowes 2001,* Belle Aventure, *designed by William Fife III (Photo: J. Taylor).*

BELOW: *Cannes 2000,* Belle Aventure *under sail (Photo: J. Taylor).*
BOTTOM: *AJC Cowes 2001, all sails windward (Photo: J. Taylor).*
BOTTOM RIGHT: *Cockpit and steering wheel (Photo: A. Tringali).*

resold to an English owner who, in 1979, had the boat restored at the McGruer naval shipyard in Scotland. This involved the replacement of the stempost and reconstruction of the deck, which was originally made of pitch pine.

From then onward, *Belle Aventure* was heavily employed on charters in the Mediterranean and Caribbean. It was refitted once again in 1987 by Southampton Yacht Service in England, when work included the replacement of the deck.

Belle Aventure was sold to its present owner in 1996, and in 1977 it took part in the Atlantic Challenge Cup. It was then transferred to Fairlie Restorations in Scotland, where Fife's specialists saw to a more thorough refitting job. Thanks to the original drawings the boat's interior was also restored to its original splendor; the saloon was completely stripped, restored, and then reorganized as it had originally been. Restoration also involved considerable work on the hull and the steering system, all of this supervised by Lloyds Register.

After its re-launch in 1998, *Belle Aventure* set sail for a two-year voyage, reaching Sydney, Australia, in time for the new millennium celebrations. It was then present at the America's Cup in Auckland, New Zealand, and sailed off on cruises round Polynesia, the Caribbean, and the east coast of the United States.

At Imperia, *Belle Aventure* has raced with *So Fong* and the boat has taken part in fall regattas held in the Mediterranean. Its spacious deck, characterized by a great many skylights, features a beautiful, perhaps unique, windlass (with two warps) at the bow, which fits in perfectly with the graceful, comfortable surrounds. A fine boat indeed.

Belle Poule

ABOVE: *The training ship* Belle Poule *(Photo courtesy of Ed Jos le Doare, Chateaulin).*

elle Poule, together with its twin *Étoile*, was launched in January 1932 by the Normandy naval shipyard at Fécamp, France, on behalf of the French Royal Navy. The two schooners are used as training ships and are based at Brest in Brittany. The two hulls are perfect copies of the "Palamboise"-type schooners, which up until 1935 were used for cod fishing off Iceland. During the training cruises, the two boats regularly take place in the Tall Ships Race, as well as the occasional vintage yacht regatta.

With its streamlined hull made of copper-lined double-oak and its long bowsprit, *Belle Poule*, like its twin, is an elegantly shaped boat. It features an Oregon pine deck. During World War II the two schooners caught up with the Free French Forces at Portsmouth, England, and can thus fly the tricolor flag with the Cross of Lorraine.

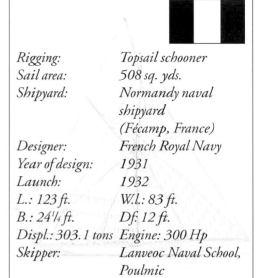

Rigging:	Topsail schooner
Sail area:	508 sq. yds.
Shipyard:	Normandy naval shipyard (Fécamp, France)
Designer:	French Royal Navy
Year of design:	1931
Launch:	1932
L.: 123 ft.	W.l.: 83 ft.
B.: 24¼ ft.	Df. 12 ft.
Displ.: 303.1 tons	Engine: 300 Hp
Skipper:	Lanveoc Naval School, Poulmic

Black Swan

*aunched under the name *Brynhild*, the *Black Swan* was one of Charles Nicholson's best projects, and, after a lifetime of regatta victories, *Black Swan* is about to be given a second life.

In 1899 the boat, commissioned by Major Selwyn Calverley (its first owner), was launched as a trysailed yawl. In 1905, *Brynhild* was sold to Lord James Pender who, after having commissioned Charles Nicholson to build him a new cutter bearing the same name, resold the boat in 1907.

Between 1912 and 1922 the boat was renamed *Swan* and transformed into a ketch. It took part in a number of regattas, competing with famous boats such as

Valdora and *Sumurun*. From 1928 to 1936 *Swan* was bought and sold a number of times, during which time it was renamed *Black Swan*. During the 1950s it was known as *Changrilla*, but it reverted to being called *Black Swan*. The 1960s saw the hull undergo numerous modifications that altered the deck and the deckhouse (which was extended).

In 1984, ship-owner Alain Mechoulam transferred the yacht to Turkey, where an amount of refitting work of substandard quality was carried out (especially as regards the sails). Towards the end of the 1980s, *Black Swan* was transferred to the south of France, where it remained until 1993, when

Rigging:	Trysail ketch
Sail area:	577 sq. yds.
Shipyard:	Camper & Nicholson (Gosport, England)
Designer:	Charles E. Nicholson
Year of design:	1899
Launch:	1899
L.: 109 ft.	W.l.: 84 ft.
B.: 20 ft.	Df: 14¼ ft.
Displ.: 146.6 tons	

it was taken to the Beconcini shipyards in Italy for a check-up and some interior restoration. After a further four years of activity, the boat returned to the same shipyard, and in January 2001 radical restoration work was begun by the Faggioni company to eliminate modifications that had altered the original appearance of the yacht.

During the initial phase of restoration the deck and rudder fittings were dismantled, together with the interior furnishings, and as much of the original material as possible was preserved. The stempost and the keel were partially rebuilt using iroko, but the ribs were still in good condition. Replacement of the hull planking with 2½ inch-thick iroko timbers fastened to the ribs using galvanized steel splines proved challenging. The transom was rebuilt, and the wooden sections of the deck were restored. The restoration envisaged a trysail ketch rigging; the two new masts, boom, bowsprit, gaff, and the gaff topsail yard were all constructed from Colombian pine.

So it is that another yacht with trysail rigging will grace the seas once again, and remind us what sailing was all about at the beginning of the 20th century.

BELOW: *VBR 1991, a superb shot of* Black Swan, *one of Charles Nicholson's most successful designs (Photo: J. Taylor).*

BELOW RIGHT: *VBR 1991,* Black Swan *under sail (Photo: J. Taylor).*

Bohème Deux

Rigging:	Bermudan schooner
Sail area:	419 sq. yds.
Shipyard:	Denmark
Year of design:	1930
Launch:	1930
L.: 117¼ ft.	W.l.: 101½ ft.
B.: 22 ft.	Df.: 12 ft.
Displ.: 176.4 tons	Engine: 250 Hp
Skipper:	George Riffe

*B*ohème Deux is a Bermudan schooner launched in Denmark in 1930. At present we know very little of its past, apart from the fact that it has cruised extensively in the Mediterranean and Caribbean and has completed a number of transatlantic crossings. It is used exclusively for charter purposes and features excellent living and sleeping quarters for its guests — in the dining room at least ten people can be seated around a large oak dining table. A number of films have been shot on board, and the 180 square yards of deck space is room enough for conferences, lunches, and buffets to be organized. Each year, *Bohème Deux* takes part in the Nioulargue race.

This schooner features teak planking covered in copper leaf, oak framing, and a lead keel. Its home port is Cannes in the south of France.

RIGHT: *VBR Porto Cervo, 1999,* Bohème Deux *under sail (Photo: J. Taylor).*

BELOW: *VBR Porto Cervo, 1999, the sail plan and the hull's lines no longer match (Photo: J. Taylor).*

Bolero

Rigging:	*Bermudan yawl*
Sail area:	*283 sq. yds.*
Shipyard:	*Nevins Yacht Yard (City Island, New York, USA)*
Designer:	*Sparkman & Stephens*
Year of design:	*1949*
Launch:	*1949*
Restoration:	*1995*
L.: 73½ ft.	*W.l.: 50¾ ft.*
B.: 14¼ ft.	*Df: 9 ft.*
Displ.: 55.12 tons	*Engine: 140 Hp*
Skipper:	*Jim Teague*

*B*olero, one of the most famous 1940s American ocean racers, was launched by John Nicholas Brown, commodore of the New York Yacht Club, in 1949. It was basically designed by Sparkman & Stephens as a racing boat, and as such it is a powerful, fast yacht.

It has a double skin in mahogany and cedar, and it was one of the very first boats to have aluminum masts. Carlo Sciarelli called it a *"large, beautiful thoroughbred of a boat,"* while *Yachting* magazine voted it the *"Miss America of Ocean Racers."*

Its victories in the 1950, 1954, and 1956 Bermuda Race were quite spectacular; the record it set in the last of these was held for the next 18 years. Its other victories include the Newport–Annapolis Race in 1953, the Storm Trysail Club's Block Island Race in 1950 and 1951, and two wins in the Astor and King's Cup. It often raced against *Stormy Weather* and *Catherina*, both of whom also competed for the United States. *Bolero* is part of American and international yachting history.

In the mid-1990s, the boat had urgent need of refitting; 60 percent of the planking had to be replaced due to the corrosive action of the mixture of metals present in the hull. The deck and deckhouse were also sorely in need of repair.

After half a century of sailing, *Bolero* has gone back to sailing between the Caribbean and New England on the east cost of the United States.

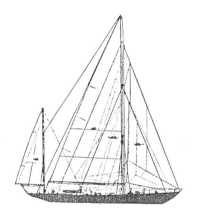

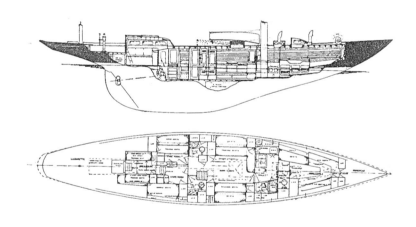

Bruma

Rigging:	*Bermudan sloop*
Sail area:	*144 sq. yds.*
Shipyard:	*Van de Woorde (Antwerp, Belgium)*
Designer:	*W.R. Murdoch*
Year of design:	*1944*
Launch:	*1945*
Restoration:	*1988–92*
L.: 54 ft.	*W.l.: 39 ft.*
B.: 12¾ ft.	*Df: 7½ ft.*
Displ.: 24.25 tons	*Engine: 80 Hp*
Skipper:	*Fabio Vespa*

I first encountered *Bruma* in 1994, and I was immediately struck by its dashing shape. Rigged as a Bermudan sloop, it has a steel hull with overlapping sheets nailed to ribs set at 16 inches from each other so as to limit their thickness. The boat was designed by William Rupert Murdoch and his brother Frank, both naval architects and builders as well as excellent yachtsmen.

The designs drawn up just before World War II were for two identical hulls, classified in the II RORC (Royal Ocean Racing Club) Class and launched in 1945 at the Murdoch's shipyard in Antwerp, Belgium. At the time the two boats were named *Wyvern II* and *Flying Mist*. Both are still sailing, but not even Frank Murdoch, who was contacted in 1988, was capable of distinguishing which is which any longer.

The boat was purchased in 1988 in a sorry state, brought to Italy and dismantled completely in order to sand the inside of the hull. It was completely refitted in 1992, regaining its pace and vitality, winning numerous trophies including every single edition of the Trofeo Durand de la Penne held so far (a race between La Spezia and Capraia in Italy in all types of weather and seas). In 1994 it won its class at Imperia, and came third in 1996 despite problems with the sails. A sturdy, comfortable vessel, it is at its best sailing close-hauled or on a beam reach, thanks to its considerable ballast; it moves smoothly across the waves and performs well even in a very light breeze. *Bruma* now has a Burmese teak deck screwed directly onto the beams below, the mast and boom are of silver spruce, while the interior is in mahogany and solid teak. The excellent quality steel used for the hull has meant that the range of thickness of the plates has been preserved, even half a century after the boat's launch, and nothing structural has ever had to be replaced.

Alas, *Bruma* sank in the port of La Spezia in November 2000 during a storm. The boat was recovered, but its future remains uncertain.

LEFT: *An old photograph of* Bruma *(Photo courtesy of F. Vespa).*

TOP LEFT: *September 1994, close-up of* Bruma, *a sturdy, fast yacht well looked-after by its owner (Photo: A. Tringali).*

BELOW: *Close-up of the steering wheel (Photo courtesy of F. Vespa).*

By Albatros

Rigging:	Cutter
Sail area:	173 sq. yds.
Shipyard:	De La Gironde
	(Bordeaux, France)
Designer:	The shipyard
Year of design:	1903
Launch:	1946
Restoration:	1990, 1993
L.: 53³/₄ ft.	W.l.: 40¹/₄ ft.
B.: 13³/₄ ft.	D.: 10 ft.
Displ.: 23.81 tons	Engine: 40 Hp
Skipper:	Gérard Bani (1987)

This boat's old documents have been lost and the present ones date only from 1946, the year in which the boat, which had been completed just before World War II, was finally launched. *By Albatros* has cruised a number of times off Africa, and for a considerable time it was used as a training ship by the Bordeaux School of Sailing.

A film from the 1950s (*La Croisière de la Goélette*) gave the yacht a lot of publicity. At the time, it was skippered by Captain M. Demousseaux, who sailed it on a cruise around the western Mediterranean together with the owner, his wife, and their 18 month-old son. The boat was subsequently purchased by Gérard Bani, director of the sailing magazine *Capian*, and was restored by the Fédération Méditerranéenne pour la Culture Maritime, who look after its maintenance at the Trapani shipyard in Cassis, France.

An *ex-voto* conserved in the Sailors' Chapel in Saint Tropez recalls the time the stern of *By Albatros* was hit and dismasted by *Puritan*; fortunately it seems that nobody was injured. In 1990 the boat was rigged out as a cutter, to make it faster and easier for a small crew to maneuver.

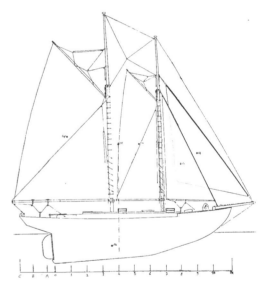

ABOVE: *September 1987, a view of* By Albatros *(Photo: L. Lauren).*

RIGHT: By Albatros *in French waters (Photo courtesy of G. Bani).*

Caroly

The name *Caroly* is dear to several generations of naval officers and yachtsmen. In 1982, *Caroly*, a winner of numerous regattas, began its service for the Italian Navy, 30 years on from its launch in the Ligurian waters of Varazze at the famous Baglietto shipyard, and in the company of *Vespucci, Palinuro, Corsaro II*, and *Stella Polare*, the other members of the prestigious fleet of training ships employed by the Italian naval academies.

It was "enlisted" in accordance with the wishes of the heirs of the owner, Commodore Riccardo Preve, a descendant of a family of sailors from Laigueglia in Liguria, Italy. His heirs donated the boat to the navy on one condition: that its unique personality be thoroughly respected. In other words, its name was not to be changed (it had been named after the owner's wife), despite the fact that it was an unusual one for a naval vessel, no modifications were to be made to certain important features of its original fitting out (such as the ward room), and it was to be used for the benefit of trainee naval officers. Thus it was that *Caroly* was to continue its sea adventures, which had started back in 1948, for many years to come.

The boat left Genoa in Italy on October 16 of that year with an Italian–Argentine crew of yachting enthusiasts, crossed the Atlantic, reached the American continent at Recife in Brazil on December 26, and then arrived at its destination, Buenos Aires, Argentina, on February 6, 1949. This was during the difficult years of the post-war period, during the rebuilding of an Italy reacting to its defeat and ensuing disasters. *Caroly* made its own small contribution to the new national image and was the first Italian yacht to cross the Atlantic after World War II. It remained in Buenos Aires until 1955 before returning to Genoa on September 19, 1956.

At the time of its departure from Genoa the crew was made up of Riccardo Preve (the owner), Emilio Gariazzo (a frigate captain on leave who acted as captain), Raul Boero, Piero Balducci, Carlo Gariazzo, Alberto Chiozza (a boatswain from Pegli), Luigi Marra (a mainsail enthusiast from Laigueglia), and Francesco Ghigliazza and Giulio Tassara (two sailors from Varazze). When the boat moored at Cannes, France, for three days, sailor Gerolamo Vasallo from Porto Maurizio in Italy joined the crew.

During the return journey, Giulio Tassara took over as boatswain. Many episodes from that unforgettable voyage are contained in the pages written by Giannetto Beniscelli from Alassio in Liguria, who came on board in Buenos Aires. The following is a moving extract from those writings.

Caroly's second Atlantic adventure

Caroly is aground now in the Varazze shipyards for a long winter rest. The hull, the masts, and the installations need a thorough check-up after the boat's Atlantic voyages and years of uninterrupted sailing. The engineers and carpenters at the Baglietto shipyard are currently sifting through the installations and rigging, both on board and below board, in order to discover any defects due to the age of the boat and its intense sailing activity over the years.

When Caroly sets sail once again this coming spring, it will be as if it is a new boat, yet one that has been thoroughly run-in over the previous years. Those sailors of Liguria, both young and old, who know the history of the boat all come to see it as it stands there tall and proud at the quayside, and they admire it as you would a thoroughbred stallion in its famous enclosure.

This is a famous boat all right. Its specifications are those dictated by the modern tendency towards yachts designed to cope with long cruises: rigged as a yawl, it boasts an overall length of 77½ feet, a waterline of 56 feet, and a beam of 15¾ feet. When needs be, it can resort to an Alfa Romeo 75 Hp diesel engine, and it has a diesel generator for the production of electric current. It also has the standard installations normally seen on a boat of this size (a radiophone, a radio compass, an echo sounder, etc.) as well as some extremely modern equipment such as the automatic pilot.

Rigging:	Bermudan yawl
Sail area:	251 sq. yds.
Shipyard:	Baglietto (Varazze, Italy)
Designer:	Vittorio Baglietto
Year of design:	1946
Launch:	1948
Restoration:	1997–98 Porto Cervo shipyards (Sardinia)
L.: 77½ ft.	W.l.: 56 ft.
B.: 15¾ ft.	Df.: 6 ft.
Displ.: 57.32 tons	Engine: 110 Hp
Skipper:	Marco Pistelli (1986), Francesco Tedeschi (1988–90), Giovanni Piaggio (1991), Luigi Castro (1998)

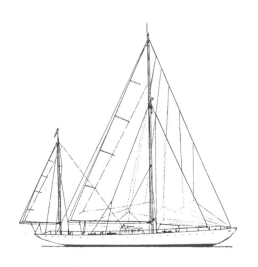

However, the fact is that Caroly *is a yacht that performs best when powered by the wind. Its 70 Hp engine is small given the size of the boat, whereas its large sails – the jib, the foresail, the mainsail, the mizzen, and others, suitable for all weathers – are raised to gather up the breath of God, the infinite wind guaranteeing unlimited sailing.*

After its launch in 1948 and a test run in the Ligurian sea and the Mediterranean, Caroly *set sail from Genoa on October 16 in the direction of Buenos Aires. Leaving in its wake the homely seas of the Mediterranean, enclosed by the Straits of Gibraltar, it called at Tangiers and Casablanca during its first voyage, then Madeira, the Canaries, and the Cape Verde Islands, and it managed the Atlantic crossing to the north Brazilian coast in just 12 days of sailing, thanks largely to the trade winds constantly blowing in its favor. It arrived at Rio de la Plata in Argentina on February 16, 1949.*

After seven years of a mixture of river and ocean sailing, Riccardo Preve decided to bring the boat back to Italy, choosing a more ambitious and difficult route this time. Starting from Buenos Aires, Caroly *sailed via Brazil, the Antilles, New York, Portugal, and Gibraltar to its destination, Genoa. A distance of more than 13,000 miles – an important voyage for a great yacht.*

Caroly's *second great adventure was to begin in December of that same year. After making careful technical and logistical preparations, we left the milky coffee-colored waters of Rio de la Plata on Boxing Day for the deep blue of the ocean beyond Montevideo. The weather was bad during the initial phase of the voyage, with an unusually hostile summer of north-eastern winds blowing into our faces, while the head sea slowed down* Caroly's *progress considerably, and we were forced to tack for considerable distances at up to 150 to 200 miles from the invisible Brazilian coast. These proved difficult days and nights that truly tested both the boat and its crew. After the battle against the wild gusts from the north, and the sudden about-turns of the cold "pampero" from the south, life on board had to be quickly and effectively organized.*

On January 13 we reached Rio de Janeiro, and on January 31 we were at Recife. We got a glimpse of the lesser known aspects of Brazil when we reached the latitude of Pernambuco and the villages of the local fishermen and, further to the north, at the mouth of the Amazon, during a stop at the river port of Belém. When we had gone past Capo San Roque, the extreme eastern spur of South America, the sailing became much calmer. We were able to take the trade winds abeam, which enabled us to maintain a good average speed, well above what we had managed during the first stages. My memories of Belém and the Equator are of the violent colors of the horizon heavy with rain, of the humid heat of the day, often accompanied by a becalmed sea, of sails drenched by frequent squalls, and of treacherous, low coastlines. The voyage from Belém to Trinidad is 1,200 miles long, off the Guyana coast and the mouth of the Orinoco River.*

When we reached the southernmost of the Antilles we entered an unforgettable blue and green landscape of water and islands that preserved the essence of a wonderful, primitive environment – the "paradise on earth" of the English West Indies, "discovered" via the menacing Dragon's Mouth on February 27. This was the first of the many lands we visited in the Central American archipelagos. Further north, Caroly's *main ports of call included Tobago, Robinson Crusoe Island, Barbados, Grenada, Saint Vincent, Saint Lucia, the green French Martinique, Antigua (to pay homage to the memory of Nelson and the ancient British Navy), Saint Thomas, and Puerto Rico.*

One of the sentimental aims of this voyage was to retrace the steps of Christopher Columbus in a kind of pilgrimage in reverse, traveling to seas and places where famous historical discoveries were made. From Trinidad upwards, we came across wonderful reminders and names from the days of Columbus on every shore and beach. A truly eloquent, fascinating experience for sailors who could pretend that time had stopped and that they were living in a continuum with the ghosts of the past.

Caroly *anchored at Puerto Plata, in the ancient Hispaniola, which is today divided between the Dominican Republic and Haiti, and then proceeded on to San Salvador, the island of discovery, which appeared before us at sunset on April 16.*

In a little over two days, leaving the first of the Bahamas to our left, we sailed from San Domingo to the desolate harbor of Cockburn, where, on a fateful October day in 1492, Columbus' caravels anchored, and where we had been preceded by Corsaro *under Captain*

ABOVE: Caroly *under sail (Photo courtesy of the UDAP Office, Naval Ministry).*

OPPOSITE PAGE: *VBR 1991,* Caroly *in a regatta (Photo: J. Taylor).*
BELOW: *VBR 1999, close-up of the stern section (Photo: J. Taylor).*

ABOVE: *A fine aerial photo of Caroly (Photo courtesy of the UDAP Office, Naval Ministry).*

BELOW: *VBR 1999, the spinnaker bearing the coat of arms of the four Maritime Republics (Photo: J. Taylor).*

De Albertis, on a pilgrimage cruise completed way back in 1893. Then we reached the northern Bahamas and the natural paradise of Nassau, where we encountered the Gulf Stream, before sailing along the Florida Channel to reach Miami; then on up northwards, along the Georgia coast, past South and North Carolina, as far as Morehead, where we turned into the perfect, navigable waterways of the United States so as to carefully avoid Cape Hatteras, and to sail through the forests and green pastures of the state of Virginia. Our inland journey took us 360 miles on, to Norfolk and Chesapeake Bay, with a stop at Annapolis and Delaware Bay, from where we returned to the Atlantic Ocean in order to reach New York City.

Our transatlantic crossing began on June 14, 1949, when we headed for Bermuda, which we reached on June 19. Ahead of us lay the 2,000 miles to the Azores. In 16 days, during which we encountered every possible kind of weather ranging from the highly exasperating "cippa" to extremely rough seas and strong winds, Caroly reached the port of Punta Delgada on the island of San Miguel. From the Azores, we sailed on to Europe, and docked at Lisbon in Portugal, followed by Cadiz in Spain, Gibraltar, the Balearic Islands, and Monte Carlo. On August 19, with perfect timing with regard to the timetable we had set ourselves, the voyage terminated at Genoa, and Caroly anchored in its home waters, in front of the headquarters of the Italian Yacht Club, in the tiny harbor of Duca degli Abruzzi.

During its last voyage, Caroly sailed some 13,150 miles, from the 35° parallel in the southern hemisphere to the 41° parallel in the northern hemisphere, and to the west as far as the Mediterranean. If we add this latter voyage to the first transatlantic crossing (7,150 miles), the total distance traveled is a considerable one for a yacht. We anchored in 34 different ports in 14 different countries. Everywhere we sailed we were offered genuine, spontaneous friendship and support from sea-faring people from all over the world, and hundreds of Italians greeted us everywhere we went with truly moving joy and enthusiasm.

The technical experience we gained deserves a special mention. At all latitudes we tried to sail during the best possible season, starting in Central America when the frightening hurricanes with their attractive female names are usually dormant. The ocean crossing was completed between June and July, when weather conditions should be ideal. However, seas and winds were obviously not always 100 percent kind to us – we were buffeted by gales and becalmed on more than one occasion – but this return to old-fashioned sailing proved a truly exciting test of our ability.

In an age when engines have arrogantly canceled the real distances between continents, reducing the size of the earth to that of a magic box, being propelled along by the four winds in such an immense area of open sea proved to be a genuine privilege for us all. This purest of sea-faring experiences was a tiring yet emotionally satisfying one, accompanied by the marvelous spectacle of marine nature at its purest and most harmonious, all from the tiny surface area of a small yacht.

Emilio Gariazzo was the untiring, ever-vigilant captain. Already back in 1949, after having watched over the birth and construction of Caroly, he had accompanied and skippered this boat from Genoa to Buenos Aires. His proven ability, the result of a brilliant career in the Italian navy, together with his vast sailing experience, fairly guaranteed the success of the adventure. The owner, Riccardo Preve, was visibly rejuvenated during this voyage (he was accompanied for long stretches by his wife, Caroly Preve, and two of their children – one during the American part of the voyage and the other during the European section). The crew was completed by Carlo Gariazzo, "the lawyer," with two transatlantic crossings to his name; the Argentinian doctor Raul Boero, who fortunately was not called upon to offer his professional services; Jorge Balerdi, another Argentine – nicknamed "el cieco" (the blind) – a man of limitless energy and resources; and myself, the writer of this diary. Other members included the faithful Giulio Tassara of Varazze, boatswain, cook, fisherman, and a truly irreplaceable member of the crew; Antonio Costa Ros, a Catalan from Ibiza – a real sailor; and young Beppe Riolfo from Laigueglia in Italy. Given the various nationalities present on board, albeit all of Latin origin, the language we used was virtually a new one, created ad hoc and immediately understandable to all.

The Italian flag flew from the stern of Caroly throughout our journey across the seas of the western hemisphere, while the red-and-white burgee of the Italian Yacht Club flying from the mainmast indicated the wind direction.

Cerida

uilt in Poole in 1938, and based on 12 drawings by Laurent Giles, *Cerida* is a splendid yacht with a mahogany skin, an 8.818-ton lead keel, oak beams and ribs, and a teak deck and interior. The original drawings are conserved at the National Maritime Museum in Greenwich, London.

The British flag was replaced by the Italian one during the early post-war years, when the boat was the property of the Milanese industrialist De Angeli Frua (the 1955 Register of Yachts, boat no. 1199). Subsequent buyers, including the owners Tarragoni, Cameli, Ribbi, and Grossetti, kept the boat moored at the Italian Yacht Club moorings in the port of Genoa, with one sailor constantly stationed on board.

Over the years, *Cerida* underwent a series of restoration operations at the Sangermani shipyard in Lavagna, Italy, and in Sardinia, where it was mainly chartered by its new owner, Michele Amorosi (the owner from 1987 to 1992). Amorosi lived on board and saw to routine maintenance work himself.

The interior layout has remained virtually unchanged from when the boat was launched (apart from the portholes on either side of the deckhouse, which are not original), as have the furnishings. Around the year 1970, significant restoration work was carried out that partially altered the silhouette of the boat. The deckhouse was modified, fortunately not in height but in width, with an extension into the keel and framefloor. The skylights, on the other hand, have remained the same as those shown in a beautiful photograph taken by Beken in 1948. If you look carefully at this photo you can make out the boomed foresail and a longer boom, as well as a steering mechanism featuring a tiller.

During the 1970s, *Cerida* featured a seven-eighths rig – a wooden mast and boom (later replaced by shorter aluminum ones). The new rigging, designed by Silvio Lami, still had a staysail, but rigged at the top of the mast and not boomed, as well as larger genoas that were originally envisaged and

Rigging:	*Gaff-rigged cutter*
Sail area:	*120 sq. yds.*
Shipyard:	*R.A. Newman & Sons (Poole, England)*
Designer:	*Laurent Giles*
Year of design:	*1937*
Launch:	*1938*
Restoration:	*1972, 1999 Argentario naval shipyard (Italy)*
L.: *43 ft.*	W.l.: *34 ¼ ft.*
B.: *10 ½ ft.*	Df.: *6 ft.*
Displ.: *16.27 tons*	Engine: *50 Hp*
Skipper:	*Sergio Grossetti (1986), Michele Amorosi (1987–92), G. Giordano (1998–2000)*

BELOW: *ASW June 2001,* Cerida *sailing close-hauled brilliantly (Photo: J. Taylor).*

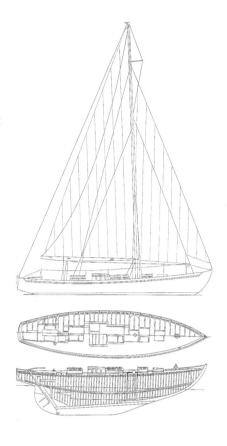

were now necessary given the smaller size of the new gaff sail.

Cerida has also taken part in numerous races. It came fourth in the 1953 Giraglia and took part in the Fastnet Race, flying the burgee of the Royal Corinthian Yacht Club. It has also taken part in various vintage yacht regattas, often crewed by members of the "Venturieri" association, and it has served as a training boat for the latter organization.

Over the years, Michael Amorosi got to know the boat and treated it with loving care. *Cerida*, an extremely smooth mover when under sail, was designed for ocean racing, and it is at its very best in high seas, thanks largely to the gentle streamlining of the stempost, which enables it to drive forward, opening up the waves rather than penetrating them and being slowed as a consequence. *Cerida* has not been part of the fleet of the "Venturieri" for some years now.

Amorosi eventually sold the boat to a new owner, who immediately decided to restore it to its former splendor at the Argentario naval shipyards in Italy. The continual changes in ownership had had negative repercussions for the boat, with a series of modernization operations destroying its original simplicity.

As has already been mentioned, the streamlined wooden mast with seven-eighths cutter rigging, steering wheels, and boomed staysail had been replaced by a shorter aluminum mast (10 feet tall), gaff-rigged at the masthead. The original central skylight and the adjacent skylight had been merged to form one large, flat deckhouse, with the original spacious, simple deck but a distant memory. The cockpit and steering gear had also been modified. However, the restoration work carried out at the Argentario naval shipyards was designed to be in total keeping with the original project drawn up by Laurent Giles.

Cerida has red mahogany skin laid over steam-curved oak ribs and forged iron frame-floors. The historical restoration of the boat, which started in November 1998, was completed the following summer. It was a long, complicated job: the iron frame-floors, seriously compromised by the formation of rust and over the years reinforced with metal crosspieces, were almost all replaced by new hand-forged pieces of the shape and size indicated by Giles in his designs. The new frame-floors are made

from red-lead-treated steel and fastened to the keel by silicon bronze bolts. Many of the hull's original mahogany strakes (80 percent) were replaced by new ones nailed to copper and caulked with cotton. The heart-shaped transom, which had previously been remade using marine plywood, was completely rebuilt using the overlapping-plank method (three planks overlapped and glued using a special epoxy glue). With the exception of a few beams (fortunately including the one bearing the serial number), all the beams were rebuilt from Slovenian oak using dovetail joints. Teak planks of an average length of 26 feet, and 1 inch thick, were then laid across the beams. The missing skylights were rebuilt according to the specifications contained in the original drawings. The mast, gaff-sail boom, spinnaker pole, staysail boom, spreaders, and jumpers were all made from Sitka spruce and silicon bronze fittings, as shown in the original drawings.

In July 1999, *Cerida* set sail once again, refitted according to its original design with a new spruce mast (back to its original length), a new rudder with tiller, and the provisional deckhouse removed for good. With this exciting new look, *Cerida* was awarded the much sought-after Maltese Cross and granted its class, despite the fact that restoration work below deck was still going on.

Here then are the honors won in the 1999 season: second place in its class in the Almirante Conde de Barcelona Cup; second prize for the best restored yacht; first place in its class in the Porto Cervo Regatta; third place in its class at Cannes; first place in its class at Saint Tropez; first place overall in the Prada Challenge Trophy for vintage sloops; and first prize in the Leroy Trophy at Saint Tropez. Furthermore, in 2000 it won first prize in its class at Porto Santo Stefano in Argentario, Italy. A brilliant start to *Cerida*'s new life.

Cheone

Rigging:	Bermudan cutter
Sail area:	299 sq. yds.
Shipyard:	Jas N. Miller & Sons (St. Monance, Scotland)
Designer:	Robert Clark and W.E. Forester
Year of design:	1937
Launch:	1937
Restoration:	1989–90 Argentario naval shipyard (Italy)
L.: 72 ft.	W.l.: 56 ft.
B.: 15³/₄ ft.	Df: 9¹/₂ ft.
Displ.: 77.16 tons	Engine: 90 Hp
Skipper:	Marcello Murzilli

RIGHT: *Argentario 1992,* Cheone *under sail (Photo: J. Taylor).*

BELOW: *Argentario 1992,* Cheone *during a regatta (Photo: J. Taylor).*

This boat was launched under the name *Tresca* in 1937. It has had a number of different owners, including Colonel Robert Low (during the mid-1950s), who registered the boat in the port of Valencia in Spain. The boat arrived in Italy from Madagascar, skippered by an English owner. However, it lay abandoned at Porto Santo Stefano in Argentario, Italy until it was discovered by its present owner, who immediately decided to have it restored. Renamed *Cheone*, its refitting included a new teak deck and the re-caulking of the entire skin. This work was carried out according to the original plans received from the Scottish shipyard, which is still in business. The cockpits and the sails were furnished by the two English suppliers Harry Spencer and Ratsey & Lapthorn, respectively.

Thus it was that the completely renewed *Cheone* took place in the Round the World Rally, an around the world regatta-cruise via the Panama and Suez Canals. It left Gibraltar on January 6, 1991, and completed the round-the-world voyage on April 15, 1992, the only vintage boat among the 20 cruise-class boats and the 13 regatta-class vessels. *Cheone*, with its wooden mast and seven-eighths rig, also took part in the vintage yacht regatta at Porto Santo Stefano in September 1992.

Chérie

ABOVE: *September 1990, a fine shot of* Chérie *(presently in the Adriatic) (Photo: S. Pesato).*

This boat arrived in Italy in 1968, when it was purchased by the architect Biuso of Rome, who in turn sold it to Roberto Brucci from Castiglioncello in Tuscany. Under its second owner, *Chérie* underwent a lengthy, complete refitting, which was not finished until it was sold to its present owner, Leonardo Bagni, in 1989.

The Adriatico shipyard in Rimini completely restored the boat. The deck was completely rebuilt in 1 inch-thick solid teak, and all the skylights, the deckhouse, the cockpits, and the toerail have been restored according to the original plans. The layout of the space below deck has been redistributed in order to make it more liveable. Some of the stempost and the sternpost has been replaced, together with the helmport and the rudderstock, while the rudder blade has been rebuilt in iroko.

Chérie has a clear deck with low toerail, a harmonious hull plan that ends at the bow in a fine, sturdy bowsprit. It is a stable boat shaped for speed, with an 12.13-ton bulb, and is currently available for charter.

Rigging:	*Bermudan ketch*
Sail area:	*239 sq. yds.*
Shipyard:	*Monzone & Son (Monaco)*
Designer:	*Monzone & Son*
Year of design:	*1954*
Launch:	*1955*
Restoration:	*1988–89 Adriatico shipyard (Rimini, Italy)*
L.: 57¼ ft.	*W.l.: 42½ ft.*
B.: 11 ft.	*Df: 8 ft.*
Displ.: 26.46 tons	*Engine: 78 Hp*
Skipper:	*Leonardo Bagni (1990)*

Clever

Clever was built in a boatyard in La Rochelle, France, that no longer exists. Specifically designed for the long Atlantic waves, it has graceful, sleek lines and is extremely stable. It has oak planking and ribs, mahogany beams, a teak deck, and Douglas pine masts and boom. Someone, on seeing the layout of the deck plan, thought the boat may have been the work of the famous designer William Fife III, but closer inspection reveals that it does not have those sleek lines astern so dear to that family of Scottish boat designers.

Clever has undergone a series of restorations over the years, and it is now an elegant vessel with a comfortable, light interior. It flew the Monaco flag up until 1976 and was then bought by an Italian, Gianni Loffredo, who kept it for nearly six years.

Around about 1981 the boat was sold once again, this time to Franco Torrini, who looked after it lovingly. The sails, which are a faithful reproduction of the original design (albeit in heavy-duty white dacron), generate maximum power in a fresh breeze and when sailing close-hauled or on a beam reach. During the course of 1996, the new owner, Ernst Grasser, had the boat's hull and masts serviced at Guido del Carlo's boatyard in Viareggio, Italy.

Rigging:	*Gaff-rigged yawl*
Sail area:	*251 sq. yds.*
Shipyard:	*La Rochelle shipyards (France)*
Designer:	*The shipyard*
Year of design:	*1927*
Launch:	*1927*
Restoration:	*1996 Del Carlo shipyard (Viareggio, Italy)*
L.: 48¾ ft.	*W.l.: 40½ ft.*
B.: 12¾ ft.	*Df: 7 ft.*
Displ.: 30.09 tons	*Engine: 93 Hp*
Skipper:	*Franco Torrini (1981–96), E. Grasser (1996)*

RIGHT AND FAR RIGHT:
Two shots of Clever *at the 1991 VBR (Photos: J. Taylor).*

BELOW: *Close-up of the sheerline and the transom (Photo: C. Borlenghi).*

Clio

(formerly Sheevra)

*C*lio, launched in 1921, was William Fife Jr.'s own personal yacht that he designed specifically for regattas and cruises in the 40-foot Class. During its first year, *Clio* won 12 of the 13 regattas it took part in, racing against other yachts in its class.

It was also one of the last works of this great designer, who was now at a venerable age and was forced to sell the boat to a Welsh yachtsman, who remained its owner for the following 27 years. Subsequently, it was resold, under the name *Sheevra*, to Peter Neidecker, chairman of the Bank of America and member of the New York Yacht Club. The new owner sailed it to the Mediterranean and adopted Cannes in France as its home port. The boat was relatively fortunate in that it had only three owners from the time Fife sold it in 1926 until 1983.

It was in 1983 that two young American admirers of Fife, Jeffrey Law and Donn Costanzo, saw the boat for the first time. It was in obvious disrepair, with the planking in desperate need of servicing. After long, drawn-out negotiations with the then owner of the boat, who was reluctant to let this noble, elegant vessel go, the two Americans finally managed to buy *Sheevra* (as it was still called) and transfer it to the Argentario naval shipyard in Italy for initial reconstruction operations.

While in the shipyard, the two met Olive Adshead, an English friend of theirs who was in the process of overseeing the construction of a new mast for *Puritan*. The upshot of their meeting was that the three decided to create a company for the purpose of restoring *Sheevra*, and personally to carry out the necessary servicing themselves with the support of the shipyard.

In the meantime, in order to bear the considerable cost of restoration work, the three business partners decided to do the restoration work on *Altair* as well. So it was that slowly but surely *Sheevra* regained its original natural splendor, thanks to the efforts of these three young people, who at the end of the day became experts in the restoration of vintage yachts.

The deck was rebuilt, the frame-floor and several ribs were replaced, the bulb was remounted using new bronze bolts, and the apron and mast step were rebuilt. *Sheevra* has a cosy interior, with antique furniture made of mahogany, iroko, and cedar, and a very clear deck, which together evoke distant memories and the true Fife style. It also has mahogany planking, oak and elm ribs reinforced with bronze plates, and a mast made from Norwegian pine.

Thanks to the refitting carried out at the Argentario yard, *Sheevra* is once again a magnificent boat that would please any vintage boat purist; a stable, fast yacht that elegantly glides over the waves. When it has failed to win outright at the vintage yacht regattas held off the coast of Imperia, it has always managed to get among the honors.

Sheevra has recently been sold once again, and is now called by its original name, *Clio*. At present it sails off the coast of Maine in the United States.

Rigging:	Bermudan sloop
Sail area:	120 sq. yds.
Shipyard:	W. Fife & Son (Fairlie, Scotland)
Designer:	William Fife Jr.
Year of design:	1919
Launch:	1921
Restoration:	1983–84 Argentario naval shipyard (Italy)
L.: 46 ft.	W.l.: 34 ¾ ft.
B.: 9 ¾ ft.	Df: 6 ft.
Displ.: 15.43 tons	Engine: 89 Hp
Skipper:	Donn Costanzo (1988–91), Timo de Vries (1994)

BELOW: *The elegance and beauty of one of William Fife Jr.'s most noble of creations (Photo: F. Taccola).*

Coaster

Rigging:	Trysail schooner
Sail area:	383 sq. yds.
Shipyard:	F.F. Pendleton (Wiscasset, Maine, USA)
Designer:	Murray Peterson
Year of design:	1934
Launch:	1935
Restoration:	1987–93
L.: 41½ ft.	W.l.: 33½ ft.
B.: 12 ft.	Df.: 6½ ft.
Displ.: 9.92 tons	Engine: 85 Hp
Skipper:	Stephen Royce (1987)

This superb schooner was built by the architect Murray Peterson for his personal use. He sailed *Coaster* along the eastern seaboard of the USA for about ten years before selling it to the Royce family from California, who sailed it along the west coast for 40 years. In 1952 the boat completed a fast Pacific crossing to Hawaii.

In 1982, under the management of the third generation of the Royce family, the boat began a round-the-world voyage via the Panama Canal, the Caribbean, the Azores, and then Europe. Given its age, it was thought wise to have the boat restored, and the work was carried out in the port of Cannes in France.

It has Philippine mahogany planking and oak ribs. In a fresh breeze, the boat can reach a speed of eight knots. *Coaster* is a member of the San Diego Yacht Club in the United States.

ABOVE: *A shot of* Coaster *(Photo courtesy of S. Royce).*
BELOW: *September 1987,* Coaster, *the splendid creation of Murray Peterson based on the American schooners of Maine (Photo: R. Minervini).*

Coch y Bondhu

The story of this yacht is one of two lives – a fascinating story that begins with a Bermudan cutter named *Coch y Bondhu* (Gaelic for "Red and Black"), which, with its canoe stern (or "pointed stern"), was launched in 1936 by the Berthon Boat Company in England. This 13.23-ton boat, with fairly slender lines, a low draft, and Bermudan seven-eighths rig, led the way in that happy age of the Gauntlet Class, taking numerous honors over the years in the Channel Race and Solent regattas off the south of England. At that time, *Coch y Bondhu* had a flush deck with steps going below in the center so as to insulate the after-cabin, teak planking, a pitch pine deck, and a silver spruce mast.

The boat has had several owners over the years: G.H.B. Wilson, J.H. Corah, W.E. Kendrick, and, finally, Lord Astor (owner of *The Times*), who gave it to his wife as a gift. After a number of other regattas, and after World War II (during which the boat played an important part in Operation Dynamo when thousands of troops were shipped to safety from the beaches of Dunkirk), *Coch y Bondhu* was transferred to Italy (in 1952) to the area of Portofino.

In 1955, according to the Register of Yachts, the boat belonged to Enrico and Franco Beghe and was registered no. 1366. However, it was not until 1967 that the boat began its second life, thanks to the actions of a man from Monza who had bought the boat in 1957 and had had the innovative, courageous idea of transforming a Gauntlet Class yacht into a Laurent Giles creation. Mario Dotti, son of the present owner, describes events at that time: "…*Giles' modifications began in 1967 and were completed by the following year. From a 41-foot cutter with a canoe stern,* Coch y Bondhu *was transformed into a 50-foot ketch (the mizzen-sail was rigged a year later) with the immediately identifiable lines of the great designer's hulls, but with its harmonious flush deck left intact. Work was carried out at the Camogli shipyard in Italy by Felice Raggi, currently technical manager at the Riva Trigoso shipyard. The boat was*

not rebuilt, but simply modified, since the hull, with the exception of the addition of bow and stern overhangs, remained unchanged. In fact, the size of the largest beam is exactly the same, and all the timbers, with the exception of an additional three feet at the bow and five feet at the stern, are exactly the same as they were in 1936 and have never been replaced…"

The transformation of the vessel was controlled by Giles himself until it had been completed. In my view, the boat is a different one from the original version, both in terms of the length of its hull and its rigging, and its sailing capabilities, which are very different from what they were.

A few years later, *Coch y Bondhu* was sold to a yachtsman in Italy, who used it as a charter and training yacht. After a period of fitting out in the Adriatic, it was bought by the present owner, who in 1986 entrusted it to Cesare Sangermani. He carried out a partial refitting, replacing some of the planking strakes together with 18 stainless-steel keel bolts. Regular servicing has given the boat a new lease of life, and it now often takes part in vintage yacht regattas, where it always gets among the honors.

Coch y Bondhu is an extremely responsive, seaworthy boat, with its teak and iroko planking, oak framing, teak deck, Douglas fir mainmast, silver spruce mizzenmast and boom, and oak interior.

Rigging:	Gaff-rigged ketch
Sail area:	323 sq. yds.
Shipyard:	Berthon Boat Company (Lymington, England)
Designer:	Paul Rodney
Year of design:	1936
Launch:	1936
Restoration:	1967–68 Camogli (Italy)
Restoration designer:	Laurent Giles
L.: 49½ ft.	W.l.: 38¼ ft.
B.: 11¼ ft.	Df: 8¾ ft.
Displ.: 17.53 tons	Engine: 100 Hp
Skipper:	Mario Dotti (1987–94)

THIS PAGE: *Imperia, September 1990, two shots of* Coch y Bondhu *(Photos: J. Taylor).*

Conti Bernardi

Rigging:	Gaff-rigged yawl
Sail area:	309 sq. yds.
Shipyard:	Luke Brothers (Hamble, England)
Designer:	A.R. Luke
Year of design:	1927
Launch:	1928
Restoration:	1990 Valdettaro shipyards (La Spezia, Italy)
L.: 70¼ ft.	W.l.: 49½ ft.
B.: 14 ft.	Df: 10 ft.
Displ.: 41.08 tons	Engine: 200 Hp
Skipper:	Vincenzo Lamberti (1990–93)

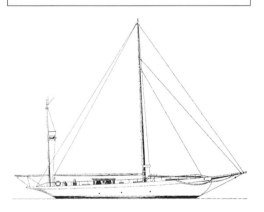

This boat was launched with the name *Gladoris II* and is registered in this name in the 1955 Register of Yachts at the port of Southampton, England, the property of V.H. Dorée. Built for an English lord, it almost immediately became the property of a wealthy American who named it *Gladoris*, a combination of the names of his two daughters, Gladis and Doris.

Thanks to his American nationality, the owner was not required to surrender the boat to the British Royal Navy during World War II (the sad destiny of many such yachts). During the post-war years, the owner's heirs sold the boat to an Italian, who soon realized the costly nature of maintaining a yacht of this kind, and, in order to cover the costs, was forced to use it as a means of transport in the Gulf of Naples. For 15 years this beautiful yacht was reduced to doing short, motor-powered trips, until the day it was noticed by Paolo Angelini, who decided to restore the boat to its original splendor.

This was the era of the "dolce vita," when famous people from the worlds of cinema, theatre, and industry came on board in search of thrilling new experiences. That period ended in 1989, the year in which the company that looked after the image of the prestigious Azienda Agricola Conti Bernardi, producer of fine wines, decided to purchase the boat. This marked the rebirth of the boat under its new name, *Conti Bernardi*, after extensive restoration and refitting work had been completed.

The interior was conserved as it had been in the original drawings, with its elegant and imaginative furnishings. The steering wheel and binnacle are the ones fitted for its launch, although on deck seven winches of the original 12 were replaced. Finally, the mizzenmast was shortened, and a number of pitch pine planks from the bottom were replaced, together with some teak planks from the topside. Some of the refitting work was carried out by skipper Vincenzo Lamberti, who remained on board from 1984 through 1993.

Today, *Conti Bernardi* is one of the most highly appreciated boats of its kind in the entire Mediterranean. Its sails cover nearly 310 square yards, sub-divided as follows: mainsail 135 square yards mizzensail 30 square yards, mizzen-staysail 65 square yards, boomed staysail 35 square yards, jib 40 square yards, and moonsail 32 square yards.

RIGHT: *1992,* Conti Bernardi *during a regatta* (Photo: J. Taylor).

BELOW: *Details of the owner's cabin* (Photo: F. Michienzi).

Creole

reole, creation no. 340 from the Camper & Nicholson shipyard, and a compound structure, was launched on September 14, 1927 as *Vira* on behalf of Alec Smith Cochrane, an American yachtsman who already owned the schooners *Westward*, *Warrior*, and *Vanitie*. When he ordered *Vira* (which turned out to be his last yacht), Cochrane was already a very ill man.

Obsessed with the idea of keeping the crew to a bare minimum, he forced Charles Nicholson to reduce the height of the masts by 30 feet. Such a radical reduction should have meant the elimination of the best part of 99.21 tons of lead in the keel. "*In this way*," Charles Nicholson was to write in *Yachting World and Power Craft* in March 1944, "*the* Creole *of my dreams was completely ruined…*" Thus it was that the boat started life with a revolutionary sailing plan that enabled it to be sailed by a limited crew (this plan can still be seen to this day).

As soon as it had been fitted out, *Vira* sailed from England towards Monte Carlo. It had a crew of just 21: two technicians (pilots), three deck-officers, six restaurant staff (waiters, chefs, and cooks), and ten sailors – a limited number of people for a yacht of this size. Yet everyone was surprised on that voyage at just how the yacht managed to do 11 knots with just a light breeze and such mutilated rigging. Encounters with *Vira* in the Mediterranean inspired other boat-owners to order two more similar vessels from Nicholson: *Ailee* and *Sonia*.

In the meantime, the owner's health had worsened considerably, and the boat was ordered to return to England, where in 1928 it was purchased by Major Maurice Pope of the Royal Yacht Squadron, who promptly renamed it *Creole*. He immediately had the masts lengthened by 10 feet, and added a further four cabins below deck. He kept the boat for nine years, using it for sailing or motor trips in the waters of the Solent off the south coast of England.

In 1937 *Creole* was sold once again, this time to Sir Connop Guthrie, a keen yachtsman who wished to restore the boat to its original design. The bases of the masts were lengthened by a further 10 feet (17 feet in the case of the mizzenmast), draft and ballast were returned to their original values, and the rigging and sails were replaced. With its unique overhangs, *Creole* sailed all over the Mediterranean between 1937 and 1939. The boat returned to Scottish waters before the war began and then sailed to Gosport, England, where it was requisitioned by the Royal Navy in September 1940 to transport troops and supplies under its new name, *Magic Circle*. The boat's owner only got it back in 1947, and, four years later, in 1951, he sold it to Stavros Narchos, a famous Greek shipping magnate who was to use it for many years in the Mediterranean.

Significant refitting work was carried out in the Kiel shipyard, where the deckhouses and the interior were replaced, with Salvador Dalí getting involved in their decoration. During this period, the *Creole* often raced in both the Mediterranean and the North Sea, and it also figured regularly in exclusive jet-set gatherings. Its guests included King Juan Carlos of Spain and Queen Sofia, who spent part of their honeymoon on board.

Towards the end of the 1970s the boat was sold to a Danish consortium who were to use it as a training boat up until 1983, when it was bought by its present owners who had found it in Denmark in desperate need of loving care and attention.

In order to restore *Creole* to its former splendor, the professional services of the Italian architects Giorgetti & Magrini were sought. Its rebuilding, after numerous patching-up operations, seemed a rather complex, albeit fascinating, task, a true challenge that was met with the highest degree of professionalism.

Work began with the stripping down of the Burmese teak hull, which proved to be in excellent condition, followed by the ribs, beams, and the frame-floor. The abnormally large engine was removed (for a boat designed to reach a top speed of 11.5 knots,

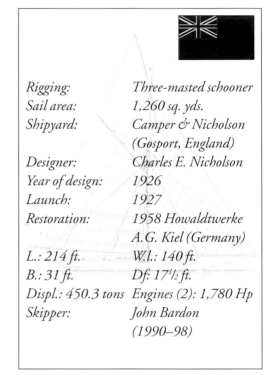

Rigging:	Three-masted schooner
Sail area:	1,260 sq. yds.
Shipyard:	Camper & Nicholson (Gosport, England)
Designer:	Charles E. Nicholson
Year of design:	1926
Launch:	1927
Restoration:	1958 Howaldtwerke A.G. Kiel (Germany)
L.: 214 ft.	W.l.: 140 ft.
B.: 31 ft.	Df: 17½ ft.
Displ.: 450.3 tons	Engines (2): 1,780 Hp
Skipper:	John Bardon (1990–98)

this engine had it traveling at 15 knots, thus risking weakening the masting). The spruce masts, also found to be in good condition, were kept, while the bottom was newly lined with copper as it had been back in 1927.

Creole's new interior reflects a clear division between the working area and the cabin quarters. The sailors' cabins feature wooden staves and light oak mouldings, while the owner's quarters are designed in classic 19th-century French style, thanks to the contribution of the French architect Albert Pinto.

So it was that *Creole* returned to racing and long-distance cruising. In 1991–92 it sailed into the Pacific for the first time ever, there to support the Italian team in the America's Cup and sailing out to sea each day during the course of the competition.

ABOVE: *Close-up of the deckhouse (Photo: G.C. Tagliafico).*
BELOW: *Imperia 1990,* Creole*'s sleek lines and magnificent sails (Photo: S. Piano).*

Croce del Sud

Croce del Sud, a truly sumptuous and mythical steel-hulled, three-masted schooner, is the only period boat that has not only maintained its original name but can also boast the unique record of having belonged to just one owner from the day of its launch. The boat-owner concerned, still sprightly considering his 86 years, said in a statement issued to Vincenzo Zaccagnino: *"…This boat has always welcomed me on board, with the exception of the five years of war. Every year since 1935 I have kept a written log telling of the crossings, the guests, the sea adventures. There are 50 volumes that I keep and cherish…"*

The boat was commissioned by Ezio Granelli, an industrialist in pharmaceuticals who ran it until his death in 1957. Since then *Croce del Sud* has been maintained with tender-loving care by his son-in-law, Bruno Mentasti (Cavaliere del Lavoro – Italy's highest honor), the proprietor and chairman of San Pellegrino, the well-known mineral water company, and his wife Maria Luisa Granelli. In the period immediately following World War II it was this boat that "discovered" the splendid, deserted, and sheltered bays of the Emerald Coast of Sardinia – *"White beaches with herds of animals and aquatic birds, limpid water…"*

During the war, *Croce del Sud* was requisitioned by the German Navy and transformed into lodgings for officers. It was well respected; before boarding, the officers would take off their boots and they wore special slippers on deck. In 1946 it was certainly the first pleasure craft to leave an Italian port (Venice), thanks to the assistance of the British ambassador to the Vatican, a keen yachtsman. Flying a British flag and in the wake of a "Liberty," the boat safely crossed the Adriatic, but it had to sail carefully in the Tyrrhenian Sea off the west coast of Italy to reach the port of Olbia in Sardinia, due to the danger of mines.

The interiors stay true to the beauty of the boat: magnificent furniture, real antiques, and armchairs bound in leather, all given a sparkle by glistening silverware and crystal glassware. In recent years *Croce del Sud* has been a star participant in various vintage boat rallies. Its sail plan has maintained the characteristics of its glorious past. Six electric winches have been fitted for the halyards of the boom foresail and six manual winches for halyards and sheets.

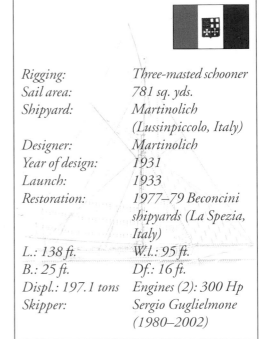

Rigging:	Three-masted schooner
Sail area:	781 sq. yds.
Shipyard:	Martinolich (Lussinpiccolo, Italy)
Designer:	Martinolich
Year of design:	1931
Launch:	1933
Restoration:	1977–79 Beconcini shipyards (La Spezia, Italy)
L.: 138 ft.	W.l.: 95 ft.
B.: 25 ft.	Df.: 16 ft.
Displ.: 197.1 tons	Engines (2): 300 Hp
Skipper:	Sergio Guglielmone (1980–2002)

TOP AND BOTTOM: *Details of* Croce del Sud *(Photos: R. Minervini and G.C. Tagliafico).*

LEFT: *Imperia 1992,* Croce del Sud *(Photo: S. Pesato).*

Croix des Gardes

Rigging:	Gaff-rigged cutter
Sail area:	126 sq. yds.
Shipyard:	Bonnin (Arcachon, France)
Designer:	Henri Dervin
Year of design:	1945
Launch:	1947
Restoration:	1993–94 Imperia shipyards (Italy)
L.: 50 ft.	W.l.: 41 ft.
B.: 12 ft.	Df.: 7 ft.
Displ.: 17.64 tons	Engine: 82 Hp
Skipper:	Mario Quaranta (1994)

Rarely do we see boats as perfect as *Croix des Gardes*, Henri Dervin's creation. After lying abandoned for ten years, this boat was found by Ernesto Quaranta, its third owner. Its original name had been *La Voie Lactée* and it had undertaken various Atlantic crossings.

Its restoration by Ernesto and Mario Quaranta at the Imperia shipyards involved two years' work: a complete reconstruction. Every part was dismantled, overhauled, and subsequently reassembled, respecting its designer's original specifications. It was possible to conserve all the planking – not a single board was replaced. A gaff-rigged cutter, *Croix des Gardes'* hull and deck structures are made of Burmese teak, and it has mahogany and oak furnishings. The mast and boom are pitch pine.

With its 6.063 tons of ballast, it has considerable stability: a stupendous boat, comfortable and safe. *Croix des Gardes* was on sale in the year 2000.

RIGHT AND BELOW: *Cannes 1998,* Croix des Gardes *(Photos: J. Taylor).*

Daphne

When, in September 1988, *Daphne* arrived at the quay in Imperia, I believe it went unnoticed by most people, including yours truly. Certainly no one at the time thought of connecting this old hull to a history of 20 years of roving the Mediterranean, committed to print in a famous book by Göran Schildt entitled *Vent'anni di Mediterraneo* (*Twenty Years of the Mediterranean*), published in 1969 by Edizioni Mursia of Milan.

Daphne was launched as a sloop in the Abö shipyard in Finland in 1935 for Madame Bandler of Helsingfors. By 1947 it already had a new owner, Christoffer Ericsson of Brando (opposite Helsinki), a Finnish historian and writer on maritime matters who set sail one day for Madeira but ended up in Copenhagen instead.

That same year, Schildt, a friend of the owner, managed to persuade him to sell the boat that he had often sailed from Finland around the Aalands Islands and into the various harbors of the Baltic. So it was that the new owner and his wife left Sweden, reaching the Mediterranean to embark upon a new way of life. It was their way of opting out of the pressures of a highly technical, consumer society, to leave behind the atrocities of war and seek a classical, Homeric life, one that only the old Mediterranean could offer.

On May 17, 1948 *Daphne* set sail from Stockholm for England, then headed south through the French canal system to the Ligurian Riviera. It reached Rapallo, then in Lavagna found a winter resting place at the Sangermani shipyards, where it was to return on many occasions in the years that followed. Then came a regular succession of cruises to Greece, the Adriatic, North Africa, Turkey, and the Lebanon, which provided the inspiration for a volume of memoirs that is also an analysis of the customs and civilizations encountered during many years at sea.

Daphne arrived at Imperia with cotton sails, original spruce masting, a Swedish pine deck, oak frames and keel, and teak planking. As in the original plan, the boat has a central cockpit between two deckhouses. Every detail clearly reveals the sophistication, craftsmanship, and professionalism of its builder, who has also made abundant use of "peroba" – a type of Brazilian wood that is in no way inferior to teak in terms of hardness and durability, to the extent that the planking has never allowed even a drop of water to filter through. In 1978 *Daphne* was sold to Fritz Jaokin, who acquired it in the port of Rhodes.

Initially used as a charter vessel, *Daphne* has left the Mediterranean and currently resides in the Caribbean. It reaches a good rate of knots, especially with trading winds.

Rigging:	*Gaff-rigged ketch*
Sail area:	*66 sq. yds.*
Shipyard:	*Båtvarf (Abö, Finland)*
Designer:	*Jarl Lindblom*
Year of design:	*1934*
Launch:	*1935*
Restoration:	*1987*
L.: 35 ft.	*W.l.: 28½ ft.*
B.: 9 ft.	*Df.: 5 ft.*
Displ.: 7.17 tons	*Engine: 50 Hp*
Skipper:	*Roberto Sartori (1988)*

LEFT: *Imperia 1988, the ketch* Daphne, *built in Finland, in its last Mediterranean appearance (Photo: S. Pesato).*

Desirée

Rigging:	Gaff-rigged ketch
Sail area:	275 sq. yds.
Shipyard:	Anker & Jensen (Asker, Norway)
Designer:	Anker & Jensen
Year of design:	1912
Launch:	1913
Restoration:	1947, 1984 Carlini shipyards (Rimini, Italy)
L.: 66 ft.	W.l.: 19¼ ft.
B.: 12½ ft.	Df.: 10 ft.
Displ.: 26.46 tons	Engine: 120 Hp
Skipper:	Leonardo Bagni (1986–87)

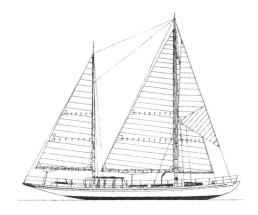

THIS PAGE: *VBR 1999, two shots of* Desirée *(Photos: J. Taylor).*

Another boat rich in history. Elegant, with very high overhangs (26 feet of difference between the overall length and that of the waterline), *Desirée* has participated in the first two boat rallies in Imperia. It was built in Norway in 1913, designed by Anker & Jensen, a firm that is well known for having built hundreds of boats. *Desirée* was commissioned by the Hohenzollern family, related to Kaiser Wilhelm II, and was called *Sibyllan*. It was a 12-meter SI, rigged as a trysail cutter, with mahogany planking and interiors, and covered in teak and steel framing.

When it came to Italy in 1928, still rigged as a cutter, the boat went by the name of *Sirocco*. It was renamed *Scirocco* and, shortly afterwards, *Dux* by the Compagnia della Vela of Venice, who had acquired it to use in cruises and regattas. *Dux* performed well in these on various occasions (such as the International Regatta of the Balearics).

In 1930 it made a cruise from Venice to Tripoli and back, and in 1939 it won the Lussino–Zara Regatta. In that year *Dux* was moved to the Galeazze Pavilion in the Arsenal in Venice, where it remained until 1943. Returned to the water when the Pavilion was ordered to be emptied by the Germans, the boat, with its seams opened by its long dry period, sank shamefully. Recovered and taken to Mazzorbo, in the Laguna in Venice, it remained there until the end of the war, after having even the lead plundered from its keel.

In 1947 the wreck (only the hull and the boom existed) was acquired by the Venetian Francesco Boratto, a partner of the Compagnia della Vela, who rebaptized it *Marisetta*. The new owner carried out considerable restructuring work. The boat was transformed into a ketch, a deckhouse was built, two davits were fitted on the starboard side, and the bow and stern were lengthened by 20 inches. Also, for the first time, the boat was equipped with an engine. The missing bulb was replaced with a lighter cast iron one, while the deck was endowed with a small, wooden toerail.

Marisetta had other owners: Giancarlo Zacchello (1953) and Torquato Gennari of Pesaro. The latter raised the deckhouse and changed the name again to *Valeria*. In 1970 Torquato Gennari sold the boat to the agricultural entrepreneur Giancarlo Lenzi of Bologna, who renamed it *Desirée*, as it was much desired by him. He restored it completely, carrying out many important works including instaling new stainless steel tanks and shrouds, renovation of the interior and exterior furnishings, an overhaul of the engine, and fitting new navigation equipment. *Desirée* finally regained its lustre of old.

In 1976 the boat was sold to the publisher Malipiero of Bologna. In 1983 the boat had yet another new owner, Leonardo Bagni, who used it for chartering. But the waltz of changing ownership for this boat does not seem to be over yet.

Dorade

orade, design no. 7, a yawl by the Stephens brothers, who were very young at the time, opened a new page in yacht design with its innovations. It was certainly this hull, with its unmistakable, well-deployed lines, that created the most renown for its constructor, Olin Stephens, at the tender age of 21.

The first results were outstanding: victory in the Transatlantic Race of 1931 and in the Fastnet Race the same year, and again in 1933. Nobody could have imagined that such a small, narrow boat (the hull was at least 6 feet shorter than those of its adversaries) would be able to race so naturally in the North Atlantic, managing to win resoundingly (two days in real time and four after handicaps). "*You are first!*" was the famous answer when the lonely, bewildered Stephens brothers asked their position on arrival. This unbelievable victory had been influenced by the choice of route followed by *Dorade*, much more to the north, and therefore shorter.

At that time *Dorade*, with its 52 feet overall, was defined by *The Times* as "*the most prodigious small ocean-regatta yacht ever built*," and the well-known critic Uffa Fox was also of the same opinion. The Stephens brothers also earned themselves a ticker-tape parade on their return home. *Dorade* contained several other innovations: the narrow, deep hull; its famous windsails; and the spruce masts that were hollow. The rudder had a tiller, and the limited main beam (10¼ feet) did not help provide much living comfort in a hull that was born to race.

Dorade won something of everything: two Bermuda Races and, in 1936, the San Francisco–Honolulu Race. After so many successes, however, it remained in the Seattle area in Washington state, used as a training vessel, until once again Federico Nardi, who is responsible for rescuing various historic boats, managed to take it to Italy for restoration at the Argentario naval shipyard.

Rigging:	Bermudan ketch
Sail area:	135 sq. yds.
Shipyard:	Minneford Yacht Club (City Island, New York, USA)
Designer:	Olin Stephens
Year of design:	1929
Launch:	1930
Restoration:	1996 Argentario Naval shipyard (Italy)
L.: 52 ft.	W.l.: 37¼ ft.
B.: 10¼ ft.	Df.: 8 ft.
Displ.: 16.53 tons	Engine: 50 Hp
Skipper:	Giles McLoughlin (1998), P. Frech (2000)

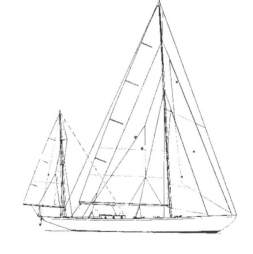

TOP LEFT: *Imperia 1998, close-up of Olin Stephens on board* Dorade *(Photo: R. Minervini).*

LEFT: *ACJ Cowes 2001,* Dorade *at a regatta (Photo: J. Taylor).*

The interventions were not all-embracing, and many components were returned to their original splendor. Only the deck, originally made of American cedar, was redone in teak. In September 1998 *Dorade* visited Imperia, and with it came Olin Stephens, now an elderly man, who was able to enjoy the historical exhibition in his honor and to race successfully.

The presence of the great Olin, still active and dynamic despite his age, rendered even more evocative the Imperia Boat Rally, which enabled him to visit the Shipbuilding Room of the International Naval Museum. His damp eyes betrayed his emotion in this room devoted to the wood craftsmanship and memories of his distant youth.

After four years of flying the Italian flag, *Dorade* has recently been acquired by a Dutch boat-owner.

TOP: *ASW 1999, a vessel born to race* (Photo: J. Taylor).

ABOVE: *Close-up of a deck without encumbrances* (Photo: J. Taylor).

RIGHT: *Imperia, September 2000*, Dorade *during a close-hauled stage* (Photo: J. Taylor).

Dyarchy

The name of this vessel, *Dyarchy*, has never changed. According to my friend Carlo Sciarelli, it is "*the most beautiful cruise boat that is still afloat.*" That is an opinion shared by many personalities in the yachting world. Indeed, though not having competitive successes behind it, *Dyarchy* has for years been accompanied by fame, due simply to the beauty and functionality of its sophisticated lines. Again, Sciarelli, who devoted no less than four pages of his book to the boat, defined it as the "character boat" of the century, that is the ambition of skippers who hate regattas.

Dyarchy was designed by Laurent "Jack" Giles for Robert Pinkney, Commodore of the Royal Cruising Club and formerly owner of a "pilot cutter" from Bristol, England (from 1901) bearing the same name. Compared to the earlier boat, *Dyarchy* was longer, a little narrower, and had more sail, but was still practically the same boat with the same lines. The boatowner's idea was to have the old *Dyarchy* in a modern version, taking account of the fact that the new one was to be conceived so as not to remain at sea in winter like the "pilot" boats.

Dyarchy, project no. 37 by Giles, was built in Sweden, with a hull completely made of oak. The spacious interior was designed by the boat-owner, an architect who, in partial payment of *Dyarchy*, designed a house for Giles in which he lived for the rest of his life. The boat needed a transom stern in order to remove the rudder easily when it came to be in low water over mud. The bow, on the other hand, is very high on the water. The hull has a solid construction; the framing consists of steam-bent oak that is planked with Swedish oak – very sturdy and close.

The launch was in 1939, but World War II prevented the owner from moving the boat to England, so it remained on land for five years. This caused *Dyarchy* to sink during the sea launch due to leaking between disconnected seams. In July 1945 the boat set sail without a motor and was registered in the port of Southampton.

From 1947 through 1950 *Dyarchy* cruised in the Baltic Sea and around Spain. It was mentioned by *Yacht Monthly* as a "*beautiful flush deck, gaff-rigged cutter, with the mast moved slightly astern.*" This was to reduce the main sail to less than 60 square yards and so make it maneuverable by a single man. The mast is a single piece of poplar, that is, without a pole, and the gaff sail is put out by itself with a single hoisting, since the halyard is guided. It has ample space and few subdivisions, following the owner's wishes, because the boat had been conceived for two people, hence the name *Dyarchy*.

Regarding its behavior at sea, the owner had this to say: "*...at sea Dyarchy is extraordinarily dry, the bow that widens at the top seems to roll away the sea and practically nothing comes astern, and the movement is soft and sweet.*" Roger Pinkney sailed *Dyarchy* for 22 years, and subsequently sold it to Bill Batten, who held it for a further 20 years. The boat made cruises throughout northern Europe and a voyage to the Lesser Antilles.

In 1982 *Dyarchy* changed owners. The current boat-owner, Peter Wieser, took it to Italy and, though flying an Austrian flag, it made its base at San Giorgio di Nogaro. The boat has recently undergone extraordinary maintenance at the Upper Adriatic naval shipyards, under consultation with Carlo Sciarelli. The planking was in a good state of repair, but the teak deck, the large, oak deckhouse, and interiors were completely redone using Canadian cedar.

Dyarchy currently cruises in the Adriatic and occasionally participates in regattas, but without any competitive commitment, almost out of respect for the first boatowner who brought it into being.

Rigging:	Trysail cutter
Sail area:	157 sq. yds.
Shipyard:	Sture Truedsson (Listerby, Sweden)
Designer:	Laurent Giles
Year of design:	1937
Launch:	1939
Restoration:	1995 Upper Adriatic shipyards (Monfalcone, Italy)
L.: 46 ft.	W.l.: 38 ft.
B.: 12½ ft.	Df.: 7¼ ft.
Displ.: 26.68 tons	Engine: 50 Hp
Skipper:	Peter Wieser

FOLLOWING PAGE: *A shot of* Dyarchy *enjoying a relaxing life of cruising in the waters of Trieste off Italy (Photo: M. Marzari).*

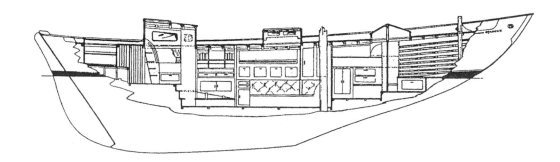

Eileen

It has not been possible to learn more about the history of this boat, launched in Norway in 1938, probably from a design by Christian Jensen, although it seems that it has never changed its name.

Eileen is a 12-meter "cruising" boat (a Scandinavian cruise version of the 12-meter SI). In 1959 it was owned by Niels Cristad, with Oslo in Norway as its port of registration. The boat was then owned by Sonia Henie, the great Norwegian skating champion, until her death in 1969. Sold in Sweden, *Eileen* was transformed into a ketch. It returned to Norway in 1985 with its new owner Erling Storm, and it was restored by him and used for charter activities. In 1997 the boat was transferred to a Dutch boat-owner. The architect Cees van Tongeren, of the Van de Stadt studio, was commissioned to restore it and return it to its condition at the time of its launch.

The restoration work was performed in France and was completed following the original design, but the interior, the equipment (battened gaff-sail), and the deck layout were redesigned in a rather too modern manner, with a large number of "self-tailing" winches. The boat appeared at the Imperia Boat Rally for the first time in 1998, where it performed well in competition, winning its class.

Rigging:	*Bermudan cutter*
Sail area:	*239 sq. yds.*
Shipyard:	*Soon Glip og Baat A/S (Soon, Norway)*
Designer:	*Christian Jensen*
Year of design:	*1938*
Launch:	*1938*
Restoration:	*1996*
L.: 61 ½ ft.	*W.l.: 41 ft.*
B.: 12 ft.	*Df.: 9½ ft.*
Displ.: 23.15 tons	*Engine: 80 Hp*
Skipper:	*Timo de Vries (1998), C. Manager (2000)*

LEFT: *Imperia, September 2000,* Eileen, *a 12-meter cruising boat (Photo: J. Taylor).*

BELOW: *Imperia, September 2000, shot of the cutter* Eileen, *a fast hull built in Norway (Photo: J. Taylor).*

Ellen

Rigging:	Gaff-rigged sloop
Sail area:	219 sq. yds.
Shipyard:	Bonnin Frères (Arcachon, France)
Designer:	Talma Bertrand
Year of design:	1930
Launch:	1931
Restoration:	1980
L.: 63 ft.	W.l.: 43 ft.
B.: 11½ ft.	Df.: 8 ft.
Displ.: 27.56 tons	Engine: 90 Hp
Skipper:	Marco Avazeri (1988)

ABOVE: Ellen *close-hauled (Photo courtesy of M. Avazeri).*

This sloop can be considered one of the first French 12-meter SIs. In the 1930s it was captained and owned by Baron De Turckheim, who wanted to make it a regatta and cruise vessel.

Ellen remained in the Atlantic until 1958. After this time, Marseilles in France became its port. The boat has participated in numerous regattas – at Porto Cervo and Imperia in Italy, and at the Nioulargue, the Coupe Phocea, and the Porquerolles Cup.

Emilia

Rigging:	Gaff-rigged schooner
Sail area:	221 sq. yds.
Shipyard:	Attilio Costaguta (Genoa, Italy)
Designer:	Attilio Costaguta
Year of design:	1929
Launch:	1930
Restoration:	1988–90 Beconcini shipyards (La Spezia, Italy)
L.: 68¾ ft.	W.l.: 57 ft.
B.: 12½ ft.	Df.: 9¾ ft.
Displ.: 30.86 tons	Engine: 72 Hp
Skipper:	Giulio Ricci (1990), Francesco Dazzi (1992), Lucia Pozzo (1998), M.R. Gastaldi (2000)

RIGHT: *ASW 1999, view of the deck of* Emilia *while maneuvering (Photo: J. Taylor).*

Emilia is the oldest Italian boat bearing the pennant of the Italian Yacht Club. Its history began in 1929, a time in which the Costaguta naval shipyards of Genoa Voltri began the construction of a 12-meter boat based on the designs of Nathaniel Herreshoff. The vessel, a sloop of 70 feet overall, was a gift from Senator Giovanni Agnelli to his son-in-law, engineer Carlo Nasi, a keen yachtman.

Looking ahead to the launching of this new regatta craft, the French programmed a series of competitions reserved for this larger category, in which boats that became renowned over the years would participate, such as *Spina*, owned by the Marquis Spinola (the first 12-meter to be built in Italy, again in 1929, by the Baglietto shipyards in Varazze), *Doris*, *Iris*, etc.

However, due to a sudden move to the USA, Nasi had to abandon his plans for *Emilia* when the construction of the boat was already at an advanced stage. It was then acquired by Attilio and Mario Bruzzone, who transformed it into a fast

27.56-ton gaff-rigged schooner. The boat, plated in copper, was put to sea on September 16, 1930 as *Emilia*, the name of Attilio Bruzzone's mother. For ten years *Emilia* was to take part in the cruise races that were in vogue in that period, competing with Italian and French vessels, obtaining success and good placings.

In 1950 the boat changed owners again to Commander Alfredo Coppola. The new

ownership is shown in the Register of Yachts of 1955 under no. 2114. Between 1975 and 1987, it moved to Venetian waters with its newest owner, Giorgio Trani, until August 1988, when it was decided to return the boat to its former splendor, entrusting this task to the Beconcini shipyards at La Spezia, Italy.

The restoration project was entrusted to architect Ugo Faggioni. Around 80 percent of the steel floor plates, 40 percent of the elm wood frames, and 60 percent of the mahogany planking was replaced. The deck was restored to health, while the sail plan was returned to the original design.

In 1998 *Emilia* changed owners again, and the current boat-owner took it to the Côte d'Azur for a new restoration (1998–99). At the regatta in Marseilles, France, in July 1999, *Emilia*, the absolute winner, won the André Mauric Trophy.

ABOVE: *2000, details of the stern (Photo: R. Minervini).*

LEFT: *VBR 1999,* Emilia, *designed by Attilio Costaguta (Photo: J. Taylor).*

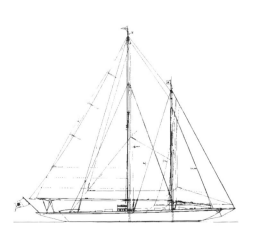

Escapade

Rigging:	Bermudan yawl
Sail area:	538 sq. yds.
Shipyard:	Luders (Stamford, Connecticut, USA)
Designer:	Philip Rhodes
Year of design:	1937
Launch:	1938
Restoration:	1980
L.: 75 ft.	W.l.: 55 ft.
B.: 16 ft.	Df.: 8 ft.
Displ.: 42.99 tons	Engine: 130 Hp
Skipper:	Gil Frei (1986)

Escapade is one of the most famous vessels of all time: its name has considerable weight in the history of yachting, both in the United States and worldwide. *Escapade* (never was a name more appropriate) can be considered one of the most beautiful boats existing today, and not only from the purely aesthetic standpoint. Philip Rhodes considered it a most unexpected and amazing result from his favorite project.

Well known in every ocean for its harmonious lines, streamlined hull, fast equipment, and long deckhouse, just raised above the deck, *Escapade* has a record of race victories that has now become the stuff of legend. Completely reconstructed between 1966 and 1984, the boat is in a general condition today that can be considered better than that of the day of its launch. Mahogany planking with oak frames and a teak deck help make up a quality hull that has new bronze bolts for the keel and an extremely solid set of equipment that easily enables it to cover 5,000 miles of ocean every year. The masts and boom were reconstructed in 1984.

The boat is currently used for exclusive charter trips in the Caribbean and the Mediterranean. Among its legendary victories, we can mention the Port Huron–Mackinac Race (1947, 1948, 1949, 1951, 1952, and 1953), the Miami–Nassau Race (1941, 1950, 1951, 1952, 1954, and 1963, a record for the race), the Chicago–Mackinac Race (1950, 1951, and 1954), the Bermuda Race (third place in 1938, 1948, 1950, 1952, and 1954, and fourth in 1946), the Transatlantic Race (Bermuda–Marstrand, 3,500 miles in 1960), the Transpacific Race (1959), the Annapolis–Newport Race (1965 and an unbeaten record), the Channel Island Race (1962), the Miami–Jamaica Race (1961), the Nioulargue (1985), and an impressive number of victories in lesser races and dozens of placings.

Escapade's most resounding successes were between 1950 and 1951, over 12 years after its launch. Called the "Queen of the Great Lakes" after winning the Rochester Regatta, the longest freshwater race (377 miles), in

the 1950s *Escapade* was owned by Wandel Anderson (who had acquired it from H.G. Fowes). Under his ownership it claimed 15 victories, two second places, and four thirds in 21 races, always under the command of Captain Alden Sewel.

In the 1960s, the boat had a new owner in the person of a Mr. Baldwin. *Escapade* won everything it was possible to win in the races in which it took part. At Imperia too, it was the fastest boat ever: when it reached its moorings, the other competitors in its class were still racing!

RIGHT: *Imperia, September 1986, shot of* Escapade, *one of the most famous racing vessels of all time (Photo: F. Semeria).*

Estella

The boat was launched in Pola, Croatia, by the experienced shipwright, Lino Puia, who added sturdiness and excellent seagoing qualities to the classical lines of the hull, transom stern, and powerful masting. *Estella* has oak frames and beams, larch planking, a pitch pine deck, and interiors in okoume, oak, and mahogany. Commissioned by an Italian notary, it ended up in Liguria in the 1950s, where it sank one day in the port of Duca degli Abruzzi.

From the few documents examined, it was possible to find the allocation of the sail number (2612) by the Italian Union of Sailing Associations (USVI), dated March 13, 1963, and a Certificate of Tonnage dated May 8, 1964, attesting to the ownership of the boat by Carlo Barbini of Milan. Finally, in February 1964, a Certificate of Tonnage from the USVI according to the 1957 Regulations of the Royal Ocean Racing Club, assigned its registration to the Yacht Club Tigullio.

In 1969–70 it was towed to Le Grazie after reconstruction work on the mast by Vibio Mestrom. The boat then remained abandoned for a long time in La Spezia. In 1976 *Estella* was noticed by Gianni Giorgi, who moved it to Anzio, where the deck was rebuilt. In 1979 the boat was sold to a family from Milan, before coming into the possession of its current owner, who operated for a time with the "Venturieri" association.

In recent years, *Estella*, with its maco cotton sails, has carried out charter activities in the Mediterranean. It has an unmistakable hull because of the presence of portholes on the broadsides. *Estella* once had a toerail receding towards the stern, but this has vanished today due to all the restoration work that has been done. In October 1996 the boat underwent further restoration at the Del Carlo shipyard in Viareggio. All the beams, stringers, deckhouses, and masting were replaced, and the deck was completely reconstructed.

Rigging:	Gaff-rigged ketch
Sail area:	160 sq. yds.
Shipyard:	Lino Puia (Pola, Croatia)
Designer:	Rikus Van De Stadte
Year of design:	1945
Launch:	1946
Restoration:	1970, 1996
L.: 45 ft.	W.l.: 34½ ft.
B.: 11½ ft.	Df.: 7 ft.
Displ.: 20.94 tons	Engine: 90 Hp
Skipper:	Carlo Belenghi, Maurizio Tremolada (1987)

BELOW: *Aerial shot of* Estella *(Photo: E. Taccola).*

Eva Maria

Rigging:	Bermudan schooner
Sail area:	478 sq. yds.
Shipyard:	Anker & Jensen (Oslo, Norway)
Designer:	J. Auker
Year of design:	1930
Launch:	1931
Restoration:	1992–93 (Piraeus, Greece)
L.: 79³/₄ ft.	W.l.: 59 ft.
B.: 15¹/₂ ft.	Df.: 12¹/₂ ft.
Displ.: 54.01 tons	Engine: 210 Hp
Skipper:	Piero Ruspini (1996–98)

This boat, launched as *Albatros* for a Swiss boat-owner, was almost certainly a gaff-rigged boat. From the North Sea it sailed to the United States, where it stayed with its new American owner for many years. The subsequent owner, an American lawyer with offices in London, found the boat abandoned and in poor condition in the port of Piraeus in Greece. Here it underwent restructuring work (the masts were remade and today are made of Douglas fir and a new hydraulic rudder was fitted). *Eva Maria* sailed around the world twice, via Cape Horn, before once again settling in the Aegean Sea where it was used for family cruises.

Very much a beating vessel, it behaves excellently in high seas and tends to plow through the waves. It has iroko planking and an iroko deck, and oak and steel frames. Only two winches are left from the original hardware. Further major restructuring work took place in 1999, and *Eva Maria* was again for sale in June 2000.

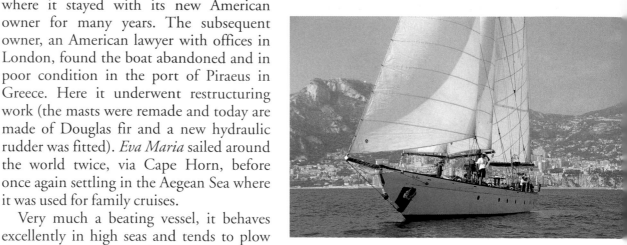

ABOVE: *Monte Carlo 1997, shot of* Eva Maria *(Photo: P. Maccione).*

Fair Weather

Rigging:	Trysail schooner
Sail area:	359 sq. yds.
Shipyard:	Port Royal (Jamaica)
Designer:	Murray Peterson
Year of design:	1936
Launch:	1952
Restoration:	1982
L.: 72 ft.	W.l.: 57 ft.
B.: 14¹/₄ ft.	Df.: 7 ft.
Displ.: 30.86 tons	Engine: 100 Hp
Skipper:	Stephen Horner (1992)

RIGHT: *Imperia 1992,* Fair Weather, *a splendid schooner designed by Murray Peterson (Photo: A. Tringali).*

I came across *Fair Weather* in the quay at Porto Ferraio in Italy and admired its splendid line and the classic stern of this American schooner from the turn of the century. The skipper, Stephen Horner, kept his promise to be present at the Imperia Boat Rally, so I had the opportunity to go out racing on this schooner with its harmonious deck and powerful masts that always need plenty of wind.

The interior of *Fair Weather* evokes exotic memories because in the furnishings can be seen work performed by Oriental craftsmen during long stays in the ports of China. These are reminders of a long voyage around the world completed 30 years ago by its first famous skipper, Suttie Adams, who left San Francisco in the United States with a team made up of his four children and two friends.

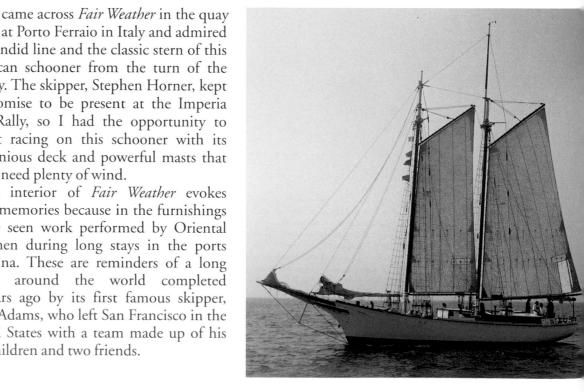

Four Winds

*F*our Winds is an American trysail schooner, built in California in 1923 and inspired by the traditional boats of Nova Scotia and New England that are used for fishing on the Grand Banks of Newfoundland. It is clearly derived from the lines of boats from the 1920s and 1930s, like *Malabar* by the great John Alden. A boat with a powerful midship section and a hull with double Alaskan cedar planking and oak frames, it was entered in the Registers of the Hawaiian Islands for many years.

The schooner was transformed into a ketch in the 1940s, during its long stay in the Pacific. In 1963 it was acquired by Captain George De Balkani in Honolulu; it reached the Mediterranean after a period spent in the Red Sea and ended up in Fiumicino, Italy, where it was noticed for the first time in 1986 by Gian Marco Borea, who subsequently acquired it with Enrico Casonato.

The boat was in a pitiful state: it was rigged as a gaff ketch with its paintwork neglected, salvaged sails, and the interior covered with carpeting and formica. Shocked by such foolishness (the bilge could not be inspected because the flooring under the carpet could not be lifted and the wood under the formica was in danger of rotting), the two new boat-owners carried out an initial restoration in Chioggia, Italy. On the basis that the old masts were still present, architect G.C. Coppola returned the boat to its original rig: two new masts made of Douglas fir were fitted. Under Italian registration, the schooner returned to its original name of *Four Winds*. Previously it was called *Nirvana*.

This restructuring, with the construction of masts, boom, and gaffs, the understanding of the many maneuvers that this boat involves, and preparation of part of the interior, were all carried out by Casonato and Borea at the Perinetti and Casoni shipyards at Chioggia, members of the "Venturieri" association.

After almost two years, *Four Winds* was ready to sail. The cedar hull, painted emerald green, became unmistakable in the Mediterranean because of the harmony and rarity of its lines. A heavy and sluggish boat, it was well suited to the training and cruises that the "Venturieri" undertook in the upper Adriatic and around Greece. After three years of activity and a couple of seasons of training cruises, *Four Winds*, commanded by skipper Andrea Vigni, reached the Ippolito shipyard in Livorno, Italy, where parts of the planking, by now worn-out, were replaced. The huge internal ballasts, consisting of a mix of cast iron and cement, were replaced with lead ingots, arranged at bilge level.

In around 1992 the boat was sold to a new owner.

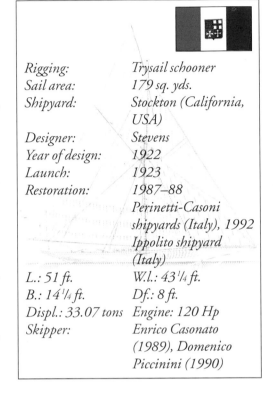

Rigging:	Trysail schooner
Sail area:	179 sq. yds.
Shipyard:	Stockton (California, USA)
Designer:	Stevens
Year of design:	1922
Launch:	1923
Restoration:	1987–88
	Perinetti-Casoni shipyards (Italy), 1992
	Ippolito shipyard (Italy)
L.: 51 ft.	W.l.: 43¼ ft.
B.: 14¼ ft.	Df.: 8 ft.
Displ.: 33.07 tons	Engine: 120 Hp
Skipper:	Enrico Casonato (1989), Domenico Piccinini (1990)

BELOW: *Imperia 1990*, Four Winds, *a gaff schooner that evokes nostalgia for the famous fishing schooners of the Grand Banks of Newfoundland (Photo courtesy of the Venturieri).*

Gabbiano
(sometime Yanez I)

Rigging:	Gaff-rigged cutter
Sail area:	54 sq. yds.
Shipyard:	Beltrami (Genoa Vernazzola, Italy)
Designer:	Vittorio Beltrami
Year of design:	1931
Launch:	1934
Restoration:	1981, 1987 Manzoni shipyard (Bocca di Magra, Italy)
L.: 28½ ft.	W.l.: 21¾ ft.
B.: 8 ft.	Df.: 5¼ ft.
Displ.: 6.34 tons	Engine: 16.5 Hp
Skipper:	Salvatore Sgarellino (1990–91), Pier Enrico Pompili (1998)

This boat was discovered run aground near Bocca di Magra, Italy, in 1980 by lawyer Aldo Spinosa. In a state of complete abandonment, with all its components cannibalized, it seemed to be simply waiting for a compassionate funeral pyre. Its first name was in fact *Gabbiano*. It was registered in Livorno, Italy, but its history was lost in the waters of Viareggio, also in Italy, where it seems it once sank due to carelessness.

After acquiring the boat, the enthusiasm of its new owner started a series of restoration projects in the Manzoni shipyard, again in Bocca di Magra. A new deckhouse – certainly taller than the original one – was built, the height of the mast was reduced by 5 feet, the empty interior was redesigned, and, finally, the old planking was restored and caulked. From 1983 through 1987 the boat changed owners and was renamed *Silvia*. There followed another abandonment, until, again in Bocca di Magra, the boat was noticed by a petty officer from the Italian Navy, who took on the work of restructuring it and rebaptized it *Yanez I*.

The rudder has a tiller where a brass plate, which has miraculously survived so many changes, still shows the lettering of the Beltrami shipyard (which has produced famous boats such as *Nina V*, *Pazienza*, and *Swallow*) and the launch date. *Yanez I* is a boat that needs wind to perform best. The hull, which still has a beautiful stern rake, has mahogany planking, iroko frames, and an acacia keel; the mast and boom are spruce. For a few years now the boat, which has regained its old name, has had a new owner, who, in 1997, had restoration work done at a shipyard in Lavagna, Italy.

Galashiel

Rigging:	Trysail ketch
Sail area:	419 sq. yds.
Shipyard:	Alexander Stephens & Son, Glasgow, Scotland
Designer:	Alfred Mylne
Year of design:	1932
Launch:	1934
Restoration:	1984 Valdettaro shipyards (La Spezia, Italy)
L.: 94 ft.	W.l.: 73 ft.
B.: 17 ft.	Df.: 11¼ ft.
Displ.: 92.59 tons	Engine: 170 Hp
Skipper:	Andrea Rolla (1986–87)

This is a beautiful vessel, launched in 1934. Going by the name of *Gialesa*, it had belonged to the Countess Feltrinelli. For a long time, from the early 1950s, the boat had been moored at Le Grazie in Italy. When it was acquired in 1983 by engineer Dr. Rolla, it did not look in good condition, particularly the hull, which was painted black and which showed marks on the planks. The interior had been adapted many years earlier by the Baglietto shipyards in Italy and had laminated plastic furniture with linoleum on the floor.

Transfered to the Valdettaro shipyards in Italy, the boat was dismasted and underwent a meticulous refit: the planking was found to be in excellent condition, as was the composite structure (frames with angled steel on 1½-inch Burma teak planking); all the original oak panels were polished with

RIGHT: *Imperia 1986, shot of Galashiel, designed by Alfred Mylne (Photo: G. Baldizzone).*

spirit, while the floors were covered with dark oak staves. The deck, no longer original, was also remade; the steering gear also had to be reconstructed, although the original silver spruce masts remained.

With the hull repainted pale turquoise, *Galashiel* – as it was renamed in 1984 – had the opportunity of sailing again with reborn beauty, its mainmast 85 feet high and a sail plan dating back to the 1930s.

In the interior, everything makes you think time has truly stopped: the barometer, compass, and chronometer are original pieces from the Cooke Company. One of the drawers in a drawing table is of particular interest; the reverse of it still bears the indication written in pencil by a worker from half a century ago ("left hand drawer") and the project number – 542. Also splendid is the dark oak saloon with a mobile bar with briarwood interiors.

A fast and maneuverable boat, today it has been resold and sails the seas around Japan. In its second appearance at Imperia, *Galashiel* was awarded the Italian Association of Vintage Yachts plate as the "best interpreter of the sailing tradition."

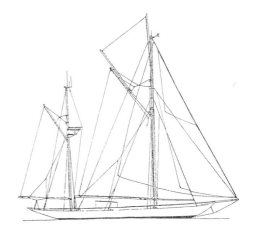

BELOW: *Imperia 1987, a wonderful image of* Galashiel *(Photo: S. Piano).*

Gaudeamus

Rigging:	Trysail cutter
Sail area:	90 sq. yds.
Shipyard:	Rostock (Germany)
Designer:	Barg
Year of design:	1914
Launch:	1914
Restoration:	1982–92, 1992–97, 2001 Nautical Center Marina One (Imperia, Italy)
L.: 51½ ft.	W.l.: 30 ft.
B.: 9 ft.	Df.: 5¼ ft.
Displ.: 7.72 tons	Engine: 20 Hp
Skipper:	Raimund Deibele (1992–2002)

BELOW: *The streamlined hull of Gaudeamus. During 2001 the boat underwent structural modifications according to the original design: modification to the stern transom, lengthening of the boom and the gaff, and reduction of the height of the deckhouse (Photo: J. Taylor).*

This boat was built in 1914 in Rostock from a project by the architect Barg on behalf of a sailing circle in Königsberg. It was given the name of *Gaudeamus*. For many years there was no news of the boat, apart from during World War II when it was bombed and sunk. In 1950 it was found reduced to just a hull in the inland waterways near Berlin and was recovered by a certain Karl Heinz Friering.

There followed restoration work at the Wolgast shipyards in Germany. It left there in 1953 with the name of *Rugia* and was moved to Stralsund. During this period, the trysail rig was changed to a gaff rig; the boat's measurements were kept as when it was built in 1938, to avoid problems for her owner.

In 1961 it was sold to Klaus Schroeder, who, in view of the political situation and the construction of the Berlin Wall, decided to flee with his whole family. One night in 1962 Schroeder embarked with his wife and two children, raised the sails (the boat had no motor), left the port of Rostock, and headed for West Germany. Fortune would have it that, during the voyage, the fugitives encountered a flotilla of Danish fishing-boats who positioned themselves around the boat and, thanks also to limited visibility, protected it from the Communist patrol boats' radar and escorted it to the port of Kiel in West Germany.

Schroeder needed money to start a new life and was forced to sell the boat to Hans Sellmer, who changed its name to *Question Mark*. In 1983 it was sold again to a new owner, who restored its old name of *Rugia* and moved the boat to Lake Constance on the border of Germany, Austria, and Switzerland.

In 1992 Raimund Deibele discovered the boat on the lake and decided to buy it. He transported it by lorry to Mentone in Italy, and then to Imperia. Finally, in 1993, after many adventures, the boat reacquired its original trysail rig and its former name of *Gaudeamus*.

Germania V
(sometime Corpus Christi)

This splendid vessel, which appeared at Imperia under the name of *Corpus Christi*, today bears its original name, *Germania V*. It was launched in May 1955 by the reconstructed shipyards of Abeking & Rasmussen on commission from Alfred Krupp, who, before becoming the king of German steel, was a keen yachtsman.

The boat, which was the representation of the rebirth of German yachting, easily won races in the Elbe, the North Sea, and at Kiel Sailing Week for some years. Its participation in the Bermuda–Marstand Regatta in 1960 was noteworthy; this was eventually won by the great *Escapade* but *Germania V*, with all the sails trimmed (around 360 square yards), kept up an average of 11 knots for many stages of the race.

In 1961 certain modifications were made to the interior at the wishes of Krupp, although he insisted on the traditional separation between the rooms for the owners and those reserved for the crew (consisting of two full-time sailors). In 1962 the boat was again outstanding in the Buenos Aires–Rio de Janeiro Race, gaining sixth place. *Germania V* was followed in September 1963 by the great yawl *Germania VI*, built by the Abeking & Rasmussen shipyards from a design by Sparkman & Stephens. The boat was 72½ feet in length, had a waterline of 52¾ feet, and a sail area of around 790 square yards, plus three spinnakers, giving a total of 960 square yards. At this time, the steel magnate donated *Germania V*, which had been so successful, to the Hansa Open Sea Sailing Association, to which he generously handed over the new Gluecksburg Sailing School establishment.

During the 1980s, *Germania V* underwent radical restoration work, with the rebuilding of the partner and the boom, as well as reinforcement of most of the steel hull. Afterwards, from 1983 to 1991, the boat was transferred to a private owner, René Talbot, with whom it made an appearance at the first Imperia Boat Rally in 1986, after having moored in the dock at Porto Maurizio in Italy the previous year. Its new name was *Corpus Christi*. In 1991 the boat was bought by Roswitha Buchner and a Mr. Pfänder.

In 1992–93 the hull again underwent repairs with the replacement of various planks, which were now considered too thin. The interior was also renewed and today the boat, which in 1991 was given back its original name, has regained its streamlined hull and the form of its best days.

Other German boats have proudly borne the same name: we should mention *Germania I* owned by Dr. Gustav Krupp, which was launched on the eve of World War I, together with the famous *Meteor* and *Hamburg*. *Germania II* appeared on the sailing scene in Kiel in 1934. And finally there is *Germania IV*, an 8-meter SI class, already launched when World War II began.

Rigging:	Bermudan yawl
Sail area:	205 sq. yds.
Shipyard:	Abeking & Rasmussen (Lemwerder, Germany)
Designer:	Rasmussen
Year of design:	1955
Launch:	1955
Restoration:	1992
L.: 66 ft.	W.l.: 44¼ ft.
W.: 15¼ ft.	Df.: 9 ft.
Displ.: 38.9 tons	Engine: 95 Hp
Skipper:	René Talbot (1986)

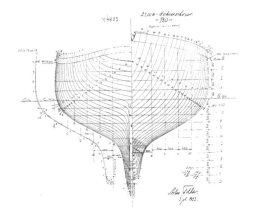

LEFT: *Imperia 1986, the phantasmagoria of sails and colors that was* Corpus Christi, *now* Germania V *(Photo: F. Semeria).*

Gioanna

Rigging:	Bermudan sloop
Sail area:	79 sq. yds.
Shipyard:	Sangermani (Lavagna, Italy)
Designer:	Cesare Sangermani
Year of design:	1948
Launch:	1950
Restoration:	1995–96
L.: 35½ ft.	W.l.: 25 ft.
B.: 8 ft.	Df.: 6 ft.
Displ.: 8.6 tons	Engine: 18 Hp
Skipper:	Giovanni Lasio (1998–2000)

Gioanna came about from a 1948 design by Cesare Sangermani, along with three other identical boats, two of which are still sailing: *Fantasia* and *Alcione*. Launched in 1951, its first owner was Casa Gavarone. The boat has always sailed the waters of the Tigullio in Italy, where it has also been used for training.

Gioanna had a second name, *Arc en ciel*. In 1994 *Gioanna* was acquired by its current owner, who submitted it for two successive restructurings, in 1995 and 1996. It has had a few internal modifications and new winches, but nothing more.

It has returned to its old name and for a few years now has regularly appeared at the boat rallies of the Italian Association of Vintage Yachts. It came second at Santa Margherita in 1997, third at Porto Cervo in the same year, and third at Argentario and second at Imperia in 1998. The boat is looked after by shipwright Mauro Balanzoni, who has built a new sitka spruce mast after a dismasting in 1999.

ABOVE: *Imperia 2000, shot of* Gioanna, *launched by Sangermani in 1950 (Photo: S. Pesato).*

RIGHT: *Porto Santo Stefano 1998,* Gioanna *during a close-hauled stage (Photo: J. Taylor).*

Halloween

Halloween was designed and built by William Fife for Colonel Baxendale and is, in many ways, similar to a 15-meter Class, if we leave aside the fact that it was conceived to resemble the typical, elegant models of the Scottish builder.

Designed and built specifically to win, immediately after its launch in 1926 *Halloween* obtained an unbeaten record in the old Fastnet Race, with a real time of 93 hours, 38 minutes. A few years later, the boat began to race in the Mediterranean.

Later it returned to the Atlantic and, with the name of *Magda XII*, was the leading yacht of the Royal Norwegian Racing Club. Often found at its helm was Prince Olaf, a great sailor and the future King of Norway. With World War II imminent, the boat remained active in the United States, where in 1952 it was acquired by one of the greatest North American ocean-racing yachtsmen, Walter Wheeler, who decided to call it *Cotton Blossom IV*. Driven by the enthusiasm

of its new owner, the boat achieved an unbelievable record of victories in regattas. Among its many trophies, *Cotton Blossom IV* can boast the Annapolis–Newport Race, the Astor Cup, the Vineyard Race (five times), and the Larchmont Long Distance Race (three times), as well as two second-placings in the Bermuda Race.

The boat was launched with a gaff-cutter rig but was subsequently changed to a trysail rig by Colonel Baxendale for a short time, then transformed into a yawl by fitting a mizzenmast. A very fast boat, with a spacious flush deck and low deckhouse (the skylights are barely noticeable), it is one of Fife's most perfect vessels, so much so that, referring to his creation, he had this to say: *"She is the perfect gentleman's all-rounder: she is a jewel!"*

Despite its successes, in 1986 Walter Wheeler decided to withdraw the boat from races; the ghost of retirement haunted *Halloween*, still called *Cotton Blossom IV*.

Rigging:	*Gaff-rigged cutter*
Sail area:	*359 sq. yds.*
Shipyard:	*W. Fife & Son (Fairlie, Scotland)*
Designer:	*William Fife III*
Year of design:	*1926*
Launch:	*1926*
Restoration:	*1986–91, 1993 Beconcini shipyards (La Spezia, Italy)*
L.: 81 ft.	*W.l.: 46 ft.*
B.: 14¾ ft.	*Df.: 11½ ft.*
Displ.: 44.09 tons	*Engine: 79 Hp*
Skipper:	*Kevin Byrne (1992), Nigel Blackbourn (1998), Pane Vanderbyl (2001)*

BELOW: *Cannes 1999, a famous boat by William Fife III,* Halloween *(Photo: J. Taylor).*

The boat-owner hoped to guarantee a future for the boat, donating it to the Classic Boat Museum in Newport, Rhode Island, but the foundation did not have sufficient resources to maintain the boat, much less restore it. However, fate stepped in and a patron financed the restoration under the supervision of the Museum's engineers, guided by Adrian Persall.

Between 1986 and 1991, the boat was completely restructured, with new equipment, sails, and rudder, maintaining William Fife's interior furnishings, meticulously finished and faithful to the original. The hull frames were found to be in perfect condition and, piece after piece, it was possible to reuse the various original teak components. A new pine mast, older than the boat, was made available by the above museum, while on deck four bronze winches were fitted to make maneuvering easier.

In 1991 *Halloween* returned to the world, honored with its original form and name. In 1993 a new English boat-owner decided to restore the boat to its original rig as a gaff-rigged sloop, undertaking several months of work in a dry dock in Barcelona, Spain. A new boom of considerable dimensions was built in England, faithfully respecting Fife's designs.

Today *Halloween* participates at vintage yacht regattas as one of the most elegant sailing boats currently in existence, distinguishing itself for being without a genoa. It is used for charter in the Mediterranean and the Caribbean.

At the end of a prolonged period of cruising in almost every corner of the Mediterranean, the owner of *Halloween* initiated a further series of restorations, under the supervision of Captain Nigel Blackbourn. The mast and bowsprit have now been restored to their original dimensions following the golden rule of the Fife family: "*All materials used shall be of the highest quality in their category and shall be finely worked and finished in the best possible way and to the full satisfaction of the customer or his representative.*"

The boat was sold to a Dutch owner in 1999.

LEFT: *Cannes 1999,* Halloween, *one of its builder's best-loved boats (Photo: J. Taylor).*

Helen

This is the first boat designed by Laurent Giles. It was launched in March 1935. It belonged to retired Lieutenant-Commander Hobart, who kept a full-time crewman on board and flew the pennant of the Royal Yacht Squadron with the same St. George Cross as units of the Royal Navy. The last English owner was a certain E. Edlmann.

The boat was acquired in Lymington, England, in 1955 by Marchese Giulio Centurione and moved by sea to the port of Viareggio in Italy. In the same year, *Cerida*, another vessel by Laurent Giles, arrived in Italy. In 1957, after making various cruises around Corsica and Sardinia and entering a few races, *Helen* was transferred to Edoardo, Visconti di Modrone and subsequently to a Piedmontese impresario.

Among the races entered, it is interesting to mention the Saint Tropez–Ajaccio Race of August 1950, recalled in *Yachting Italiano* by Bruno Veronese, who was a member of the crew, together with Commander Centurione and his wife Lisetta. Also participating in that regatta were the great Spanish yachts *Orion* and *Altair*, and the boat *Alvée* by the Ravano brothers. *Helen* won in real and corrected time for Class III after 19 hours, 17 minutes, with an average speed of over seven knots, and was placed second in the general placings in corrected time. Throughout the voyage, sea and wind had not been favorable; there were many withdrawals and several yachts were damaged.

In the mid-1960s *Helen* was sold to Antonio Amelotti, who carried out restoration work on the interior and remade the deck in 1969.

A sturdy boat, seaworthy and docile at the helm, *Helen* has pitch pine planking, a teak deck that terminates in a narrow, tall cockpit where the original tiller is located, a spruce mast, and cotton sails. Some of its parts have been replaced, such as the lead bulb and the 16 inch-long bowsprit. From 1974 through 1989 the boat found a new owner in Giuseppe Cagelli. After lying up for years in the little Duca degli Abruzzi dock in Genoa, Italy, it has reached the seas of Turkey sailing with its latest owner.

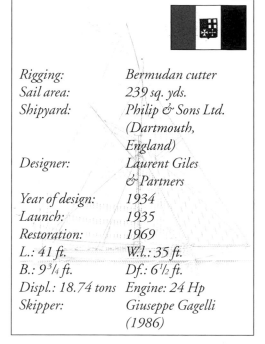

Rigging:	*Bermudan cutter*
Sail area:	*239 sq. yds.*
Shipyard:	*Philip & Sons Ltd. (Dartmouth, England)*
Designer:	*Laurent Giles & Partners*
Year of design:	*1934*
Launch:	*1935*
Restoration:	*1969*
L.: 41 ft.	*W.l.: 35 ft.*
B.: 9³/₄ ft.	*Df.: 6¹/₂ ft.*
Displ.: 18.74 tons	*Engine: 24 Hp*
Skipper:	*Giuseppe Gagelli (1986)*

ABOVE: *Dartmouth 1935,* Helen *soon after its launch (Photo courtesy of G. Gagelli).*

LEFT: *An old image of* Helen, *taken by K. Beken. This is Laurent Giles' first design (Photo courtesy of G. Centurione).*

Hygie

Rigging:	Gaff-rigged ketch
Sail area:	347 sq. yds.
Shipyard:	Le Marchand (Minihic, France)
Designer:	D. Severi
Year of design:	1928
Launch:	1930
Restoration:	1987, 1992
L.: 78³/₄ ft.	W.l.: 53 ft.
B.: 16¹/₄ ft.	Df.: 10 ft.
Displ.: 66.14 tons	Engine: 135 Hp
Skipper:	André Costa (1987), Bertrand Danglade (1992–94)

Hygie was launched in 1930 by the Le Marchand shipyard in Minihic, near Saint Malo, France, on behalf of the pharmacist M. Verliac (the former owner of *Forban I*), who wanted to give it the name of the goddess of health.

For four generations the Landriais naval shipyard, established in 1850, had been in the hands of the Le Marchand family, and it had known periods of great activity, particularly in the construction of the famous "Bisquines" of Cancale, when 70 workers simultaneously worked on the construction of 14 of these units. In 1930 *Hygie* was the port's greatest yacht, before a gradual decline in local construction. Pre-war, the boat took part in many regattas and won an edition of the Fastnet Race.

In 1955 the boat was owned by a certain Paul Collin, and its fitting-out port was Saint Malo. There followed years without a history, during which it seems to have been used in smuggling operations. In 1970 *Hygie* came under the ownership of Daniel Baillant, who used it for charter activities in the Antilles.

In 1979 the new owner, Bertrand Danglade, took the boat back to the Ile de Rè, France, for a total restoration. It then returned to the Antilles to continue charter activities until 1985. In that period *Hygie* was sold again, to Gérard Simonetti and André Costa, who transferred it to the port of St. Florent in Corsica, where it is still to be found today. With André Costa as skipper, the boat continued charter activities in the Antilles, the Balearics, and Greece. In 1990 it got a new owner, Eric Lavigne, who rebuilt the teak deck and deckhouse in 1992.

A very sturdy and well-built boat, it has a pitch pine topside and oak hull. The frames are alternated oak and acacia, at 2-inch intervals, while the masts are built of Oregon pine. *Hygie* is a good cruise boat and needs a full wind for good speeds.

RIGHT: *Cannes 1998, a photograph of the ketch* Hygie, *a good cruise boat (Photo: J. Taylor).*

Ice Fire

Before talking about *Ice Fire* we should first mention that Nathaniel Herreshoff was commissioned by the New York Yacht Club to produce a one-off boat for all the members of the circle; this was called the "New York 30," of which *Linnet* was one. In late 1935 the board of directors of the club decided that the time had come to build a new boat to enable the associates to participate in regattas with equally matched yachts, as well as to represent the association in sailing events on the east coast of the United States. So it was that in 1936 the Commander of the New York Yacht Club, W.A.W. Stewart, announced a full-blown competitive bidding process for the creation of the "official" vessel of the circle, just 20 of which would be built.

The five most well-known naval design studios were involved and invited to present a design to the members of the board: Alden, Luders, Ford & Paine, Belknap & Paine, and, finally, Sparkman & Stephens. The design selected was the one by Sparkman & Stephens, which envisaged a fast, powerful sloop, capable of handling even demanding ocean voyages.

Conforming to the directives received, the boat was conceived as slightly larger than the New York 30. Its construction was personally supervised by Rod Stephens, in line with the rules of the Cruising Club of America and Lloyds of England.

Once the commission was received, the firm quickly began to construct the boats, all with hulls with a single mahogany plank, screwed onto white oak frames, and keels with "Everdur" silicon bronze screws. The boat-owner was only allowed to choose between rigging the boat as a sloop or yawl (there were only three of the latter). The 20 boats were finished during 1936–37.

The design of the New York 32, as it was known, is a combination of the best of *Dorade* (design no. 7 of 1929) and *Stormy Weather* (design no. 27 of 1934), both by Sparkman & Stephens. The New York 32 can be compared to a large 6-meter SI Class, with characteristics specific to the cruise vessel. Its sections are slender, the overhangs and hollow bow are noteworthy (typical of Olin Stephens), and there was meticulous research to reduce the wet surface, factors that are reminiscent of *Starlight* (design no. 66 of 1934), a vessel that won many times in open-sea races. In his fundamental text, *Choice Yacht Designs*, Richard Henderson has defined the New York 32 as "…*an all-time classic*." Of the 20 vessels built, 19 are still in existence, with just one in Europe.

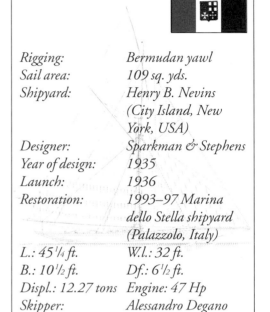

Rigging:	*Bermudan yawl*
Sail area:	*109 sq. yds.*
Shipyard:	*Henry B. Nevins (City Island, New York, USA)*
Designer:	*Sparkman & Stephens*
Year of design:	*1935*
Launch:	*1936*
Restoration:	*1993–97 Marina dello Stella shipyard (Palazzolo, Italy)*
L.: 45¼ ft.	*W.l.: 32 ft.*
B.: 10½ ft.	*Df.: 6½ ft.*
Displ.: 12.27 tons	*Engine: 47 Hp*
Skipper:	*Alessandro Degano (1992–2002)*

LEFT: *An image of* Ice Fire *(Photo courtesy of A. Degano).*

BELOW: *Trieste 2001, a foreshortened image of the yawl* Ice Fire *still flying the United States flag (Photo: P. Maccione).*

This is the third vessel, *Ice Fire* (formerly known as *Swell*, *Old Salt*, *Lord Jim*, and *Reverly*), now restored and flying the Italian flag. Having finished this long, but necessary, introduction, we can now tell the story of *Ice Fire*.

In 1992 the boat was discovered laid-up in the shed of a shipwright in Maine in the United States. It was in a terrible condition, but not completely compromised. Out of the original hull the interior fittings and furnishings, deck, and deckhouse had been dismantled; almost all the original hardware was lost or had vanished; and only the planking was in relatively good condition. However, it was love at first sight.

This is how the current owner remembers that first sight of *Ice Fire*: "... *The deck has been removed, we can only see the frames and the beams, and one or two interior walls. I go down into her belly, I touch it, I cut it, I tap it... While the others are absorbed in reading various documents, I sneak down again (taking a camera) inside* Ice Fire: *I like her, she has a familiar air, I take some photos, caress her, I like her more and more, but I feel intimidated (perhaps at the thought of the massive amount of work there is to be done to restore her), as though this were my first date. I sit down inside her, I think: it's madness, but I want to do it!...*"

The boat-owner was able to return to Italy with documents declaring him to be the owner of a piece of the glorious history of United States yachting: *Ice Fire*. In Italy, the boat was placed in the imposing sheds of the Marina dello Stella shipyards in Palazzolo, near Udine, and was entrusted to the fond care of naval carpenter Silvano Stefanuto. The work carried out can be summarized as follows: two mahogany planks were replaced, the wooden plugs and original silicon bronze screws were removed, and all the boards were re-fastened with new stainless steel screws.

The two crossed internal bronze faces (the "strapping") that transmit powerful forces from the mast to the keel, via the chain plates to which they are attached, were dismantled and, once structural soundness had been checked, they were put back in position. Plywood was laid on the beams – almost all the original ones have been conserved – and covered with a mat impregnated with epoxy resin.

Above this, a deck of teak heartwood boards and a mahogany deckhouse were created. On its launch, in 1936, the deck had pine planks covered with a painted canvas. The interior is completely new because it was non-existent. *Ice Fire* was equipped with modern self-tailing winches and stainless steel blocks instead of the original bronze ones.

With its 52½ foot-sitka spruce mast, pronounced rakes, limited freeboard, and spoon-shaped prow, *Ice Fire* has not lost any of its beauty and elegance. It has now returned to race in the upper Adriatic.

BELOW: Ice Fire *flying the Italian flag (Photo courtesy of A. Degano).*

Ilex

This is a splendid vessel with slender, harmonious lines, designed by Charles Nicholson and launched back in 1899 in Gosport, England. For more than 20 years it was owned by the British Royal Army Engineers Yacht Club. It is the only boat to have completed the Fastnet Race nine times, winning it in 1926 and always getting a good placing (including third place in 1929, 1930, and 1935). *Ilex*, which has crossed the Atlantic twice (in spring 1931 and fall 1933), also competed in many international regattas between 1929 and 1935.

In 1971 it was acquired by John Peter Moore, Salvador Dalí's private secretary. Before being registered in Spain, the vessel remained in Gibraltar under the British flag. During 1972–73, *Ilex* was transformed into a ketch, while its deck and interior were completely replaced.

In 1991 the boat was acquired by German Ruiz and transferred to Torrevieja (in Alicante, Spain) for repairs. These continued up to 1994, at which time it reached the Vatesa shipyards in Santa Pola, Spain, to have its original look restored.

In May 1996 *Ilex* resumed its youthful appearance, with its distinguishing free and spacious deck. It could not help but win the XIV Almirante Conde de Barcelona Trophy in 1999, when it won the award for the best, conserved vessel.

Rigging:	Gaff-rigged sloop
Sail area:	197 sq. yds.
Shipyard:	Camper & Nicholson (Gosport, England)
Designer:	Charles E. Nicholson
Year of design:	1898
Launch:	1899
Restoration:	1994 Vatesa shipyards (Alicante, Spain)
L.: 50½ ft.	W.l.: 42¼ ft.
B.: 11 ft.	Df.: 8½ ft.
Displ.: 20.94 tons	Engine: 120 Hp
Skipper:	German Ruiz

BELOW: *An image of* Ilex *(Photo: N. Martinez).*

Iska

Rigging:	Bermudan ketch
Sail area:	146 sq. yds.
Shipyard:	Groves & Guttbridge Ltd. (East Cowes, England)
Designer:	Laurent Giles & Partners
Year of design:	1947
Launch:	1948
L.: 54³/₄ ft.	W.l.: 42 ft.
B.: 13 ft.	Df.: 8¹/₂ ft.
Displ.: 33.07 tons	Engine: 120 Hp
Skipper:	Luigi Lang (1987–91)

Laurent Giles was commissioned to build *Iska* in 1947 by Jacques Segard, one of the best-known French cotton manufacturers. Segard actively collaborated in the design, being a friend of Giles and having a considerable amount of sailing experience.

After seeing *Iska* at boat rallies, I lingered to look at it one afternoon in Genoa, Italy, while the boat was gently cradled in the sheltered dock of the Yachting Club. It is a sturdy boat with mahogany planking and oak frames (every third one alternating with one of galvanized iron), a teak deck, and spruce masts.

Iska was the first yacht of a certain size to be launched in Cowes, England, after World War II. The Groves & Guttbridge shipyard was selected on account of the quality and experience of its carpenters. Special care was devoted to the choice of the timber, using teak that had been stored before the war. Designed in 1947, and built in 1948, *Iska* was launched in November of the same year.

Between August and April 1949, the boat was taken to the Mediterranean, via Cherbourg in France and Lisbon in Portugal. It had illustrious guests on board, such as Reynaud, Pinay, Cuve de Murvile, and various members of the House of Savoia. For many years *Iska* flew the Portuguese flag (in 1955 the Register of Yachts showed it as no. 3363 under the ownership of Carlos Farinha, probably a friend of and front for Segard). It sailed under Armand Léon (subsequently the skipper of Edmond de Rothschild's *Gitana*) and then of Angelo Biggi.

In 1969 it was acquired by the current owner, who made gradual modifications to it over time, fully respecting the original plans. Indeed, the whole hull and rig have always been the object of conscientious maintenance in order to conserve its age-old splendor. Though not having been built as a regatta boat, with its 33.07 tons *Iska* is certainly undersailed; with a fresh wind it performs soundly and holds well at sea.

Like other boats that have had the privilege of limited changes of ownership, *Iska* survived the ravages of time until 1995. It is currently in very poor condition in the Duca degli Abruzzi dock in Genoa.

Ivanhoe

Rigging:	Bermudan yawl
Sail area:	215 sq. yds.
Shipyard:	T. Holm (Gamleby, Sweden)
Designer:	Tore Holm
Year of design:	1938
Launch:	1938
Restoration:	1991 Belliure (Spain)
L.: 69¹/₂ ft.	W.l.: 47 ft.
B.: 13³/₄ ft.	Df.: 9 ft.
Displ.: 35.27 tons	Engine: 170 Hp
Skipper:	Markus Schweiger (1998)

Ivanhoe was launched with the name of *Havsörnen* (Sea Eagle) on behalf of the famous yachtsman Sven Salen, who had an ambition to compete in the 1939 Gotland Round, a race he ended up winning.

Ivanhoe was the largest yacht ever to be built in the Holm shipyard and had innovative characteristics that were very advanced for that time (such as stainless steel components). In the early years of its life, the boat was transformed into a sloop in order to return to its original rig. It was only in the 1950s, after changing owners several times, that it received its current name.

From the seas of the north, it ended up sailing in the eastern Mediterranean, participating in races in Greece and Italy. On one or two occasions it even had King Constantine of Greece as its skipper. Subsequently the boat returned to northern Europe and, in 1970, it underwent changes by designers from Sparkman & Stephens, after which it returned to the Mediterranean with a new owner, yachtsman Guillermo Cryns.

So it was that it was discovered by the current owners, who immediately wanted a complete restoration of the boat after so many years of activity and racing. It was taken to the Belliure shipyards in Spain, where many components of the hull were replaced and strengthened with the intention of returning the boat to its original design.

Today *Ivanhoe* has two masts and a boom made of Oregon pine, a 1¹/₂-inch Honduran mahogany hull, and oak and steel frames. The deck is Burmese teak and the interior mahogany.

Entirely renovated, *Ivanhoe* won the special edition of the Almirante Conde de Barcelona Trophy in 1992 and 1994.

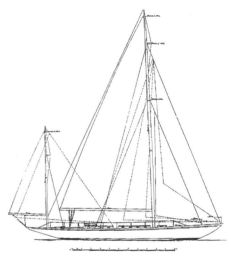

LEFT: *A bird's eye view of* Ivanhoe *(Photo: N. Martinez).*

ABOVE AND BELOW: *Cannes 1998, images of* Ivanhoe *racing (Photos: J. Taylor).*

Jalina

Rigging:	Bermudan sloop
Sail area:	128 sq. yds.
Shipyard:	P. Jouet
	(Sartrouville, France)
Designer:	Eugène Cornu
Year of design:	1946
Launch:	1946
Restoration:	1975, 1993
L.: 44 ft.	W.l.: 30 ft.
B.: 10½ ft.	Df.: 6 ft.
Displ.: 10.47 tons	Engine: 40 Hp
Skipper:	Petra Wolker (1989)

Le Yacht magazine of October 1953 defines this creation by the architect Eugène Cornu with the following words: "*Jalina is a magnificent race animal.*" And it could not be otherwise considering the ability of the greatest French architect of the last 50 years, the creator of famous boats that all have something special in common, such as *Glianne*, *Crazy Cloud*, *Morniz*, *Laer Mor*, *Striana*, *Kriss III*, *Pie Chris*, *Forban VI*, *Hallali*, *Marie-Berthe*, *Ondine*, *Janabel*, and many more besides. *Jalina*, which has an abundant career of successes behind it, stood out on its appearance in the competitive field.

In 1947 it was victorious in the Cowes–Dinard and the Cannes–Portoferraio races. In the first edition of the Giraglia (Cagnes–Giraglia–San Remo, 196 miles), the boat won clearly in its class, leading *Cerida* (in fourth place) by almost seven hours. It won the Giraglia again in 1954, and again with owner-skipper Jacques Barbou, accompanied by his wife Eliane, both owners of the more famous *Janabel* (on board which they competed in the Fastnet Race immediately after the Mediterranean regatta). That year, the crew of *Jalina* was composed as follows for the Giraglia: Monsieur and Madame Barbou,

Mr. Roger Breasange, Dr. Marcello Celloni, and a sailor, François.

In 1955, the boat distinguished itself again in the third edition of the race, taking second place. In 1958 it won the Ajaccio–Monaco Race. However, it was in the Giraglia that *Jalina* remained at its best: third in 1959, fourth in 1960 (with skipper Jacques Legrè), and seventh in 1964. *Jalina* continued to distinguish itself with its third owner, Dr. Maurice Legris, until in 1975 it came into the possession of André Hardy, who transformed the boat for peaceful cruising. The mast and deck were replaced.

In 1982 the boat was acquired by Philippe Mazella and, finally, in 1989, it was bought by the current owner Petra Wolker, who was so enamored of *Jalina* that she decided to live on board. The interior has not been changed since 1975: it is mahogany and pine and white-lacquered. *Jalina* has mahogany planking, acacia frames, and an aluminum mast (the original was 6½ feet taller). Under sail, especially close to the wind, it is a "wet" boat: it is at its best with a crosswind and flies along easily, even if it is hard work to stay at the helm. Despite the burden of the years, *Jalina* earned itself an honorable fourth at the Imperia Boat Rally in 1989.

ABOVE: Jalina, *designed by Cornu (Photo: S. Pesato).*
RIGHT: Jalina *at good speed (Photo: F. Taccola).*

Janabel

*J*anabel, the creation of Eugène Cornu, was launched five years after the famous *Jalina*, designed by the same architect. Its first owner was Jacques Barbou, the owner of *Jalina*. The boat-owner, accompanied by his wife Eliane, won the 1954 Giraglia with *Jalina*, and then participated immediately afterwards in the Fastnet Race with *Janabel*. It secured fourth place in the Giraglia in 1957 and sixth place in 1959.

This was a period of intense racing activity for *Janabel*, participating in competitions such as the Newport–Bermuda Race and the transatlantic Bermuda–Plymouth Race. A dynamic youth (*Janabel* was a splendid racing boat), it competed with the most famous yachts of the period, such as *Lutine*, *Bloodhound*, and *Samuel Pepys*.

However, after these frenetic years among the thoroughbreds of sailing, there followed years of neglect and abandonment. *Janabel* underwent painful transformations; the beautiful cabin top that extended partly over the cockpit to form an inviting deckhouse was cut to build an ugly, asymmetrical companionway.

In this condition, the boat arrived in Sicilian waters and was later abandoned, run aground on a beach opposite Sciacca in Sicily by its last French owner. Pulled ashore and checked out by Roberto Parisi, an enthusiast from Palermo in Italy, *Janabel* returned to life and racing, appearing at the Porto Cervo Boat Rally in Sardinia in 1985.

In 1989 it was acquired by its current owner, struck by the purity of the boat's lines. After two family cruises, *Janabel* arrived at the Sangermani shipyards in Italy for a complete restoration. This began with the demolition of all the alterations and the altered deckhouse. The hull was returned to wood, constructed with a technique that was rather advanced for the period: three layers of planking, two of which crossed at 45° with one longitudinal, interposed with impregnated and waterproofed canvases and copper-riveted.

The interior was then redesigned for greater living comfort. After around three years of work (1992–94), and thanks to drawings and photographs from the French magazine *Le Yacht*, Cornu's original project was fully restored. All the installations are modern, housed and fitted so as not to upset the originality and style of the boat. Today *Janabel* has a spruce mast and stainless steel hardware.

As anticipated, *Janabel* has attended a number of vintage yacht rallies. At the vintage yacht rally in Porto Cervo (in 1985), it took second place in Class B, with skipper Dario Lo Bue.

A few years later, in the Sahara Route Race, it had the best corrected time, once again showing its ever-aggressive pace on long stretches of open sea.

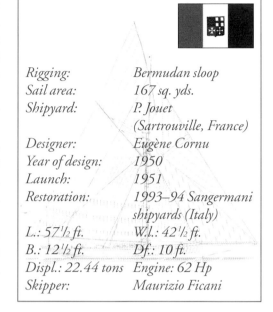

Rigging:	Bermudan sloop
Sail area:	167 sq. yds.
Shipyard:	P. Jouet (Sartrouville, France)
Designer:	Eugène Cornu
Year of design:	1950
Launch:	1951
Restoration:	1993–94 Sangermani shipyards (Italy)
L.: 57½ ft.	W.l.: 42½ ft.
B.: 12½ ft.	Df.: 10 ft.
Displ.: 22.44 tons	Engine: 62 Hp
Skipper:	Maurizio Ficani

THIS PAGE: *Shots of* Janabel, *today flying the Italian flag (Photos: F. Taccola and courtesy of M. Ficani).*

Jetta

Rigging:	Gaff-rigged ketch
Sail area:	156 sq. yds.
Shipyard:	Jas A. Silver Ltd.
	(Rosneath, Scotland)
Designer:	John Bain
Year of design:	1938
Launch:	1939
Restoration:	1995
L.: 48 ft.	W.l.: 43 ft.
B.: 11½ ft.	Df.: 6 ft.
Displ.: 28.77 tons	Engine: 50 Hp
Skipper:	Michel Martini
	(1996–2000)

*J*etta is the prototype of a series of vessels called "Western Isles," which show for the first time the intention of John Bain in conceiving pure sailing boats and not "motor sailers."

Ordered by an English lord, *Jetta* was requisitioned during World War II and used to patrol the Scottish coastline. The boat has only known four boat-owners and, at least until the late 1950s, it sailed under the name of *Ornum*, with Greenock in Scotland its fitting-out port. Since 1995 it has belonged to Sandrine and Michel Martini, who moor it at La Napoule, near Cannes, France.

Besides once again calling it by its original name, the current boat-owners have begun systematic interior and exterior restoration work, aiming to return *Jetta* to its condition at launch. The boat has mahogany planking, oak framing, teak superstructures and a teak deck, and Oregon pine masts.

Joyette

Rigging:	Bermudan schooner
Sail area:	880 sq. yds.
Shipyard:	Camper & Nicholson
	(Gosport, England)
Designer:	Charles E. Nicholson
Year of design:	1906
Launch:	1907
Restoration:	1966–68 Camper &
	Nicholson (Gosport,
	England), 1987–88,
	Valdettaro shipyards
	(La Spezia, Italy),
	1992, Amico
	(Genoa, Italy)
L.: 106½ ft.	W.l.: 64 ft.
B.: 17 ft.	Df.: 11 ft.
Displ.: 99.21 tons	Engine: 300 Hp
Skipper:	Giancarlo Basile
	(1990–94)

*"I*f a sailor these days wishes to see with his own eyes what is understood by the true beauty of a ship, he should take the train or the steamboat and go to Falmouth (England), where the* Cutty Sark *is still moored, polished, and preserved as in her most glorious days."* That is what Basil Lubbock wrote in his classic work *Sail: the Romance of the Clipper Ships.* The same expression can be used for *Joyette,* one of the masterpieces by Charles Nicholson from the early years of the 20th century, the golden age of yachting that declined with the Great War.

Joyette, with seemingly endless overhangs, a completely unencumbered deck (now the only one of these vintage boats left to testify to the style that characterized an age), masts that touch the sky, and an arcane charm that emanates from works of art.

Joyette, the favorite design of Nicholson, one of the greatest naval architects of the period, the yacht whose elegance of lines made him famous and sought-after like no other. His son John wrote in a book that his father considered it his "prettiest design" and that the model of the yacht, together with that of *Brynhild,* always remained in his office to testify to his affection for his creation. Today, *Joyette* is still the subject of degree theses in a naval architecture faculty. It has an ancient lineage, this elegant "lady of the seas."

Construction no. 176 from the Camper & Nicholson shipyards in Gosport, the splendid schooner had been commissioned for regattas in the waters of the Solent off southern England. A marvelous image by Beken from 1919 depicts it in the full splendor of its lines and sails, a sail plan that is demanding and striking, which, as for all the great yachts – including the British Royal Family's former yacht *Britannia,* with which it was often compared – underwent transformations required by the development of techniques and by fashion. I have personally been able to ascertain that all the rest has remained original, including the interior with period furniture, suspension lamps, prints and etchings, and all those precious furnishings that remain faithful to the original design, making the visitor feel

OPPOSITE PAGE: *September 1991, the lines of Joyette, one of Charles Nicholson's masterpieces (Photo: S. Navarrini).*

as if he or she is in the fascinating, lost world of yachting of the turn of the 19th century. The trophies won form a beautiful display in the old saloon, together with other period objects and solid silver jugs recently received as a gift from the White House.

Joyette was designed in 1906, the year when International Tonnage was also established. It was a period when narrow-beamed boats with a large draft were in vogue; these performed best on a beam reach or close reach. The boat was launched with the name of *Almara*, which it retained for just a couple of years; its second and last name,

BELOW: *Spectacular photograph of the bowsprit of* Joyette *(Photo: S. Navarrini).*

Joyette, seems very atypical: the French diminutive of the word for "joy," it may allude to pleasure and frivolity. In spite of its long career, the boat has had very few owners. Each has tended to keep it for an average of ten to 15 years with the exception of one, who sailed it for 30 years.

But let us continue with its history: the boat was launched in 1907, from the same port where *Orion* was launched three years later. Its first owner was Major Calverley, a keen yachtsman, as were many of his colleagues in the British Army. It was registered in the Royal Yacht Squadron of Cowes, England, the highly selective club of the British Royal Family. It was soon acquired by Sir Osborne Hondell, KBE, who kept it for 30 years, keeping the structure intact, though he did install a small petrol motor (the boat had been designed without a motor, and so it had remained for more than 30 years).

Joyette sailed on the English side of the Channel until its acquisition by an Italian entrepreneur, who, before transferring it to the port of Santo Margherita Ligure, where the boat was to have its new home, sent it for restructuring work to the same shipyard that had built it. This was between 1966 and 1968. In those years old boats were not "vintage" boats (the concept arose in the early 1980s with the regattas in Porto Cervo in Sardinia and Saint Tropez in France), but only "old," so a boat such as *Joyette* was merely of value for its size and capacity to handle any sea conditions. The ultra-slim stern was therefore shortened by 5 feet; the bowsprit was eliminated; the masts shortened; the ballasts modified; and sturdy, monstrous pulpits built, with a stainless steel handrail and balcony, plus seating, hatches, and air and light inlets on the deck to make the boat more comfortable. Fortunately the interior and the equipment on deck remained intact.

These aesthetic changes to *Joyette* were not insignificant: it maintained the beauty of its lines but lost out (with its mutilated hull and masts) in terms of the elegance of its seemingly endless rakes – all for the benefit of calm ocean-cruising.

It was 1987 when the next owner, keen on seafaring and at the height of the awakening of a traditional seafaring culture, became aware of this magnificent vessel, which, despite its changes, emanated an appeal that was difficult to resist. He realized that it was necessary to dig into its past and, following a diametrically opposite path to that of his predecessor, went to England and discovered that *Joyette* was one of England's most famous boats. He then recovered whatever might be useful for the restoration: the original designs conserved at the National Maritime Museum in Greenwich, London (they no longer existed in the shipyard since they were burnt in a great fire); information on the construction and history at the Camper & Nicholson shipyard in Gosport; and original photographs of the time taken by Beken and the Royal Yacht Squadron in Cowes, England.

There then began an enthusiastic restoration, not performed with the boat given to the shipyard "keys in hand," as often happens, but lasting several years, with the various jobs divided up over time and supervised by experienced and keen personnel. In fact, *Joyette* was perfectly preserved in terms of its soundness, had always sailed, and was complete with all its equipment (not, as in many cases, a boat extracted from the mud or abandoned in a shipyard). The restoration work therefore revolved around its elegance and traditional maneuvers, and not its sturdiness and functionality. Between one regatta and another, the work was carried out at the Valdettaro shipyard at Le Grazie and, in recent years, at the Amico shipyard in Genoa, both in Italy, which, bringing together precious shipwrighting skills and endowing itself with quality equipment, came to the forefront for high-level restoration work.

With time the bowsprit was put back; the stern was reconstructed according to the original designs; the pulpit, handrail and balcony, and seating were eliminated; the deck was rebuilt with a single, well-seasoned teak mast; the masts were lengthened, the foremast to 92 feet and the mainmast to 105 feet (the original, including the mast, pole, and boom of the gaff sail reached 120 feet); the ballast was reconstructed; the sails remade; the rudder blade reconstructed; all the installations remade; and finally the motor replaced. This, calibrated on the lines of the hull, ensured a maximum speed of 12 knots (unusually high for a sailboat), confirming

the quality and power of the lines designed by Nicholson.

The only aspect that is different today from Beken's photograph is the rig, which was in fact modified by the shipyard. To restore the original sail arrangement was unthinkable for two reasons: the difficulty of maneuvering and the quantity of crew members required. In fact, the Bermudan sail plan, with the change of the 14 sails available (created by Murphy & Nye), allows good speeds under all conditions, with a higher quantity of cloth than the original. Today, *Joyette* can change from a sail surface for medium–heavy weather, with 145–290 square yards of just low sails (jib, foremast, stay sail, reduced fisherman, broad reach fisherman, high stay sail, and large gaff sail), to another that includes a 215 square yard genoa and a 290 square yard fisherman. With all the sail cloth aloft in light weather (seven sails), the boat offers the impression of a training ship.

Another considerable advantage of this sail arrangement is the possibility of reducing the crew to practically a single helmsman if only the boomed foremast, the stay sail, and the small gaff sail mounted on the reduced mainmast boom are used. All four flying shrouds are blocked, practically becoming backstays, and the boat changes tack as though it had a centerboard.

Among the boat's mechanisms and equipment, almost all original, the steering gear can be seen astern. Equally original are the two warp winches, used for maneuvers in port, identical to some that have completely disappeared today but that are clearly identifiable in the famous photo of Nicholson on board *Candida*. Something else that has now remained and is unique are the old bow cleats, which unscrew to allow air into the crew's quarters.

When the masts were lengthened, the original gold coin that the English shipyards would always leave for good luck was found in the mainmast step; needless to say, the same coin was put back in position at the time of the ceremony of reinstallation of the mast.

Created with Burmese teak planking that was well seasoned at the time, *Joyette* has the sturdy, classic construction of the 19th century: double frames side by side and oak beams, steel floor plates, crossed steel bars to reinforce the main braces of the masts,

ABOVE: *Close-up of the onboard bell (Photo: S. Navarrini).*

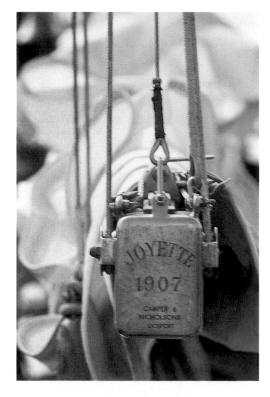

BELOW: *The boom head with the name of the boat and launch date etched on it (Photo: M. Sassone).*

external chain plates, and a stern terminal made of handcrafted teak heartwood. Deckhouses, skylights, stringer, toerails, and gunwale are still the original teak heart-wood. All the maneuvers are still manual (there are winches on deck); the sheets are hauled aft with flying tackle attached to the belay pins inserted in the eye bolts of the toerail, and with stopknots on the sheet. The same system is used to haul aft the halyards, after the crew have moved along the deck to hoist the sails.

Joyette already performed well at the regatta at Porto Cervo, Sardinia, in 1987, during its first phase of restoration. Heavy weather gave rise to a now-famous match race with *Puritan* around the Maddalena archipelago. Since then, the boat has always performed honorably during races, winning awards of various types from the cup for the most sporting crew, to that for the best conservation of the characteristics of the period, to first place in its class for coming out to race, uniquely in the class of large boats, when the others preferred to remain in port on account of the difficult weather conditions.

Most of the merit of *Joyette*'s performances is due to its exceptional skipper, Commander Giancarlo Basile, who is devoted to the boat. It was he, incidentally, who commanded *Stella Polare* when it won the famous Giraglia of 1966 (and produced a record unbeaten for 24 years) and the transatlantic Bermuda–Travemunde Race of 1968, from among another 33 fiercely competitive boats.

Commander Basile and *Joyette*, a pure family boat that has never done an hour of chartering in its whole, long life, are happy to play host to students of the Naval Academy for important regattas so that they can appreciate the differences in maneuvering to the training ship *Amerigo Vespucci*. *Joyette* may not be imposing like its bigger sisters (those still active) by the same designer – *Orion*, *Candida*, *Astra*, *Endeavour*, and *Shamrock* – and neither does it have the trysail arrangement displayed by Fife's *Altair* or Alden's *Puritan*, but it has an inexplicable charm that makes it unique. The same charm that Charles Nicholson, designer of dozens of famous boats, must have felt when every day he admired the model of his elegant "lady of the seas."

ABOVE: *The sophistication and warmth of the interior of* Joyette *(Photo: S. Navarrini).*

RIGHT: *The richness of the saloon (Photo: L. Fioroni).*

Karenita

This is one of the most beautiful boats to plow through the waves of the Mediterranean; it has a very slender bow with huge overhangs, a pure "racer." Its history is almost a legend.

Karenita was launched in 1929 at the Neponset shipyard in the United States, the 422nd creation of the naval architect who was all the rage in those years and dominated the scene of ocean regattas: John Alden. With its 75-foot length, the boat was inspired by the great racers – the legendary "J Class." A cruise and racing ketch, it is the masterpiece of a shipwright at the peak of his art and experience, a unique testimony to a style that had reached its height.

After nine years, five different owners, and as many names, *Karenita* became linked with the name of Errol Flynn, who acquired it in Boston: "*We were in Boston to buy a sailing boat. One should never rename a boat, but for this one I did a foolish thing…*"

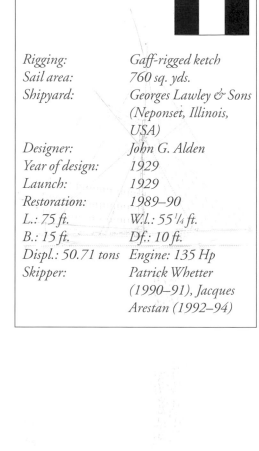

Rigging:	*Gaff-rigged ketch*
Sail area:	*760 sq. yds.*
Shipyard:	*Georges Lawley & Sons (Neponset, Illinois, USA)*
Designer:	*John G. Alden*
Year of design:	*1929*
Launch:	*1929*
Restoration:	*1989–90*
L.: 75 ft.	W.l.: 55¼ ft.
B.: 15 ft.	Df.: 10 ft.
Displ.: 50.71 tons	Engine: 135 Hp
Skipper:	*Patrick Whetter (1990–91), Jacques Arestan (1992–94)*

LEFT: *John Alden's* Karenita, *under sail, 1992 (Photo: J. Taylor).*

BELOW: *Close-up of the wheel and the binnacle (Photo: J. Taylor).*

ABOVE: _Skylight and warmth of the wood (Photo: J. Taylor)._

BELOW: Karenita, _1992 (Photo: J. Taylor)._

So, in 1938, Errol Flynn changed the name of the boat, which was called _Avenir_, to _Sirocco_, like the old one that the actor possessed in New Guinea. There followed cruises along the Atlantic coasts. Flynn sold _Sirocco_ in 1942.

Like all Alden's boats, _Karenita_ was built very solidly. It had an oak keel and hull with double mahogany planking bolted onto the frames; these too were oak. Nevertheless, the boat began deteriorating slowly. In 1985 it was found high and dry in Tortola in the Virgin Islands, without a deck and in the open air; nothing remained of the luxurious fittings and furnishings of the past. One night on the beach, for fun, someone had made a big bonfire of it. In April 1988, Patrick Khayat, creator of the "Blanc Bleu" mark, discovered the boat undergoing restorations. Within 48 hours he took the decision to buy it, out of the blue, after various boat-owners had tried to save it. In a short time the most qualified artisans arrived from Florida, from England, and from the Pacific.

The reconstruction took place under the responsibility of Bill Coffman, director of the Woodworks shipyard on Tortola. Everything had to be rebuilt, or almost. The search for the original plans began, and these were gradually found one after the other. Seventy frames were replaced with the same number of brand-new laminated oak ones, and the whole topside was replaced. From nearby Venezuela came Angelica wood; this is very hard, perfectly suited to the construction of the deck. Patrick and his friends commenced the search for naval antiquities from all over the Caribbean.

The final problem arose in May 1989. The local shipyard did not have the necessary means to position the heavy hull on the slide. From the neighboring island of Saint Thomas, Patrick succeeded in bringing over a tow, a barge, and a 70-ton crane. On June 3, 1989 _Karenita_ was lifted by the crane. A year later, on May 28, 1990, the boat left Tortola for Europe: the determination of one man enabled this dream boat that was considered doomed, to live again!

So it was that _Karenita_ rediscovered the polish, purity, rakes, and elegance of its best times. Once more a cruise and racing boat, it rediscovered the passion of competition. After its arrival in Europe in 1990, _Karenita_ won two races and two prestigious trophies. At Imperia and Saint Tropez in France it received awards; in summer 1993 it came outright first in the general placings of the Almirante Conde de Barcelona Trophy in Palma de Mallorca.

Years of greatness and oblivion, triumphs paid for at a hard price, follies and dangers; _Karenita_ has traversed passions and oceans so that its legend may continue. Today its sail surface is distributed as follows: "yankee" and large foresail (275 square yards), large sail (120 square yards), "yankee" two (55 square yards), "yankee" three (36 square yards), large foresail (62 square yards), spitfire (25 square yards), storm trysail (40 square yards), genoa (141 square yards), etc. In short, it is one of the most fascinating vessels to have reappeared in recent years in the evocative fleet of vintage yachts.

Kenavo II

K *enavo II* is a cutter designed and built by André Mauric in 1942 and inspired by the plans of an English pilot boat. It is a heavy, yet fairly fast boat. The current owner, the fourth in the life of *Kenavo II*, has paid meticulous attention to its every detail for 13 years. The 1955 Register of Yachts mistakenly shows its launch date as 1941.

ABOVE: *Close-up of the deck of* Kenavo II *(Photo: F. Ramella).*

RIGHT: *Shot of* Kenavo II *(Photo courtesy of P. Rouveret).*

Rigging:	*Bermudan cutter*
Sail area:	*96 sq. yds.*
Shipyard:	*André Mauric (Marseilles, France)*
Designer:	*André Mauric*
Year of design:	*1942*
Launch:	*1942*
Restoration:	*1982–85, 1990 Beconcini shipyards (La Spezia, Italy)*
L.: *39¼ ft.*	W.l.: *28½ ft.*
B.: *10 ft.*	Df.: *6½ ft.*
Displ.: *12.13 tons*	Engine: *40 Hp*
Skipper:	*Pierre Rouveret (1990–92)*

Kentra

Rigging:	*Trysail ketch*
Sail area:	*437 sq. yds.*
Shipyard:	*W. Fife & Son*
	(Fairlie, Scotland)
Designer:	*William Fife III*
Year of design:	*1923*
Launch:	*1923*
Restoration:	*1995 Fairlie*
	Restorations
	(Fairlie, Scotland)
L.: 84 ft.	*W.l.: 60 ft.*
B.: 17¼ ft.	*Df.: 10 ft.*
Displ.: 71.65 tons	*Engine: 145 Hp*
Skipper:	*Paul Jonkers (1996)*

RIGHT: *The boom head (Photo: A. Tringali).*
BELOW: *Imperia 1996, another Fife boat from 1923,* Kentra *(Photo: A. Tringali).*

uilt in six months, *Kentra* was launched on June 24, 1923. Its captain, Archie Hogart, had been the skipper of the first *Shamrock*, a competitor in the America's Cup and built in 1899 by Fife for Sir Thomas Lipton. *Kentra*'s first owner, the wealthy Scotsman Kenneth Clark, possessed about 30 yachts, all designed by G.L. Watson and William Fife.

Kentra, a comfortable and elegant cruise ketch, was acquired by its current owner (preceded by no fewer than 11 owners) through a sudden impulse, without even having seen the boat. He dreamt of acquiring *Belle Aventure*, another yacht by Fife, which was similar to *Kentra* but not for sale.

Kentra was transferred to the Fairlie Restorations shipyard in Scotland, completely dismantled, and subjected to major restructuring work. The new boat-owner was keen to give the restoration a very rare patina of authenticity, urging the shipyards to find period trimmings. Endowed with a rig and a sail plan identical to the original ones, *Kentra* sails a great deal between the Mediterranean and the Antilles.

In 1998, for the first time since 1993, the boat rediscovered the green waters of the Solent off the south coast of England after the Benodet Boat Rally, during which no fewer than ten vintage yachts celebrated the 100th birthday of *Pen Duick*. This boat rally in late May 1998, composed totally of vessels by Fife (*Clyde, Kentra, Lotus, Magda IV, Moonbeam III, Pen Duick, Solway Maid, Starlight, Tuiga,* and *Viola*) was the very last occasion that Eric Tabarly attended before his tragic death the following month.

Kentra usually winters at Cap d'Ail in southern France, and spends its summers on the seas of Greece and Turkey. The boat is currently sailing around the world.

Kipawa

This beautiful boat, which has not changed its name since the day of its launch, shows in its interior the noble origins of a past still waiting to be discovered. In the 1990s *Kipawa* was abandoned for a couple of years in low water on the beach between Milazzo and Messina in Italy. It was found by Santo Panté, who managed to give it a new life after four years of meticulous work and personal care. With its noble overhangs and 11-foot maximum beam, *Kipawa* is such a good plyer and so fast that it has always gained good placings in races.

During the long restoration, the new owner reconstructed all the elm frames and replaced the galvanized iron floor plates, by now worn-out, with new stainless steel

ones. *Kipawa* has cedar planking, a spruce mast and boom, and a teak deck, where the four original bronze winches can still be admired. Among the innovations, attention is drawn to the graceful wind sleeves, replacing the original "mushrooms," and a new electric winch instead of the manual one. Stanchions and stays had been fitted many years earlier.

With its ivory-colored hull, *Kipawa* is very manageable, sliding through the waves in a high sea and close to the wind. It almost always has a dry deck.

It was truly worthwhile to save this boat, so noble that for quite some time it had a bathtub in the washroom and a double cabin with two berths. The boat is currently for sale.

Rigging:	*Bermudan cutter*
Sail area:	*148 sq. yds.*
Shipyard:	*Dansnsen (Sweden)*
Designer:	*Christian Jensen*
Year of design:	*1938*
Launch:	*1938*
Restoration:	*1993*
L.: 54 ft.	*W.l.: 34 ft.*
B.: 11 ft.	*Df.: 8 ft.*
Displ.: 15.98 tons	*Engine: 47 Hp*
Skipper:	*Santo Panté*

BELOW: *VBR 1999,* Kipawa, *a history to be discovered (Photo: J. Taylor).*

Lasse

Rigging:	Gaff-rigged cutter (10-meter SI)
Sail area:	254 sq. yds.
Shipyard:	Stubbekobing (Denmark)
Designer:	Johan Anker
Year of design:	1938
Launch:	1940
Restoration:	1974–79 (Lacchini shipyards, Italy)
L.: 60 ft.	W.l.: 51 ft.
B.: 11 ft.	Df.: 8 ft.
Displ.: 18.74 tons	Engine: 90 Hp
Skipper:	Claudio Billi (1990–98)

This boat was launched in August 1940 in Stubbekobing, Denmark, the time the vessel was registered. Its history has not yet been completely determined, but from recent investigations it has emerged that *Eva* (its original name) was given as a gift by the King of Denmark to Eva Braun on the occasion of her visit before World War II. She had expressed her admiration for a similar boat that she had seen, designed by Johan Anker in 1931. In homage to her and for the sake of gallantry, the Danish monarch had a twin boat built by the same designer.

It is not known how much the boat was used in Germany (the war was near), but, from a volume published in Canada, which has in the text an image of Eva Braun and Hitler shown aft, it seems that it was actually active for short cruises. In any case, as a "state boat," *Eva* was moored at the Naval Academy in Flensburg, Germany, and miraculously escaped the Allied bombing, to the extent that for a few months Midshipman Karl Vattrod, today resident in Porto Cervo, Sardinia, learned his first sailing maneuvers on it. Probably sold by auction at the end of the war, *Eva* was

acquired by Mrs. Gurli Marie Larsen who, subsequently, on May 17, 1945, resold it to her husband P.T. Grosserer Larsen. Under his ownership, with the new name of *Lasse* and moored in Copenhagen, the boat was entered on the Danish Naval Register on September 27, 1952.

The vessel is one of the very few existing examples of a 10-meter SI class dating back to before the war. *Lasse* was acquired in the 1960s by Professor Paride Stefanini and in 1969 by the current owner who, from 1974 to 1979, submitted it for restoration work at the Lacchini shipyards in Viareggio, Italy. During this time the boat had an accident in port, when it was involved in a collision with a large boat that was maneuvering.

With considerable damage, *Lasse* ended up in a shed awaiting restructuring. In the meantime, many people, who had found out that this was "Hitler's boat," felt obliged to take away a piece of it. Even the berths disappeared!

Under Stefanini, *Lasse* sailed the Mediterranean and stopped off for a time in Cannes, France, where it was used for a feature film starring Alain Delon. In Viareggio the stempost was rebuilt and some oak frames were replaced, so that it now has some steam-bent beech ones instead. *Lasse* has an oak hull, mahogany planking above the waterline, a teak deck, a pitch pine mainmast (original), a spruce mizzenmast, and a pitch pine boom.

All the superstructures are original (including the wheel and the binnacle), while the planking has been partially replaced with boards whose dimensions and wood types are identical to those at the launch. The bulb, around 12 tons, is lead-cast iron, with a support held by four stainless steel keys.

Finally, the boat has an overhanging bow, with a recently fitted metal pulpit and a slender stern. Engraved on the central beam is the wording: "EVA 15.50 RTN 1940." During the works phase the beam was replaced and kept as a souvenir by the shipwright Bertolucci.

BELOW: *VBR 1991, an image of* Lasse, *a much-admired vessel (Photo: J. Taylor).*

Latifa

L atifa is another beautiful vessel designed and built by William Fife. In describing it, it would be unforgivable not to report Uffa Fox's description of the boat: "Latifa *is a great delight for those who love sailboats because it is one of the most beautiful sailing boats ever seen. I see it now as it darts through the Solent with a breeze from the north-west, running free, almost all hoisted, including the mizzen-staysail, and the whole cloud of its sails seems to lift it out of the water…*" And also: "*Light on the water like a chick with just its feet grazing the water…*" No less interesting is the description by Carlo Sciarelli: "*A big boat, with the class that we know. The width is greater than in the older boats and there is an unusual characteristic in an ocean racer, the canoe-like stern, the conclusion of a normal long stern rake…*" In fact, *Latifa*'s lines seem very pure and are reminiscent of many of Fife's previous boats. The rakes are very accentuated and seaworthy, with deep, V-shaped

sections that enable it to plow through the waves easily, and they join up sweetly with the mighty main section, which makes it float like a gull. Its canoe-like stern, very rare for large boats of the time (only to be found on its old adversary *Evenlode*), is the natural conclusion of the long stern rake and makes the whole hull even more graceful.

Latifa's first owner was Michael Mason. Immediately after its launch, it completed a 5,000-mile cruise along the western coast of Africa, overcoming heavy weather. It then successfully participated in many races, including the Fastnet Race where it was placed second in 1937. Two years later it challenged for supremacy, again at the Fastnet Race, with *Nordwind* of the German Navy, coming first in real time and fourth after handicaps. After World War II it was the only English yacht at the 1946 Bermuda regatta. In 1947 it won the Queen's Cup in the triangle race and won

Rigging:	Bermudan yawl
Sail area:	244 sq. yds.
Shipyard:	W. Fife & Son (Fairlie, Scotland)
Designer:	William Fife III
Year of design:	1936
Launch:	1936
Restoration:	1996 Beconcini shipyards (La Spezia, Italy)
L.: 70 ft.	W.l.: 52 ft.
B.: 15¼ ft.	Df.: 10 ft.
Displ.: 47.4 tons	Engines (2): 40 Hp
Skipper:	Mario Pirri Ardizzone

BELOW: *ASW 2001,* Latifa, *one of the best vessels in the yachting hierarchy (Photo: J. Taylor).*

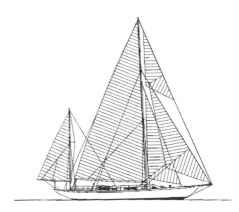

the Fastnet Race again in real time, defeating the famous *Bloodhound* and the corsair *Myth of Malham*.

In 1955 *Latifa* had a new owner, Jack Salem, who installed a 35 Hp engine on board. It then changed owners for a third time, ending up in 1976 in the hands of the Italian architect Pirri, a sailing-boat enthusiast. In 1977 and 1978 the boat underwent restructuring work at the Beconcini shipyards in La Spezia, Italy, who were to continue to have the honor of keeping it in good condition. But *Latifa* has been lucky to have had only four owners, who have always put the utmost importance on boat maintenance. The results are still evident today.

From November 1994 through March 1996 *Latifa* sailed round the world via the Panama and Suez Canals, returning to La Spezia after 26,000 miles in perfect condition and after various lone voyages by the skipper-owner.

Latifa still has its original binnacle and wheel, spruce masts and boom, original bronze hardware on the deck, and steering gear. Today, it continues to represent an ideal combination of beauty, speed, power, and nautical quality, as well as comfort. The grace and harmony of the lines are accompanied by sturdiness and quality of construction, which these days is found in very few vintage yachts. At the moment *Latifa* is undergoing restoration work.

ABOVE: *Close-up of the original winches, 2000 (Photo: F. Ramella).*

LEFT: *Shot of* Latifa *during a pleasant crossing (Photo: A. Andrews, courtesy of M. Pirri).*

OPPOSITE PAGE: Latifa *under way (Photo: A. Andrews, courtesy of M. Pirri).*

Laura III

Rigging:	Bermudan ketch
Sail area:	359 sq. yds.
Shipyard:	Jas N. Miller & Sons (Saint Monance, Scotland)
Designer:	W.G. McBryde
Year of design:	1929
Launch:	1929
Restoration:	1963, 1980
L.: 70¾ ft.	W.l.: 55 ft.
B.: 15¾ ft.	Df.: 8½ ft.
Displ.: 58.97 tons	Engines (2): 145 Hp
Skipper:	Raffaele Schiano di Cola (1987–91)

This boat was launched as *Ceol-Mara II*; there is not much information about its first years of life. In 1955 it is shown on the Register of Yachts with the simple name of *Ceol Mara*, probably under the same owner, Lieutenant Commander D.G. Silcock, who kept Glasgow in Scotland as its fitting-out port. In 1963 it was acquired by Pippo Dufour, the son-in-law of Achille Lauro, who rechristened it *Chevito*. It would seem that in the same period *Saharet* also arrived in Italy from England, acquired by Ercole Lauro.

The boat underwent a first restoration at the Barbagelata shipyard in Genoa, Italy, shifting the mizzenmast forward (the original mast-step still exists) and shortening the main boom. In 1977 further work was carried out.

In the meantime, the boat was called *Laura I*, later taking the name of *Laura III*. In 1980 it was acquired by its current owner, Giorgio Manfellotto, who himself performed regular maintenance work, rebuilding the deck. The boat has mahogany planking, oak frames, and (original) spruce masts. It hugs the wind well when close-hauled, while a stern wind is not ideal on account of its heaviness and its 12.13 tons of ballast.

THIS PAGE: *Two images of* Laura III, *1992 (Photos: J. Taylor).*

Lelantina

*L*elantina, which formerly sailed under a French flag, was designed in 1929 by the most famous architect of the first half of the century, a helmsman and tactician of famous oceanic races: John Alden. The boat is no more than an improved version of one of the schooners that the great Alden was so fond of, and it is the designer's 448th creation (*Puritan* bears the number 435).

The first vessel to bear the name *Lelantina* was built in the Netherlands by the famous De Vries shipyards on behalf of the American Ralph Peverly. The boat made its debut at the 1937 Fastnet Race. The owner, an admirer of Alden's creations, decided to commission an identical schooner, but with superior displacement, and so *Lelanta II* was born and subsequently renamed *Lelantina*. The boat had various owners, ending up in Brittany and then in Florida, where it was involved in marijuana trafficking. In 1955, when it belonged to the Siamese Prince Bira, it was nearly shipwrecked on entering the port of Capraia in Tuscany, Italy.

In 1986 *Lelantina* underwent a period of significant restoration: the deck was completely rebuilt, while the two original spruce masts were kept. Its hull, made of steel with riveting, was carefully inspected and found to be in excellent condition. The fore deckhouse that can be seen in a famous photo by Beken from 1938 has disappeared today, while the sail plan has remained almost identical. The new owner furnished the very bright interior with great passion, thanks also to crystal-glass light points sunk into the deck (now completely free from any encumbrance).

Under sail *Lelantina* is a model of sweetness and equilibrium; the perfection of the lines of the steel hull is closely tied to its stability and power. With its 480 square yards of sail, it bears winds of up to 30 knots very well. In fact, when it has to leave the port of Saint Tropez in France, its normal mooring place, it waits for the Mistral to blow to feel the thrill of the sails under their top conditions.

The magic proportions of this schooner rig made Uffa Fox write: "*The combination of sails that will withstand a dead calm or a sudden rush of wind is better than any other rigging I know…*"

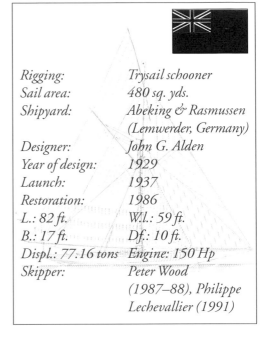

Rigging:	Trysail schooner
Sail area:	480 sq. yds.
Shipyard:	Abeking & Rasmussen (Lemwerder, Germany)
Designer:	John G. Alden
Year of design:	1929
Launch:	1937
Restoration:	1986
L.: 82 ft.	W.l.: 59 ft.
B.: 17 ft.	Df.: 10 ft.
Displ.: 77.16 tons	Engine: 150 Hp
Skipper:	Peter Wood (1987–88), Philippe Lechevallier (1991)

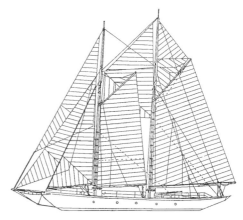

THIS PAGE: *Cannes 1998,* Lelantina, *the big, beautiful creation of John Alden (Photos: J. Taylor).*

FOLLOWING PAGE: *Cannes 1998, power, grace, and speed (Photo: J. Taylor).*

L'Iliade

(sometime L'Iliade et l'Odyssée)

This boat was placed on the slipway in the Normandy shipyards (in Fécamp, France) in October 1934 and was launched the following July. Its first owner was Fernando Rey of Paris, who had commissioned it from architect François Camatte, known for having built many boats in Cannes and Arcachon in the 1930s and 1940s. *L'Odyssée* – this was its first name – immediately distinguished itself in all the races in which it participated before it became stuck in the port of Cannes throughout World War II.

In 1950 the boat was sold to Marius Durbec of Marseilles, France, who carried out an initial restoration for conservation purposes. In 1960 the new owner was Roger Castella, with whom *L'Odyssée* made numerous cruises in the Mediterranean. The boat underwent restoration in 1972 by the famous architect André Mauric, who modernized all the onboard equipment,

replacing the original masts and winches, as well as rebuilding the teak deck. It was Mauric again who, in 1973–74, went on a long cruise to the Caribbean before returning to Marseilles. In 1987 the new owner, Michel Roy, gave the boat the name *L'Iliade et l'Odyssée* and restructured the interiors.

An extremely strong boat, with abundant use of oak, it underwent careful refitting in 1993, which underlined the excellent condition of the planking and framings. *L'Iliade* has an oak hull, and a teak deck and super-structures that are still original. The interior, on the other hand, was modernized to meet the demands of chartering. The boat has sailed a great deal along the English and French coasts, in the Mediterranean and the Caribbean, and has no fewer than a dozen Atlantic crossings to its name. The latest modernization, undertaken at the wishes of the new owner of the boat, dates back to 1999.

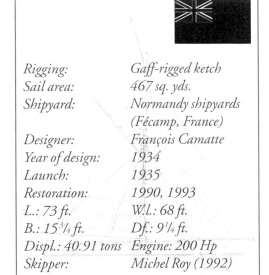

Rigging:	Gaff-rigged ketch
Sail area:	467 sq. yds.
Shipyard:	Normandy shipyards (Fécamp, France)
Designer:	François Camatte
Year of design:	1934
Launch:	1935
Restoration:	1990, 1993
L.: 73 ft.	W.l.: 68 ft.
B.: 15¾ ft.	Df.: 9¼ ft.
Displ.: 40.91 tons	Engine: 200 Hp
Skipper:	Michel Roy (1992)

THIS PAGE: *Cannes 2000,* L'Iliade *at a regatta* (Photos: J. Taylor).

Lily IV

Rigging:	Gaff-rigged sloop
Sail area:	81 sq. yds.
Shipyard:	Pierre Foces (Les Mureaux, France)
Designer:	Henri Dervin
Year of design:	1946
Launch:	1946
Restoration:	1996
L.: 33¼ ft.	W.l.: 24 ft.
B.: 10 ft.	Df.: 6 ft.
Displ.: 10.32 tons	Engine: 35 Hp
Skipper:	Enrico Monaco (1994–2002)

Based on a diagram by Henri Dervin, this boat was launched under the name of *Anitra Pierre III* on October 25, 1946 in the Pierre Foces ship-yard in the north of France. Until the early 1950s, it was registered at the port of Nassau (in the Bahamas). It was subsequently called *Ioawi* and in 1955 was transferred to a boat-owner in Nice, France.

Abandoned for a long time in the waters of Villefranche, France, and with considerable damage caused by negligence, it was lucky to be noticed by the shipwright Joseph Masnata, owner of a shipyard in Villefranche, who decided to acquire and restore it. It was during this period that the boat was given its current name of *Lily IV*. The interior was reconstructed and a bowsprit was added.

In 1994 *Lily IV* was acquired by the current owner, who at that time replaced the heavy motor, restored the deck, and returned the boom to its original length (16½ feet).

Today, *Lily IV* has mahogany planking, a silver spruce mast, acacia frames, and an oak keel. The boat is very manageable and stable, with its tiller and boomed fore staysail.

Limnoreia

Rigging:	Bermudan schooner
Sail area:	197 sq. yds.
Year of design:	1928
Launch:	1929
L.: 49 ft.	W.l.: 39¼ ft.
B.: 11 ft.	Df.: 8 ft.
Displ.: 24.25tons	Engine: 75 Hp
Skipper:	Paul Kroiss (1987)

There is limited information on this boat, which sails under a French flag. Launched in 1929, *Limnoreia* stands out at a distance on account of its aft balustrade and long bowsprit. Its deckhouse and toerail are painted with a wood effect.

RIGHT: Limnoreia *in light winds* (Photo: Sbriscia).

Linnet

On September 1998 two boats arrived in the waters off Imperia: *Dorade* and *Linnet*. The latter is a true gem of a yacht, designed in 1904 by Nathaniel Greene Herreshoff. It is one of the survivors of the "New York 30" – the first to reach the Mediterranean.

Linnet was discovered by chance in the Cape Cod area by Federico Nardi, technical manager of the Argentario naval shipyard. It can be considered to be the first one-design in sailing history, the first mass-produced hull, and one of the very few (of the 18 launched) to have competed for nearly a century in sailing regattas.

The début of the "NYYC 30" Class was a rather unusual event. Following a request from a group of members of the NYYC, a committee was set up to create a new class (covering yachts with a waterline length of less than 30 feet and a sufficiently spacious deck and cockpit that these boats could race against the club's larger yachts). As soon as this project had been drawn up and approved, orders for these boats came pouring in, and their owners quickly saw the outcome of the new design – they were incredibly stable, fast boats.

Linnet was the first to be launched and is one of 13 such yachts still sailing. When Nardi came across it, *Linnet*'s hull was missing some equipment and the deckhouse and cockpit had been modified. Thanks partly to Bertelli, who already owned *Nyala*, *Linnet* has been completely restored by the Argentario naval shipyard and is now a much admired, successful racer.

Its restoration, mainly designed to conserve the boat's original characteristics, involved, among other things, the replacement of a number of planking strakes; the removal of the bulb and its remounting using new bolts; and the rebuilding of the mast, boom, gaff, and spinnaker pole strictly according to Herreshoff's original drawings. A new white cedar deck was laid, and the skylights and the interior were also restored.

Over the years, *Linnet* had been poorly transformed into a gaff-rigged yacht. The deck rigging had all been recast in bronze, and, as Nardi pointed out at the time in an interview he gave to Giuliana Fratnick, the only original equipment left was "a cleat and a chock." After seven months' work, *Linnet* reacquired its original appearance, much to the satisfaction of all trysail yacht enthusiasts. During the Prada Classic Week held at Porto Santo Stefano, *Linnet* displayed its natural talent as a fast, dashing vessel.

Rigging:	Trysail sloop
Sail area:	109 sq. yds.
Shipyard:	Herreshoff boatyard (Bristol, Rhode Island, USA)
Designer:	Nathaniel G. Herreshoff
Year of design:	1904
Launch:	1905
Restoration:	1998 Argentario naval shipyard (Italy)
L.: 43¼ ft.	W.l.: 32 ft.
B.: 8½ ft.	Df.: 6¼ ft.
Displ.: 8.82 tons	Engine: 18 Hp
Skipper:	F. Nardi (1998)

BELOW: *Cannes 1998,* Linnet *during a regatta, having just been fully restored (Photo: J. Taylor).*

OVERLEAF: *Imperia 1998, a fine shot of* Linnet, *a light, fast NYYC 30 designed by Nathaniel Herreshoff (Photo: J. Taylor).*

Loki

A fast yacht designed by Olin Stephens, *Loki* has been described by Carlo Sciarelli as the "typical small American yacht" – i.e. long, heavy, comfortable, and quite capable of winning regattas. In fact, it has won one edition of the Bermuda Race (in 1947) and came third in the 1953 Fastnet Race. It has also taken part in regattas on the Côte d'Azur (in October 2001).

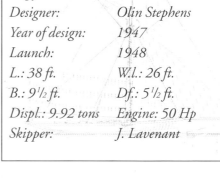

Rigging:	Gaff-rigged yawl
Sail area:	299 sq. yds.
Shipyard:	Albert Limos
Designer:	Olin Stephens
Year of design:	1947
Launch:	1948
L.: 38 ft.	W.l.: 26 ft.
B.: 9½ ft.	Df.: 5½ ft.
Displ.: 9.92 tons	Engine: 50 Hp
Skipper:	J. Lavenant

THIS PAGE: *VBR 2001, three shots of* Loki *during the regatta (Photos: J. Taylor).*

Lord Jim

Rigging:	*Bermudan schooner*
Sail area:	*299 sq. yds.*
Shipyard:	*M.M. Davis & Son (Solomons, Maryland, USA)*
Designer:	*John G. Alden*
Year of design:	*1930*
Launch:	*1930*
Restoration:	*1960*
L.: 78 ft.	W.l.: 63 ft.
B.: 15 ft.	Df.: 8 ½ ft.
Displ.: 35.27 tons	Engine: 120 Hp
Skipper:	*Lionel Cazé*

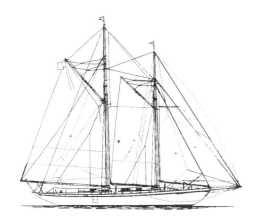

Design no. 476 by John G. Alden, *Lord Jim* was launched as a trysail schooner on behalf of Paul Nevin of New York and Bar Harbor, Maine in the United States. At least three of Alden's boats have had the same name. This one was launched in the same year as the smaller schooner, *Malabar X*, and the interiors of the two yachts were very similar. Designed for offshore cruising or sailing the open seas, *Lord Jim* had somewhat stronger framing than *Malabar X* (which had curved framing) and sawn ribs that, in its early days, enabled the boat to successfully survive the November storms in the waters around Cape Hatteras.

In June 1959, with skipper and owner E. Ross Anderson (at that time Commodore of the Boston Yacht Club) at the helm, *Lord Jim* was invited to escort Admiral Donald B. MacMillan's schooner *Bowdoin* during its voyage of exploration in the Arctic. A coast-guard cutter accompanied the two schooners on the voyage. At that time, *Lord Jim* was a splendid sight with its trysail rig.

Just off the coast of Rhode Island, the two schooners sailed into thick fog, with their radar not working properly. The two boats were both proceeding cautiously when Catumb's Rocks suddenly appeared below the bows of the *Bowdoin*, which just managed to avoid running aground. However, it did not manage to warn *Lord Jim*, which was sailing astern, in time, and the latter was not quite so fortunate and crashed into the rocks. Twenty minutes later *Lord Jim* sank. The seven crew members were all saved, but of the boat itself only the bell, the compass, and the flag survived.

Like other boats designed by Alden, *Lord Jim* was resuscitated, albeit in rather obscure circumstances. The sunken yacht was recovered, and Mervin Briggs spent four years putting it back together in a shipyard in New Hampshire. However, he was unable to finish the job completely and in 1964 had to sell the boat, which was then transported to another shipyard. During the 1970s it was seen again at Gloucester, fitted out for fishing and with the rig unaltered, and, as R. Carrick

and R. Henderson recollect in their biography of Alden, they were lucky enough to see one of his schooners return to its roots.

The most famous of the three versions of *Lord Jim* was probably the second one, which began life as the *Meridian* and which was subsequently renamed *Blue Water*, *Shoal Water*, *Genie*, and *Shoal Water* once again. This 72-foot hull (drawing no. 614) was launched in 1936 at the George Lawley & Son shipyard in Neponset (in Massachusetts) on behalf of the Knight brothers. The schooner had a considerable displacement for an offshore cruiser, and, like the first *Lord Jim*, had not been designed for racing since speed had been considered of secondary importance. It had double-cut ribs, thick yellow-pine planking, and a teak flush deck (even though the original sail plan envisaged a rather pronounced deckhouse).

The schooner, sailing under the name of *Blue Water*, was used as an anti-submarine patrol boat during World War II, at the end of which it was purchased by Rescoe Prior from Boston. The new owner promptly saw to properly restoring the boat before entering it (under its new name of *Shoal Water*) in the 1948 Marblehead–Halifax Race, where, against all odds, it came second behind the Herreshoff ketch *Ticonderoga*.

It was then donated to the New York State Maritime Academy and subsequently took part in the 1954 Bermuda Race. It gained notoriety, nevertheless, when it was bought by E. Ross Anderson to replace the first *Lord Jim*. Anderson, with the help of a shipyard and the sail-maker Ted Hood, transformed the boat into a staysail schooner for racing purposes only. With its new 86-foot aluminum foremast, *Lord Jim* became extremely competitive and immediately won the Lambert Cup (in 1961) and the Marblehead–Halifax Race.

In 1966 it was sold once again and was chartered in the West Indies, with mixed fortunes including running aground on the coral reef of Antigua. In 1975 it was bought by Holger Kreuzhage, a photographer and TV producer who gradually restored it to its former state.

In 1970 *Lord Jim* took part in the Round Grenada Race. Then, after work carried out in 1989, it raced in the 1993 Antigua Classic Yacht Regatta, where it came first of all the boats taking part, and first of its schooner class despite its handicap. Used as a charter yacht, it would seem that it was sold in 1993 (according to my friend Mike Horsley) and sailed in the Caribbean.

I believe, as does Niels Helleberg of Alden Design in Boston, that the picture shown in the present volume is of the hull launched in 1936. However, some doubts remain, in particular as to what exactly happened to the first *Lord Jim*.

BELOW: Lord Jim, *Alden's famous schooner, photographed taking part in the Antigua regatta (Photo: B. Villani).*

Lulù
(sometime Gunga Din)

Rigging:	Trysail cutter
Sail area:	108 sq. yds.
Shipyard:	Texier, France
Designer:	Rabot
Year of design:	1897
Launch:	1897
Restoration:	1986, 1987–90
L.: 49 ft.	W.l.: 31 ft.
B.: 9¹⁄₂ ft.	Df.: 6 ft.
Displ.: 10.76 tons	
Skipper:	Gerard Naigeon (1996),
	J. Duchatelier (2000)

*L*ulù is quite simply a fantastic boat! This trysail cutter with an overall length of 50 feet was designed by Rabot and launched in 1897. It has a pine, teak, and mahogany hull with a spruce mast, and was discovered in 1984 near Montpellier in France by Petty Officer Morgan Thierry of the French Navy. In 1993 it was included among France's maritime heritage, and as a result the French government regularly finances its servicing. This has enabled Morgan Thierry to transfer the boat to Brittany, where it has been carefully restored over a period of three years.

At Imperia, *Gunga Din* (the boat was called by this name at that time) won the honors in its class, beating boats of the caliber of *Tonino* and *Tuiga*. It has also taken part in the Nioulargue. At present it is based in Toulon, France.

RIGHT: *Cannes 1998, a close-up of Lulù, a yacht with extremely harmonious lines (Photo: J. Taylor).*

BELOW RIGHT: *Imperia 1987, Maddalena II at its moorings (Photo: S. Pesato).*

Maddalena II

Rigging:	Gaff-rigged ketch
Sail area:	275 sq. yds.
Design and shipyard:	Martinolich (Tacoma, Washington, USA)
Year of design:	1938
Launch:	1938
Restored:	1983 Argentario naval shipyard (Italy)
L.: 52¹⁄₂ ft.	W.l.: 45¹⁄₂ ft.
B.: 12¹⁄₄ ft.	Df.: 7 ft.
Displ.: 23.81 tons	Engine: 130 Hp
Skipper:	Oliviero Foschi (1987)

*M*addalena II has a reasonably shaped hull, albeit one that is not enhanced by the false deckhouses and the figurehead beneath the bowsprit. It is clear that a number of modifications have been performed over the years that have altered the teak deck and the Douglas fir masts.

In 1983 it underwent considerable restoration work, with the replacement of the garboard strake, the controtorello and the floor timbers, and the rebuilding of the transom. In 1987 the boat took part in the vintage yacht regattas held at Porto Cervo in Sardinia, Imperia, and Saint Tropez in France.

Manihiki

Sailing under the Panamanian flag, *Manihiki* was purchased at Pola (now part of Croatia) in 1973 and for 27 years was used for cruising purposes by its owner. As often happens, the history of the boat remains a mystery, although it would seem that it was used by the French Navy for training purposes and that it has completed two round-the-world voyages.

It has a flush deck, teak planking, oak ribs, and aluminum masts (the original masts were in Douglas fir). The boat underwent substantial refitting during the 1980s at the La Bussola shipyard at Fiumicino in Italy, where the deck was completely replaced.

Manihiki has taken part in one vintage yacht regatta at Porto Cervo in Sardinia and is presently to be found in a shipyard at Viareggio, Italy.

Rigging:	Bermudan ketch
Sail area:	335 sq. yds.
Shipyard:	Bordeaux naval shipyard (Bordeaux, France)
Designer:	The shipyard
Year of design:	1932
Launch:	1932
Restoration:	1980, 1990 La Bussola shipyard (Fiumicino, Italy)
L.: 55³/₄ ft.	W.l.: 46¹/₂ ft.
B.: 13¹/₂ ft.	Df.: 8 ft.
Displ.: 33.07 tons	Engine: 90 Hp
Skipper:	Luigi D'Angelo

BELOW: Manihiki, *built in Bordeaux in 1932 (Photo courtesy of L. D'Angelo).*

Manta

Rigging:	Gaff-rigged cutter
Sail area:	141 sq. yds.
Shipyard:	Tarabocchia
	(Lussinpiccolo,
	Croatia)
Designer:	Tarabocchia
Year of design:	1934
Launch:	1935
Restoration:	1980–89
L.: 45 1/4 ft.	W.l.: 36 1/4 ft.
B.: 11 1/4 ft.	Df.: 6 3/4 ft.
Displ.: 25.35 tons	Engine: 90 Hp
Skipper:	Ernesto Irace
	(1990–2002)

*M*anta is one of the few cutters launched at Lussinpiccolo in Croatia that have come to Italy. It has remained very much as it was the day it was launched but for the addition of winches from an earlier period; every single part of the hull has been perfectly conserved.

It was originally designed for transatlantic crossings, but during its inaugural voyage it was forced ashore in the Canary Islands, and has remained in the Mediterranean ever since. Very little is known about the boat's history. *Manta* is one of the keenest competitors in current vintage yacht regattas.

BELOW: Manta *during a regatta (Photo: C. Borlenghi).*
RIGHT: *Argentario 1992 (Photo: J. Taylor).*

Mariella

Mariella, a splendid yacht designed by Alfred Mylne, caused quite a stir when it arrived in the port of Imperia. It is a composite structure consisting of a hull and deck built from 1½-inch teak planking, and beams and ribs in steel. The interior is also in teak with the exception of the lounge, where English oak is greatly in evidence. The boat was launched just before the outbreak of World War II, but its first owner, coffee merchant James Paterson, was unfortunately not able to enjoy it, quickly disappearing from the scene. The boat was subject to the usual problems associated with wartime: unrigged, it was moored on the River Clyde and used as a patrol boat warning of imminent attacks by the German Luftwaffe – a sad destiny common to a great number of yachts during that time. It was Baron Ronald Teacher, the whisky magnate, who was to benefit from this splendid Fife

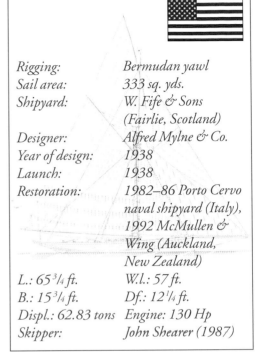

Rigging:	Bermudan yawl
Sail area:	333 sq. yds.
Shipyard:	W. Fife & Sons (Fairlie, Scotland)
Designer:	Alfred Mylne & Co.
Year of design:	1938
Launch:	1938
Restoration:	1982–86 Porto Cervo naval shipyard (Italy), 1992 McMullen & Wing (Auckland, New Zealand)
L.: 65¾ ft.	W.l.: 57 ft.
B.: 15¾ ft.	Df.: 12¼ ft.
Displ.: 62.83 tons	Engine: 130 Hp
Skipper:	John Shearer (1987)

LEFT: *VBR 2001,* Mariella, *designed by Alfred Mylne (Photo: J. Taylor).*

BELOW: *Porto Cervo, the yacht in a regatta in the 1990s (Photo: C. Borlenghi).*

creation and he remained its owner for over 32 years.

The boat was subsequently sold to three other owners before being purchased by Vincenzo De Domenico, a sixth-generation Italian–American from San Francisco whose family had made its fortune selling chocolate and pasta. The new owner split his leisure time between *Mariella* and another Fife creation, *Kentra*, built in 1923. *Mariella*, which never changed its name, is very well-known in the Channel ports and the Mediterranean. In 1982, in an attempt to cover its significant running costs, the boat

was equipped for charter purposes and restored at Porto Cervo in Sardinia. The spaces below deck were reorganized in order to make it more habitable and functional, although the original oak lounge was left intact; the construction serial number is engraved at the base of the skylight. It was also during the 1980s that *Mariella* completed a round-the-world voyage and, in between periods of restoration work, managed to take part in a number of regattas and meetings. At the McMullen & Wing shipyard in Auckland, New Zealand, a number of beams were replaced and the teak deck was completely rebuilt. At the end of 1992, the boat was bought at auction by Antigua's Italian Vice-Consul, Carlo Falcone. The former skipper, after having serviced the boat and maintained the crew at his own expense for a year, and not having had any further news of the then owner, arranged for the sequestration of *Mariella*, which was then sold by public auction on October 6, 1993.

Mariella won the Antigua Classic Yacht Regatta outright in 1994 and 1995, but in 1996 and 1997 it only managed to come first in its class. It had already won one Antigua Race Week sailing in this part of the ocean.

The boat has conserved its original masting: Oregon fir masts and a spruce boom. The deckhouse is attractively set into a clear stern deck; the cockpit features a splendid binnacle. The sleek bow and the power of the boat's massive rigging mean that in a strong wind it can easily reach 12 to 14 knots. During its last term in New Zealand waters (where it took part in the Schooner Cup), *Mariella* took on and beat its more highly esteemed rivals.

THIS PAGE: *VBR 2001,* Mariella *pictured twice during a regatta (Photos: J. Taylor).*

Mariette

Mariette is without any doubt one of the most beautiful and prestigious boats that have ever sailed into the port of Imperia. Designed by Nathaniel Greene Herreshoff, it bears one of the most important hallmarks of naval architecture in the world. Herreshoff was a true genius, and *Mariette* continues to be one of his best calling cards.

Launched in 1915, it had a series of different owners and names prior to being requisitioned by American coastguards at the beginning of World War II. The boat came out of military service in a sorry state, was sold once again, and was renamed *Gee Gee*. Bought by a Canadian, it was used as a luxury charter yacht in the Caribbean. Several years later, the boat was noticed in the Antilles by Erik Pascoli. He advised a group of Italian and Swiss bankers to buy the boat, without knowing that they would ask him to take over command of the yacht at a later date. *Mariette* was given its original name back in 1979, thanks to the publisher Alberto Rizzoli, who proved to be one of its best owners.

The yacht was subsequently taken to the Beconcini shipyard for restoration work, which was to last until 1983, under the guidance of the architect Ugo Faggioni and Erik Pascoli. Originally designed as a trysail schooner, the boat has since been transformed into a Bermudan schooner and has started to win regattas throughout the Mediterranean. The present-day *Mariette* is one of the greatest works of restoration of a vintage yacht ever seen in Italy.

Eleven years after the restoration had been completed the boat was sold to Wolf Chitis, and then bought in 1995 by the American Thomas J. Perkins, who decided to refit its original rigging. He asked the Herreshoff Foundation for a copy of the initial sail plan, together with technical

Rigging:	Trysail schooner
Sail area:	1,236 sq. yds.
Shipyard:	Herreshoff boatyard (Bristol, Rhode Island, USA)
Designer:	Nathaniel G. Herreshoff
Year of design:	1914
Launch:	1915
Restoration:	1980–83, 1995 Beconcini shipyard (La Spezia, Italy)
L.: 110 ft.	W.l.: 79½ ft.
B.: 23½ ft.	Df.: 13¾ ft.
Displ.: 181.9 tons	Engines (2): 150 Hp
Skipper:	Frederic Vergue (1996), Chris Gartner (1998–2002)

LEFT: *Cowes 2001, the trysail schooner* Mariette *by Herreshoff (Photo: J. Taylor).*

OVERLEAF: *Cowes 2001, the legendary* Mariette *sailing on the edge (Photo: J. Taylor).*

RIGHT: *ASW 2001, detail of the stern cockpit (Photo: J. Taylor).*

ABOVE AND BELOW: *Cowes 2001, snapshots of* Mariette *during a regatta (Photos: J. Taylor).*

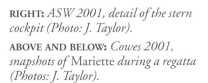

drawings of the masting and fittings. The English company Harry Spencer won the tender for the construction of the masting, while the Beconcini shipyard saw to refitting the deck and part of the interior. *Mariette* is once again the vintage racer of old. The two new masts, the boom, and the bowsprit have all been made from Columbia pine; the mainsail's gaff and the gaff topsail's yard, on the other hand, have been made from silver spruce. A few of the original features of the interior have disappeared, although the Honduran mahogany furniture between the berths has been restored to its original splendor, and the lounge has been preserved exactly as it was when the boat was launched, with splendid Circassian walnut paneling, red-tasseled divans, and a beautiful Honduran mahogany staircase. With more than 1,200 square yards of sails, *Mariette* slides through the water in an elegant, secure manner. Its perfect shape is truly breathtaking. With 30 people taking the greatest care over its every maneuver, *Mariette* displays great power and pace to an admiring public.

The boat is presently a member of the New York Yacht Club.

Marjatta

I first saw this yacht one fall afternoon in 1990 in the calm waters of Santa Margherita harbor in Italy; moored just a few meters away from *Marjatta* were *Samadhi* and *Joyette*. *Marjatta* had a dark blue, sleek hull that gave it a Nordic appearance and simplicity.

Immediately after its launch, the boat was transferred to Stockholm then, in 1948, to London where it was registered. In fact, details of the boat are to be found in the 1955 Register of Yachts (where it is registered as yacht no. 4668 – the property of H. Ahlström) and in the writing engraved on the main beam dating from 1950.

Marjatta remained in England up until the 1960s, when it was sold and transferred to Italy. Restoration work was begun in 1989 at the Tigullio shipyard at Santa Margherita. The electrical system was completely redone and the deck rebuilt, without altering the rigging or the interior at all. In fact, the boat's name and rigging have remained as they were when it was launched; likewise the masts, rudder, winches, furnishings, and anchor. Only the mainsail boom has been remounted in aluminum.

Marjatta is a rather fast, responsive yacht when sailing close-hauled or on a beam reach, but it requires careful handling when sailing with the spinnaker. At the 1990 Imperia Regatta, *Marjatta* performed extremely well and was awarded a special prize for having the youngest crew.

Rigging:	Gaff-rigged yawl
Sail area:	175 sq. yds.
Shipyard:	Båtvarf (Abö, Finland)
Designer:	J. Lindblom
Year of design:	1939
Launch:	1943
Restoration:	1989 Tigullio shipyard (Santa Margherita, Italy)
L.: 59 ft.	W.l.: 41 ½ ft.
B.: 13 ft.	Df.: 8 ft.
Displ.: 26.46 tons	Engine: 90 Hp
Skipper:	Guido Broggi (1990–96), Stefano Beltrando (1998)

BELOW: *ASW 2001, one side of* Marjatta, *ever-present at vintage yacht regattas (Photo: J. Taylor).*

Mehalah

Rigging:	*Bermudan sloop*
Sail area:	*75 sq. yds.*
Shipyard:	*Berthon Boat Ltd.*
	(Lymington, England)
Designer:	*M.G. May*
Year of design:	*1939*
Launch:	*1947*
Restoration:	*1960, 1993*
	(Gino d'Este)
L.: *41 ft.*	W.l.: *32½ ft.*
B.: *9½ ft.*	Df.: *5¾ ft.*
Displ.: *15.43 tons*	Engine: *40 Hp*
Skipper:	*Francesco Castaldi*
	(1994–96)

This Bermudan sloop, designed by M.G. May, was launched in 1947 at the Berthon boatyard in Lymington, England, where the designer worked. It reached Italy during the mid-1950s after having been the property of D.M. Jones of Southampton. Compared with the vessel shown in a famous photo taken in 1949 by Beken, the boat no longer features a seven-eighths rig and now has a wheel rather than the original tiller. The stern deckhouse has also been extended somewhat. The spruce mast is the original, albeit moved slightly astern. *Mehalah* has a teak deck and deckhouse, oak ribs, mahogany planking, and steel floor plates.

THIS PAGE: *VBR 1995, two photographs of* Mehalah *(Photos: J. Taylor).*

Membury

Membury was registered with the Lowestoft Custom House in England by R.H. Riley immediately after it had been built. It then sailed off the Norfolk coast. During its early years, the boat changed hands a number of times. Up until 1953, *Membury* was regularly registered in the Lloyds Register of Yachts, but then the boat inexplicably disappeared.

In 1965 the boat became the property of a Mr. Anscomb. It was not until 1985 that the present owner, Nick Douch, discovered the boat in a bad state on the River Adur at Shoreham, England, and bought it from a Mr. Sullivan. The purchase completed, the boat was put in for three years of refitting work, including the replacement of 24 ribs and the construction of a completely new deck. Once it had been fully restored, *Membury* began to sail once again off the southern English coast and then moved into the Mediterranean for a six-month cruise.

In the summer of 1993 the boat lost its mast due to an extensive crack, and the owner consequently decided to convert it to a trysail cutter, thus reverting back to the rig it had when purchased in 1985. The boat currently has a pitch pine skin and oak ribs, mahogany deckhouse and hatches, and a spruce mast. Greatly admired at regattas for its noble looks, *Membury* recalls boat designs from the late 19th century.

Rigging:	*Bermudan cutter*
Sail area:	*72 sq. yds.*
Shipyard:	*T. Martin*
	(Southwold, England)
Designer:	*T. Martin*
Year of design:	*1928*
Launch:	*1928*
Restoration:	*1985–89*
L.: 40 ft.	*W.l.: 28 1/2 ft.*
B.: 10 1/2 ft.	*Df.: 4 1/2 ft.*
Displ.: 8.23 tons	*Engine: 30 Hp*
Skipper:	*Nick Douch (1989)*

LEFT: *A shot of* Membury *under sail. Its lines are those of a typical English yacht from the end of the 19th century (Photo courtesy of N. Douch).*

Merry Dancer

Rigging:	Bermudan sloop
Sail area:	120 sq. yds.
Shipyard:	W. Fife & Sons (Fairlie, Scotland)
Designer:	W. Fife Jr.
Year of design:	1936
Launch:	1938
Restoration:	1994
L.: 51½ ft.	W.l.: 34¼ ft.
B.: 11 ft.	Df.: 7 ft.
Displ.: 17.64tons	Engine: 45 Hp
Skipper:	Albert Arrigon (1994–2000)

THIS PAGE: *Cannes 1998,* Merry Dancer *during a regatta (Photos: J. Taylor).*

"She sails beautifully, like her name says."

There can be no doubting that *Merry Dancer* was the last original design produced by William Fife Jr. (Plan no. 814-1936). Launched in the spring of 1938, it was considered, rather unusually, to be a 35-foot RORC (Royal Ocean Racing Club) Class. The present owner (the fifth so far) has had the boat for 16 years and maintains it in keeping with the style and spirit of its builder.

At the end of World War II, *Merry Dancer*, together with its twin yacht *Evenlode*, which belonged to the famous sail-maker Ratsey, successfully took part in numerous regattas held in the Solent at Cowes, England. For a few years the boat was rigged as a yawl, probably for reasons of tonnage, before going back to its original Bermudan-sloop rig. It has been used above all for family cruising, although it has occasionally taken part in Mediterranean regattas. It has been, and continues to be, excellently cared for, which is the reason why, up until now, there has been need to restore it. All components are original, and it remains one of William Fife Jr.'s finest creations.

Merry Dancer has Honduran mahogany planking over American elm ribs – which had already been seasoned for more than 20 years before the boat was launched. Above the waterline the planking rests on oak; the bottom is in Burmese teak, as are the deck and superstructures. *Merry Dancer* appears the epitome of sturdiness, with its abundant bronze and copper features. The interior furnishings in oak differ from Fife's usual choice and are the very best the carpenters of Fairlie could produce.

The new mast, built in 1994 by Harry Spencer of Cowes from seasoned sitka spruce, is in full keeping with Fife's original design. All the accessories and the original fittings were carefully saved and re-employed in the construction of the new mast. Congratulations, *Merry Dancer*!

ABOVE: *Cannes 1998, the graceful stern of* Merry Dancer *(Photo: J. Taylor).*

Migrant

This boat was the brainchild of David Hillyard and was built in the shipyard of the same name (set up in 1903). Lloyds 1952 Register of Yachts lists the boat at no. 4743 under its old name, *Taeping*. When the present owner bought it in 1975, it was sailing under the French flag and was registered in Cannes.

Compared with the original project, this vessel now appears very different, with the addition of a cabin between the deckhouses in place of the central cockpit. The masts and boom are original, as are the materials the boat is built from: the hull is of pine and oak, the deckhouses and interior are of mahogany, and the deck is made of teak. *Migrant* appears to be a rather sturdy boat, one that copes with the sea very well even in rough weather. Being quite heavy for its size, it requires a fresh breeze to perform well.

The original boat, with its sail plan and mainsails touching the deck, no longer exists, however. If you look closely at the boat's splendid lines, its sheerline, the thrust of the bow, and the harmonious shape of the stern, you can immediately see the contrast resulting from a transformation that the boat and its original sail plan certainly did not deserve.

Rigging:	Bermudan schooner
Sail area:	84 sq. yds.
Shipyard:	D. Hillyard (Littlehampton, England)
Designer:	David Hillyard
Year of design:	1930
Launch:	1934
Restoration:	1976
L.: 40 ft.	W.l.: 33¼ ft.
B.: 11 ft.	Df.: 4¼ ft.
Displ.: 19.84 tons	Engine: 26 Hp
Skipper:	Enrico Madia (1988–96)

Molly

Rigging:	Trysail yawl
Sail area:	90 sq. yds.
Shipyard:	Chapman (Filey, England)
Designer:	Robert Cole
Year of design:	1914
Launch:	1914
Restoration:	1982–84
L.: 39¼ ft.	W.l.: 36 ft.
B.: 9 ft.	Df.: 5¼ ft.
Displ.: 9.33 tons	Engine: 10 Hp
Skipper:	Franco Bosia (1989–2000)

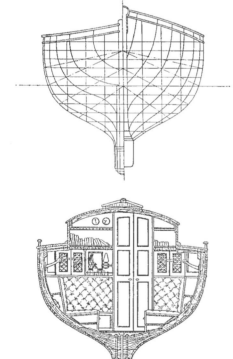

I think that this gem of a boat represents more than any other the idea of what a vintage yacht should be. Every single detail has been conserved according to the original design. Its lines seem particularly versatile: the topside, weighty or slender depending on the angle you look at it from; a powerful, darting hull; and a deck devoid of any concessions to modern living. All this makes it perhaps a unique boat of its kind. It has no radio or electrical installation, but effective oil lamps. In 1992 *Molly* celebrated its 78th year, the same age its designer, Robert Cole (Albert Strange's favorite pupil), was in 1934, the year its present proud owner was born. What a coincidence!

In 1928 the boat belonged to one Matthew Botteril. In 1955 the Register of Yachts showed *Molly* registered as yacht no. 5075, the property of a certain A.M. Oakes. In 1981 it was purchased by Franco Bosia and Titta Locatelli, who then sailed it to Lisbon, Portugal, to have it completely restored. This work, which began in 1982, was completed in 1984 with the occasional help of two fine carpenters. Every little detail was checked and re-checked, from the truck to the very last bolt in the keel, then restored and, where necessary, replaced strictly according to the original design. Four sheet-winches (from the 1920s), which apparently belonged to the yacht *Hispania IV*, are the only "modernizations" on board; the halyards and steering wheels are still operated using tackle.

With its fast, elegant style, *Molly* has fully repaid the faith placed in it by its final owners (with luck their place will only be taken, when the time comes, by a maritime museum), as I witnessed for myself in 1992. It has become part of the family, at times a mother or friend, at others a daughter or lover – or even a petulant old aunt – but, nevertheless, it always manages to generate incredible passion and, at times, suffering.

The welcoming interior is like a drawing room from yesteryear: it contains dishes, door handles, instruments, and furniture from a distant past, all of which is a delightful surprise. There is a green-enameled oil stove, a galvanized work surface, a white-enameled sink, an ancient two-stroke diesel engine, and, above all, Franco and Titta Bosia's love for everything that surrounds them, which enables you to understand the true fascination of this boat and the loving respect that it usually engenders.

RIGHT: *Imperia 1992, the harmonious hull of* Molly, *one of the very few completely original vintage yachts. Below deck oil lamps are still used (Photo courtesy of N. Famà).*

Moonbeam

On 1903, when this truly beautiful boat slid into the water off the Fairlie Slip in Scotland beneath the watchful eye of William Fife Jr., people still traveled through the streets of London in horse-drawn carriages, Marconi had only just invented the radio, and the Wright brothers had still not performed their historical flight. Yet *Moonbeam* has remained a surprisingly modern boat. It was ordered by Charles Plumtree, an eminent London lawyer and member of the Royal Thames Yacht Club, as well as the son of Queen Victoria's personal physician. He had commissioned William Fife Jr. to design the boat after a positive experience with the original *Moonbeam*, which he purchased in 1893 and which was designed by Fife's father, William Fife Sr., way back in 1858, and which Plumtree, enamored of the name, had raced for six years.

The new *Moonbeam* was rigged as a yawl, contrary to the regatta fashions of that time, but it still proved successful and won honors on a number of occasions. With this boat Fife had wanted to produce a unique combination of a fine racing yacht and a splendidly furnished and decorated interior, and he was so successful in this that Dixon Kemp defined it as "one of the best-ever regatta yachts produced by Fife."

The history of the boat was to continue under the guidance of its second owner, M.F. Marconi, who transferred *Moonbeam* to Brest in France. Designed as a racer, in 1920 it won the Coupe Anton before moving to the Mediterranean, where it continued to take part in regattas during the 1920s and 1930s. In 1928 it won the Course Croisière de la Méditerranée. Little is known of the boat's movements during the obscure war years. However, we do know that it was purchased in 1948 by the French aviation pioneer Felix Amiot, who sheltered it in his Cherbourg boatyard for

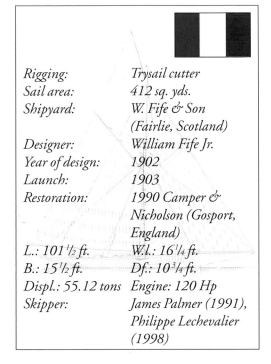

Rigging:	Trysail cutter
Sail area:	412 sq. yds.
Shipyard:	W. Fife & Son (Fairlie, Scotland)
Designer:	William Fife Jr.
Year of design:	1902
Launch:	1903
Restoration:	1990 Camper & Nicholson (Gosport, England)
L.: 101½ ft.	W.l.: 16¼ ft.
B.: 15½ ft.	Df.: 10¾ ft.
Displ.: 55.12 tons	Engine: 120 Hp
Skipper:	James Palmer (1991), Philippe Lechevalier (1998)

BELOW: *Cannes 1998,* Moonbeam *sailing in strong winds (Photo: J. Taylor).*

23 years, an incredible length of time that no one has ever really been able to explain. After a brief foray into the eastern Mediterranean, the boat returned to England where it underwent substantial restoration work, especially below deck. Afterwards, it made its comeback in racing regattas, and in 1988 *Moonbeam* won the Round the Island Race. It adopted cutter rig once again, but it had undergone a number of modifications during its long years of racing: for example, the rudder tiller no longer exists, having been replaced by the steering wheel, and a small cockpit has been built that was not there before. Apart from these changes, however, the original structure has remained largely unaltered. The last refitting, completed in 1990 at the Camper & Nicholson yard in England, saw *Moonbeam* regain its original glory.

The boat has a teak deck and planking (2 inches thick), elm framing, and mahogany paneling below deck embellished by mirrors and padded sofas. On deck a series of new winches have been installed to make maneuvering easier for a crew that needs great experience and has to take care when getting used to the height of the heavy boom, which almost touches the deck and on jibing could quite easily push someone overboard.

PRECEDING PAGE: *The fascination of* Moonbeam *running free; you can clearly see the long boom, which is very low and potentially dangerous when jibing (Photo: F. Taccola).*

ABOVE AND TOP: *Details of one corner of the drawing-room featuring fine mahogany paneling, delightful fittings, and a padded leather sofa (Photos: S. Navarini and G. Tagliafico).*

RIGHT AND ABOVE RIGHT: *Cannes 1998 and 2000, two images of* Moonbeam *racing (Photos: J. Taylor).*

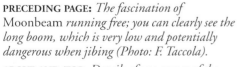

Moya

*M*oya was built in 1910 by the W. Crossfield shipyard in Morecambe Bay, England, a yard that produced working boats as well as yachts that raced in the Walney Channel. Many of these boats were traditional English cutters with an elliptical stern, much like the present-day *Moya*.

The boat's first four owners were English, until it reached Italian waters in 1988. During the 1930s, *Moya* was rigged as a yawl and sailed up and down the River Clyde in Scotland. In 1973 it was found abandoned in a canal in Lancaster and purchased by C.M. Waddington, owner of a shipyard in Fareham, who then restored the boat with the idea of entering it for regattas. At that time the sail plan returned to a cutter rig.

Thus it was that *Moya* started racing once again. It took part in numerous regattas in the Solent off the south coast of England, including the 1975 Fastnet Race, where it came second in its class. Its present owner had gone to England in the hope of finding a boat to buy and was fortunate enough to find *Moya* still in good condition. One month later the boat was ready to sail to Italy, commanded by Frank, a professional skipper.

Since 1988 *Moya* has taken part in numerous vintage yacht regattas: it won the Louis Vuitton Trophy during the Nioulargue held at Saint Tropez in France, and it has also won at Imperia, La Spezia in Italy, and Porto Cervo in Sardinia with skipper Giambattista Borea, a navy officer on leave and the son of the famous Gian Marco Borea, charismatic Chairman of the "Venturieri."

The boat, which up until 1992 had a green hull and brick-colored sails, is an unmistakable, much-admired vessel. The rudder and tiller make the boat highly sensitive, while the crossbeam for maneuvering the sails, situated behind the cockpit, does not get in the way of other maneuvers. The boat features pitch pine planking, a teak deck, a low deckhouse with a skylight at the center illuminating the comfortable quarters below, and a drawing-room that has been almost completely rebuilt according to a photograph that appeared in a 1911 copy of *Yacht Monthly*.

In 1988, *Moya*, with Carlo Sciarelli on board, came first in Class D (the smallest vintage yachts). In 1989 it came second out of 15 boats at La Spezia, just behind *Arcangelo*, a 6-meter SI, beating boats of the caliber of *Cerida*, *Elpis*, and *Alzavola*. According to the skipper, *Moya* sails well even in light breezes and is very strong in a leading wind with a spinnaker; when sailing close-hauled with little wind and a calm sea it is a little slower than more modern boats, and it is penalized by a short sea.

Moya makes a truly splendid sight when seen side-on: a long boom beneath the mainsail and gaff topsail balances a perfect sail plan featuring a staysail, jib, and moonsail, all a brick-red color that perfectly matches the slender bows of the green hull, giving it a true North Sea appearance. Today, *Moya* has taken to the sea once again, this time with a white hull; it is registered with the Adriatico Yacht Club of Trieste, together with *Sorella*.

Rigging:	Trysail cutter
Sail area:	96 sq. yds.
Shipyard:	Crossfield (Arnside, England)
Designer:	William Crossfield
Year of design:	1910
Launch:	1910
Restoration:	1992 Alto Adriatico shipyard (Monfalcone, Italy)
L.: 43 ft.	W.l.: 36 ft.
B.: 11 ft.	Df.: 6 ft.
Displ.: 14.33 tons	Engine: 75 Hp
Skipper:	Giambattista Borea d'Olmo (1988–90)

BELOW: *VBR 1991, a fine shot of* Moya *as it glides through the waves. It is currently registered with the Adriatico Yacht Club of Trieste (Photo: J. Taylor).*

OVERLEAF: Moya *when it sailed under the British flag (Photo: L. Fioroni).*

Nagaïna

On November 11, 1950, the prestigious French magazine *Le Yacht* wrote: "...*On the morning of Friday October 20, the 20-ton 'racer cruiser'* Nagaïna *was launched in the port of Cannes. This splendid, elegant yacht was built for a group of youthful, keen yachting enthusiasts – M. and Mme. Auberge, Mlles. Andrée and Susanne Combastet, M. Michel Combastet, M. and Mme. Laforgue.*"

The writer at that time (André Pierre Boison), went on to say that: "*The fine hull with its harmonious and seaworthy lines does justice to Camatte's original design, given not only the beauty of its shape, but also its modern conception. The clearly visible mark of a designer who has successfully created more than 60 hulls of international tonnage, for both French and foreign owners, is there for all to see...*"

The congratulations at its launch were also directed towards Attilio Chiesa and his sons, who had surpassed themselves in producing a vessel of such finesse and elegance, praised by the Lloyds inspector present at the launching ceremony. The mahogany hull was plated with copper; the deck was of Burmese teak; the fittings and riveting were of bronze; the sail set was made of English cotton. The boat's interior was spacious and light and took up the entire width of the hull.

Half a century has gone by since that day, but *Nagaïna* has not been substantially modified. Since 1969 it has been the property of M. and Mme. Berthoz, who restored the boat between 1991 and 1993 by simply having the deck and a number of planking timbers replaced.

Rigging:	Gaff-rigged cutter
Sail area:	167 sq. yds.
Shipyard:	Attilio Chiesa (Cannes, France)
Designer:	François Camatte
Year of design:	1949
Launch:	1950
Restoration:	1992–93 (Sanary sur Mer, France)
L.: 54½ ft.	W.l.: 38¼ ft.
B.: 12 ft.	Df.: 7½ ft.
Displ.: 24.25 tons	Engine: 55 Hp
Skipper:	Nathalie Berthoz (1998)

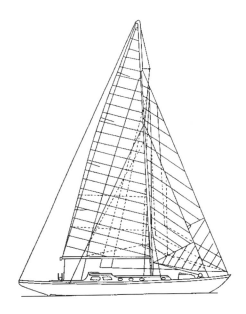

LEFT: *Cannes 1998,* Nagaïna, *a fast racer designed by François Camatte, as it sails close-hauled (Photo: J. Taylor).*

Nausicaa

Rigging:	Bermudan sloop
Sail area:	179 sq. yds.
Shipyard:	Genova naval shipyard (Sturla, Italy)
Designer:	Bruno Veronese
Year of design:	1950
Launch:	1955
Restoration:	1983
L.: 52½ ft.	W.l.: 39½ ft.
B.: 12½ ft.	Df.: 8 ft.
Displ.: 20.72 tons	Engine: 90 Hp
Skipper:	Luigi Bellini Trinchi (1988)

BELOW: *A shot of* Nausicaa, *designed by Bruno Veronese and the first steel-built Italian yacht (Photo courtesy of B. Veronese).*

Designed by my dear friend the late Bruno Veronese, *Nausicaa* was launched from Sturla beach in Italy on September 5, 1955. It was the first welded steel hull ever built in Italy for a motor sailer that performed well under sail, a yacht highly suited to summer cruising in the Mediterranean. The specialized international magazines (*Yacht Monthly*, *The Rudder*, *Yachting World Annual*), and Italian publications such as *Vela e Motore*, were full of praise for the boat.

Nausicaa began life as a cutter. Its hull-sheathing, not coming up as far as the deck, created a temperature difference between the inside of the submerged part of the hull and the upper sections of the sides, producing a current of air that in turn kept the boat cool below deck. The deck, also in steel, was lined with teak, while the deckhouse and the mast were wooden.

Nausicaa has won numerous honors in the past. It took part in the first ever Brooking Cup in 1986, where it did very well, despite its age, against more modern yachts. In fact, it held the lead right up until the Azores but was then forced out of the race by broken stern-rigging. In more recent times *Nausicaa* has been used to experiment with solar paneling by the Italian environmental association Lega Ambiente, and for research purposes in the battle against the pollution of the Italian coastline.

The shape of the boat's hull produces a relatively limited displacement and constitutes a successful compromise for a boat designed for mixed navigational purposes. Despite a number of changes made over the years, *Nausicaa* would still make the famous "Captain Black" – the late Bruno Veronese – extremely proud of her.

Navara

Navara, originally rigged as a yawl and launched at Fairlie in Scotland in 1956, is based on a design by William Fife dating back to 1936. Its original owner and builder was Archibald Macmillan. It closely resembled two of Fife's other famous creations, *Latifa* and *Evenlode* (albeit with a smaller hull). It was slightly larger than its two twin-hulls, *Nyatoga* (1951) and *Nyachilwa* (1952). Its first regatta was the centenary edition of the Plymouth–Santander Race (in 1956). Its light hull (it can be sailed comfortably by just two people) was designed so that it could race in the smaller RORC (Royal Ocean Racing Club) Class. During the early stages of its racing career, it took part in regattas in Scotland and in the Solent off southern England up until 1963, at which point its owner replaced it with *Navara II*, an even smaller hull that he kept rigged until his death.

Under the Spanish flag since 1990, *Navara* regularly takes part in the Almirante Conde de Barcelona Trophy, winning in 1999.

ABOVE: *Picture of* Navara *(Photo: N. Martinez).*

Rigging:	Bermudan sloop
Sail area:	56 sq. yds.
Shipyard:	W. Fife & Son (Fairlie, Scotland)
Designer:	W. Fife III
Year of design:	1936
Launch:	1956
L.: 34¼ ft.	W.l.: 27 ft.
B.: 8½ ft.	Df.: 6 ft.
Displ.: 10.47 tons	Engine: 40 Hp
Skipper:	Luis Olaso

Niña Luisita

Niña Luisita is a familiar sight in my home waters; in fact, for several years it was moored along the east jetty at Porto Maurizio in Imperia, just a few meters from another vintage yacht, *Romeo*.

Pofì – as she was known in 1932 when launched as an "auxiliary schooner" – was design no. 488 by Vincenzo Baglietto, designer and builder at the Baglietto shipyard in Varazze, Liguria, which was once part and parcel of life in this small Italian town. The Baglietto family's skills have been passed down from generation to generation, starting from the progenitor Pietro (affectionately known as "u Muntagnin" – literally "the mountain dweller"), who used to build racing yachts and cruisers. Launchings consisted of the traditional celebration attended by the local priest and the christener, with the

bottle of champagne broken against the boat's hull as it glided down the slipway into the awaiting waters.

Under the guidance of Vittovio Baglietto, who graduated in naval engineering from Glasgow University, Scotland, a series of 6-meter and 8-meter SI yachts were constructed that were to dominate the most important Mediterranean regattas over the years. These vessels were commissioned by the most famous yachtsmen of the time – people like Francesco Giovanelli, Marquis Paolo Pallavicino, and the brothers Max and Giuliano Oberti – the winners of regattas throughout Europe. This yachting nobility entrusted the Baglietto yard with the job of building their families' yachts.

Pofì belonged to the Counts Bruzzo, and remained their property until 1971 (as

Rigging:	Bermudan schooner
Sail area:	239 sq. yds.
Shipyard:	Baglietto shipyard (Varazze, Italy)
Designer:	Vittorio V. Baglietto
Year of design:	1929
Launch:	1932
Restoration:	1987, 1988–90 Baglietto shipyard
L.: 68¼ ft.	W.l.: 48¼ ft.
B.: 14 ft.	Df.: 8 ft.
Displ.: 60.63 tons	Engine: 115 Hp
Skipper:	Hengel Haasler (1987), Attilio Colombo (1988–92), A. Sario (2000)

shown by the entries in Lloyds Register), lovingly cared for in the port of Rapallo, Italy. It took three years of effort by a young Argentine woman, Cristina, wife of the Genoan Count Tagliaferri, to convince the elderly owner to sell his favorite boat, and he only agreed to do so knowing that it was going to be in safe hands.

Thus it was that the boat was renamed *Niña Luisita* and became a family boat that was soon to embark on a series of long and winding voyages throughout the Mediterranean. When it eventually returned to Varazze to be restored, there were celebrations once again; a truly moving moment for those who had worked on the boat some 60 years before.

Restoration work included the careful rebuilding of the deck (for the third time), but everything else on board remained as it was when the boat was first launched. The boat was rigged as a Bermudan schooner once again, with loose shrouds and sails hauled by hand. On the deck is a combination of teak, brass, and bronze. There is only one winch used to raise the mainsail.

The interior has remained as it was in the 1930s – the advantage of having only two owners in all these years, both of whom were totally enamored of the perfect styling of the time. The wardroom is spacious and light, featuring trumeaux and writing cabinets (chosen by Count Bruzzo) set against the light-colored walls. Since the day the boat was launched a small statue of the Virgin Mary made of Murano glass has overlooked the entire interior.

Nowadays, *Niña Luisita* is able to compete against the reborn *Joyette*. It passes the winters in the quiet port of Imperia, its masts silhouetted against the sky amid the annoying metallic tinkling made by the neighboring modern yachts. Its elegant hull, still clad in copper, barely moves in the swell as it patiently awaits the racing season ahead.

BELOW: Niña Luisita *in the middle of a regatta (Photo: F. Pace).*

Nirvana

Nirvana is a very beautiful yawl designed by John Alden and built at the Southwest Harbor in Maine in the United States in 1950. Its original owner, Harry G. Haskel, kept the boat for only three years before selling it to Governor Nelson A. Rockefeller, who used it as a family yacht for about 25 years and kept it moored at the Northeast Harbor, also in Maine. In 1978 the boat was put up for sale and subsequently purchased by David Warren, founding member of the Newport Museum of Yachting.

Nirvana is currently in great shape, mainly due to the fact that it has had only three owners, all of whom have luckily had sufficient financial and cultural resources to keep it in the best possible condition.

This seven-eighths-rigged Bermudan yawl still has all its original equipment and rigging, from the interior to the deck equipment, the tackle included. It has a double skin of mahogany over cedar, and oak ribs. The rest of the boat is in teak, from the deck to the deckhouse.

The interior has been embellished with white wooden furnishings and the warmth of solid teak. The masts are in sitka spruce, with rigging specially designed and manufactured by Morriman Brothers. *Nirvana* also possesses a vintage wooden tender, which is both sleek and fast and has two sets of oars, a small mast, and a sail.

Nirvana was "baptized" at the 1950 Bermuda Race and in recent years has always taken part in the regattas organized by the New York Yacht Club, as well as in the various editions of the Newport Classic Yacht Regatta. In 1993 it also took part in the Antigua Classic Yacht Regatta and came first in its class.

Rigging:	*Bermudan yawl*
Sail area:	*211 sq. yds.*
Shipyard:	*Henry R. Hinkley & Co. (Southwest Harbor, Maine, USA)*
Designer:	*John Alden*
Year of design:	*1950*
Launch:	*1950*
L.: 65 ft.	*W.l.: 49 ft.*
B.: 14 ft.	*Df.: 8 ft.*
Displ.: 41.89 tons	*Engine: 100 Hp*
Skipper:	*Henry Hinckley (2001)*

OVERLEAF: *VBR 2001,* Nirvana, *designed by Alden (Photo: J. Taylor).*

BELOW: *Antigua 1993, a picture of* Nirvana *(Photo: B. Villani).*

Nocturne

arely have I ever come across a boat that has not been modified in any way from the original design: *Nocturne*, however, after 63 years of life at sea, still appears as it did in Beken's old photograph (see below). A sturdy, weighty boat, it needs a good wind and strong arms, all maneuvers still having to be done by hand. It was launched in October 1937 (no. 163094) on behalf of Count Edward T. Greenekelly, who kept it for only 15 months.

It had three different owners up until 1942, and it would appear that the boat played an active part in the evacuation of British troops from Dunkirk in May 1940. In April 1942 *Nocturne* was sold to the Count of Warwick, who subsequently sold it to Sir Philip Eric Millbourn.

In 1957 the boat changed its name (to *Margherita*). It was used as a training yacht by a Cardiff shipping company up until 1966. In that year it was purchased by an Englishman, who decided to call it *Malika*. The boat remained in England or cruised the Atlantic during these next few years.

In 1973 another new English owner chartered the boat in Greece. It was only in 1975 when Captain Jean Claude Lehöerff bought the boat that it reacquired its original name and work was begun restoring it. Restoration work was often done by the new owner himself, and not always with the right tools, but in the end he managed to complete the task without having to alter a single item on board.

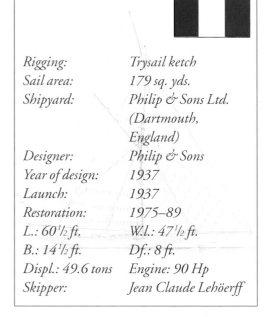

Rigging:	*Trysail ketch*
Sail area:	*179 sq. yds.*
Shipyard:	*Philip & Sons Ltd.*
	(Dartmouth,
	England)
Designer:	*Philip & Sons*
Year of design:	*1937*
Launch:	*1937*
Restoration:	*1975–89*
L.: 60½ ft.	*W.l.: 47½ ft.*
B.: 14½ ft.	*Df.: 8 ft.*
Displ.: 49.6 tons	*Engine: 90 Hp*
Skipper:	*Jean Claude Lehöerff*

LEFT: Nocturne *(in 1952), currently skippered by the master mariner Jean Claude Lehöerff. It is the best preserved and most completely original yacht in the entire Mediterranean (Photo: K. Beken of Cowes).*

BELOW: Imperia 1991, the skipper of Nocturne *(Photo: Mengatti).*

Nordwind

Rigging:	Gaff-rigged yawl
Sail area:	550 sq. yds.
Shipyard:	Burmester (Bremen, Germany)
Designer:	Henry Gruber
Year of design:	1938
Launch:	1939
Restoration:	1982, 1989
L.: 85½ ft.	W.l.: 59½ ft.
B.: 17¼ ft.	Df.: 13 ft.
Displ.: 71.65 tons	Engine: 280 Hp
Skipper:	Antoine Duarte Silva (1987–1991)

This is an ocean-racer that should have done the German Navy proud for a long time but which managed to do so for only a brief period. It was built from drawings by Henry Gruber, who designed three other similar boats: *Ostwind*, *Sudwind*, and *Wastwind*, boats that were not to be very successful as a result of the impending war. *Ostwind* was sunk off the Miami coast, *Sudwind* is currently on display in a German museum, and *Wastwind* disappeared without trace.

Nordwind's career got off to an amazing start at the 1939 Fastnet Race. The boat to beat was the famous *Latifa*, designed by Fife, although all eyes were on this new German creation. That Fastnet Race, the fastest ever at that time, saw a whole series of exciting overlaps that continued for nearly four days in a very rough sea. In the end, just a short distance from

Fastnet Rock, a brilliant maneuver enabled *Nordwind* to turn first at the famous lighthouse. It won the Lizzy Mac Trophy, and, after a further 275 miles it was the first over the line to take the race itself. *Latifa* was left trailing by over half-an-hour, thus losing the Erivale Cup, which went to *Nordwind*, which covered the 635 miles in three days, 16 hours, and 28 minutes, a record that remained unbeaten until 1984.

In 1945 the boat was literally snatched from its German owners as part of war reparations. It was bought by Lord Astor (it was still his property in 1955), and for 20 years he raced it in the waters of the Solent. In August 1950, *Nordwind* won the XVIII Cowes–Dinard Cruise Regatta. This marked a period of intense racing activity, which was followed by years of abandonment in a warehouse in Plymouth,

RIGHT: Nordwind *in a superb photograph by Beken (1939). This is the year it won the Fastnet Race with a crew from the German Navy.*

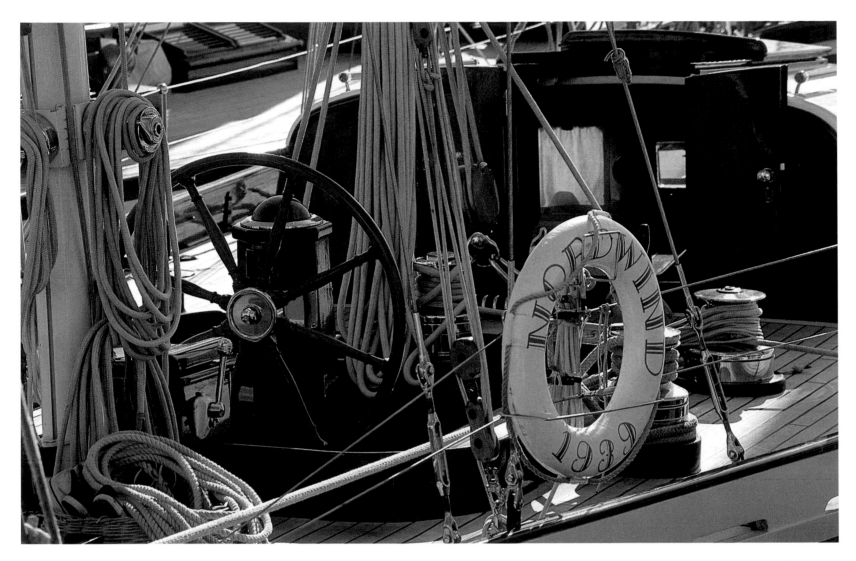

England, until two Dutchmen bought it, paying just the price of the lead in its keel. This, unfortunately, has been the sad destiny of many a yacht in the past.

Nordwind was taken to the Camper & Nicholson yard in England for initial restoration work, consisting of the replacement of the mahogany planking with iroko timbers covered in a thin layer of copper. The masts were also replaced by two new aluminum ones. This was in 1976. The inner, galvanized steel structure remained, but in 1979 a Dutch designer redesigned the deck, the sail plan, and the interior. At that time it seemed that the Dutch, in the opposite manner to the English, were persisting in doing away with all original interior fittings. With the final touches put to the new rigging, and the interior furnishings in solid teak, very little remained of the original German vessel apart from the binnacle and the compass.

In 1984, restoration work was completed and *Nordwind* set sail elegantly once again.

The superstructure has not been significantly modified, and the deck is partly clear and offers considerable visibility, as Henry Gruber would have wished himself having trained in the United States under Stanley Burgess. Both mainsails are fitted with wheels, and in normal winds winches make maneuvering the boat a relatively simple operation. Below deck, each room is lit by the original skylights, or by more modern prisms set into the teak deck timbers.

From 1986 *Nordwind* was the property of Ugo Baravalle, a true vintage yacht enthusiast, who recently took the boat to the Sangermani shipyard in Italy for refitting, and who intended to restore it to its original splendid condition in the near future, starting with the masting, which was to be rebuilt in wood. The boat was sold during the course of 2000. It has recently been resold to the owner of *Veronique*, who is having the boat completely restored at Palma de Mallorca.

ABOVE: *Imperia 1992, close-up of* Nordwind*'s stern. In wartime the boat was used by the German Navy (Photo: F. Ramella).*

Noroît

Rigging:	*Bermudan yawl*
Sail area:	*239 sq. yds.*
Shipyard:	*Craft (Quimper, France)*
Designer:	*The shipyard*
Year of design:	*1921*
Launch:	*1922*
Restoration:	*1977–83 Sestri Ponente naval shipyard (Italy)*
L.: *48¹/₂ ft.*	W.l.: *43¹/₂ ft.*
B.: *11³/₄ ft.*	Df.: *6¹/₄ ft.*
Displ.: *26.46 tons*	Engine: *100 Hp*
Skipper:	*Luciano Locci (1987–89), Adriano Frassinetti (1998–2002)*

At the beginning of the 1970s this boat arrived in Italy, sailing under the French flag, and was immediately seized by the Maritime Authorities under suspicion of smuggling. This was followed by a long period during which *Noroit* was virtually abandoned and eventually sank in the port of Savona. This old boat, probably rigged as a trysail yawl at the outset, was eventually restored by 1982, the year in which it was bought by its last owner, who then transformed it into a gaff-rigged yawl.

The boat was built without due concern about the amount of wood used: its ribs are oak and its planking pitch pine painted green; the masts are made of spruce and were retained when the boat was transformed. In 1976 the bowsprit was rebuilt in iroko. On its third appearance in Imperia *Noroit* collided with *San Guido* and was seriously damaged as a consequence, rendering it unfit to compete in the subsequent regattas. The unfortunate *Noroit* was literally crashed into by the massive *San Guido*, which smashed through the left side, cutting through the mizzen-sail shrouds and destroying the binnacle and rudder wheel: fortunately no one was hurt. *Noroit* sportingly remained moored at the quayside for the rest of the racing week.

The boat has since been completely restored and at the time of writing was for sale at the Sestri Ponente naval shipyard, managed by Adriano Frassinetti.

RIGHT: *Imperia 2000,* Noroit *during a regatta* (Photo: S. Pesato).

Ohio

This sloop, belonging to the "Hocco" series, built in mahogany and teak by the Corsier-Poet shipyard in Geneva, still has all its original cotton sails (a mainsail, genoa, spinnaker, jib 1, jib 2, and spitfire), its silver spruce mast and boom, and its rudder tiller. The boat was constructed by the famous Swiss yard, one that was already specialized in building 18-foot and 20-foot hulls before World War II. *Ohio*, which originally belonged to Diane Alice de Rothschild, has seen its deck made heavier with the replacement of plyboard with solid teak. "Hocco" boats can still be seen taking part in regattas on Lake Geneva, but the old boatyard no longer exists.

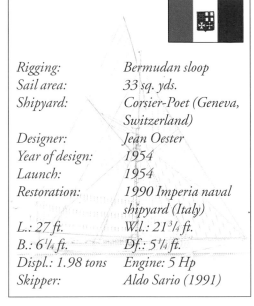

Rigging:	Bermudan sloop
Sail area:	33 sq. yds.
Shipyard:	Corsier-Poet (Geneva, Switzerland)
Designer:	Jean Oester
Year of design:	1954
Launch:	1954
Restoration:	1990 Imperia naval shipyard (Italy)
L.: 27 ft.	W.l.: 21³/₄ ft.
B.: 6¹/₄ ft.	Df.: 5¹/₄ ft.
Displ.: 1.98 tons	Engine: 5 Hp
Skipper:	Aldo Sario (1991)

Oiseau de Feu

(formerly Firebird X)

Between 1935 and 1937, Charles E. Nicholson designed four hulls that were to become famous; the last of these was registered as "Cutter Yacht no. 447" and was named *Firebird X*. This very fast ocean-racer had been ordered by Ralph Hawkes, a member of the Royal Thames Yacht Club and already owner of *Diadem*. In 1937 *Firebird X* took part in the Fastnet Race, where it came eighth. The following year it came fourth in the Dover–Kristiansund Race and won the Copenhagen–Warnemunde Race ahead of *Silberkonder*, a yawl rigged by the Luftwaffe. These were years of growing international tension, although both the German airforce and navy fitted out a number of boats for officer training at the regattas held in the Baltic Sea. Many such yachts were subsequently seized and taken to England as war reparations – boats such as *Nordwind* and *Pelikan*.

In 1938 *Firebird X* came third in the Cowes–Dinard Race. It subsequently won four first places and six second places in

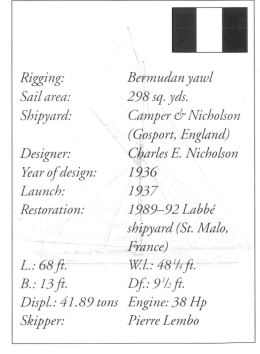

Rigging:	Bermudan yawl
Sail area:	298 sq. yds.
Shipyard:	Camper & Nicholson (Gosport, England)
Designer:	Charles E. Nicholson
Year of design:	1936
Launch:	1937
Restoration:	1989–92 Labbé shipyard (St. Malo, France)
L.: 68 ft.	W.l.: 48¹/₄ ft.
B.: 13 ft.	Df.: 9¹/₂ ft.
Displ.: 41.89 tons	Engine: 38 Hp
Skipper:	Pierre Lembo

ABOVE: Ohio *(Photo courtesy of A. Sario).*
LEFT: Oiseau de Feu *yawl-rigged at Cannes, 1999 (Photo: J. Taylor).*

ABOVE: *The splendid interior (Photo courtesy of P. Lembo).*

BELOW: *A close view of* Oiseau de Feu, *a very fast yacht (Photo: J. Taylor).*

English regattas. It raced against Fife's *Lady Anne* and *Taiga*, as well as against three other yachts designed by Nicholson: *Foxhound* (1935), *Bloodhound* (1936), and *Stiarna* (1937). Nicholson's four yachts were rigged differently: *Firebird X* and *Foxhound* as cutters, *Bloodhound* as a yawl, *Stiarna* as a sloop.

During the post-war years, *Firebird X* was sold to Hugh M. Crankshaw and took part in the Round the Island Race. Then, in 1951, under its third owner, it took part in the Cowes–Dinard Race and the Britannia Challenge Cups and was a constant presence at regattas. The boat was transformed to a yawl and still flying the British flag, *Firebird X* remained the property of its newest owner, J.E. Green, until 1962. It was in excellent condition when it was bought by Pierre Cointreau, a French yachtsman who changed its name to *Flame II* and used it for eight years as a Mediterranean cruiser.

Between 1970 and 1973 the name of the boat was changed once again, this time to *Vindilis II*, under the ownership of Henry Rey. The next owner, Michel Perroud, called it by its original name but translated into French: *Oiseau de Feu*. The boat subsequently returned to Southampton in England, but it was seriously damaged during a storm while moored in the harbor. It was saved with some difficulty, and then repaired.

The present owner, Pierre Lembo, transferred the boat to Brittany and had it restored at the Raymond Labbé boatyard in Saint Malo. The boat was completely rebuilt according to the original drawings under the guidance of Guy Ribadeau Dumas. A number of planking timbers were replaced with teak timbers for the hull, and mahogany for the topside. The pine deck was completely rebuilt in teak, while the Oregon pine masts were replaced by new spruce ones. *Oiseau de Feu* was equipped with completely new rigging. Work was finally completed in 1993, and the boat is now more beautiful than ever. Recently it has been transformed into a sloop.

Old Fox

This is another splendid boat, a top performer in ocean regattas that in the past raced in the Solent off the south coast of England against the likes of *Latifa* and *Bloodhound*. Its first owner, a retired English admiral, gave it the name *Old Fox*, and it has kept this name ever since.

In 1940, due to World War II, the boat was sold to John Basil Goulandris, who kept it until 1948. During the post-war years, *Old Fox* successfully took part in various regattas (particularly those held in the English Channel), such as those organized for Cowes Week, as well as the Admiral's Cup, the Fastnet Race, and others.

In 1948 the boat was purchased by Pierre Matisse, son of the painter Henri Matisse. It is said that Henri Matisse spent a lot of his time on board the boat in its customary port, St. Jean Cap Ferrat. During the mid-1950s, the boat belonged to Leight Newton and was based at Brixham, England. In 1972 it was sold to Gabriel Fabre, and its port of mooring was Jounieh in Lebanon. During the war in Lebanon the boat was used to evacuate refugees and the injured to Cyprus and various Turkish ports.

Old Fox's hull boasts an elegant line similar to that of *Alzavola*, and the similarity is even greater given that both boats have the same colored freeboard (black). In November 1989 the boat was taken to the Argentario shipyard in Italy for a complete refitting after many years of sailing. This operation, which took some nine months, involved the rebuilding of the deck in teak, the replacement of some of the ribs, the organization of new chain plates and

Rigging:	Bermudan yawl
Sail area:	161 sq. yds.
Shipyard:	Jas N. Miller & Son (St. Monance, Scotland)
Designer:	O. Watts
Year of design:	1938
Launch:	1939
Restoration:	1990 Argentario naval shipyard (Italy)
L.: 65 ft.	W.l.: 53 ft.
B.: 14¼ ft.	Df.: 9 ft.
Displ.: 34.17 tons	Engine: 115 Hp
Skipper:	Christian Sauvageot (1990–92)

BELOW: Old Fox *(Photo courtesy of G. Fabre).*

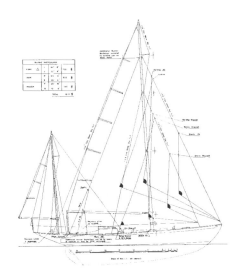

partners, the relaying of the teak topside planking, the caulking of the hull, and the rebuilding of all the superstructures – including the skylights – with the exception of the deckhouse. The spruce masts and the Austrian oak interior were not touched. *Old Fox* has taken part in a number of vintage yacht regattas at Porto Cervo in Sardinia, Saint Tropez in France, and Imperia.

The boat's present, proud owner has looked after it with loving care for all of 28 years now.

RIGHT AND FAR RIGHT: *Below deck on* Old Fox *(Photos: J. Taylor).*

Ondine

Rigging:	Bermudan sloop
Sail area:	24 sq. yds.
Shipyard:	Rallu (Ile de la Jatte, Paris, France)
Designer:	Eugène Cornu
Year of design:	1943
Launch:	1946
Restoration:	1975
L.: 21¼ ft.	W.l.: 19 ft.
B.: 7¼ ft.	Df.: 1½–4 ft.
Displ.: 3.19 tons	Engine: 6 Hp
Skipper:	Christophe Nurit (1987)

Ondine, the work of French architect Eugène Cornu, creator of famous boats such as *Jalina*, *Janabel*, and *Jadic*, was built during the course of the winter of 1946–47 at the boatyard on the Ile de la Jatte situated along the Seine in Paris. It was designed three years earlier, when Albert Lebrun, the Olympic sailing champion, asked Cornu to design him a dinghy a little longer than *Sharpie*, but with a small cabin for two people and with the potential to accommodate more on board when racing.

The sail plan at that time envisaged a trysail rig: an 18 square yards cotton mainsail, a 5 square yards jib, and a 10 square yards genoa. The "Belouga" Class, which must have been produced in the hundreds – a national series that remained French offshore cruiser champion until 1975 – was a creation of that period.

In 1954 there were 462 "Belouga" Class boats in France, compared with only 11 in Italy and 22 in Great Britain. In 1958 the number had increased to 597, against 185 Requins, 122 Dragons, and 142 Stars. Cornu, who many consider to be the inventor of the modern dinghy, had created a boat that was to remain in the hearts of generations of French yachtsmen.

Ondine was sold to Charles Nurit in 1948 and has not been sold again since. Its moorings over the years have included Menton, Saint Raphael, and Saint Tropez, all in France. In 1975 the boat underwent a series of alterations: the sliding keel was replaced by a 440-pound dagger-board, the deck was coated with plastic, and the original mast was replaced by an aluminum mast recouped from another "Belouga" Class boat.

From 1975 through 1988 *Ondine* continued to sail around the bays of Hyères and Urins on the French Riviera. In 1986 it came second in the Nioulargue behind *Coppelia*, out of a total of 50 boats. It has always performed extremely well (with a crew of five and a spinnaker it has reached a speed of 12 knots), but it really comes into its own with a good crosswind.

Orianda

This beautiful Bermudan staysail schooner was built in 1937 according to a design by Carl Andersen for Duke Oresund.

Orianda, a solid oak-built boat with a teak deck and cast-iron keel, was discovered at Tortola in the Virgin Islands by Peter Phillips, who for years had been looking for a classic wooden boat. It was initially equipped as a charter yacht, but only two days after its purchase it was badly damaged by a fire on board while moored in the port of West End at Tortola. The deck and superstructures were seriously compromised as a result.

A number of local inhabitants rushed to put the fire out, but the proud owner of the boat, Peter Phillips, was badly shaken by the incident, and, among other things, he realized that the insurance company would cover only 50 percent of the damage to the boat. However, he did not lose heart completely, and ten days after the fire he covered the damaged area with sheets and held a party on board. He also managed to persuade numerous people and tour operators to contribute towards the cost of restoration work. In the end, he succeeded in restoring *Orianda* to its former splendor in the space of just five months: part of the deck and the deckhouse were rebuilt in teak, and the cockpit area, which had been particularly badly damaged by the fire, was also completely restored.

The boat came to Imperia for the 1990 meeting, where it greatly impressed onlookers. It took part subsequently in the Nioulargue, where it won first prize for the best restoration work.

Rigging:	Staysail schooner
Sail area:	237 sq. yds.
Shipyard:	Rasmus Moller (Faaborg, Denmark)
Designer:	Carl Andersen
Year of design:	1936
Launch:	1937
Restoration:	1988
L.: 85 ft.	W.l.: 74 ft.
B.: 17 ft.	Df.: 11¼ ft.
Displ.: 99.21 tons	Engine: 200 Hp
Skipper:	Jonathan Oretorius (1990)

BELOW: *Imperia 1990, the schooner* Orianda *during a regatta (Photo: F. Pace).*

Orion

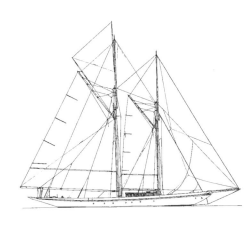

Rigging:	Trysail schooner
Sail area:	1,179 sq. yds.
Shipyard:	Camper & Nicholson (Gosport, England)
Designer:	Charles E. Nicholson
Year of design:	1910
Launch:	1910
Restoration:	1974, 1978 Valdettaro shipyard (La Spezia, Italy)
L.: 147 ft.	W.l.: 90 ft.
B.: 23½ ft.	Df.: 13¾ ft.
Displ.: 280 tons	Engines (2): 230 Hp
Skipper:	Ignazio Torrente (1988–98), Renzo Castagna (2000)

When all its sails are hoisted, *Orion* is one of the most spectacular yachts in the entire Mediterranean. It certainly has not led a boring life these past 90 years or so: it has had five different names, flown the flags of five different nations, and has had a dozen or more owners during this time.

It was commissioned by Lieutenant Colonel C.E. Morgan, and was launched from the Camper & Nicholson shipyard in Gosport, England, was based in Portsmouth, and sailed under the British flag. It was originally called *Sulvana* – a name it kept until 1913 when sold to Commanding Officer Jean De Polignac (hence a change to the French flag and to Brest as its home port).

In 1919 it was renamed *Pays de France* (its new owner was Bunan Varilla), and it still bore this name in 1920 when it was purchased by the newspaper *Le Matin* and sent back to the shipyard that had built it, Camper & Nicholson.

In 1922, under its new owner, Captain Cecil W.P. Slade, it was renamed *Diane* and was based at Portsmouth. This continual changing of names and owners was to continue: in 1927 it was renamed *Vira* and became Argentinian (Raul C. Monsegur was its new owner). Finally, in 1930 it was given the name *Orion* (which it has kept ever since) by its new owner, Miguel De Pinillos, who transferred it to Cadice in Spain under the Spanish flag. Sixteen years later it changed its owner again (to Manuel Beltran Mata). In 1949 it was purchased by the Fagesco Company and transferred to Barcelona, and then in 1968 it was sold to Lebo Enterprise of Panama and moved

RIGHT: *Imperia 1991,* Orion *with all sails hoisted. For several years the boat has flown the Spanish flag (like* Altair*) and was owned by Miguel Mora, Commander of the Real Club Nautico of Barcelona (Photo: S. Piano).*

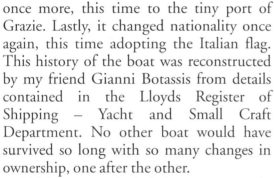

once more, this time to the tiny port of Grazie. Lastly, it changed nationality once again, this time adopting the Italian flag. This history of the boat was reconstructed by my friend Gianni Botassis from details contained in the Lloyds Register of Shipping – Yacht and Small Craft Department. No other boat would have survived so long with so many changes in ownership, one after the other.

1966 was a particularly important year in the life of *Orion*: it set sail from Barcelona for Marseilles on March 17 (skippered by Gaetano Morlè from Ponza, Italy), but when it reached Cap Creus, and as it was sailing close-hauled at 7 knots in a strong north-easterly wind, the foremast's forestay broke and two of the masts collapsed onto the deck and into the sea. The unmasted boat had to be towed by a passing vessel and then, using its engines, managed to reach the port of La Spezia, Italy. The architect Ugo Faggioni redesigned the sail plan, transforming *Orion* from a trysail schooner into a staysail schooner, but preserving the mainsail gaff and shortening the masts by several meters.

After the boat had been completely refitted, *Orion* began a series of cruises. On one voyage between Monte Carlo and Cape Corse, it managed to reach a speed of 17 knots with all sails trimmed.

In 1974 *Orion* underwent further work and inspections by Lloyds. The copper-clad hull was stripped down to the wood (mahogany and green walnut), the deck was rebuilt, and even the 960 square yards of sails were replaced by Hood. The interior, which during the years that the boat was laid up at La Spezia had been ruined by being lacquered white, was restored to its original splendid condition, as was some of the superb antique furniture that Miguel De Pinillos had used to furnish the boat back in 1930.

Today, *Orion*'s sleek white hull can often been seen at vintage yacht regattas, and, since 1978, when it underwent a complete refitting at the Valdettaro shipyard in Italy, as the property of the Braghieri brothers and flying the Italian flag, transcends those former tumultuous years.

During the course of 1999, the boat returned to the Beconcini yard at La Spezia to have the riveting removed from the skin. In the meantime, the boat changed owners once again and returned to its trysail rig of old, with the masts being replaced. Once again, architect Faggioni, who had always wished for a return to its original rig (with mast, masthead, and pole), was involved. Thus the masts were shortened and made thinner, and worked to take the new fittings and rigging at the masthead. The poles were designed to be "struck" as in the past. Nowadays, *Orion* is faster and more beautiful than ever.

TOP LEFT: *Imperia 2000,* Orion *gets ready for the start (Photo: J. Taylor).*

ABOVE AND TOP: *Details of the interior (Photos: J. Taylor).*

BELOW: *An aerial view (Photo: L. Fioroni).*

Palinuro

Rigging:	Schooner ship
Sail area:	1,134 sq. yds.
Shipyard:	Dubignon shipyard (Nantes, France)
Designer:	The shipyard
Year of design:	1932
Launch:	1934
Restoration:	1951–54, 1984–86
L: 226 ft.	W.l.: 164 ft.
B.: 33 ft.	Df.: 16 ft.
Displ.: 1,478 tons	Engine: 375 Hp
Skipper:	Antonio Carminati (1987–88), Gioacchino Chieffi (1989–90)

alinuro is a vintage ship rather than a vintage yacht, and as a schooner can take part in the periodically held Tall Ships Races. This particular tall ship has taken part in the Imperia regattas on a number of occasions, competing against old navy boats.

It was launched in 1934 under the name *Commandant Louis Richard* and was designed for fishing off the Banks of Newfoundland in North America. As a result of its naval specifications, the ship was bought by the Italian Navy in 1950 and subsequently refitted, an operation that totally transformed the appearance of the ship into a vessel designed for training young seamen.

It began active service on July 16, 1955, replacing the old, rather small *Ebe* (a brigantine rig). We can only hope that when the time comes for the ship to be retired from naval service the Italian state decides to transform it into a naval museum, as Italy is the only European nation without such a ship. After the sad loss of the *Giorgio Cini*, we hope that our "nation of navigators" manages to prevent *Palinuro* being taken from us (and by the French again)!

RIGHT: *A detail of the figurehead (Photo: Perino).*
BELOW RIGHT: *Endurance (Photo: Ansaldo).*
BELOW: *Imperia 1996, the training ship* Palinuro *(Photo: F. Ramella).*
OPPOSITE PAGE: *The training ship* Palinuro *in a fresh breeze (Photo courtesy of the Italian Navy's UDAP office).*

Partridge

Rigging:	Trysail cutter
Sail area:	299 sq. yds.
Shipyard:	Camper & Nicholson (Gosport, England)
Designer:	J. Beavor Webb
Year of design:	1885
Launch:	1885
Restoration:	1979–99
L.: 71³/₄ ft.	W.l.: 49 ft.
B.: 10¹/₄ ft.	Df.: 8¹/₄ ft.
Displ.: 30.86 tons	Engine: 40 Hp
Skipper:	Alexander Laird (2000)

THIS PAGE: *Cannes 2000,* Partridge *during a regatta (Photos: J. Taylor).*

A splendid boat has recently made its appearance at regattas: the trysail cutter *Partridge,* designed by J. Beavor Webb and launched at the Camper & Nicholson yard in England in 1885 in the presence of Mrs. Lora Napthorn. It is a typically Victorian-style yacht, very popular at its time for one-day cruises and the occasional regatta.

We do not have a complete history of the boat: it was recorded in the Lloyds Register of Yachts only up until 1923. From 1885 through 1923 the boat had three different names and a series of diverse owners, including a certain Ebenezer Southgate, who in 1915 was also owner of the trysail cutter *Marigold.* In 1923 the boat was sold to a Belgian owner, who used it as his living quarters.

It was finally re-discovered in 1979 by Alex Laird and Peter Saxby at Tollesbury in Essex (on the east coast of England), abandoned in the mud of the River Blackwater. At the time of its rediscovery, only two historical facts were uncovered: one was that the boat had once been called *Tanagra,* and the other that at another time it sailed under the name of *Harry 1885* (as witnessed by the name engraved in an old frame-floor timber). However, armed with these two new pieces of information, it ultimately proved possible to retrace the history of the boat.

Beginning in 1979, the boat underwent a long refitting operation under the constant surveillance of Alex Laird and in strict accordance with the original specifications dating from 1885. The original central keel was preserved, together with the teak stringers and a fair amount of the planking. The long list of work done includes the reconstruction of all the deck beams, the stempost, and the rudderstock. The 11 sails were made by Ratsey & Lapthorn, the sail-makers who had provided the original sails back in 1885. *Partridge* now has a pitch pine and teak deck (95 percent original) and oak framing (completely rebuilt). The rigging was supplied by Harry Spencer of Cowes.

The refitted boat is a wonderful sight, a real flashback to former times, and has won prizes and acknowledgement from such prestigious publications as *Yachting World,* which in November 1999 stated that: "Partridge *is one of the prettiest gaff-rigged cutters in existence… And she's fast, very fast."* So she has proved to be, winning a host of honors: the XV Admirante Conde de Barcelona Trophy (first among the trysail yachts, voted the best restored yacht, second among the vintage yachts); Monaco Classic Week (winner of the Prada Trophy, and of the first prize in the technical trials and in the elegance competition); Cannes Régates Royales (second place in its category in the Prada Trophy); and Les Voiles de Saint Tropez (first prize for trysail yachts, winner among the trysail yachts, and first in its category in the Prada Cup). An excellent start indeed to the boat's new life!

Pen Duick

en Duick was one of the most photographed and admired boats during the Seventh Imperia Week. It has belonged to the Tabarly family since 1937, by which date it was already an old boat with quite a history. "Pen Duick *was my boat,*" Tabarly recounted. "*For me it represented my idea of a certain maritime oil-painting I was very fond of. It was a 50-foot 'cotre franc' designed by Fife… and it was on that boat that I gained my first experience of sailing.*"

During World War II the boat was laid up on a launching cradle with no servicing, and this marked the beginning of its period of decline. The ribs were rotten, but in 1957 Tabarly decided to try and save the boat at all costs and threw himself headfirst into an operation that others considered to be completely crazy at that time: he built a fiberglass shell over the old planking, the first time this had ever been attempted.

After having dismantled every single onboard item, including the deck, the ballast, and the rigging, *Pen Duick* was laid upside down on a barge. In the words of Tabarly himself: "*I spent all my leave working on this project and managed to construct a new shell consisting of seven layers of fiberglass.*" The Costantini shipyard subsequently added the framing, the frame-floor timbers, and then a marine-plyboard deck. "*Thus it was that I started to sail the boat in 1958 even before the final layer had been put in place.*"

So it was that *Pen Duick* was brought back to life after a series of different owners and names. During its lifetime, it has been called *Yum*, *Grisèlidis*, *Magda*, *Cora V*, *Astarte*, *Panurge*, *Butterfly*, and, finally, *Pen Duick* (which in Breton literally means "black head," the name given to the black-headed swan). This boat loves light breezes, when it performs at its very best.

Today *Pen Duick* can boast a new Oregon pine deck with traditional-style fittings. The sail plan, redesigned by Tabarly, enables the boat to glide elegantly across the waves as it must have done in former times. Very sadly, it is currently in search of a new skipper.

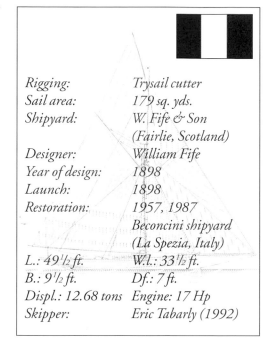

Rigging:	*Trysail cutter*
Sail area:	*179 sq. yds.*
Shipyard:	*W. Fife & Son (Fairlie, Scotland)*
Designer:	*William Fife*
Year of design:	*1898*
Launch:	*1898*
Restoration:	*1957, 1987 Beconcini shipyard (La Spezia, Italy)*
L.: 49½ ft.	*W.l.: 33½ ft.*
B.: 9½ ft.	*Df.: 7 ft.*
Displ.: 12.68 tons	*Engine: 17 Hp*
Skipper:	*Eric Tabarly (1992)*

BELOW: *Nioulargue 1992,* Pen Duick *with Eric Tabarly at the helm (Photo: L. Fioroni).*

TOP RIGHT: Pen Duick*'s prow (Photo: L. Fioroni).*

RIGHT: *Imperia 1992, the unbeatable*
Pen Duick *with Eric Tabarly at the helm
(Photo: R. Minervini).*

BELOW: *Imperia September 1992,* Pen Duick
during a regatta (Photo courtesy of R. Bigi).

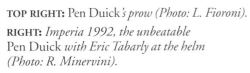

Phantom Light

*P*hantom Light, one of three identical boats designed by Robert Clark (the other two were called *John Dory* and *Serica*), was called *Mary Richmond* when it was launched just before World War II having been commissioned and completed by a Mr. Boothman. Nevertheless, the owner was not able to use the boat for a number of years, and it ended up being stored in a shed during this period. It was only in 1972, when a Mr. McColl bought the boat, that it finally emerged from storage and was used by the new owner and his family for cruising off the coast around the Hamble Estuary in England. In 1985 it was sold to James Robert Gale who kept it in Normandy until 1988 and then moored it in the South of France.

The present owner, in honor of this beautiful boat by Robert Clark, has turned it into a fast, user-friendly pleasure yacht. The hull of *Phantom Light* features teak planking, while the topside planking is in Honduran mahogany: the seasoned oak ribs are steam-curved, while the mast is made of spruce.

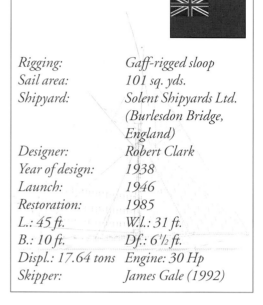

Rigging:	Gaff-rigged sloop
Sail area:	101 sq. yds.
Shipyard:	Solent Shipyards Ltd. (Burlesdon Bridge, England)
Designer:	Robert Clark
Year of design:	1938
Launch:	1946
Restoration:	1985
L.: 45 ft.	W.l.: 31 ft.
B.: 10 ft.	Df.: 6½ ft.
Displ.: 17.64 tons	Engine: 30 Hp
Skipper:	James Gale (1992)

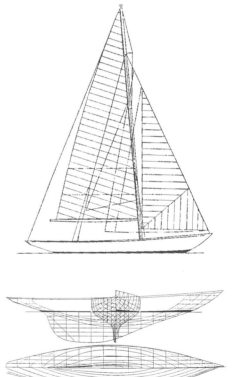

LEFT: Phantom Light *was designed by Robert Clark (Photo courtesy of R. Gale).*

Piraña

Rigging:	*Bermudan sloop*
Sail area:	*72 sq. yds.*
Shipyard:	*Scheep (Amsterdam,*
	The Netherlands)
Designer:	*G. De Vries Lentsch*
	(Amsterdam,
	The Netherlands)
Year of design:	*1938*
Launch:	*1938*
Restoration:	*1991, 1994*
L.: 33¾ ft.	W.l.: 31½ ft.
B.: 8½ ft.	Df.: 6 ft.
Displ.: 7.72 tons	Engine: 13 Hp
Skipper:	*Micollet Benoît*
	(1991–96)

aunched in The Netherlands, the original design of *Piraña* has not been modified at all. It was originally named *Thalassa* (in 1938). In the early 1950s its new French owner, Caston Deferre, entered it for numerous regattas in the Mediterranean, including the Giraglia, when it sailed under the name *Palynodie*. It was sold for a second time in 1960, and little is known of its whereabouts for the following 30 years. Then, in 1990, it was purchased by Micollet Benoît, who sailed it all the way from Corsica (its home port being Calvi) to Turkey.

A very attractive boat, with a teak deck and planking and an oak keel, it was restored in 1991 and a new mast was mounted. The crew of *Piraña* currently consists of a pleasant young couple with a very young child, the youngest heir to the helm ever encountered on Imperia quay.

RIGHT: *A photo of* Piraña *moored at the quayside (Photo courtesy of M. Benoît).*

Puritan

he present-day *Puritan* is extremely faithful to the original design by John Alden. This trysail schooner has a steel hull, a teak deck, and an adjustable keel, and is one of the most fascinating vintage yachts in circulation. It is one of its designer's best projects (design no. 455-B), possibly his masterpiece, and is a boat inspired by the large New England fishing schooners.

This vintage yacht, one of the few that has always kept its original name, was commissioned from the prestigious Boston designer by a rich American businessman, H.J. Curtis, but during the infamous Wall Street Crash it seemed that it would never get past the drawing-board stage. However, a few days later, Edward M. Brown, a member of the New York Yachting Club, turned up to take over the order, only to be involved himself in the economic crisis shortly afterwards.

At this point, a third candidate for ownership appeared (by now the entire project was being closely monitored by a number of sailing clubs) who entrusted the task of finishing the boat to the New London shipyards, who also worked for the US Navy. So *Puritan* had already had three owners before it was even launched!

The first effective owner of the yacht, though, was the Californian Henry J. Bauer, who looked after it very carefully and had it regularly serviced while it remained his property. During the war it was sold to the US Navy, and then afterwards it went to Mariano Prado Sosa, son of the President of Peru. Subsequently it was resold to William Bolling, a vintage yacht restorer from Fort Lauderdale, who serviced the boat at a time when it was in a critical condition. Once it had been restored to its former splendor, *Puritan* was bought by an Austrian, Oscar Schmidt, who wasted no time in transferring the boat to England to have it undergo major refitting work.

With an English skipper and crew, the boat returned to the United States to be a spectator at the America's Cup; it also took part in the Classic Yacht Regatta, where it won first prize in its class. The return voyage from the USA was a truly dramatic one: in April 1981 *Puritan* sailed into an exceptionally violent storm during which the mainmast snapped. At this point there was nothing else to do but shelter in the Canaries while the boat was repaired so that it could sail again. Afterwards it headed for the Mediterranean, and the Argentario shipyards in Italy where the broken mast was rebuilt.

Towards the end of 1990 *Puritan* was bought by Arturo Ferruzzi, the majority shareholder in the Ferruzzi Group. All the sails were replaced and the steel hull inspected (it was found to be in excellent condition), again at the Argentario shipyards.

Puritan's interior is completely original and has been given a certain warmth by the Oregon pine furnishings. The boat's maneuvers are traditional: a good deal of brute force is required but the results are often excellent, thus amply repaying the crew for its efforts.

In the opinion of Carlo Sciarelli, *Puritan* "*is the best looked-after boat in the world!*"

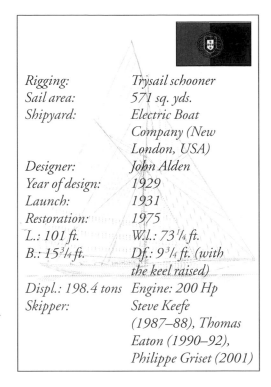

Rigging:	*Trysail schooner*
Sail area:	*571 sq. yds.*
Shipyard:	*Electric Boat Company (New London, USA)*
Designer:	*John Alden*
Year of design:	*1929*
Launch:	*1931*
Restoration:	*1975*
L.: *101 ft.*	W.l.: *73¼ ft.*
B.: *15¾ ft.*	Df.: *9¾ ft. (with the keel raised)*
Displ.: *198.4 tons*	Engine: *200 Hp*
Skipper:	*Steve Keefe (1987–88), Thomas Eaton (1990–92), Philippe Griset (2001)*

BELOW: *October 2001,* Puritan *seen from the stern (Photo: F. Ramella).*

ABOVE: *Below deck on* Puritan
(Photo: S. Navarrini).

RIGHT: *A spectacular view of the deck*
(Photo: S. Navarrini).

BELOW: *During a regatta (Photo: A. Tringali).*

Romeo

This boat, originally named *Heti*, was designed and built in 1912 by Max Oertz, the most famous of German yacht designers. Today, the boat is called *Romeo* and has been somewhat mutilated by alterations made over the years.

In 1919 the sail plan was modified to adapt the boat for cruising purposes; first it was given a trysail-yawl rig, then a Bermudan-yawl rig. The boat changed hands a considerable number of times, until just after World War II when, having fortunately avoided being requisitioned for war reparations as happened to a great many beautiful German yachts, it finished up at the Gludesburg Sailing Club on the German Baltic coast, where it was subsequently used for training purposes under its new name, *Seeschwalbe*.

In 1965 it was sold to a private owner who changed the rigging once again, this time transforming it into a sloop and deepening the keel. Once again, it had a change of name and was now called *Saturn*. For the first time ever the boat was raced in a regatta, and in 1970 and 1971 it won a number of victories.

Despite still being a fast boat, it is strange to see a slender, streamlined hull beneath a boom that should be twice its actual length. In September 2000, as a result of a collision, *Romeo*'s mast was broken and had to be replaced completely.

Rigging:	Bermudan sloop
Sail area:	167 sq. yds.
Shipyard:	Max Oertz
	(Hamburg, Germany)
Designer:	Max Oertz
Year of design:	1912
Launch:	1912
Restoration:	1970
L.: 62½ ft.	W.l.: 49¾ ft.
B.: 11½ ft.	Df.: 10¼ ft.
Displ.: 39.68 tons	Engine: 130 Hp
Skipper:	Friedrik Goebel
	(1991–2000)

ABOVE: *Imperia 2000,* Romeo *returns to port after being unmasted as the result of a collision (Photo: G. Pittaluga).*

LEFT AND BELOW: *Two shots of* Romeo *racing in the waters of Argentario in 1992 (Photos: J. Taylor).*

Rondine II

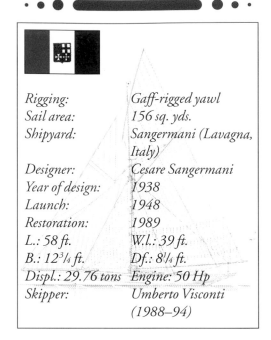

Rigging:	Gaff-rigged yawl
Sail area:	156 sq. yds.
Shipyard:	Sangermani (Lavagna, Italy)
Designer:	Cesare Sangermani
Year of design:	1938
Launch:	1948
Restoration:	1989
L.: 58 ft.	W.l.: 39 ft.
B.: 12³/₄ ft.	Df.: 8¹/₄ ft.
Displ.: 29.76 tons	Engine: 50 Hp
Skipper:	Umberto Visconti (1988–94)

BELOW: *A shot of* Rondine II, *one of the most famous creations of the Sangermani shipyard (Photo: J. Taylor).*

first came across *Rondine II* after the boat had begun to winter at the Medaglie d'Oro quay in Porto Maurizio, Italy. Apart from its tall, slender masts, I was particularly struck by the attractive bench abaft the wheel. I later met the boat's skipper, Umberto Visconti, an interesting, old-fashioned character whom I immediately became friends with.

The boat had been commissioned in 1947 by Mario Pratolongo, a true sailing enthusiast, and was launched the following year (design no. 17) with the name *Fiammetta II*, perhaps the same as that of the owner's daughter. The August 1948 edition of the Italian sailing magazine *Vela e Motore* had the following to say about the event: "… *An ocean racer of great class is born… In test-runs, with a fresh breeze and running free, the log*

registered 14 knots!" A photograph taken at that time clearly shows the stern section of the boat at the water's edge, flanked by *Radiosa Aurora*, complete with the yawl rig envisaged in the original design (when *Rondine II* was bought by the present owner in 1982 it had no mizzenmast).

The 1955 Register of Yachts lists the boat as no. 6361, the property of Paolo Materazzo, and now sailing under the name *Rondine II*. For about 15 years the boat remained in Sicilian waters, but in 1965 it appears to have belonged to the Italia Sailing Club of Naples, and in 1968 to three Roman friends. Around 1971 the boat was bought by a Bank of Naples executive and returned to the port of Naples before being sold once again in 1975 to Giorgio Paruffo, a pilot from Vicenza, who exchanged the boat for a tourist-class aircraft.

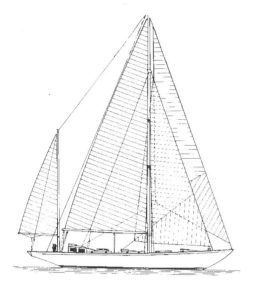

Rondine II was now based at Monfalcone in Italy, and it sailed in Adriatic waters until 1982, when it was sold again. At that time, *Rondine II* was not in very good shape and had to be taken to the Santa Margherita shipyard at Caorle to have the planking checked and restored (of both the hull and the topside), to have a provisional deckhouse superstructure demolished, and to refit the mizzenmast.

Finally, in 1983 the boat reached the familiar waters of the Ligurian coast. At the Sangermani shipyard I once again encountered my old friend, Mariano Topazio, who had fitted the larch planking on the former *Fiammetta* years before and who now runs his own boatyard. He could not hide his emotion when he recognized the old hull of what had been the first ever large ocean-racer built at the Sangermani yard.

During the boat's construction, a number of modifications had been made to the original design, and in particular to the shape of the deckhouse, the stern cockpit, and the interior. When it was finally refitted, the interior was made more luminous, using a generous quantity of mahogany, and great care was taken over details, the redesigned version of the boat being completed at the Imperia shipyard. Thus it was that *Rondine II*, and the man who had skippered the boat

for 11 years, Umberto Visconti, got their second wind.

The boat has a considerable sailing area in relation to the slender lines of the hull and its small, wetted surface. The mainmast (75 feet) enables a 70 square yards spanker to be used, while there is up to 155 square yards of canvas area exposed to the wind (yankee, staysail, spanker, mainsail, and mizzen-sail). The boat responds well in all sailing conditions, especially from sailing close-hauled to running free, and it thoroughly repays the considerable effort required with a truly thrilling performance. On the other hand, it performs poorly when sailing close-hauled in a short sea or a following sea given the limited volume of the stern. This is the only time that steering the boat becomes a tiring task.

On the whole *Rondine II* is a splendid boat that is a credit to its builders. It is extremely popular at vintage yacht meetings, accompanied by its skipper and his "second-in-command," Loris Bellani. *Rondine II* was sold in 1997 and is currently based in the port of Ravenna, Italy, after having been partially refitted (a new rudder, mast fittings, etc.). In 1999–2000 it took part in the vintage yacht meetings held in Venice and Trieste. In 2002 it returned to the Tyrrhenian Sea off the west coast of Italy.

Rosalind

This extremely elegant yacht was launched in 1904 in the south of England by Charles Helleyer of Yorkshire, who ordered the boat from the Stow & Son shipyard in Shoreham, a boatyard famous for having built such prestigious yachts as *Roma* and *Harbinguer*. Originally designed as a trysail yawl with no engine or electricity, it was built in beautiful, strong Burmese teak with robust oak ribs, a simple interior in Cuban mahogany, and an equally simple cabin. At the end of World War I it was registered in Gibraltar and Barcelona.

The first engine was installed in 1934. In 1948 the boat's last English owner, Lieutenant-Colonel C. Morrison, transferred the boat to Spain, and since 1951 it has flown the Spanish flag and has been the property of the Conde Godò family. It was recently refitted as a ketch with carbon-fiber masts.

In 1990, its skipper, Javier Ayala, saw to the restoration of the boat according to the original design with a completely renewed Cuban mahogany interior. In the same year, it took part in the XV Almirante Conde de Barcelona Trophy, the boat currently being registered with the city of Barcelona's Royal Yachting Club.

Rosalind has a twin, *Mohawk II.*

Rigging:	Trysail yawl
Sail area:	287 sq. yds.
Shipyard:	Stow & Son (Shoreham, England)
Designer:	H.J. Stow
Year of design:	1904
Launch:	1904
Restoration:	1996–97 Monty Nautic (Barcelona, Spain)
L.: 118 ft.	W.l.: 86½ ft.
B.: 15 ft.	Df.: 11¼ ft.
Displ.: 93.7 tons	Engine: 238 Hp
Skipper:	Javier Ayala

LEFT: *A spectacular shot of the trysail yawl* Rosalind *in 1999 (Photo: N. Martinez).*

OVERLEAF: *A fascinating aerial shot of* Rosalind *(Photo: N. Martinez).*

Royono

Rigging:	Gaff-rigged yawl
Sail area:	261 sq. yds.
Shipyard:	Herreshoff Manufacturing Co. (Bristol, Rhode Island, USA)
Designer:	John Alden
Year of design:	1935
Launch:	1936
Restoration:	1975–77, 1988
L.: 71¼ ft.	W.l.: 51 ft.
B.: 15¾ ft.	Df.: 9 ft.
Displ.: 44.09 tons	Engine: 130 Hp
Skipper:	Bill Wallace (1989), Simon Nighy (1990), Steve Willins (1992)

This fantastic boat is the result of a transitional period in the work of the famous boat-designer John Alden, whose schooners were at the forefront of American ocean racing during the years immediately after World War I. It was commissioned by Spencer Berger, one of the regular entrants in the Bermuda Race, and was registered no. 9623 under the name *Mandoo II*. On close inspection, one can easily make out the lines of the typical Gloucester fishing schooner in its relatively low freeboard and the typical overhangs of the stempost.

In the original drawings, *Royono* had a boomed staysail and a short bowsprit that was added at a later date. For reasons of time and money, the hull was a composite construction: the keel was in oak, while the framing was in Swedish steel with intervals of 18 inches. The hull had Honduran mahogany planking, while the interior was fitted out using Port Orford cedar: the latter only grows in Oregon and California, has few knots, and is just a little heavier than European fir. It is widely used in the United States for boat construction, and Alden recommended it be used because of its pleasant fragrance.

Mandoo II was launched on May 15, 1936, and by June 22 it was ready to take part in the 13th edition of the Bermuda Race. Unfortunately, it had to withdraw from the race due to a broken forestay.

In 1938 the boat was purchased by the famous yachtsman Alfred F. Loomis, who refitted it as a cutter. Under a series of subsequent owners, *Mandoo II* (which was renamed *Royono*) took part in all the editions of the Bermuda Race up until 1965. 1950, the year in which the boat was donated by John B. Ford to the Annapolis Naval Academy, marked the beginning of an intense period of racing. Skippered by Frigate Captain Frank Siatkowski, director of the Academy's yachting section, *Royono* won the 1952 Bermuda Race, 16 years after the boat was launched. The plates decorating the door leading to the boat's map-room commemorate the victories and its participation in the Newport–Annapolis and the Buenos Aires–Rio de Janeiro Regattas. When Senator John F. Kennedy visited the

RIGHT: *Imperia 1990,* Royono *always finishes among the honors in regattas (Photo: F. Ramella).*

Naval Academy he fell in love with the boat (which had in the meantime been reconverted to a yawl), and, after his election as US President he often sailed on it in the company of the five regular crew members. The Naval Academy sold the boat in 1967 for US$25,000 to Julian Elfenbein, who subsequently chartered it in the waters of Antigua.

The life of *Royono* continued under its next owner, Elmer Dion, who transferred the boat to his boatyard at Kittery in Maine. Here, more than 65 feet of planking was replaced. The next change of ownership marked the beginning of a dark period in the existence of the boat: in 1975 a cargo of marijuana was found on board by the coastguards, and the boat was consequently towed to Florida. Several years went by before the boat was discovered at St. Thomas, Florida, by Philip Bommer in November 1987. At the time, it seemed impossible to restore the boat given that it had not been serviced at all during this long period of forced abandonment. However, Bommer was determined to save the boat at all costs, and he had it towed to the West End Slipway Yard at Tortola in the Virgin Islands, where its reconstruction was completed under the supervision of Captain Simon Nighy.

The hull showed no signs of corrosion, but, as often happens, some of the wood had rotted around the rivets. The money spent on restoring *Royono* would have been enough to build two new similar yachts. The entire operation took ten months to complete, and involved the construction of two new spruce masts, rigged by Harry Spencer of Cowes, England, while the new set of sails were made by Hood.

Thus it was that at the Nioulargue *Royono* could once again compete against its old rivals such as the famous ketch *Ticonderoga*, launched the same year as *Royono* by L. Francis Herreshoff and with an impressive number of victories to its name. This boat, winner of a series of regattas held on the Great Lakes and during the various editions of the Chicago–Mackinac, got to be known as the "Queen of the Mackinac Race."

Weighing in at 44.09 tons (39 percent of which is made up of the lead in the keel), *Royono* is essentially a flush decked yacht with the deck only interrupted by two small deckhouses and a stern hatchway.

LEFT: *A snapshot of* Royono *as it hits a wave (Photo: F. Taccola).*
BELOW: *VBR 1991, the boat sailing at full speed (Photo: J. Taylor).*

Saharet of Tyre

Rigging:	Bermudan ketch
Sail area:	478 sq. yds.
Shipyard:	Camper & Nicholson (Gosport, England)
Designer:	Charles E. Nicholson
Year of design:	1931
Launch:	1933
Restoration:	1985–86 (Malta)
L.: 100 ft.	W.l.: 67½ ft.
B.: 11 ft.	Df.: 9 ft.
Displ.: 62.39 tons	Engine: 236 Hp
Skipper:	Jan Staniland (1991)

BELOW: *Close-up of the end of the stern and the jib pole (Photo: S. Navarrini).*

RIGHT: Saharet of Tyre *(Photo: F. Taccola).*

Saharet of Tyre, a splendid Bermudan ketch, was one of Charles Nicholson's fine creations, designed for an American owner, Woodbury Parsons. Nowadays it is rather difficult to recognize it from the original drawings given the difference between the present deck superstructures and those of its creator.

In 1947 it flew the Italian flag and sailed under the name *Lily*. In 1955 it became the property of the engineer Carlo Pesenti, and, in subsequent years, of Captain Lauro, with whom it navigated mainly by engine and indeed with no bowsprit – a strange way of doing things for the old Captain of Cape Horn fame! In 1980 it was sold to the German Hans Papst, and then to a Mr. Bassoul.

The current-day *Saharet of Tyre* is an extremely elegant, fascinating streamlined boat, the result of a rather difficult series of "cosmetic" restorations (due to the lack of any original drawings, all of which were lost during the war). Restoration work was carried out in Malta in the period from 1985 to 1986, during which the old English oak keel and the frame of steel ribs and beams were saved but the planking was completely replaced with 2 inch-thick teak planks mounted using over 6,000 copper nails specially made in England.

In order to make the boat easy to manage and suitable for ocean cruising, some of the winches were also replaced given that the original single-speed ones were not really suited to a smaller crew. The original sail plan was preserved, as were the original masts in laminated Columbia pine, the ideal wood in terms of lightness and strength, together with the mainsail boom made from Oregon pine.

Saharet of Tyre, a boat designed for running on a beam wind, is comfortable in light breezes and suffers when sailing close-hauled due to its limited draft. Its sailing surface, consisting of a basis of eight sails, six of which can be trimmed at the same time, can be anything up to 478 square yards.

Saint Briac

aint Briac is a delightful ketch designed by Henri Dervin. A special book has even been written about this boat.

In 1960 it set sail from Cannes, France, on a round-the-world voyage that was to last 80 months, with Didier Depret and his young wife Bernadette on board enjoying the most romantic of honeymoon journeys. This voyage covered some 35,000 miles across all of the world's seas, with entertainment provided in the form of Bernadette's piano-playing. Their journey was completed in 1966, and, over the following years, *Saint Briac* was often seen in the Antilles, the Pacific islands, Australia, and Ceylon, having been transformed into an ocean cruiser for charter purposes. At Imperia, the boat appeared full of people entertained by an accordion player and made a suitably good impression with Michel Dejoie and his wife, Cristina Borgogna, unfortunate protagonists of the 1985 Portofino–New York Race.

The boat has an iroko hull with oak and acacia ribs, as well as, alas, a plastic-coated deck. Other distinguishing features include the metal topside chain-plates, its long bowsprit, and the typical inclined wheel astern of the mizzenmast. It was sold in 1989 at Cowes, England, and currently flies the English flag in the waters of the Canary Islands.

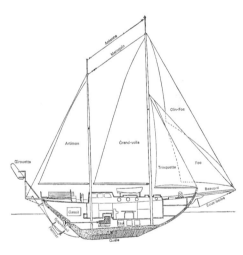

Rigging:	Gaff-rigged ketch
Sail area:	215 sq. yds.
Shipyard:	Roux (Brest, France)
Designer:	Henri Dervin
Year of design:	1944
Launch:	1951
Restoration:	1981–82
L.: 62¼ ft.	W.l.: 37¾ ft.
B.: 14 ft.	Df.: 8½ ft.
Displ.: 24.25 tons	Engine: 80 Hp
Skipper:	Michel Dejoie
	(1986–88)

LEFT: *A photograph of* Saint Briac *(Photo: S. Piano).*

Samadhi

Rigging:	Bermudan sloop
Sail area:	144 sq. yds.
Shipyard:	Otero Terni Orlando
	(Leghorn, Italy)
Designer:	A. Rouger
Year of design:	1938
Launch:	1939
Restoration:	1972 Agostino
	Moltedo shipyard
	(Santa Margherita
	Ligure, Italy)
L.: 47 ft.	W.l.: 32½ ft.
B.: 11 ft.	Df.: 6½ ft.
Displ.: 13.01 tons	Engine: 70 Hp
Skipper:	Alfredo Martini
	(1989–96)

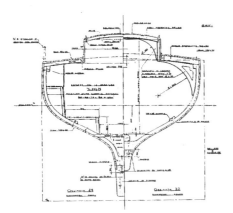

RIGHT: *Imperia 1989, the sloop* Samadhi *(Photo: R. Minervini).*

Launched in 1939, this boat belonged to an engineer at the Odero Terni Orlando shipyard in Italy who kept it moored in the port of La Spezia. Its original name was *Marilli II*. Towards the end of World War II it was sunk by the Germans, as were all the other vessels inside the port area, creating a depressing mass of wreckage. However, *Marilli II* was recovered straight after the war and bought by Pietro Bertollo who had it taken to the Costaguta shipyard at Voltri in Italy for the necessary repairs. The hull was rigged as a sloop, with three wooden cross-tree masts that were longer than the boat itself. An old photograph shows the boat in the port of San Remo with the tender arranged on deck on the roof of the deckhouse as was once the custom.

The boat was renamed *Pinta III* (the Bertollo family had already owned two boats of that name), but during the 1940s, given that the Naval Register already featured another *Pinta*, the name was changed once again to *Kea*. In the late 1960s the boat regularly cruised in the Mediterranean and to the island of Porquerolles (virtually a desert island at that time) where it was welcomed by the "Mayor," who came on board to greet the crew of perhaps the first Italian boat to appear in those waters after the war.

As a result of Bertollo's work commitments, *Kea* subsequently went through a rather sad period of decline, during which it was left abandoned in a garden in the town of Pietra Ligure. It was here that the engineer Alfredo Martini first saw the boat. Martini was the owner of a successful company producing landing stages and, despite the fact that the boat, short of a mast and resting on a cradle, had turned into a hen-house complete with chickens and roosters (as witnessed by a photograph from that period), he was nevertheless attracted towards this poor vessel and, in June 1971, decided to buy it. A year's restoration work carried out by Agostino Moltedo's shipyards in Genoa was enough to restore it to its former seaworthy self.

So it was that *Kea*, still with a sloop rig, and with its name changed to *Samadhi*, was given a new sail plan designed by the architect Davide Castiglioni, together with a new metal mast and a refitted deck, interior (the latter designed by Martini), and cockpit. Finally, a steering wheel replaced the old tiller, which nevertheless was kept on board. *Samadhi* has a teak deck and deckhouse, elm-oak-ash ribs, an oak keel, and a lead false keel.

The boat has recouped its original splendor, thanks to the organizational energies and creative inspiration of its owner, and is now a well-equipped, comfortable yacht. With its skipper at the helm aided by a crew of good friends, *Samadhi* is taken out into the open sea every spare moment they have.

San Guido

*S*an Guido is a vintage yacht designed by pasquale Carmosino and built in Italy. Originally a trysail rig, over the years it has undergone a series of transformations. It has excellent pine planking, Douglas fir masts, a 1 inch-thick teak deck, oak floor timbers, and doubled elm ribs.

The deck installations have been largely conserved according to the original drawings: the four steering wheels, the wooden blocks, and the inclined wheel with steering chain. Beneath the bowsprit (made of Douglas fir) there is an attractive carving of a snake with a wolf's head. In 1989 the boat collided with *Noroit*, whose deck was half destroyed as a result.

San Guido has had a variety of different owners but has recently gone back to flying the Italian flag with its new owner from Amalfi. The boat is presently at the Argentario naval shipyard in Italy for internal refitting and the replacement of some of the planking.

Rigging:	Wishbone ketch
Sail area:	359 sq. yds
Shipyard:	Carmosino (Santa Margherita Ligure, Italy)
Designer:	Pasquale Carmosino
Year of design:	1939
Launch:	1939
Restoration:	1986, 1989, 1994 Argentario naval shipyard (Italy)
L.: 72 ft.	W.l.: 55³⁄₄ ft.
B.: 15 ft.	Df.: 8¹⁄₂ ft.
Displ.: 37.46 tons	Engines (2): 170 Hp
Skipper:	Carl De Parèdes (1989)

THIS PAGE: *Imperia 1989, two snapshots of* San Guido *during a regatta (Photos: F. Taccola).*

Santa Maria II

Rigging:	*Gaff-rigged ketch*
Sail area:	*316 sq. yds.*
Shipyard:	*J. van Dam (Onde, The Netherlands)*
Designer:	*Audgaarden*
Year of design:	*1950*
Launch:	*1951*
Restoration:	*1974*
L.: 59 ft.	*W.l.: 53³/₄ ft.*
B.: 13³/₄ ft.	*Df.: 9 ft.*
Displ.: 49.6 tons	*Engine: 126 Hp*
Skipper:	*Aldo Martinetto (1988–2000)*

BELOW: *Imperia 1988, the ketch Santa Maria II: a sturdy cruiser with a steel hull (Photo: S. Pesato).*

I used to watch this particularly attractive, solid yacht when it was moored at Imperia's Porto Maurizio east quay. Subsequently, I had the chance to observe its performance close-hand when my friend Aldo Martinetto invited me to spend a few enjoyable hours on the boat.

This ketch with a steel hull was commissioned by a certain P.M. Hendriks of Scheveningen, The Netherlands, who had planned a round-the-world voyage. It was launched at some point in the year 1951. *Santa Maria II* is a boat with a considerable displacement, and the stability given by its weight is only slightly greater than that given by its shape. The wood-paneled interior is arranged according to the English system, that is, along the line of the keel. By its very nature, the boat is well suited to long-distance voyages both in summer and winter.

For a number of years nothing more was heard of this boat, except for the fact that a Genoese sailor remembered having sailed on it in 1954 from The Netherlands to Genoa, where the Panamanian flag was raised. Years later the boat was seen moored in the port of Venice bearing the name *Ala Magica*. It was also mentioned in a book written by Nantas Salvalaggio set, in fact, in Venice. It was also in the port of Venice that, in 1959, the boat was given its original name back – *Santa Maria II*.

Changing ownership, it sailed in the Adriatic and Aegean Sea. It was then sold again and moved to France, where it underwent extensive refitting. In 1974 it was sold yet again, and, after more restoration work, was once again sailed on the open sea.

This boat performs best when sailed close-hauled or running on a beam reach, although it is not quite as effective when running before the wind. In the 1950s it had a large square cotton mainsail, a sail that was traditionally used on the trade winds route.

Santa Rosa

This boat was designed to race in the Buenos Aires–Rio De Janeiro ocean regatta and for ocean cruising. After several years of racing, and numerous victories gained in national and international competitions, and having sailed along the coast of South America, *Santa Rosa* was bought by the Nicolini family in the late 1950s and transferred to Peru. They kept the boat for the next 35 years. The boat's original name, when it had been owned by an Argentine doctor, had been *Rosaines*.

The Nicolini family really looked after the boat and in 1988 decided to prepare it for the European classic-yacht circuit. Thus it was that *Santa Rosa* underwent a complete refitting designed to restore it as much as possible to its authenic state: the original fittings, winches, and masting were all conserved. Restoration work got under way in August 1988 and was completed by July of the following year. Twenty-nine hull planks were replaced by new ones weighing exactly the same and of exactly the same dimensions. The cockpit, deckhouse, and mahogany interior were also either restored or replaced by an exact copy of the original; only the teak deck was completely rebuilt, although under expert guidance.

In August 1989, *Santa Rosa* crossed the Atlantic and reached Leghorn in Italy in September, having previously been purchased by an Italian boat-owner. During a regatta inspection in Sardinia, Olin Stephens, the boat's designer, confirmed that the restoration work had been carried out perfectly. Today, the boat has reacquired that original splendor and its much-admired copal-finished hull. At its first regatta in the Veteran Boat Rally held at Porto Cervo in Sardinia, *Santa Rosa* surprised everyone by winning its class from among a field of 63 boats. It did the same at the VII Almirante Conde de Barcelona Trophy held in August 1991. At Imperia it finished second behind Tabarly's *Pen Duick*.

Despite being quite wide (with a square stern), and having a high freeboard, it manages to capitalize on the edge it has when running free or sailing with a trading wind. A seaworthy, stable boat, it cannot manage to hug the wind to any great extent, despite its bronze canting keel, which is raised when running free.

The boat has composite framing with steel ribs, and, rather unusually, a stern hatchway that can be slid along the keel in both directions by moving a metal pin (embossed with the words "*designed by Sparkman & Stephens*" – as is the dinette's skylight). Another interesting detail is that the boat does not have a windlass.

Rigging:	Gaff-rigged yawl
Sail area:	136 sq. yds.
Shipyard:	San Isidro (Rosaines, Argentina)
Designer:	Olin Stephens
Year of design:	1948
Launch:	1949
Restoration:	1988–89
L.: 50 ft.	W.l.: 35¼ ft.
B.: 13 ft.	Df.: 4¼ ft.
Displ.: 15.98 tons	Engine: 60 Hp
Skipper:	Lorenzo Orrù (1991–94)

THIS PAGE: *VBR 1991, two snapshots of* Santa Rosa *flying the Peruvian flag (Photo: J. Taylor).*

Selamat

Rigging:	Bermudan cutter
Sail area:	48 sq. yds.
Shipyard:	Mu Berman shipyard (Perak, Malaysia)
Designer:	Thomas Harrison Butler
Year of design:	1948
Launch:	1948
Restoration:	1996
L.: 29½ ft.	W.l.: 22½ ft.
B.: 8½ ft.	Df.: 5 ft.
Displ.: 9.04 tons	Engine: 8 Hp
Skipper:	Gian Battista Borea d'Olmo (1995–2002)

RIGHT: *A historical photograph of* Selamat *(Photo courtesy of B. Borea).*

On Sardinian waters you may come across an unusually shaped cutter by the name of *Selamat*. It was designed by Thomas Harrison Butler and built in 1948 on behalf of John Campbell Edwards, an Englishman residing in Penang who remained the boat's only owner for the next 30 years until 1978.

In 1948 the boat reached Port Said, Egypt, stowed aboard the *City of Khartoum*.

It then set sail from that port on a long sail-powered voyage (it had no engine at the time), which took it to various parts of the Mediterranean before its final destination, Portimao in the Algarve. Subsequently, the boat spent many years in English waters. In 1951 it was fitted with a two-stroke Stuart-Turner engine.

On Edwards' death, the boat was taken over by skipper Ken Gregson until 1995, when it was bought by Gian Battista Borea d'Olmo. A completely reliable, seaworthy boat, *Selamat* was restored by the English carpenter Felix Oliver.

Many original parts are still on board (for example, the winches, lights, and oil lamps). The original engine was successfully restored, while the sail plan was completely renewed.

The boat is easy to maneuver. It has an agile hull with marked sagging, a canoe stern, and a low, continuous deckhouse stretching as far as the stern cockpit.

Shenandoah

Rigging:	Trysail three-masted schooner
Sail area:	approx. 960 sq. yds.
Shipyard:	Townsend & Downey (Shooter's Island, USA)
Designer:	T.E. Ferris
Year of design:	1901
Launch:	1902
Restoration:	1986, 1994–96 McMullen & Wing
L.: 145 ft.	W.l.: 100 ft.
B.: 23½ ft.	Df.: 15¼ ft.
Displ.: 330.7 tons	Engine: 480 Hp
Skipper:	J.F. Bertholet (1986–1998)

This steel-hulled schooner was the biggest vintage yacht present at the first seven editions of Imperia Vintage Yacht Week. It was designed by Theodor Ernest Ferris, who created numerous boats during the first 25 years of the 20th century, including a series of navy ships.

Shenandoah was commissioned by Gibson Fahnenstock, a New York financier, who decided to name it after a native American Indian chief mentioned in an old sailor's song ("The Old Capstan Shanty"). *Shenandoah* was built alongside the famous *Meteor III* of the German Kaiser at the Townsend & Downey yard on Shooter's Island in Newark Bay, just a short distance from Staten Island. Under its first owner, the boat sailed in the Mediterranean for a decade, before being sold in 1912 to Landrat Walter von Bruining, a German who decided to rename it *Lasca II* and base the boat in the German port of Kiel (which just happened to be the home port of *Meteor III*, built and launched in the same year from the same yard). However, while sailing in English waters the boat got caught up in the beginning of the war and was subsequently confiscated by the British.

In 1919 *Lasca II* ended up in the hands of Sir John Esplen of London, who renamed it *Shenandoah* and sold it two years later to G.H. Williams of Southampton. The

new owner kept the boat in English waters for about nine years, and during that time it had a paraffin engine installed.

In 1928 it was sold to the Italian Ludovico Potenziani, who renamed it *Atlantide* and kept the boat moored at the port of Fiumicino near Rome. Up until 1930 the boat was sailed on Mediterranean cruises, but then it was sold again, this time to the Duke of Copenhagen. It remained in Scandinavian waters, where it was used as a cruiser for about 20 years. In 1935 it was fitted with electricity, and three years later with two diesel engines.

Following World War II, *Atlantide* flew the Honduran flag and was the property of the Compañia de Navigacion San Augustin, which chartered it for various purposes. After a few years in South America, the boat reappeared in the Mediterranean once again, but this marked the beginning of a rather dark period in the boat's history. In 1962 it was confiscated by the French authorities for tax reasons and was neglected at its mooring for about ten years.

It was saved from a certain bad end by Baron Bich, who finally managed to purchase it in 1972. With the help of the New York Yacht Club and the Gibson Fahnenstock family, Baron Bich managed to procure the original drawings of *Shenandoah* and began a large-scale refitting operation designed to restore it to its original splendid condition. The deck was rebuilt, the masts and mizzen-boom shortened, and modern navigational instruments were installed.

Finally, in 1974 the boat, which had been given back its original name by the Baron, made its triumphant re-entry into Newport harbor after nearly 70 years – a great return that was reported in all the world's papers.

Another vintage yacht enthusiast, Philip Bommer, subsequently bought the boat, which currently belongs to Yachtord Ltd. of St. Helier (in Jersey) and is registered with the Monaco Yacht Club. After many years of absence, the boat entered Porto Maurizio in Italy in September 1998.

PRECEDING PAGE: *Cowes 2001, a poetical image of a trysail beauty (Photo: J. Taylor).*

THIS PAGE: *Cowes 2001, two shots of* Shenandoah *racing (Photos: J. Taylor).*

Sif

This splendid schooner took part in the first vintage yacht meetings held at Imperia under the name of *Icicle IV* and flying the British flag. It was designed by its first owner, L. Hansen, and built at the N.F. Hansen shipyard in Odense, Denmark.

It was launched in 1894 under the name *Sif*, a Norse goddess and wife of Thor, and was registered as a 9.921-ton trysail cutter. It was still registered as such in Lloyds Register of Yachts in 1911 and had no engine at that time.

No further news of the boat is available until the year 1934, when it was abandoned in Plymouth, England, by three young Danish yachtsmen who had intended to sail around the world in it (at that time *Sif* was already rigged as a trysail schooner, albeit still without an engine). That same year it was bought by W.J.W. Modley, an ice-manufacturer who had a two-stroke engine installed and certain parts of the interior modified. The boat began to fly the British flag in 1938, under the name *Icicle IV*, but it was then stripped for the entire wartime period and was only able to sail again after the war.

In 1954 the schooner was purchased by Anthony Williams who, together with his brother Trevor and his wife Zetta, transferred *Icicle IV* to the port of Saint Tropez in France in 1961. The boat was easily recognizable at this time as it remained the only yacht in the harbor for some while. With the opening of Port Grimoud in France, the Williams family, who lived aboard the yacht, found another familiar mooring for the boat while restoration work continued.

Then, in the winter of 1985, Mike MacInnes discovered the boat: behind those rusty chain plates, old sails, and obsolete shrouds, he perceived the boat of his dreams and lost no time in negotiating its purchase. After changing its name back to the original, he registered it under the American flag (in 1988) and entered it for the first time in the Nioulargue, where it won the Corum Trophy for the First Class (Saint Tropez boats).

Sif's lines are very similar to those of Herreshoff's cutter *Gloriana*: it is one of the first designs for a Danish hull with a straight clipper bow. Similar lines can be seen on *Pen Duick* (1898) and *Cicely* (1902), although these are boats of a different size.

Rigging:	Gaff-rigged schooner
Sail area:	96 sq. yds.
Shipyard:	N.F. Hansen (Odense, Denmark)
Designer:	L. Hansen
Year of design:	1894
Launch:	1894
Restoration:	1985–89
L.: 51½ ft.	W.l.: 31 ft.
B.: 9½ ft.	Df.: 6 ft.
Displ.: 9.61 tons	Engine: 98 Hp
Skipper:	Trevor Williams (1987), Enrico Caretti (1988), Mike MacInnes (1989–91)

BELOW LEFT: *The graceful lines of the schooner* Sif *(Photo: F. Pace).*

BELOW: *The beautiful stern (Photo: R. Minervini).*

The hull is robust, with oak ribs alternated at intervals with other pitch pine steam-curved ribs, held together by galvanized steel bars. The planking is in $1\frac{1}{4}$ inch-thick pitch pine and features a few of the original bronze rivets. During the 1950s, Trevor Williams replaced several planking timbers while the boat was afloat. The deckhouse, cockpit, and covering boards are all in teak, as is the new skylight, which is longer than the original one so as to provide more light and better ventilation when sailing in the Mediterranean. The few remaining original features below deck are also in teak, with engraved pine paneling. The simple oak rudder was completely rebuilt in 1922.

As we have said, the boat was originally rigged as a gaff cutter. The mizzen-fittings are the original ones from when the boat was launched; the present heavy main-gaff is the cutter's original one and has been made shorter to take the mainsail. When Trevor Williams tried to refit the boat in 1959, he only found the fittings of the masts, which had been burnt. He therefore had two new masts made quickly by planing two telegraph poles to size, in preparation for the journey across France towards the Mediterranean.

The present owner has lengthened the mainmast to 40 feet (the mizzenmast is less than 33 feet). The majority of the blocks are original parts from the boat's cutter days. In 1989 the stempost and the sternpost were both rebuilt, while the sail plan was redesigned in 1986 when new sails were put in place (bought at Port Grimoud).

At present *Sif* is still without winches. Restoration work proceeds in a systematic fashion, thanks to the enthusiasm of Mike MacInnes and his partner Thérèse Nurit, who have invested all their energy in restoring this boat. The results are there for all to see: in 1989 *Sif* won the Phocea Cup at Marseilles in France and the Agnesi Trophy at Imperia.

In 2000 the boat celebrated its 106th birthday. Its owner wishes to ensure that his restoration work will guarantee a long future for this wonderful yacht, one that will see it solemnly gliding across the sea with that grace and elegance we have always admired.

LEFT: *Imperia 1990, a shot of* Sif *and its likeable crew* (Photo: S. Pesato).

Skagerrak

Rigging:	Bermudan yawl
Sail area:	303 sq. yds.
Shipyard:	Abeking & Rasmussen (Lemwerder, Germany)
Designer:	Henry Rasmussen
Year of design:	1938
Launch:	1939
Restoration:	1975, 1985, 1993
L.: 89½ ft.	W.l.: 65½ ft.
B.: 18 ft.	Df.: 12 ft.
Displ.: 82.67 tons	Engine: 150 Hp
Skipper:	Carlo Corbari (1994)

In 1939 a yacht was launched at the prestigious Abeking & Rasmussen shipyard in Bremen, Germany that could have taken part in the America's Cup: this boat was *Skagerrak*, a training vessel for young officers in the German Navy. This boat, which was improperly named "Hitler's yacht," was not given the chance to compete against the top American and English boats because World War II was just around the corner.

However, *Skagerrak* came through the war unharmed, was seized by the British as war reparations, and was transferred to England where all trace of it was lost until the 1950s. It was then bought by an Italian boat-owner who transferred it to the Mediterranean. In 1963 it was sold once again, this time to a Roman professional who still looks after the boat with loving care.

In its first regattas in Sardinia, *Skagerrak* was skippered by Frigate Captain Ferruccio Bomanello, a well-known yachtsman from the Italian Navy. This 90-foot yawl does not appear to have changed very much from its early years, although the mainmast was shortened during its English period. In 1975 the teak deck was rebuilt, and the original winches were recently replaced, together with the windlass.

The hull consists of 2¼ inch-thick mahogany planking (original) fixed to strong steel ribs. The interior and furnishings are exactly as they were when it was launched. At the first Italian vintage yacht meeting, *Skagerrak* came second in the overall classification and first in its class.

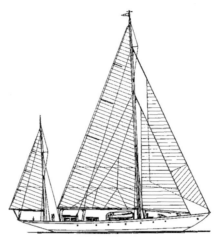

BELOW: *Porto Cervo, 1991,* Skagerrak, *the former German Navy training ship, as it surges across the waves (Photo: J. Taylor).*

So Fong

Rigging:	*Gaff-rigged schooner*
Sail area:	*300 sq. yds.*
Designer:	*Sparkman & Stephens*
Year of design:	*1936*
Launch:	*1937*
Restoration:	*1992*
L.: 89 1/2 ft.	*W.l.: 76 1/4 ft.*
B.: 16 1/4 ft.	*Df.: 11 3/4 ft.*
Displ.: 66.14 tons	*Engine: 130 Hp*
Skipper:	*Robert Verschoyle*
	(1996)

RIGHT: *Cannes,* So Fong *during a regatta (Photo: J. Taylor).*

BELOW AND BOTTOM: *Details of the deck (Photos: J. Taylor).*

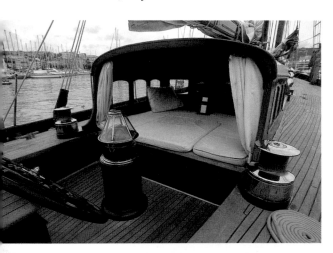

So Fong (which in Vietnamese means "easy woman") is a schooner designed in 1937 by Sparkman & Stephens. It reached the recent gathering at Imperia after having sailed 11,000 miles.

This boat made its first round-the-world trip just before the outbreak of World War II, and it played an important part during that war after having been requisitioned by the United States Coastguard. Up until 1957 it continued to sail and take part in regattas in various parts of the world. In the early 1980s it was captured in communist Vietnam, where it languished, neglected, until 1991 when it was discovered and saved by its then owner, who restored it in a small boatyard he set up in Vietnam using local materials and labor. The boat was subsequently set upon by pirates in the China Sea and in the Red Sea.

Today it is a comfortable, competitive yacht, just as it was when it was first built.

Solway Maid

*S*olway Maid, a yacht that has taken part in numerous regattas in its lifetime, was launched in 1940. Contrary to popular belief, *Solway Maid* was not William Fife's final creation, but rather the last boat he built. The last of his designs was *Madrigal*.

Solway Maid has a very interesting history: it remained in the possession of the same owner, F. Ivan Carr, for all of 34 years and was kept beached for a further 14 years by Carr's widow after her husband died.

The boat has not been significantly modified in any way but has been excellently conserved as it was when it was launched. It has a new set of sails (supplied by Ratsey & Lapthorn of Cowes, England) which David Spy has realigned, and it is now a regular presence at vintage yacht regattas from the Solent in southern England to the gulf of Saint Tropez in France.

Rigging:	*Bermudan cutter*
Sail area:	*151 sq. yds.*
Shipyard:	*W. Fife & Son (Fairlie, Scotland)*
Designer:	*William Fife III*
Year of design:	*1939*
Launch:	*1940*
Restoration:	*1989–91*
L.: 52 1/2 ft.	*W.l.: 35 ft.*
B.: 10 3/4 ft.	*Df.: 7 1/2 ft.*
Displ.: 16.53 tons	*Engine: 44 Hp*
Skipper:	*Ian McCallister (1996–2000)*

LEFT: *VBR 1999, a fine shot of* Solway Maid *with its flush deck (Photo: J. Taylor).*

BELOW AND BOTTOM: *During a regatta – details of the stern (Photos: J. Taylor).*

Sorella

Rigging:	Trysail cutter
Sail area:	78 sq. yds.
Shipyard:	Dan Hatcher (Southampton, England)
Designer:	Dan G. Hatcher
Year of design:	1858
Launch:	1859
Restoration:	1981, 1989–90
L.: 27 ft.	W.l.: 25½ ft.
B.: 9 ft.	Df.: 5 ft.
Displ.: 4.96 tons	Engine: 20 Hp
Skippers:	Giorgio Soano and Mauro Albonico (1989–91)

This yacht was launched at Southampton in 1859, on behalf of Lieutenant-Colonel F.W.J. Dugmore and was rigged as a cutter with Ratsey & Lapthorn sails (of Cowes, England) in 1887. All its details are given in the 1890 Lloyds Register, and up until that year it took part in regattas with the owner. It was then bought by the Fugjer family from Warsash in England, famous for their fishing and sailing traditions. The Fugjers had three sons, all well-known skippers.

This kind of vessel (known as the 27-foot Class) was usually prepared after work for the Town Regatta, in which considerable cash prizes were up for grabs and conspicuous bets were laid on the eventual winner. The three brothers won many regattas and became famous as a result. They subsequently passed on their skills and experience to their grandchildren, one of whom was to be the skipper of numerous boats, including Baron Bich's *Gitana*.

Sorella belonged to the Fugjer family for almost a century. A photograph taken in 1967 shows the boat with its number clearly visible on the side: SU 43. At that time it was considered the oldest boat of its kind on the River Hamble and had been used for oyster fishing, especially during the winter months. We know that its first engine was installed as late as 1932. In the 1980s, Sorella was purchased by Chris M. Waddington, who restored it in his Fareham shipyard.

Sorella is a delightful 8-meter yacht with a decked bow forming a small cabin with space for a tiny stove and two berths. It also has a roomy cockpit and a single mast with a mainsail, gaff topsail, yankee, staysail, and a genoa on the bowsprit. The sailing area is sub-divided as follows: mainsail (45 square yards), jib (18 square yards), staysail (9 square yards), and gaff topsail (6 square yards).

In 1989 *Sorella* was bought by Renato Pirota, who also purchased *Moya* from the same English owner, thus availing himself of the incredible chance to save two truly vintage yachts. Today *Sorella* is undergoing restoration work at the Alto Adriatico shipyards in Italy under the watchful eye of Carlo Sciarelli.

ABOVE: *Imperia 1989, the elegance and beauty of Sorella (Photo: J. Taylor).*

RIGHT: *VBR 1991, during a regatta (Photo: J. Taylor).*

Spartivento

S *partivento* was constructed in 1954 in the present-day Stella Maris shipyard of Castellamare, Italy, probably to an English design. It belonged to a Roman boat-owner, and in 1955 it was being restored at Riva Trigoso when it was acquired by Count Cella of San Remo. Rigged as a sloop at that time, its sails were

still made of heavy-duty cotton. In the early 1960s the boat was sold to Nuccio Bertone who used it for short offshore cruises.

The boat's hull is still in good condition, but the boat has been largely neglected after some provisional refitting, and it is in great need of a complete refitting or rebuilding by its present owners.

Rigging:	Bermudan sloop
Sail area:	144 sq. yds.
Shipyard:	Castellamare di Stabia (Italy)
Designer:	Pasquale Russo
Year of design:	1953
Launch:	1954
Restoration:	1995
L.: 35 ¹/₂ ft.	W.l.: 37 ft.
B.: 10 ft.	Df.: 3 ¹/₂ ft.
Displ.: 14.18 tons	Engine: 55 Hp
Skipper:	Nuccio Bertone (1986)

LEFT: *Imperia 1989, shot of the 1954 sloop* Spartivento *(Photo: S. Pesato).*

St. Nicolas Saxo

T his boat was found in a really bad state at Saint Tropez, France, in 1993, and little is still known about its history. Didier Mangin, the present skipper and owner, arranged for the boat to be restored in a Cannes shipyard, and thus it was that *St. Nicolas Saxo*

managed to enter the vintage yacht circuit. In fact, it went on to win the S Class category of the Régates Royales in Cannes in 1995.

The boat has teak framing, pine planking, a teak deck, mahogany superstructures, and a spruce mast.

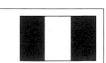

Rigging:	Bermudan sloop
Sail area:	66 sq. yds.
Shipyard:	Carantec (France)
Year of design:	1937
Launch:	1937
Restoration:	1993–94 (Cannes, France)
L.: 36 ³/₄ ft.	W.l.: 29 ft.
B.: 8 ft.	Df.: 5 ¹/₂ ft.
Displ.: 8.3 tons	Engine: 40 Hp
Skipper:	Didier Mangin (1996)

Stormy Weather

Rigging:	Gaff-rigged yawl
Sail area:	152 sq. yds.
Shipyard:	Nevins Yacht Yard (City Island, New York, USA)
Designer:	Olin Stephens
Year of design:	1933
Launch:	1934
Restoration:	2000–2001 Argentario naval shipyard (Italy)
L.: 54 ft.	W.l.: 39½ ft.
B.: 12½ ft.	Df.: 8 ft.
Displ.: 22.51 tons	Engine: 100 Hp
Skipper:	Giles McLoughlin (2000), Sandro Berti Ceroni (2001)

OPPOSITE PAGE: *Cowes 2001, Stormy Weather lives up to its fame and that of its designer, Olin Stephens (Photo: J. Taylor).*

BELOW AND BOTTOM: *Close-up of the wardroom and the deck (Photos: P. Maccione).*

Stormy Weather is a splendidly designed yacht, an Olin Stephens creation based on the lines of *Dorade*, a boat that Olin's brother, Rod, sailed to victory in both the Transatlantic Race and the Fastnet Race of 1935. Olin was only 27 when he designed *Stormy Weather*, but he was already considered the best in his field.

This boat is noticeably wider than *Dorade* (by 2 feet), but not much longer. It has the definitive shape of the ocean racer as designed by Stephens and, as Sciarelli says, is *"definitely one of the most beautiful modern boats in existence."* As dictated by tradition, the bow is much shorter than the extremely streamlined stern, and the sloping rudder follows the line of the hull. The deck is clear and tidy and is similar to that of *Dorade*, with the same kind of skylights and wind scoops. Prism skylights on deck provide light to the cabins below. The rudder is of the tiller variety, as on *Dorade*.

Stormy Weather started to win honors shortly after it was launched: in 1934 it won the Bermuda Race, in 1935 the King of Norway Cup and the transatlantic race Brenton–Riff–Bergen. Then, with skipper Rod Stephens at the helm, it went on to win the Fastnet Race. Its other victories are part of international yachting legend.

A number of yachtsmen have been lucky enough to have owned this pure racer over the years. One of these, James J. O'Neil, managed to win the Miami–Nassau Race six times and never failed to point out that this was a *"great thoroughbred"* of a boat. Naval architect John Alden, congratulating the owner and crew on the excellent form of *Stormy Weather*, declared that: *"In my opinion it would be impossible to design a better yacht."*

Carlo Sciarelli said of the boat: *"…Stormy Weather's bow, as dictated by regulations and tradition, is much shorter than the stern, which is extremely slender; the noticeably sloping rudder is a continuation of the line of the hull; the deck is clear, with the same kind of skylights and wind scoops as Dorade."* I intend to look into the much quieter period in the boat's life during the post-war years at some point in the near future.

In 1998 *Stormy Weather* entered the Mediterranean. By now, its age had begun to show. It was bought by Giuseppe Guzzoni Froscura, who was already owner of *Dorade*, and entered the regattas held during Argentario Yachting Week, where it won all three races in its category under the command of skipper Sandro Berti Ceroni.

It then underwent a complete refitting at the Argentario naval shipyard, operations being directed by Federico Nardi (the technical manager) and Piero Candieri (the head carpenter). During the course of refitting, 50 percent of the mahogany planking was replaced, as were the mizzenmast and the entire deck. The frame-floor timbers of the hull had their bolts removed, and the frame-floor timbers located mid-hull were replaced. Finally, restoration of the oak ribs, wheel, and apron was completed. On deck, the copper wind-scoops and the prism skylights set into the upper deck to provide light below deck (positioned according to the original design) remained. The original layout of the interior was also left unaltered. When completed, the entire restoration project was given the seal of approval by Olin Stephens himself, present at the re-launching ceremony. The sailing performance of the yacht has hardly changed at all: when sailing close-hauled with a wind of 20 knots, the boat manages to hug 40°, whereas when running before the wind it tends to roll somewhat. After two years of restoration, *Stormy Weather* is now in great form for forthcoming vintage yacht regattas.

Sumurun

Rigging:	Bermudan ketch
Sail area:	360 sq. yds.
Shipyard:	W. Fife & Son (Fairlie, Scotland)
Designer:	William Fife III
Year of design:	1913
Launch:	1914
Restoration:	1983, 1988, 1993, 1995
L.: 94 ft.	W.l.: 68½ ft.
B.: 16½ ft.	Df.: 13 ft.
Displ.: 95.57 tons	Engine: 150 Hp
Skipper:	Armin Fisher (1998)

BELOW: *Porto Cervo, 1991, the restored* Sumurun *(Photo: J. Taylor).*

BELOW RIGHT: *VBR 2001, a close-up of the deck (Photo: J. Taylor).*

*S*umurun, which could be defined as a "fast cruiser," must once have been a truly spectacular sight – as hinted at by a photograph taken by Beken in 1937 with its trysail rig and 720 square yards of sail billowing in the wind. When first launched, this powerful, elegant yacht designed by Fife had 2¼ inch-thick planking, an elm bottom, and a teak topside fastened to the ribs with riveted copper nails and bronze grips. Moreover, the 6 × 6 inch oak ribs set at intervals of 16 inches, together with the riveted steel frame-floor and the oak beams, all gave the boat a robustness designed to guarantee it a long life. The interior was elegantly furnished and comfortable, complete with an ice-box – a rare item on boats at that time.

Its first owner, Lord Sackville, kept the boat until 1926, when he sold it to the Vice-Commodore of the Royal Harwich Club in England. However, its home port remained Glasgow in Scotland. During the 1920s and 1930s, the yacht took part in numerous regattas held in British waters, skippered by Captain Gurten. It competed against the most famous yachts of that time, including *Rendez-Vous*, its closest rival and another Fife creation. Other adversaries in those races included *Joyette* and *Terpsichore* (thereafter *Lulworth* – another racer built by White in 1920). At the 1928 Cowes Week in south England it won the Large Yacht Handicap Class, beating *Lady Anne* and *Moonbeam* among others. It was the first yacht to have a lighting generator unit; and it was also equipped with other avant-garde equipment, the weight of which in fact made it necessary to lighten the original 44.09 tons of ballast by 6.614 tons.

In 1933 it was fitted with an engine, and in 1952 it changed its name to *Erna* and flew the Costa Rican flag. The following year it was transformed into a Bermudan ketch, partly to reduce the number of crew on board. In 1960 it was also deprived of its bowsprit.

Further changes in ownership followed, and then in 1983 a new owner, the American A. Robert Towbin, transferred the boat to the Beconcini shipyard in La Spezia, Italy, in order that it be completely restored and modernized. The masts, sails, and winches were all replaced, and little was kept of the original interior. The yacht subsequently reverted to its former name, *Sumurun*, and crossed the Atlantic once again to sail between the United States and the Caribbean, sometimes as a charter yacht.

In 1984 *Sumurun* won the Atlantic Cup at the Newport regattas, and finished first in its class at Antigua Week. Despite the fact that it now has a different sail plan, *Sumurun* remains a beautiful boat, a constant reminder of its aristocratic past.

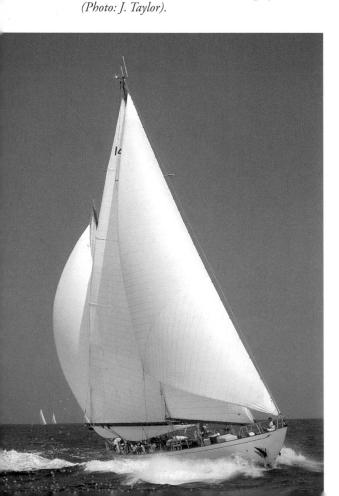

Sylphe IV

Sylphe IV, a cutter rig, was designed by André Mauric in 1940, and constructed at the Faro shipyard in Marseilles, France, during the course of World War II. It is a sturdy yacht that was designed for cruising and racing and features oak framing, copper-riveted iroko sides, a teak deck, mahogany ribs, galvanized steel fittings, and a spruce boom and spruce spinnaker pole.

It was finally launched in 1946, initially with a sloop rig and under the name *Ariel*. In 1954, for reasons of tonnage, it was equipped with Bermudan-cutter rigging and a jib pole was added. The present owners bought it in 1978 and used it for long Mediterranean cruises, as well as regularly taking part in the Saint Tropez Nioulargue and the Cannes Régates Royales in France, and the vintage yacht week in Imperia.

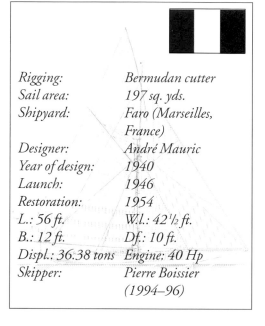

Rigging:	Bermudan cutter
Sail area:	197 sq. yds.
Shipyard:	Faro (Marseilles, France)
Designer:	André Mauric
Year of design:	1940
Launch:	1946
Restoration:	1954
L.: 56 ft.	W.l.: 42½ ft.
B.: 12 ft.	Df.: 10 ft.
Displ.: 36.38 tons	Engine: 40 Hp
Skipper:	Pierre Boissier (1994–96)

BELOW: *A shot of one of André Mauric's most beautiful creations (Photo: S. Pesato).*

Tamory

Rigging:	*Wishbone ketch*
Sail area:	*365 sq. yds.*
Shipyard:	*Nordwerft (Hamburg, Germany)*
Designer:	*Koser U. Mayer*
Year of design:	*1952*
Launch:	*1952*
Restoration:	*1954, 1974*
L.: 86 ft.	*W.l.: 65½ ft.*
B.: 19 ft.	*Df.: 9 ft.*
Displ.: 82.56 tons	*Engines (2): 350 Hp*
Skipper:	*Luigi Vietti (1990–98)*

amory is a solid steel hull commissioned by a German and constructed at the Nordwerft yard in Hamburg, Germany, only to be abandoned after a cruise to the Maddalena area of Italy and subsequently sold in 1953 to the architect Luigi Vietti, who had seen it for sale in the port of Genoa, Italy. Vietti, who was to go on to design numerous villas and entire villages along Sardinia's Emerald Coast, is still a very keen yachtsman, and it was he who gave it its present name, *Tamory*, an abbreviation of the Italian for "I love you Riccarda" ("*t'amo Riccarda*"), Riccarda being the name of his wife.

It is a heavy, extremely seaworthy boat with a harmonious sail plan. It is not particularly fast, but it has always performed honestly during the numerous vintage yacht regattas in which it has taken part, especially when there has been a fresh breeze that makes steering that much easier.

RIGHT: *The heavy, seaworthy* Tamory *(Photo: J. Taylor).*

BELOW: *Imperia 1990 during a regatta (Photo: R. Minervini).*

Tapiner

Launched by Sangermani in 1950, *Tapiner* was initially a seven-eighths sloop rig with rudder and tiller. During the course of time, however, it underwent a series of rather unfortunate modifications such as the fitting of an aluminum mast.

However, in 1981 it was discovered by Francesco Capolei, a keen boat-owner who persuaded the Gallinaro yard in Anzio, Italy, to carry out regular servicing and refitting work. In 1991 a Douglas fir mast was fitted and the planking varnished with copal. The boat made an appearance at the Porto Cervo meetings in Italy in 1985 and 1992, before being sold in 1999 on the death of its owner.

It is a very seaworthy boat that performs well when running before the wind and when running free. The boat still has its mahogany (topside) and Lebanese cedar (bottom) planking, oak ribs, and teak deck.

Rigging:	Bermudan sloop
Sail area:	179 sq. yds.
Shipyard:	Sangermani (Lavagna, Italy)
Designer:	Laurent Giles
Year of design:	1948
Launch:	1950
Restoration:	1991 Gallinaro shipyard (Anzio, Italy)
L.: 46 ft.	W.l.: 36½ ft.
B.: 10¼ ft.	Df.: 7 ft.
Displ.: 16.53 tons	Engine: 65 Hp
Skipper:	Andrea Capolei (1981–92)

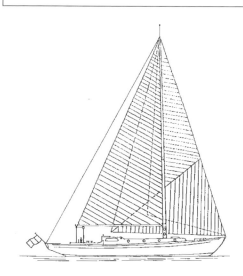

THIS PAGE: *ASW 2001, shots of* Tapiner *(Photos: J. Taylor).*

Te Vega

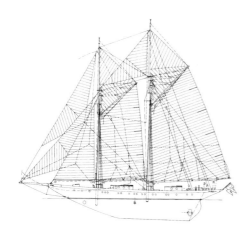

Rigging:	Trysail schooner
Sail area:	1,172 sq. yds.
Shipyard:	Krupp (Kiel, Germany)
Designer:	Cox & Stevens
Year of design:	1929
Launch:	1930
Restoration:	1995–97 Beconcini shipyards (La Spezia, Italy)
L.: 133½ ft.	W.l.: 100 ft.
B.: 28 ft.	Df.: 16¼ ft.
Displ.: 222.7 tons	Engine: 750 Hp
Skipper:	Camillo Comuni (1998)

*T*e Vega was launched, on behalf of its owner Walter Ladd, at the Krupp shipyard in Kiel, Germany, with the name *Etak* in 1930. It is a steel-hull schooner with a trysail rig and gaff topsail. It was to be called simply *Vega*, but its final name was acquired during a cruise in Polynesia when the natives showed their appreciation for this enormous, noble-looking yacht by calling out *"Te Vega!"* (meaning *"Look, the Vega!"*).

Its second owner sailed it in the Caribbean and the Pacific as a cruiser. Then in 1941 it was requisitioned by the United States Navy (and named the USS *Juniata*), who used it as a weather station. It was also fitted with an after-gun. In the mid-1950s, the boat sailed as a passenger vessel between the Polynesian and Hawaiian islands. It was subsequently used as a TV film-set and as a luxury charter yacht in the Caribbean. In 1962 it was restored by Stanford University, who then used it as an oceanographic station for approximately ten years.

In 1995 it was bought by Callisto Tanzi, who already owned the 12-meter SI *Flica II*. He decided to restore *Te Vega* to its original condition and so entrusted the boat to the famed Beconcini shipyards in La Spezia, Italy, under the supervision of the Giorgetti & Magrini company. Given that the owner wished to use the boat as a cruiser, although the restoration work aimed to maintain the boat's original style and technical character, it was made as comfortable and functional as possible.

Compared with other yachts of its age, *Te Vega* was designed according to truly avant-garde criteria: the two spanker halyards were controlled by a pair of electric winches with two warping ends designed to haul the two gaff and throat halyards at the same time, thus reducing the crew's efforts. The two masts, one 130 feet, the other 115 feet, are still the spruce originals, as is the 30 foot bowsprit. The interior, with its cherry-wood furniture and paneling, mahogany parquet-flooring, and white wood-paneled ceiling, still manages to create that historical atmosphere of old with its sober, practical style.

In September 1997, *Te Vega* made its first official appearance after refitting at the Veteran Boat Rally held at Porto Cervo, Sardinia, and the following year it took part in vintage yacht week at Imperia.

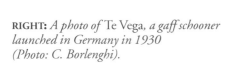

RIGHT: *A photo of* Te Vega, *a gaff schooner launched in Germany in 1930 (Photo: C. Borlenghi).*

Thalatta

<table>
<tr><td>Rigging:</td><td>Gaff-rigged sloop</td></tr>
<tr><td>Sail area:</td><td>167 sq. yds.</td></tr>
<tr><td>Shipyard:</td><td>Jhoan de Dood
(Hamburg, Germany)</td></tr>
<tr><td>Designer:</td><td>Anton Miglitsch</td></tr>
<tr><td>Year of design:</td><td>1949</td></tr>
<tr><td>Launch:</td><td>1949</td></tr>
<tr><td>Restoration:</td><td>1998–99 Walsteds
Baadevaerft (Turo,
Denmark)</td></tr>
<tr><td>L.: 47¹⁄₂ ft.</td><td>W.l.: 34¹⁄₂ ft.</td></tr>
<tr><td>B.: 11¹⁄₂ ft.</td><td>Df.: 8 ft.</td></tr>
<tr><td>Displ.: 22.05 tons</td><td>Engine: 48.5Hp</td></tr>
<tr><td>Skipper:</td><td>Rafael Serratosa</td></tr>
</table>

esigned by Anton Miglitsch in 1949 and built in Hamburg, Germany, by Jhoan de Dood that same year, *Thalatta* took part in various regattas along the east coast of the United States and in English waters between 1952 and 1960. It has also crossed the Atlantic a number of times. From 1961 onwards it moved on to German ports and took part in various regattas in the Baltic and the North Sea. It was then bought by Rafael Serratosa, who had it refitted by Walsteds Baadervaerft, the Turo shipyard in Denmark.

Thalatta, which with its sails hoisted requires a good wind, remains one of the most attractive "flush deck" yachts around. Moored at Moraira (in Alicante), it took part in the 1999 and 2000 editions of the Conde de Barcelona Trophy and in the 2001 edition of the Cadice–La Havana Race. It has two twin-hulls, both of which are currently employed by the Royal Navy as training yachts.

LEFT: *The sloop* Thalatta, *launched in Germany in 1949 (Photo: N. Martinez).*

The Blue Peter

<table>
<tr><td>Rigging:</td><td>Bermudan cutter</td></tr>
<tr><td>Sail area:</td><td>222 sq. yds.</td></tr>
<tr><td>Shipyard:</td><td>W. King & Son
(Burnham-on-
Crouch, England)</td></tr>
<tr><td>Designer:</td><td>Alfred Mylne</td></tr>
<tr><td>Year of design:</td><td>1929</td></tr>
<tr><td>Launch:</td><td>1930</td></tr>
<tr><td>Restoration:</td><td>1988</td></tr>
<tr><td>L.: 64¹⁄₄ ft.</td><td>W.l.: 52¹⁄₂ ft.</td></tr>
<tr><td>B.: 13 ft.</td><td>Df.: 9 ft.</td></tr>
<tr><td>Displ.: 29.76 tons</td><td>Engine: 140 Hp</td></tr>
<tr><td>Skipper:</td><td>Giovanni Aprea
(1990–96),
Mathew Barker
(2000–01)</td></tr>
</table>

ommissioned by Alfred Mylne, *The Blue Peter* is still a splendid racing yacht today. Its first owner, D.W. Molins, was the inventor of the cigarette-rolling machine. The boat was immediately registered as a member of the Royal Corinthian Yacht Club at Burnham-on-Crouch, the oldest yacht club in Great Britain.

The boat is built entirely from Siamese teak (the hull, deck, and deckhouse) using a batch of timbers that had already been seasoned in the boatyard for 60 years. Designed and built as a racer, *The Blue Peter* took part in numerous regattas in northern Europe, winning all of 52 races including the prestigious Scottish Trophy. Welcomed on board by Giovanni Aprea, a truly experienced skipper who had been at the helm of the boat for more than ten years, I looked round in search of signs of its past, which I quickly found.

In the center of the dinette there is a fine table with folding sides, undoubtedly an original part of the boat; the paneling is solid Prussian oak. On the deck, there is a spacious cockpit surrounding the original steering wheel that is engraved with the name of the manufacturer and date of manufacture; the powerful spanker soars above the cockpit, although at one time it must have been situated further aft.

Up until 1955 little was heard of the boat, although it seems likely that it was only used for cruising until that time. That same year,

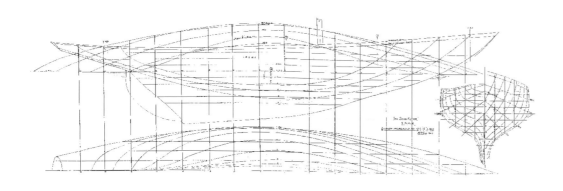

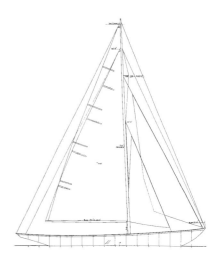

THIS PAGE: *The warmth and color below deck on* The Blue Peter *(Photos: J. Taylor).*

the Register of Yachts shows the boat registered at no. 840 and belonging still to Molins, although it was then sold to the engineer Giulio Kirsh, who used it for cruising between Sardinia and France. Shortly after the death of its owner, *The Blue Peter* sank while moored in the port of Marina di Carrara in Italy, probably as a result of a break in a pipe connected to a hull valve. After the boat had been recovered in 1978, it was purchased by Captain Giuseppe Longo, who used it as a charter yacht for the next five years.

The current owners, Daniele Fiori and Maurizio Salvadori, entrusted the restoration of the boat to master-carpenter Furio Bertolucci. However, right at the beginning of refitting operations, one of the cables attached to a crane holding *The Blue Peter* snapped, and the boat crashed to the ground from a height of 5 feet. Fortunately the boat was only slightly damaged. For safety's sake, the hull was disassembled, thoroughly checked and then reassembled. All the original bronze keel bolts were replaced.

The Blue Peter, a boat that performs well when sailing close-hauled, quickly becomes a "wet" boat when racing and loses ground when running before the wind or free, due to the length of its waterline. Given that it is also a narrow hull, in a cross sea it becomes difficult to steer, which is why the mast has been shortened by $6\frac{1}{2}$ feet. At the end of the 1970s, the boat reached a speed of 16 knots off Capo Caccia in Italy.

Having recouped its youthful spirit, this elegant, noble vessel frequently takes part in vintage yacht meetings and regattas, giving the general public the opportunity to admire one of Alfred Mylne's most successful creations.

THIS PAGE: *ASW 2000,* The Blue Peter *photographed during a regatta (Photos: J. Taylor).*

The Lady Anne

Rigging:	Trysail cutter
Sail area:	222 sq. yds.
Shipyard:	W. Fife & Son (Fairlie, Scotland)
Designer:	William Fife III
Year of design:	1911
Launch:	1912
Restoration:	1998
L.: 75 ft.	W.l.: 50 ft.
B.: 35½ ft.	Df.: 10 ft.
Displ.: 42.99 tons	
Skipper:	Alex Laird (1998), P. Mandin (2000)

THIS PAGE: *Imperia 2000,* The Lady Anne *(Photos: J. Taylor).*

The *Lady Anne* was designed and built by William Fife III for George Coats, the head of a rich family well-known in yachting circles on the Clyde, Scotland. One of the reasons behind the owner's choice of yacht was that he very much wanted to try and win the 15-meter Class, which in 1911 had been won by the German boat *Paula.* Unfortunately for Coats, Charles Nicholson was designing *Istria* at the same time, and this boat went on to win the race in 1912. However, after a few modifications, *The Lady Anne* eventually managed to come to the fore, especially in light breezes, and probably finished the racing season in second place.

Further modifications to the hull and the rigging during 1912–13 kept the boat competitive, but *Istria* always finished first. Despite its transformation to a gaff cutter, it was unable to collect any further honors due to the war in 1914. While Nicholson's yachts were generally faster, Fife's creations tended to last longer, and in fact *The Lady Anne* outlived other similar boats of its age having followed the route of many other metric yachts to Scandinavia during the war. The boat returned to racing with a smaller sail plan during the early 1920s.

During World War II the boat led a quiet life of cruising, apart from one short period of requisition when, in order to transport munitions, the lead keel was removed and its place taken by an iron one. At that time the boat was rigged as a ketch.

After a period during which it was stationed in Spain, *The Lady Anne* returned to England to await much-needed refitting operations. Its entire structure needed checking, as did the original fittings, which were corroding the planking. One section of the stern was rebuilt, the hull was meticulously restored, and the interior was reorganized according to the original drawings. The auxiliary engine was repositioned so as not to compromise the interior layout, while the propeller and the rudderstock are now retractable during regattas. The skylights and hatchways were carefully rebuilt, as were the mast, boom, and spars, which, among other things, were all reinforced internally with carbonfiber. Moreover, a new stainless steel and bronze rigging was fitted.

Thus it was that on June 16, 1999, having recouped its original good looks, *The Lady Anne* returned to the vintage yacht circuit.

Thendara

Thendara is a superb trysail ketch designed by Alfred Mylne (project no. 555) in 1936, and launched at Linthouse, Glasgow, in April 1937. It was the last yacht launched from the Stephens & Son shipyard, although the company continued to build boats up until 1950. The boat's first owner was Lord Arthur Young, a boat enthusiast who was especially keen on 6- and 8-meter SI yachts, which he had raced in various regattas in the Solent off southern England during his early sailing years.

Immediately after its launch, Thendara, with the Scottish skipper Alan McMillan at the helm, took part in the Torbay Coronation Regatta, where it won first place among the over-75-ton hulls. This success was followed by a period of constant cruising in the Baltic Sea, during which Prince Olaf of Norway was a frequent guest on board.

During World War II the boat was requisitioned and used on the River Clyde in Scotland as a buoy supporting barrage nets. This work seriously compromised the state of the boat, with a good part of the planking getting damaged in the process. It raced to a lesser extent during the post-war years, usually against much smaller boats – the era of large English yachts was at an end.

Lord Young died on board Thendara at Benodet in Brittany, and the boat had to be sold subsequently to cover funeral expenses. It was during this period that the boat was transformed into a Bermudan ketch. Over the following years the boat was sailed in Greek waters, where it was eventually bought by an Australian boat-owner.

From 1986 through 1988, restoration work was carried out at the Valdettaro shipyard in La Spezia, Italy, but when it next changed owners in 1991, Mike Horsley suggested that the boat be transferred to the Southampton Yacht Service in England, a shipyard famous for its restoration of classic boats. Thendara reached the Solent in the early hours of a September morning, when it met, ironically enough, Lulworth on its way to Italy for a further refitting.

Despite the composite structure (steel-framing and beams), the teak planking of the hull appeared to be in good condition. It underwent a complete restoration operation, with the replacement of the Columbia pine masts and a return to a trysail rig. The boat was returned to its former youthful condition, and was extremely impressive on its first appearance in the waters of Imperia in 1996.

Rigging:	Trysail ketch
Sail area:	656 sq. yds.
Shipyard:	Alex Stephens & Son (Linthouse, Scotland)
Designer:	Alfred Mylne
Year of design:	1935
Launch:	1937
Restoration:	1993–94
L.: 121¼ ft.	W.l.: 76 ft.
B.: 20 ft.	Df.: 13 ft.
Displ.: 154.3 tons	Engine: 130 Hp
Skipper:	Jacques Luovet (1996)

BELOW: *Imperia 1996, the superb* Thendara *set in a charming panorama (Photo: F. Ramella).*
OVERLEAF: *The mythical* Thendara *sailing close-hauled (Photo: F. Ramella).*

Tirrenia II

Rigging:	Trysail ketch
Sail area:	188 sq. yds.
Shipyard:	H.R. Stevens Ltd. (Southampton, England)
Designer:	Frederick Shepherd
Year of design:	1913
Launch:	1914
Restoration:	1991–92 Pitacco Luxich & Ferluga shipyard (Muggia, Italy)
L.: 60¼ ft.	W.l.: 44 ft.
B.: 12½ ft.	Df.: 7 ft.
Displ.: 33.07 tons	Engine: 93 Hp
Skipper:	Lucia Pozzo (1992), M. Di Giovanni (1996–2000)

On September 16, 1992 I noticed a boat mooring in the port of Imperia that I had never seen before: a trysail ketch with a delightful sail plan. The boat was *Tirrenia II*, a yacht that must have been at least 70 years old (as was later confirmed). The history of this boat is one long adventure, with a happy ending for both the boat and its new owners.

At that time the boat was skippered by the English broker David East, yet had an Italian name, *Tirrenia II*, of which any trace had been completely lost for many years. It was Carlo Sciarelli who managed to find the information sought by the Chairman of the Italian Vintage Yacht Association, Gianni Loffredo. Searching among his archives Sciarelli found a fascinating logbook dated 1929 in which the then owner of the boat, Guido Fiorentino, one of the chairmen of the Naples section of the Royal Italian Yacht Club, wrote of a voyage to the Balearic Islands.

The ketch, designed by Frederick Shepherd, was launched in England on behalf of the Greek envoy to the Italian government and was originally named *Sappho II*. A few years later its name was changed to *Dodoni*, and in 1924 it was changed to its present name, *Tirrenia II*.

That year it had been bought by Guido Fiorentino, who was the creator of the Coppa Tirrenia, a trophy awarded to the boat that, during the course of the year, was judged to have completed the best cruise. Fiorentino submitted the competition's regulations to Marquis Paolo Pallavicino, the then Vice-Chairman of the Royal Italian Yacht Club, and entrusted him with the cup named after his ketch.

This cup, which was awarded up until 1939, and which encouraged many yachtsmen to attempt increasingly adventurous voyages, proved a great success. The 1927 and 1928 editions were won by *Tirrenia II*, while in 1929 the winner was *Dux* (a cutter). In 1930 the ketch *Jolande* won, and from 1933 through 1935 the winner was the ketch *Mizar*.

Loffredo, who was increasingly fascinated by this yacht, asked David East for some photographs, and these clearly show the excellent condition of the interior. They also showed that it had been converted to a gaff-rigged yacht. The boat, which appeared in excellent shape, disappeared without trace after 1951.

According to the Register of Yachts, in 1955 the boat belonged to Major C.J.P. Ball and was based in London. Much later, the

RIGHT: *Cannes 1999,* Tirrenia II *during a regatta (Photo: J. Taylor).*

OPPOSITE AND FOLLOWING PAGES: *Cannes 1999 and 2000, shots of the boat at various sailing angles (Photos: J. Taylor).*

boat was rediscovered in the Caribbean and taken on a trial voyage from Santa Lucia to La Guayra in Venezuela. After the skipper had confirmed the excellent qualities of the yacht, its sale was concluded, and so *Tirrenia II*, after having wandered the seas for years – perhaps as a charter yacht – was transferred overland to the Pitacco boatyard in Muggia, Italy. Refitting operations were begun without the new owner having seen the boat.

Under Carlo Sciarelli's supervision the rigging and deck were completely refitted. When the copper covering was stripped from the hull, the teak was seen to be in good condition. The interior is still 80 percent original and is covered in beautiful briarwood panels; the steering wheel and its worm-screw mechanism (a real gem bearing the name of the manufacturer) are also original. The original 10 foot-long engine mounted astern was removed and replaced by a more modern design mounted in the center of the boat, making it possible to create a four-berth cabin in the stern section.

On July 4, 1993, *Tirrenia II* reverted to its original sail plan, making it a truly elegant and enchanting yacht that rightfully takes its place among those boats built in what was the most creative and fortunate period in the history of yachting.

BELOW: *ASW 2000,* Tirrenia II *with its crew maneuvering the jibs (Photo: J. Taylor).*

Umiak

Rigging:	Bermudan ketch
Sail area:	102 sq. yds.
Shipyard:	Sangermani (Lavagna, Italy)
Designer:	Laurent Giles
Year of design:	1954
Launch:	1955
L.: 49¼ ft.	W.l.: 40½ ft.
B.: 12½ ft.	Df.: 6 ft.
Displ.: 22.07 tons	Engine: 65 Hp
Skipper:	Giogio Corallo (1990), Lucia Pozzo (1991–92), Giorgio Campanino (1998–2002)

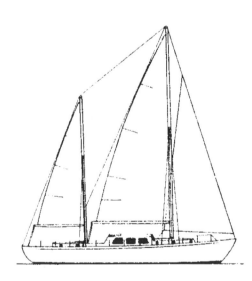

*U*miak is one of the best motor sailers Sangermani built during the 1950s. It possesses a sturdy, seaworthy hull, a "Norwegian" stern, iroko planking, and a mahogany-paneled interior. Designed as a cruiser, *Umiak* has had only three owners, the second of whom kept the boat for a period of 30 years. The lines of the hull are a slight improvement on those of *Santa Lucia*, *Arrisha*, *Muscocco*, and *Noa Noa*. In 1989 the boat was purchased in the port of Carrara in Italy by the engineer Tiberio Gracco de Lay, who conserved it in pristine condition. In fact, despite its age, *Umiak* has been excellently maintained in its original state, thanks largely to the efforts of the boat's owners (the second of whom used to unmast it every winter before carefully storing it away in a shed). It is a very stable, dry boat at sea and performs well in trading winds but obviously less well when sailing close-hauled. In other words, it is a safe boat, ideal for cruising.

Its present owner, Giorgio Campanino, began to restore it to its best possible condition in July 1999. Recently, the wardroom has been restored to its former self, the deckhouses and masts have been re-varnished using copal, the stainless-steel parts on the deck have all been replaced by chromium-plated bronze parts, and the rigging has all been renewed. It is always a pleasure to step on board such a spacious, comfortable boat once again, especially when greeted by such a welcoming skipper and owner.

Overall, I would rate *Umiak* as being one of Sangermani's best-ever creations.

ABOVE RIGHT: Umiak *with its sails hoisted but on a calm sea (Photo courtesy of M. Quaranta).*

RIGHT AND FAR RIGHT: *Two shots of the boat's interior (Photos: S. Pesato).*

Vadura

This powerful, seaworthy boat was designed by Alfred Mylne in 1925 for an Italian noblewoman. Its name comes from the gardens at the Palace of Versailles in France and means "strong and long life." In 1955 it was the property of J. Howden Hume and was based at Greenock in Scotland. It has sailed round the world three times during its lifetime, and in recent years it has taken part in numerous tall ships races. It came first in the America's Cup regatta for large yachts held in Australia, and in the Bay of Islands Classic Yacht Race in New Zealand. Moreover, *Vadura* holds the official record for the fastest time from New Zealand to Tahiti, a journey of more than 2,000 miles, which it completed in just nine days. A very beautiful, comfortable boat, at various times its guests have included Brigitte Bardot and King Hussein of Jordan.

Both the hull and deck are in teak, laid across steel ribs, while the masts are spruce and the rigging is in galvanized steel. Its spacious deck makes it easy to control navigation (as I was able to see first-hand during a recent regatta). Its sail plan is impressive, consisting of over 1,000 square yards of sails, and the boat as a whole is one of Alfred Mylne's best-ever creations.

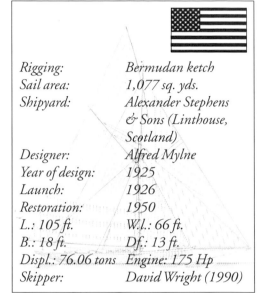

Rigging:	Bermudan ketch
Sail area:	1,077 sq. yds.
Shipyard:	Alexander Stephens & Sons (Linthouse, Scotland)
Designer:	Alfred Mylne
Year of design:	1925
Launch:	1926
Restoration:	1950
L.: 105 ft.	W.l.: 66 ft.
B.: 18 ft.	Df.: 13 ft.
Displ.: 76.06 tons	Engine: 175 Hp
Skipper:	David Wright (1990)

LEFT: *Imperia 2000,* Vadura, *an extremely beautiful yacht designed by Alfred Mylne (Photo: S. Pesato).*

Vagrant

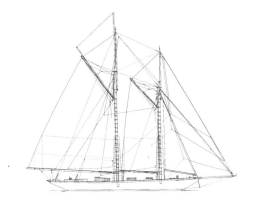

Rigging:	Trysail schooner
Sail area:	556 sq. yds.
Shipyard:	Herreshoff Manufacturing Co. (Bristol, Rhode Island, USA)
Designer:	Nathaniel Greene Herreshoff
Year of design:	1910
Launch:	1910
Restoration:	1985
L.: 107 ft.	W.l.: 56¼ ft.
B.: 18 ft.	Df.: 11½ ft.
Displ.: 74.96 tons	Engine: 195 Hp
Skipper:	Bruce Tedder (1988–1990)

BELOW: *One of the most luxurious lounge/dining rooms on a vintage yacht (Photo: C. Borlenghi).*
BELOW RIGHT: *A glimpse of* Vagrant *under sail (Photo: C. Borlenghi).*

This famous boat was "discovered" during the summer of 1985 by Peter de Savary, an America's Cup yachtsman. It was rotting on an Antiguan slipway, its 75 years of history having been forgotten since its design and construction by Nathaniel Herreshoff, the top American boat-designer. Its recovery is now part of yachting history.

The boat was originally a present from his family to Harold Vanderbilt, heir to an immense fortune left by his grandfather, Commodore Cornelius Vanderbilt. The extremely busy Herreshoff yards at Bristol, Rhode Island, received the order to begin work on the boat on March 23, 1910. Sixty days later, at a cost of US$26,800, this ocean-racer was launched by Harold, who immediately captained it to victory in the Bermuda Race.

It was an elegant, safe hull with 90-foot Douglas fir masts and a high-quality fitted interior, as one would expect from Herreshoff with his great attention for the smallest of details. In 1912 Harold sold the boat to Hendon Chubb, who renamed it *Queen Mab*, a name that was to stay with the boat for almost three-quarters of a century. *Queen Mab* had various owners – members of the East Coast Yachting Club and, in particular, A.W. Stewart, who owned the boat from 1926 through 1939.

Around 1948 the boat reached the west coast of the United States, and from 1953 through 1971 Mary Pringle and Phyllis Brunson completed nine consecutive crossings of the Pacific. It also competed in Class A regattas against great boats such as *Morning Star*, *Varuna*, *Ondine*, *Ticonderoga*, *Blackfin*, and *Windward Passage*.

Contact with the Herreshoff yard was always maintained, and in 1920 the mainmast was transformed from trysail to gaff-rigged, while the foremast was converted in 1952. This was followed by hard times for the boat and it was seen in Antigua in May 1983 in a very poor state. It was subsequently sold to a young Dutchman by the name of Hans Lammer, a real vintage yacht enthusiast who decided to give it back its original name, *Vagrant*. For about a year he chartered the yacht, and then at the end of 1984 he decided to sell it again.

Months went past, and many people thought the boat had come to the end of its days. That is, until it was discovered and saved by Peter Savary. He personally oversaw the complete refitting of the boat over a total of three years. The new rigging was created by Harry Spencer in Cowes, England, and, with its new spruce masts, *Vagrant* can now be considered to be one of the finest restoration projects in the world. It has gone back to its original trysail schooner rig, with 556 square yards of sail, which together with its impressive size and fantastic, elegant interior make it a truly wonderful boat for both cruising and racing. Its long history has really only just begun!

Varuna

(formerly White Heather)

For many years the wreckage of a once elegant hull has lain in the compound at Imperia's shipyards. I have often gone to see it, and for years hoped that someone sooner or later would decide to breathe life back into it. Well, my hopes were not in vain, because restoration work has begun.

The boat in question, *Varuna*, is a gaff-rigged cutter that was already in a terrible state when it entered the yard, powered by its engine, back in 1987. It would appear that in recent times it also spent four or five years in the port of San Remo, Italy.

It was launched in 1909 at the Philip & Sons yard in Dartmouth, England, the creation of designer A. Richardson. When it was launched it bore the name *White Heather*, and at that time it was a trysail cutter – or so it appears from one of Beken's photographs (no. 8203). In the 1930s the boat changed names to become *Varuna*. An auxiliary engine was fitted, and the trysail-cutter rig was transformed to that of a gaff-rigged sloop, as required by the fashion of that period.

Little is known about the boat's racing career; it may have been used as a "hare" to train other 12-meter yachts. The Register of Yachts in the mid-1950s shows it as belonging to two owners, Colonel S. Ward and Lieutenant-Colonel F.B. St. George. Its hull is 60 feet long (including the bowsprit) and 11 feet wide, and it has a draft of 9 feet. It would seem that the Burmese teak used to construct the hull had been bought from an eccentric English lord who, on returning to England, left the wood to season in a peat bog for more than 80 years. The precious timber was then employed in the construction of *White Heather*.

From May 2000 onwards the hull was completely emptied and the planking timbers stripped in order to check the state of the frame. All the bolts were removed, together with the respective soft-iron frame-floor. During the course of restoration, a certain number of modifications to the original design have come to light. It proved hard work revealing the bolts between the keel and the ballast, as they were all covered in a thick layer of polyester resin and sawdust. Subsequently the stem- and sternposts were replaced, together with 15 ribs from the area where they touch the frame-floor: 50 percent of the latter was replaced by galvanized iron, and all the planking, rib, and frame-floor bolts were also replaced.

In July 2001 the rudder blade was completely restored using only a part of the original rudderstock. Almost all of the hull planking (in teak) was recouped, whereas the old beams were all replaced by new oak ones. The bottom and topside were caulked, and the topside was completely relined. All the deck fittings were saved and galvanized, the upper deck and skylights were rebuilt, and the doghouse was brilliantly restored. Below deck, the cherry-wood paneling and antique washbasins and taps create a refined, elegant atmosphere.

After approximately 25,000 hours of work the newly restored *Varuna*, flying the Italian flag, is certainly going to add an extra touch of class to forthcoming vintage yacht meetings as of fall 2002.

Rigging:	Trysail cutter
Sail area:	203 sq. yds.
Shipyard:	Philip & Sons Ltd. (Dartmouth, England)
Designer:	A. Richardson
Year of design:	1909
Launch:	1909
Restoration:	2000–2002 Imperia naval shipyards (Italy)
L.: 70 ft.	W.l.: 62 ft.
B.: 12¼ ft.	Df.: 9 ft.
Displ.: 30.86 tons	Engine: 100 Hp

ABOVE: *Delightful details of the newly restored interior (Photo: S. Pesato).*

BELOW: *The new deck featuring the restored skylight and doghouse (Photo: S. Pesato).*

Vera Mary

Rigging:	*Trysail schooner*
Sail area:	*311 sq. yds.*
Shipyard:	*Berthon Boat Company (Lymington, England)*
Designer:	*J.P. Soper*
Year of design:	*1931*
Launch:	*1932*
Restoration:	*1980*
L.: *72 ft.*	W.l.: *62 ft.*
B.: *12½ ft.*	Df.: *9 ft.*
Displ.: *72.75 tons*	Engine: *75 Hp*
Skipper:	*Christian Radon (1988)*

This boat, launched with the name *Vera Mary*, was given as a gift by King George V to Sir Philip Hunloke, who for many years was Captain of the Royal Yacht *Britannia*. Just before World War II the boat was sold to a new owner, who subsequently transferred it to the south of France. During the difficult years that followed, the skipper used the boat for smuggling contraband to and from South America, and in doing so he kept it seaworthy and in excellent shape.

During the post-war years the trysail schooner was transformed into a Bermudan rig in order to make it easier to handle. Thanks to the care taken by its various owners, all of whom kept the boat for a number of years, 80 percent of the present boat is just as it was the day it was launched in 1932.

Vera Mary has teak planking on the topside and pitch pine planking on the bottom, oak beams and ribs, bronze keel bolts, and a teak deck. The masts and booms are in Oregon pine.

This is a boat that has not really changed much over time, and its solid build and elegance are still very much in evidence.

BELOW: *Imperia 1988, a glimpse of the deck of* Vera Mary *during a regatta in the waters of Imperia (Photo: F. Pace).*

Veronique

Veronique is a beautiful ketch with pronounced and graceful rakes, launched in 1907 from a design by A.R. Luke. The first boat-owner was the Marquis of Northampton, who kept it for at least 15 years. He personally supervised the selection of the construction materials, especially the wood, most of which still appears to be in good condition today.

Veronique was built with pitch pine planking in the hull and Burmese teak above the waterline; this planking is still almost entirely original and rests on cut oak frames, 80 percent of which still look as good today as on the day of the launch. The interior has been well preserved. The boat had been launched as a trysail yawl. It was subsequently transformed into a gaff-rigged yawl, then into a Bermuda cutter, and now today it is rigged as a gaff-rigged ketch. The Register of Yachts from 1935 through 1971 shows Lieutenant-Commander (British Royal Navy) L.K. Stevenson as the owner of *Veronique*, and Glasgow, Scotland, as its port of registration.

After 15 years under a French flag, *Veronique* was acquired by the current owner, who arranged a complete restoration. This lasted four winters in Palma de Mallorca, using English shipwrights. Today, *Veronique* looks like new, although a return to its original rig is planned.

Rigging:	Bermudan ketch
Sail area:	227 sq.yds.
Shipyard:	Luke Bros. (Hamble, GB)
Designer:	A.R. Luke
Year of design:	1907
Launch:	1907
Restoration:	1985, 1995 (Palma de Mallorca, Spain)
L.: 75 ft.	W.l.: 50 ft.
B.: 13 ft.	Df.: 9 ft.
Displ.: 24.91 tons	Engine: 65 Hp
Skipper:	Lionel Cazé (1994–96), X. Gomez (2000)

LEFT: *Imperia 2000*, Veronique, *a beautiful ketch with pronounced rakes (Photo: J. Taylor).*

BELOW: *VBR 1999*, Veronique *shot during a fast tack (Photo: J. Taylor).*

Vespucci

Rigging:	*Ship*
Sail area:	*2,728 sq. yds.*
Shipyard:	*Castellamare di Stabia (Naples, Italy)*
Designer:	*F. Rotundi*
Year of design:	*1929*
Launch:	*1931*
Restoration:	*1951, 1958, 1973 Naval Arsenal (La Spezia, Italy)*
L.: 399 ft.	*W.l.: 270 ft.*
B.: 52 ft.	*Df.: 57 ft.*
Displ.: 4,570 tons	*Engine: 2,000 Hp*

his is the most famous and well-loved Italian square-sailed ship of the last 70 years. In 1925 the then Italian Naval Minister, Admiral Paolo Thaon de Revel, proposed before the Naval Academy a ship whose sail plan and hull lines would keep alive the charming and imposing character of age-old vessels. The idea was put into effect by his successor, Admiral Giuseppe Sirianni, who saw the birth of two superb ships during his mandate: *Colombo* and *Vespucci*, both launched from the Castellamare di Stabia shipyard. The author of the project was Colonel G.N. Francesco Rotundi.

Designed in May 1930, *Amerigo Vespucci* entered the sea on February 22, 1931 and went into service on July 1 of the same year. Since that date it has been modernized three times: in 1951, 1958, and 1973. *Cristoforo Colombo*, which entered service in 1928, was transferred to the Soviet Union in the post-war period, under the clauses of the peace treaty. Until 1959 it sailed the Black Sea under the Soviet flag, going by the name of *Dunay* (Danube). After four years in use by the nautical school of Odessa, it was stripped permanently.

In summer 1933 the two training ships undertook a teaching cruise in the Atlantic,

captained by the Commander of the Naval Academy, Admiral Romeo Bernotti, who raised his insignia on *Vespucci*. The ships called in at the North American ports of Baltimore and New York. Their arrival in the latter city (on August 20, 1933) coincided with the presence in that port of Italian submarines and the national fleet, which had escorted the famous flight celebrating the decennial of Italo Balbo. In 1936 the two ships were together again at the Olympics in Kiel, Germany. Then came World War II and an eventful transfer from Pola (now in Croatia) to Brindisi, Italy, on September 12, 1943.

The lines of *Vespucci* are unique: with a steel hull, the ship has white bands on both sides. These corresponded to the lines of portholes for the batteries on ancient vessels and frigates. Rigged as a "ship" (that is, with three masts flying square-shaped sails), it has a long bowsprit and the traditional stern quarter that on warships completed the highly decorated gallery, onto which the aft cabins looked out.

Unlike other sailing vessels used as training ships, *Vespucci*, with its very high freeboard and considerable width, cannot hug the wind well and tacking is always difficult. Only under particular wind conditions can it take on other sailing boats. I have been able to ascertain personally that the ship holds exceptionally well at sea. It behaved memorably in early September 1974 when, in the Bay of Biscay, it battled for 50 hours against the Atlantic, which was raging at force nine. The ship continues to be admired all over the world for the harmony of its sail plan and the overall image that distinguishes it.

Amerigo Vespucci has two bridges; the fore bridge is used during motor navigation. Another jewel of the ship is the famous "council room" at the far stern, used for executive entertainment; this is a truly unique place on account of its special ornate furnishings.

During sail maneuvers, the crew usually mans the foremast, while the main and mizzenmasts are the responsibility of the

RIGHT: *The evocative square-sailed cathedral that is* Amerigo Vespucci *(Photo: L. Ronchi).*

students of the Naval Academy. Since 1932, thousands of officers and cadets have gained experience of cruise sailing in northern Europe and the North and South Atlantic on this ship. Among its commanders are famous sailing names such as Straulino, Dequal, Lapanje, Foschini, Bernotti, Di Giovanni, Iannucci, Faggioni, Colombo, Corsini, and many more. The ship has been present at many Operation Sail meetings and major marine events.

It has undertaken a number of exceptional maneuvers, such as its passage with sails unfurled along the navigable canal to Taranto in Italy (under the command of Captain Straulino), leaving the port of Brest in France, or sailing up the Thames in London, again under sail. It was present in the roadstead at Camogli (under Captain Romeo Bernotti) and in the port of Imperia (under Captain Renato Sicurezza) at the only Italian Congresses of the captains of old sailing vessels that have rounded Cape Horn, members of the AICH of Saint Malo. On that occasion, unique in its history, its deck was festively invaded by about 400 elderly captains who had the distinction of having vanquished the accursed Cape and who, though they had considerably depleted the supplies of chianti on the ship, came out on top to sing the old songs of the ocean with a youthful spirit, and with the strokes of the bell as intermezzo.

BELOW: *The training ship* Amerigo Vespucci, *which forged generations of naval officers (Photo courtesy of the UDAP Office of the General Staff of the Italian Navy).*

Viveka

Rigging:	Bermudan schooner
Sail area:	395 sq. yds.
Shipyard:	F.W. Lawley & Son (Great Britain)
Designer:	Frank Payne
Year of design:	1929
Launch:	1930
Restoration:	1992–93
L.: 73 ft.	W.l.: 16¼ ft.
B.: 14 ft.	Df.: 10 ft.
Displ.: 105.8 tons	Engine: 170 Hp
Skipper:	Merlin Petersen (1992)

Moored at the quay was an unknown schooner, with a slender, elegant shape. I found it hard to believe my eyes. The boat was a wreck; it had been dismasted in the first phase of the regatta. Its name was *Viveka* (a popular Scandinavian woman's name). The boat was skippered by Merlin Peterson, a sea captain, aged 71, from San Francisco in the United States, but of Danish origin.

The schooner was built in Boston in 1930, designed by Frank Payne for the financier Pierpoint Morgan. He used it for pleasure and to entertain until 1957, when Petersen himself, besotted with the vessel, decided to acquire it.

The boat was in good general condition. Petersen modified its sail layout, raising the mainmast by 10 feet and shortening the boom by the same amount. The result was that the mainsail surface reached 108 square yards. Conceived as a trysail rig, the boat was transformed into a gaff rig to make it a better plyer. A dream began to take shape in Petersen's mind: the passion for voyages. He ended up selling all his properties and his first cruises began.

The year was 1958. Visiting Los Angeles, Tahiti, etc., *Viveka* familiarized itself with ports till then unknown. In the Pacific, between one regatta and the next, the schooner ate up 150,000 miles, to the extent that in 1982 its skipper was named "President of the Indian Ocean." Honolulu became the American skipper's new residence.

As a calm cruise sailor, in 1989 Petersen participated in the Honolulu–Hiroshima Race. *Viveka* acquitted itself honorably, coming in third. He then took part in the race between Japan and Vladivostok in Russia, returning to Muroran on the island of Hokkaido in Japan, and won. *Viveka* then pushed on to Tokyo, Okinawa, Hong Kong, Macao, and Singapore, before entering the Mediterranean. The crew of *Viveka* was made up of unpaid volunteers, all wishing to measure themselves against the sea. This campaign, taking in northern Europe, returning to the United States, and going on to Hawaii, was not to end until 2000 because for Captain Petersen the world, with all its diversity, always has thrills to offer.

No doubt, *Viveka* will take to the seas again, with different crews, in the spirit of the Flying Dutchman.

LEFT: *Imperia 1992,* Viveka, *the American schooner, returns to port after dismasting due to a collision (Photo: R. Minervini).*

West Wind II

West Wind II is a sloop with a receding centerboard, built in 1935 using Borneo teak. In 1963–64 the deck was rebuilt with ³/₄-inch Burmese teak, placed over sheets of ¹/₂-inch marine plyboard. The boat initially flew the Belgian flag, then from 1953 through 1961 it belonged to a certain Signor Di Pietro, an official at the Italian Consulate in Nice, France, who sold it to Robert Simoni. From that moment on, *West Wind II* hoisted the French flag.

Initially registered in 1957 at the Monaco Nautical Club, the boat is currently registered at the Villefranche Sailing Club in France. After restoration work and replacement of the original mast, *West Wind II* has cruised in the Mediterranean and participated in vintage yacht regattas in Nice, France, Monaco, and Imperia.

Rigging:	Bermudan sloop
Sail area:	60 sq. yds.
Shipyard:	Langesberg (The Netherlands)
Designer:	Adolf Harmes
Year of design:	1935
Launch:	1935
Restoration:	1963–64
L.: 36 ft.	W.l.: 24 ft.
B.: 8¹/₂ ft.	Df.: 16¹/₂ ft. (with lowered centerboard)
Displ.: 7.28 tons	Engine: 35 Hp
Skipper:	Robert Simoni (1991–94)

LEFT: *A shot of the sloop* West Wind II *(Photo courtesy of R. Simoni).*

White Wings

One of the most graceful plans by John Alden (construction no. 677), *White Wings* was designed for Percy Grant of the Royal Canadian Yacht Club. The year of design and launch was 1938. The hull was built with mahogany planking on oak frames and it has a teak deck. Its lines, designed by Carl Alberg, reflect the influence of the RORC (Royal Ocean Racing Club) rules and, together with the sail plan (designed by Clifford P. Swaine), allow the boat good speed in light winds. In 1964 a number of modifications were made, such as shortening of the mast and extension of the boom, devices that led to the assigning of a "rating" for *White Wings*, which today behaves rather well in strong and light breezes.

The boat raced successfully with Percy Grant and his sons William and Robert on Lake Ontario in Canada. Its best result was achieved with a triple victory in the Freeman Cup Race, a 140-mile competition. *White Wings* also took third place in the Chicago–Mackinac Race, while it was the first Canadian yacht to win the Lake Ontario Cup. The boat remained the property of the Grant family until 1968, when it was sold to Peter Allen, who kept it registered at the Canadian Yacht Club until 1977. Its third owner, Robert Stryker of Wayne, New Jersey, transferred the boat to City Island, New York, always attending to its every detail.

Today, *White Wings* flies a German flag and sails in the Mediterranean.

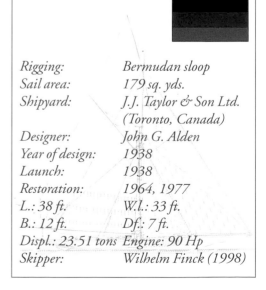

Rigging:	Bermudan sloop
Sail area:	179 sq. yds.
Shipyard:	J.J. Taylor & Son Ltd. (Toronto, Canada)
Designer:	John G. Alden
Year of design:	1938
Launch:	1938
Restoration:	1964, 1977
L.: 38 ft.	W.l.: 33 ft.
B.: 12 ft.	Df.: 7 ft.
Displ.: 23.51 tons	Engine: 90 Hp
Skipper:	Wilhelm Finck (1998)

THIS PAGE: *Cannes 1998 and 1999, images of the very successful vessel* White Wings, *designed by the great John Alden, during a regatta (Photos: J. Taylor).*

Windswept

At this time, *Windswept*, a ketch designed by David Hillyard in 1936, is in advanced stages of restoration in the Tecnomar shipyards in Fiumicino, Italy. A comfortable boat with balanced lines and a canoe stern, *Windswept* has a limited draft, pitch pine planking on an oak framing, and a bottom planked on copper.

Initially registered in Jersey, the boat had two Italian owners in the late 1960s and for a while was used for charters. During restoration, the deck and rudder blade have been rebuilt and the bolts of ballast replaced.

All the rigging and the electric and hydraulic systems have been changed. The original masts are spruce, while the interior, still very charming, has not undergone modernization work. *Windswept* was re-launched in the summer of 2002.

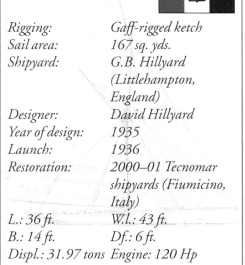

Rigging:	Gaff-rigged ketch
Sail area:	167 sq. yds.
Shipyard:	G.B. Hillyard (Littlehampton, England)
Designer:	David Hillyard
Year of design:	1935
Launch:	1936
Restoration:	2000–01 Tecnomar shipyards (Fiumicino, Italy)
L.: 36 ft.	W.l.: 43 ft.
B.: 14 ft.	Df.: 6 ft.
Displ.: 31.97 tons	Engine: 120 Hp

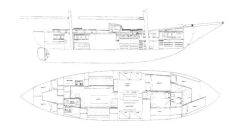

LEFT: *The hull of* Windswept *on its arrival in the shipyard (Photo courtesy of Monica della Porta).*

Yadic II

Created by Eugène Cornu, *Yadic II* has distinguished itself in many regattas, including the Cowes–Dinard Regatta of 1964. On its third appearance at Imperia, it collided with *Raphaelo* and returned to port with a broken mast. Its hull lines are very beautiful, created by the same great French architect who designed *Jalina*, *Janabel*, and several other fast vessels.

Rigging:	Bermudan sloop
Sail area:	72 sq. yds.
Shipyard:	Bonnin (Arcachon, France)
Designer:	Eugène Cornu
Year of design:	1950
Launch:	1950
Restoration:	1992
L.: 37 ft.	W.l.: 26 ft.
B.: 9 ft.	Df.: 6 ft.
Displ.: 5.51 tons	Engine: 5 Hp
Skipper:	Jean Marie Roux (1989–91)

Yali

(sometime Shaula)

Rigging:	*Bermudan ketch*
Sail area:	*355 sq. yds.*
Shipyard:	*Camper & Nicholson (Gosport, England)*
Designer:	*Charles E. Nicholson*
Year of design:	*1925*
Launch:	*1925*
Restoration:	*1986 Beconcini shipyards (La Spezia, Italy)*
L.: 78 ft.	W.l.: 60 ft.
B.: 18 ft.	Df.: 11 ft.
Displ.: 79.92 tons	Engine: 228 Hp
Skipper:	*Franco Della Pina (1990), Gian Guido Bonatti (1989–92)*

This boat was launched with the name of *Kathleen* and was rigged as a ketch. Its first owner – from 1925 through 1928 – was a certain Sir Goodson. From 1928 through 1948 it had various other owners: Herbert West (1928–31), E. Seymons Mead (1931–32), Wallace D. Roome (1932–38), and H.L. Wessel (1938–48). In 1929 the boat was converted into a yawl and thus it remained until 1948, the year when it was definitively transformed into a ketch. During World War II the boat sheltered in Denmark, where it suffered slight damage due to an air raid. In the meantime (1938) it had been rechristened *Yali*.

Up to 1956 it had four other owners, when it was acquired by Leopoldo Pirelli, who owned it until the 1970s. There then followed a period of abandonment in the dock in Lavagna in Italy.

In the late 1950s *Yali* had been noticed on the slipway at Le Grazie, Italy, by the trainee architect Ugo Faggioni, who remembers: "…*The stern was raked, it stretched out over the bottom, terminating in a transom that seemed small in proportion to the rest of the hull. Standing out on this was a name that I have never forgotten:* Yali…" Twenty-five years later, Faggioni, now an established architect, rediscovered the boat of his dreams in a state of extreme abandonment. It was dismasted, the hull had almost no trace of paint, and the deck's planks were detached and warped.

The boat now had the good fortune to be acquired by Gian Guido Bonatti, who decided to renovate it, entrusting the restoration to none other than Faggioni. As the construction plan – indispensable for hull calculations – was missing, Faggioni accurately plotted the form of the bottom, faithfully redrawing the line of the whole hull. *Shaula* (the name given it by the boat-owner at the time) slowly recovered the shape that had been lost over the years.

The boat has a teak deck and planking; elm ribs, keel, sternpost, and stempost; larch shelf-pieces and cabin planking; and lead ballast with bronze bolts. The deck is protected by a tall teak handrail. The original parts of greatest value have been kept, such as the saloon, the owner's cabin, and the deckhouse; the wood for the interior is to a large extent original and is top-quality Honduran mahogany.

To give an idea of how vast and demanding the restoration and reconstruction of a boat like this can be, it may be useful to show the note of work carried out on *Shaula*, provided by Faggioni:

1. The stripping of the copper hull cladding.
2. The replacement of a number of teak timbers from the lower section of the hull.
3. The stripping and remounting of the dead wood, and the reconstruction of the damaged or rotten sections.
4. The sealing of all the holes made by the copper nails in the copper cladding of the hull, using glued wooden pins.
5. The checking of all the ballast bolts and the replacement of some of them with naval bronze ones.

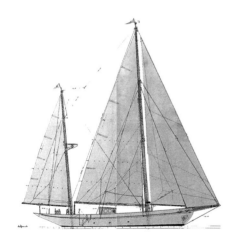
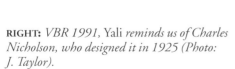

RIGHT: *VBR 1991,* Yali *reminds us of Charles Nicholson, who designed it in 1925 (Photo: J. Taylor).*

OPPOSITE PAGE: Yali *with its sails unfurled (Photo: J. Taylor).*

6. The complete reconstruction of the upper deck and of a number of the original beams which were either broken or damaged.

7. The dismounting and restoration of the original parts (deckhouse, skylights, hatchways, futtocks, toerail timbers, line and decorations, rudder and its mechanical parts), still in good condition, and their subsequent remounting.

8. The recouping of all bronze parts, and the reconstruction in stainless steel of those parts in galvanized steel that have rusted or are broken, strictly according to the original design (chain plates, eyebolts, cleats, boat davits, etc.).

9. The restoration and galvanization of the bowsprit.

10. The reconstruction of the masting in Oregon pine, according to the new sail plan, complete with collars, spreaders, and shrouds.

11. The recouping and restoration of the boom, bowsprit, and their fittings.

12. The complete restoration of all sections of the original lounge, together with the ladder and certain bulkheads.

13. The replacement of the engine and various installations.

Today, *Shaula* is a beautiful ketch that enriches vintage yacht regattas with its presence. Its white hull, with its considerable freeboard, is unmistakable, as is its splendid central deckhouse, recalling a far-off time of yachting. The boat, sold in early 1994, has been given back its old name of *Yali*.

BELOW: *VBR 1991, another image of* Yali *(Photo: J. Taylor).*

Yvette

Seeing it in the water, anyone would feel a sense of admiration for the grace and elegance of this slim vessel. *Yvette* seems to be the only surviving sailing-model of three famous scaled-down prototypes launched by William Fife for the first of his famous *Shamrock* boats, which Sir Thomas Lipton requested for the America's Cup challenge. In practical terms, *Yvette* was created for that particular competition, but is slightly less than 30 feet long! Two of these "miniature" vessels, *Yvette* and *Pierette*, were acquired by Donaldson for his children to race. These are decidedly fast hulls and naturally "wet," with a limited freeboard, as in all of Fife's creations.

In 1914 *Yvette* was sold to Captain Andrew Smith of Kirn, Scotland, which was its first base before moving to Holy Loch during the fine season. In the winter months it sheltered at the McKellar shipyard of Kilgreggan, where it was always maintained with the utmost efficiency and special care. In 1930 the rig was modified into a Bermudan under the supervision of Fife himself.

In early 1962, due to the poor health of the boat-owner's youngest daughter, *Yvette* ceased all activities and was sheltered at the Morris and Lorimer shipyard in Sandbank, still in Scotland, where in 1968 it was acquired by Donald Atherton of Drymen. It was put to sea again but took in a lot of water, even after caulking. It was therefore decided to make the hull wood and to line it with glass fabric impregnated with epoxy resin.

In 1969 the McFadyen shipyard embarked upon a meticulous overhaul and implemented the transformations required by the new boat-owner. A smaller cockpit and a deckhouse further towards the bow were built, the interior was modified using mahogany, and the deck equipment and the sails were altered. In 1975 a new aluminum mast was mounted and the bowsprit restored, as per the original design, also replacing the chain plates.

For 20 years *Yvette* sailed on Loch Lomond with its base at the Canoe Club,

and it participated in many regattas in Scotland, also achieving success in the handicap classes despite the transformations. It then ended up sheltered at the club, where, in 1991, it was acquired by the current owner, who had it restored at the La Bussola shipyard in Fiumicino, Italy, with the collaboration of the architect Mauro Sculli of Giorgini & Magretti.

Yvette's deck was rebuilt. Furthermore, after inspection of the planking (which was found to be in perfect condition), the deckhouse was eliminated and the cockpit reconstructed as it was originally. Among its original components, the boat carries the 100-year-old roller furler, which is still perfectly operational.

Finally, following the designs of the Fairlie shipyard, the mast, bowsprit, boom, and spar were also rebuilt, and the hardware was reconstructed based on the style of the period. Its current rig is with a "Portuguese" type sail, midway between a trysail rig and a gaff rig.

Rigging:	Portuguese sloop
Sail area:	58 sq. yds.
Shipyard:	W. Fife & Son (Fairlie, Scotland)
Designer:	William Fife Jr.
Year of design:	1899
Launch:	1899
Restoration:	1969, 1992
L.: 28 ft.	W.l.: 19 ft.
B.: 7 ft.	Df.: 4½ ft.
Displ.: 3.31 tons	Engine: 7 Hp
Skipper:	Francesco Bossio (1996–2000)

BELOW: *ASW 1998, shot of* Yvette *taken in the waters of the Argentario (Photo: J. Taylor).*

Zaca

Rigging:	*Trysail schooner*
Sail area:	*1226 sq. yds.*
Shipyard:	*Nune Brothers (Sausalito, California, USA)*
Designer:	*Garland Rotch*
Year of design:	*1928*
Launch:	*1929*
Restoration:	*1992–94 Toulon shipyards (France), 2002 Amico shipyards (Genoa, Italy)*
L.: 143 ft.	W.l.: 106 ft.
B.: 24 ft.	Df.: 14 ft.
Displ.: 242.5 tons	Engines (2): 320 Hp
Skipper:	*Lucia Pozzo (1996), Bruno Dal Piaz (1998–2002)*

BELOW: Zaca *has returned to the seas, even more sumptuous and beautiful than before (Photo courtesy of B. Dal Piaz).*

Zaca is a trysail schooner, designed by Garland Rotch and built by the Nune Brothers shipyard of Sausalito (in California) in 1929, for a Californian businessman. Its early years were spent plowing the waves for scientific purposes – studying fauna and flora. In 1946 *Zaca* was acquired by Errol Flynn, who made it his floating home and the venue for glamorous liaisons with personalities from the show-business world. In 1947 the schooner was used for some shots in the film *The Lady from Shanghai* (with Orson Welles and Rita Hayworth).

After his relations with Hollywood deteriorated, the actor and boat-owner spent his evenings with fashionable society in Palma de Mallorca, where the schooner was moored. Unfortunately, his critical financial situation and, ultimately, his death in 1959 forced him to separate from the schooner. For about 20 years it remained totally abandoned, gradually plundered.

There are some photographs showing it in a shed, completely broken up.

Finally, in 1991 an Italian businessman, Roberto Memmo, succeeded in saving it from oblivion. A boat enthusiast, he began the complete restoration of *Zaca*, which lasted two years, at the Toulon shipyards in France. Built of Oregon pine and teak, with pitch pine masts and an Oregon pine and oak double-hull, *Zaca* has slowly returned to life and beauty.

Sadly, many original parts disappeared during its abandonment, such as the stanchions, the binnacle, and the windsails. The aft transom has been slightly modified, while the deckhouse and steering gear have been saved. In September 1994 *Zaca* made its first official appearance at a regatta, looking even more beautiful than before.

During 2002 the schooner underwent a brief refit (with replacement of some of the planking) by the Amico shipyard in Genoa, Italy.

ABOVE: *Two shots of Zaca, a schooner launched in the United States in 1929 (Photos courtesy of B. Dal Piaz).*

LEFT: *Imperia 1996, detail of the full shape of the stern and the very long boom. The masts are the original ones (Photo: F. Ramella).*

Zephir

Rigging:	*Bermudan cutter*
Sail area:	*315 sq. yds.*
Shipyard:	*Philips & Son (Dartmouth, England)*
Designer:	*J.M. Soper & Son*
Year of design:	*1928*
Launch:	*1929*
Restoration:	*1985–90, 1994*
L.: 67 ft.	*W.l.: 47 ft.*
B.: 14 ft.	*Df.: 8 ft.*
Displ.: 39.68 tons	*Engine: 120 Hp*
Skipper:	*Carlo De Carlo (1972–2000)*

*Z*ephir, designed in 1928 and launched in 1929, is a magnificent cutter with pronounced rakes, especially in the stern. The boat came to Italy in the 1950s following its acquisition by Marquis Giacomo de Santis of Rome. The Register of Yachts of 1955 indicates a new owner, Marquis Giacomo Dusmet. Sold once again, in 1963 *Zephir* ended up at the Versilia Nautical Club of Viareggio, Italy. Then in 1969 it sailed under the Panamanian flag for the company Yen Bay Enterprise Inc. In 1972 the current boat-owner acquired the boat and returned it to the Italian flag.

The hull was in excellent condition and only the original cotton sails, by now unusable, were replaced with a new Dacron set.

Compared with its original plans (project no. 9603 of the Philips & Son shipyard), *Zephir* now has a deckhouse of larger dimensions, teak planking with steel frames, winches for the original halyards, and old davits for the dinghy.

In 1984, during a regatta for vintage boats at Porto Cervo, Sardinia, the boom (built in 1937) was broken and had to be precisely reconstructed by the Carlini shipyard in Rimini, Italy. From 1985 to 1990 all the frames were replaced with stainless steel section bars in successive phases, while in 1994 the traditional copper-leaf cladding around the hull was removed. The teak deck was also replaced ($\frac{1}{2}$-inch on a $\frac{1}{4}$-inch layer of marine plyboard) over the pre-existing one, again 1-inch teak.

BELOW: *An image of* Zephir, *a cutter from 1929; it is currently in the upper Adriatic (Photo: M. Marzari).*

Boats of the "Venturieri"

The recent death of Gian Marco Borea d'Olmo has not only deprived the sailing world of a great sailor, but it has inevitably created a moment of reflection in the planning of the activities of the "Venturieri" (the "Adventurers"). In recent years some of the boats belonging to the "fleet," such as *Estella*, *Desirée*, *Four Winds*, and *Cerida*, have had new owners and no longer belong to the association. We express our heartfelt wish for the "fleet" to return soon, as numerous and active as it once was.

In 1970, the first short training cruises on board the ketch *Vistona* (skippered by Gian Marco Borea) provided the opportunity for many enthusiasts to come into contact with the sea and to sail using methods more gratifying than those of the usual teachers, thus discovering the rich and changing charm of sailing on boats and of long voyages of historical significance. The "Venturieri" association was formed to develop the activities that were needed to realize its initial intentions: training cruises, research trips, guided visits to museums, participation in conferences, collaboration with scientific bodies and institutes, and other initiatives that prove to be useful for an increasingly in-depth knowledge of the marine environment and naval culture.

Furthermore, the association is directly committed to the restoration and construction of cruise boats based on innovative designs, albeit as the result of a careful study of historical sailing boats. This combination of experience and research makes it possible to offer associates qualified assistance and skilled consultation in a specific sector. Finally, in the association members find a meeting point, a place to swap experiences, to form crews, and to organize cruises under convoy with their own boats or in the retinue of the association's vessels.

In fall 1987, Gian Marco Borea, with a group of sailing instructors and former students, decided to create an association that had as its statutory objective: "*The spread of navigation*

under sail and the seafaring culture." Today the "Venturieri" have a fleet of about 20 vintage and classic yachts whose diversity makes them particularly suited to the association's various activities. The skippers are chosen from among those who, by virtue of experience gained from years of sailing, have acquired a high degree of professionalism and skill; this allows the "fleet" to sail any sea. A unique association, well established in the world of international sailing, the "Venturieri" now look towards Europe, offering the objectives and interests that distinguish them from others.

The training cruises, strictly on vintage yachts, exemplify the quality of the "Venturieri." A primary role is performed by the skipper-instructor, who must combine his obvious skill with human qualities that are capable of making a crew of "initiates" gel, creating a necessary understanding between the participants, each of whom in turn must perform maneuvers and duties on board. Each year the "Venturieri" also organize open-sea and ocean voyages, and participate en masse in the vintage yacht regattas.

In 1988 I had the opportunity to spend time with them at Imperia. Five boats of their fleet – three the association's and two owned by associates (all identified by the yellow and blue pennant) with crews formed by "Venturieri" – docked and offered a great demonstration of organization, genuine attachment to the sea and to sailing, and competence and friendliness. Gian Marco Borea, was everywhere, like a mother hen guiding her chicks. Some of the many boats that have been the envy of the sailing world for being models of efficiency and reliability – *Vistona*, *Four Winds*, *Estella*, *Cerida*, *Desirée*, *Elpis*, *Alzavola*, *Colomba*, *Grande Zot*, *Tamourè*, and others besides – still plow the waves and are often present at the regattas. Mindful of their cultural formation, at Imperia, as is now customary, the "Venturieri" were designated to lay a laurel crown at the feet of the International Monument to the Sailor of Cape Horn in the name of all vintage boats.

Colomba

Rigging:	*Trysail yawl*
Sail area:	*156 sq. yds.*
Shipyard:	*Auroux (Arcachon, France)*
Designer:	*The shipyard*
Year of design:	*1928*
Launch:	*1929*
Restoration:	*1986 La Bussola shipyard (Fiumicino, Italy)*
L.: 50 ft.	*W.l.: 42 ft.*
B.: 12 ft.	*Df.: 6 ft.*
Displ.: 17.64 tons	*Engine: 40 Hp*
Skipper:	*Gian Michele Sambonet (1989–2002)*

This beautiful boat, created as a trysail yawl, was transformed into a gaff rig in the 1940s. It had various owners, first French and then Italian. During the last war it was sunk in the port of Nice, France, but was subsequently recovered and repaired. Along with its initial name *Colomba*, it has had many other names: *Flirt*, *Choucoune*, and *Viura*. Finally, after a radical restoration at the La Bussola shipyard in Fiumicino, Italy, by the current owner, it had its original name restored. It has a teak deck and pitch pine planking on flexible acacia frames.

During its last restoration *Colomba* re-acquired the trysail plan that can be easily identified from the original masting, which still has the hardware of the time, repaired and used again. In the 1930s it sailed in the Antilles with owners from Nice. It currently belongs to the fleet of the "Venturieri" and conducts cruises and sailing courses for the association. In recent years *Colomba* has returned to the Tyrrhenian Sea, from where, after ordinary maintenance work, it will transfer to the "Venturieri" headquarters in Chioggia, Italy.

RIGHT: Colomba *in a regatta (Photo: S. Piano).*

BELOW: *Imperia 1989, the yawl* Colomba *(Photo: S. Pesato).*

Elpis

Though launched in 1920, this small, attractive boat is a reminder of the influence of English design at the turn of the last century, even if it does not have the typical vertical bow. In *Elpis'* case it is already more slender and pronounced, also keeping the long bowsprit of the typical English cutter. Its first name was *Kathleen*, named after the sister-in-law of the single-handed round-the-world yachtsman Sir Francis Chichester. It has been called *Elpis* since 1945. The Register of Yachts of 1955 has its owner as a certain W.D. Hawkes. Some passages of ownership are registered, however, on the back of the Certificate of British Registry, as follows:

- Glasgow May 12, 1943 – Wallace Douglas Hawkes, engineer
- Glasgow April 9, 1954 – Wallace Douglas Hawkes, engineer
- Glasgow February 11, 1963 – David Philip Keppel Gaunt, writer
- Glasgow February 2, 1969 – Alan Roderick Mackay, manager.

The history of the years that followed is not yet known. The boat was spotted by Michele Amorosi completely abandoned in the square in front of the Sangermani shipyards in Lavagna, Italy. For five years it had lain in a storage tank, prey to deterioration and plundering (everything was missing on board, even the cabin planking). The boat was to be auctioned. Struck by that slender, elegant hull, Amorosi finally became its proprietor in 1984 after various bureaucratic difficulties.

During a year of hard work that he carried out personally, Amorosi recaulked the hull, replaced some copper plates positioned on tarred felt, renewed the electrical system, mounted a new motor (the old one was an open-air pile of rust), and built a new deck. The mizzenmast was created from a 30-foot piece of Douglas fir. Then it was the turn of all the equipment, copying the original items, which had been preserved even if they were in a precarious condition. The new boat-owner also modified the cockpit to make it self-emptying.

The next winter, by kind concession of Beppe Croce, *Elpis* was accepted at the quay of the Italian Yacht Club, where preparations were made for the new tonnage, registration, and nationalization (the boat had previously been under a flag of convenience). With *Elpis* regenerated, Michele Amorosi began training activities and participated in a number of vintage yacht regattas. In 1987 he sold the boat in order to acquire *Cerida*.

The new boat-owner, another "Venturiero," Beppe Spreafico, maintained it impeccably. At the Sestri shipyards in Italy, Spreafico completed the restoration work begun by Amorosi, restoring the hand-tiller to obtain more sensitivity in maneuvers. Finally, he eliminated the copper from the teak hull.

Elpis proved to be a strong, safe boat (it has oak frames and lead ballast). It has never had winches of any type. At sea it displays considerable displacement, is powerful when running free, and likes sailing close-hauled but is very "wet." The passion, enthusiasm, and personal sacrifice of the last two boat-owners have made it a small jewel with its harmonious and much-admired sail plan.

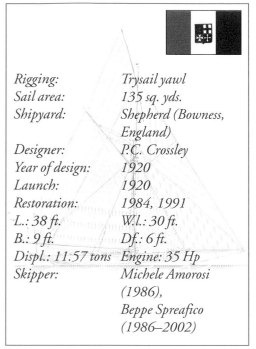

Rigging:	Trysail yawl
Sail area:	135 sq. yds.
Shipyard:	Shepherd (Bowness, England)
Designer:	P.C. Crossley
Year of design:	1920
Launch:	1920
Restoration:	1984, 1991
L.: 38 ft.	W.l.: 30 ft.
B.: 9 ft.	Df.: 6 ft.
Displ.: 11.57 tons	Engine: 35 Hp
Skipper:	Michele Amorosi (1986), Beppe Spreafico (1986–2002)

BELOW: *Porto Santo Stefano 1992,* Elpis *under sail (Photo: J. Taylor).*

FOLLOWING PAGE: Elpis *in the same regatta (Photo: J. Taylor).*

Vistona

Originally designed as a cutter, this boat was built in 1937 according to a project drawn up by the designer MacPherson Campbell, former partner (or pupil) of William Fife, and later head draftsman at A.M. Dickie and Sons. The boat was originally called *Nancy Rose*, although it appears that it never actually sailed under this name.

After World War II, it was bought by Captain Campbell, a retired Royal Navy officer, and renamed *Vistona*. During the late 1940s it sailed from Scotland to the Mediterranean, where it visited Spain, the French coasts, San Remo in Italy (where Gian Marco Borea saw it for the first time), Corsica, and Greece.

When Campbell died at the end of the 1950s, the boat was sold to a company from Panama headed by a Mrs. Potin, and with a Spanish crew it was used as a charter yacht based at Cannes in France. The 1955 Register of Yachts shows it as belonging to Steengood & Co. Ltd. During this period, the peak was removed and the trysail spanker replaced by a gaff-rigged spanker with a very long, low boom, probably to make it easier for a small crew to maneuver the boat.

When discovered by Gian Marco Borea in the port of Cannes in 1967, it was clearly in a neglected state (and had been for some five years). Although it was for sale, it lacked any sails, the original compass, and most of the rigging, which had all been stolen during this period. Thus it was that Gian Marco began a long period of hard work, lasting from 1967 through 1979, during which he lived on board the boat while he restored it. In 1969 he had it transformed from a cutter to a gaff-rigged ketch. He did most of the work himself, only occasionally calling in craftsmen or small shipyards to carry out certain jobs. The interior was refitted without making any fundamental changes to the original design, with the ancient mahogany and brass restored to its original splendor. Only the large forepeak, which had originally been used as a sail store, was partially converted into a cabin with two berths.

The teak hull laid over oak ribs had managed to survive the years of neglect and five years of constant mooring rather well. The transformation of the sail plan was done gradually, without changing the mast or its position, and as a result managing to increase the boat's speed when running free. Thus it is that *Vistona*, with well-adjusted sails, can maintain its course without anyone at the rudder at various reaches, with its 240 square yards of canvas, showing that the new rig is both practical and efficacious. The original cockpit with its small cover is shown in the photographs contained in Eric Hiscock's book *Cruising Under Sail*.

Gian Marco was very proud of the boat, which has displayed excellent seaworthiness, speed, and stability, even though it remains a very simple vessel, suited to true sailing enthusiasts. Its immense flush deck is both attractive and highly functional, providing ample space for maneuvers even in the worst of seas and winds. The spanker and jib halyard winches are not geared down and so have to be handled carefully and require physical effort. The blocks are of the traditional type – yet another feature that does not make sailing this yacht an easy task.

In 1971, the *Vistona* completed its first training cruises in the Mediterranean. At present it is a nominal member of the "Venturieri" fleet based at Chioggia, Italy, and in recent years it has taken part in numerous vintage yacht meetings. For

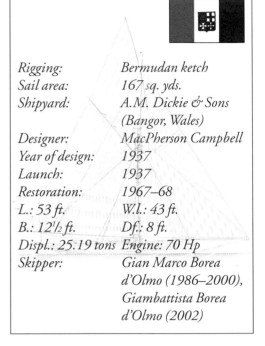

Rigging:	Bermudan ketch
Sail area:	167 sq. yds.
Shipyard:	A.M. Dickie & Sons (Bangor, Wales)
Designer:	MacPherson Campbell
Year of design:	1937
Launch:	1937
Restoration:	1967–68
L.: 53 ft.	W.l.: 43 ft.
B.: 12½ ft.	Df.: 8 ft.
Displ.: 25.19 tons	Engine: 70 Hp
Skipper:	Gian Marco Borea d'Olmo (1986–2000), Giambattista Borea d'Olmo (2002)

BELOW: *The ketch* Vistona – *the boat of my dear departed friend, Gian Marco Borea d'Olmo (Photo: S. Piano).*

over 20 years it sailed throughout the Mediterranean with Gian Marco Borea at the helm: they were not only the "perfect couple," but also represented the perfect symbiosis between man and boat. Gian Marco would have liked to have seen his *Vistona* return to its original trysail-cutter rig, but as the "patriarch" of the "Venturieri," he was waiting for a more opportune moment to carry out this project.

Up until now *Vistona* has always sailed without the aid of electronic instruments (if you exclude the echo-sounder used when dropping anchor). In fact, this is one of the attractive features of the boat together with its dark hull and aggressive-looking, sleek bow dominated by a sturdy bowsprit, and, of course, the fact that it has

had a total of only three owners in nearly 60 years of sailing.

During the course of its existence, *Vistona* has flown the burgee of the Royal Ocean Racing Club (RORC), of the Ocean Cruising Club (OCC), of the CVA, and of the "Venturieri," together with other boats like *Colomba, Alzavola, Cerida, Elpis, Four Winds,* and *Estella*. To understand just how much *Vistona* meant to Gian Marco, you have only to think about these words: "*I find her extremely attractive, I love her waterline and the warmth exuded by her old timbers with that unique smell of the sea…*"

Vistona has recently left the Adriatic to return to the Tyrrhenian Sea, and she is to undergo some important refitting in the near future, particularly on her hull.

BELOW: *Imperia 1986,* Vistona *during a regatta (Photo: F. Semeria).*

Colin Archer

During recent vintage yacht regattas, there have been few yachts derived from this type of northern European boat, which I think is worth mentioning briefly here. It could be said that since 1919, the year in which the Norwegian cutter *Oeger* reached the southern seas, a great number of cruisers have been inspired by the lines created by designer Colin Archer.

This great architect, born in Norway, was originally from a Scottish family. The Norwegian Society for the Development of Fishing commissioned him to carry out a study aimed at improving the seagoing qualities of the old, local fishing-boats. So it was that he began designing decked boats with a higher freeboard; in fact, his were almost lifeboat cutters (the famous *Redninskoite*), boats employed to safeguard local fishing-boats during the winter months.

The first of its kind was launched in 1892 and the seaworthiness and navigational qualities of these boats even in the worst conditions, like the famous Le Havre and Bristol "pilots," was to become almost proverbial. The fact that they were not very good at sailing upwind was of relatively little importance. These boats had a considerable reserve of buoyancy – with an upright keel that gave them a certain propensity towards getting stranded – a curved sternpost, and a crew that lived on board. The lines of the "Colin Archer" were of the traditional Nordic variety; the sections were based on the Viking model, and the hull ratios were similar to those of the English "pilots."

These features were partially modified over the years, but the simple lines were copied by numerous European and American designers. Boats with cutter, ketch, and yawl rigs were created, all suited to long-distance cruising; heavy, yet safe boats. The architect Alan Buchanan created *Karin III*, a boat that was to become extremely famous in the English Channel. In the yachting field, those boats based on the "Colin Archer" were never going to rival others in pure racing terms, but their qualities on the open sea were never questioned. Johan Anker, the most famous of Norwegian yacht designers, once said of them: "… *As long as there are sailing craft on our waters, their memory will live on.*" At Imperia I encountered two boats based on the "Colin Archer": *Aurura* and *Tartuga*. The former had in fact been a lifeboat during its early days: a very heavy boat that during the course of its transformation was rendered more agile, a yacht that never cut a poor figure in regattas. *Tartuga* was a more elegant vessel (I use the past tense because it no longer exists), and with a good wind even managed to perform well when sailed close-hauled.

Aurora

Rigging:	Bermudan ketch
Sail area:	126 sq. yds.
Shipyard:	Allmaysk-Yern Urust (Sweden)
Designer:	Colin Archer
Year of design:	1905
Launch:	1908
Restoration:	1979–86
L.: 35 ft.	W.l.: 33 ft.
B.: 14 ft.	Df.: 6 ft.
Displ.: 13.23 tons	Engine: 47 Hp
Skipper:	Ernesto Paesani (1987–2000)

BELOW: *Imperia 1996,* Aurora *during a regatta. The boat has an oak bottom (the original) and a pine topside. The remaining original ribs are made of Swedish pine, while the new ones are in acacia laminate (Photo: F. Ramella).*

PREVIOUS PAGE: *Imperia, September 2000, the Colin Archer boat* Aurora, *a boat that has had an adventurous life in the North Sea (Photo: J. Taylor).*

This boat has had an adventurous life that began at the turn of the last century in Sweden. It was one of the many hulls originally designed by Colin Archer as a lifeboat, and we do not know what name it was launched with back in 1908. In fact, during the early years of its life it worked as a lifeboat, and it was subsequently used as a pilot during the latter years of sailing's "golden age." After a period of being laid up, it was recouped by a yachting club and fitted out as a training boat with the name *Niagara*.

It was reorganized internally for this purpose, with the construction of 16 new bunks, but its activity as a training vessel was to come to a premature end one stormy night when it crashed into the rocks. The crew were saved, but *Niagara* was seriously damaged on its left-hand foreside. The stempost was broken and a hole was smashed through the side of the boat, with a series of ribs getting broken in the process. It returned to the shipyard but was immediately abandoned, and it was not until a yachting enthusiast rediscovered the boat some time later that the necessary repair work was completed.

The original sail plan was modified for the first time during this period, and the original Colin Archer was transformed into a gaff-rigged ketch. This was a positive period in the life of a boat that had in the meantime been renamed *Ulla* and was sailing the northern seas once again.

Then in 1968 it was bought by an Italian doctor who worked in Sweden. A small auxiliary engine was fitted and the boat was transferred during the owner's holidays, first to Germany, then to The Netherlands, and then on to Marseilles via the French inland waterways. After routine servicing, the boat sailed the last leg of its journey to the port of Grazie in Italy, where due to repeated theft and bureaucratic difficulties, it was once again left, semi-abandoned, a local attraction as it withered at the quayside. The wind, rain, and sun had bleached the colors of its flag; its end could not have been far off. A leak on its starboard side led it to sink one night, and the task of restoring the boat became difficult and costly, so much so that the owner decided to throw in the towel and have *Ulla* demolished.

At this point it seemed to be all over. However, in October 1979 the soon-to-be-demolished hull was lucky enough to be noticed by Ernesto Paesani, who could foresee that this wreck had the makings of his dream boat. He wasted no time in buying it and personally began the long job of restoring it: this took a total of six years and 6,000 working hours, taking up every free moment he had. Eighty percent of the ribs and 50 percent of the planking was replaced, new main and mizzenmasts were made from Douglas fir, and a new teak deck and deckhouse roof were fitted. In the end, *Aurora* (named after Ernesto's wife) emerged in all its splendor, the result of its owner's love and tenacity.

I could hardly fail to notice the boat and was on board during its first regatta in the waters of Imperia. That was back in September 1987: the boat slid across the rippling waves created by a fresh west wind, as stable and powerful as ever. A few days later, it was awarded a plaque as the oldest boat present at the Imperia meeting.

Gipsy

This is a beautiful hull weighing 12 tons with a limited freeboard, built at the Echevarrieta & Larringa shipyard in Cadiz, Spain, in 1927. It was built at the same time as the great Spanish training yacht *Juan Sebastiano de Elcano*. Since 1956 its owner has really looked after the boat, maintaining it in perfect condition. It was restored in 1969 at the Tarragona shipyards in Spain, where new "Hood" sails were fitted. *Gipsy* has taken part in the past eight editions of the Almirante Conde de Barcelona Trophy held at Palma de Mallorca, where it has distinguished itself by winning numerous victories and honors. In 1992 and 1995 it underwent careful refitting by the skilled staff of Escola Taller in the Port of Tarragona. It is currently a member of Tarragona's Royal Yachting Club.

Rigging:	*Bermudan ketch*
Sail area:	*132 sq. yds.*
Shipyard:	*Echevarrieta & Larringa (Cadiz, Spain)*
Designer:	*Colin Archer*
Year of design:	*1905*
Launch:	*1927*
Restoration:	*1969 Tarragona shipyards (Spain)*
L.: 38 ft.	*W.l.: 30 ft.*
B.: 12 ft.	*Df.: 1½ ft.*
Displ.: 13.78 tons	*Engine: 45 Hp*
Skipper:	*Ricardo Vilar*

BELOW: Gipsy *during a regatta (Photo: N. Martinez).*

Tartuga

Rigging:	Trysail sloop
Sail area:	60 sq. yds.
Shipyard:	Viareggio shipyards (Italy)
Designer:	Colin Archer
Year of design:	1928
Launch:	1951
Restoration:	1988 Tomei shipyard (Viareggio, Italy)
L.: 40 ft.	W.l.: 28 ft.
B.: 11 ft.	Df.: 5 ft.
Displ.: 9.59 tons	Engine: 90 Hp
Skipper:	Renzo Ricciardi (1989)

*T*artuga was designed as a trysail rig. Its owner, Riccardo Sella of Biella, sailed it all over the Mediterranean. A most valuable record of the boat's activity is contained in *The Story of Coxswain Mario Jacopini of Viareggio* (only 50 copies were published, not for public sale, in 1968), which is the story of a return voyage, from Viarregio in Italy to Ibiza, that began on June 27, and ended on August 30, 1963. Mario Jacopini, born in 1894 and a former merchant seaman, was an elderly man when he made the trip and he gives a brilliant, detailed description of the voyage, undertaken in the company of its owner.

All of *Tartuga*'s documents are kept at the Fondazione Sella in Biella, Italy. In 1988 the boat was sold to Renzo Ricciardi, who had it refitted at the Tomei shipyard in Viareggio: the mast and gaff were rebuilt, the bowsprit lengthened, and the boat re-acquired its original trysail rig (after having been converted to a gaff-rigged sloop). All maneuvers are manual, including weighing the anchor. The green hull with its light-colored deckhouse had copper riveting and an abundance of Corsican red pine.

Unfortunately, the boat is no more. On the night of February 14, 1991 it was destroyed by an arsonist as it hauled up in the small yard at Santa Teresa di Gallura. Thus these words constitute an epitaph to an elegant boat with classic "Colin Archer" lines and a harmonious sail plan.

RIGHT: Tartuga *during a regatta (Photo: S. Pesato).*

BELOW: *Imperia, 1989, the "Colin Archer" boat* Tartuga – *a meteorite that has disappeared into the void (Photo: S. Piano).*

Working Boats

The working boats are a wonderful sight at the vintage yacht meetings: these splendid historical vessels have served man well and kept him company during years of hard work and have provided considerable satisfaction as well. Former fishing boats include *Circe*, since refitted completely as a charter yacht. Likewise, *Madre Giulia* and *Isla Ebusitana*, both designed as merchant vessels. A successful transformation of the former auxiliary sailing ship *Gerlando* has given us the luxury yacht *Taitù* (later renamed *Raphaelo*). The only original part of all these boats is the shell; all the original sailing equipment has been replaced. The same goes for *Marcantonio*, *Oloforne*, and *Intrepido*, three former cargo boats. Among the working boats, *Fleur de Lys*, a former fishing boat from Camaret, France, is something of an exception in that efforts have been made to try and conserve its original sail plan.

Thus it proves rather difficult when observing the modernized versions of these boats to perceive anything of their working past (a past that among other things has rarely been documented), especially in that they have all but disappeared from the Mediterranean, with the exception of a few rare examples left in Spain and Portugal. The picture is very different on the coast of Maine in the United States, where about 30 fishing or merchant schooners have survived thanks to the importance given to that area's maritime heritage and the more favorable historical and environmental conditions present.

Bourru III

Rigging:	Trysail yawl
Sail area:	144 sq. yds.
Shipyard:	Bernard Frères (La Tremblade, France)
Designer:	Marcel Bernard
Year of design:	1958
Launch:	1959
L.: 42 ft.	W.l.: 38 ft.
B.: 13 ft.	Df.: 5 ft.
Displ.: 15.98 tons	Engine: 65 Hp
Skipper:	Michel Simon (1987)

This boat was designed in 1958, having been commissioned by a group of friends, the founders of the Connaissances Sous-Marines Research Center set up for research and explorative purposes, namely Commander Gilbert Mahé, Pierre Gaisseau of the Orinoco expedition, town-planner Paul Herbé, doctor Charles Henry, chief architect Bernard Zehrfuss, lawyer Jean-Pierre Le Mee, administrator Patrice Moulin-Ferrand, reporter Michel Simon, and Jacques Ertaud, a cameraman from the Jacques Cousteau Group. Steph Simon, who had always had contact with marine and maritime things, was given the job of overseeing the construction of the boat that was to have been the base for the group's missions. Unfortunately, the group disbanded before the project could be concluded, and thus *Bourru III* became Steph Simon's boat and is currently owned by his son, Michel.

The choice of boat was dictated by the desire for a boat shaped like the fishing boats of Charente and Oleron in France with a large hull with a low draft, cement ballast, and guaranteed seaworthiness. The boat was built quickly and was ready for launching on February 9, 1959.

Bourru III has oak framing and sides, a Burmese teak lounge and hatchways, a Javanese teak deck (the timbers were recouped from the flooring in the Wagram Room in Paris), spruce masting, Oregon pine internal furnishings, and an oak keel containing 4,180 pounds of lead.

The boat has taken part in various vintage yacht meetings (including the Nioulargue and gatherings at Imperia and Porto Cervo in Sardinia) and has been much admired for the sleek, seaworthy lines of its white hull, which perfectly match its ocher-colored sails.

RIGHT: *An aerial photo of* Bourru III *taken during the 1992 Nioulargue (Photo courtesy of M. Simon).*

BELOW: *Nioulargue 1992,* Bourru III *during a regatta (Photo courtesy of M. Simon).*

Cala Millo

Built in 1948 at the shipyards in Palma de Mallorca, this boat with a sturdy pitch pine hull has changed names a number of times (it was once *Antonio Matutes*, then *Outlaw*, then *Jola*).

From 1973 through 1977 it was repeatedly refitted at Ibiza and at Vancia and Marseilles in France. It is 140 feet long and has a tonnage of 188.5 tons. Below deck there are nine cabins with a total of 18 berths.

ABOVE: *The brigantine* Cala Millo *(Photo courtesy of N. Legler).*

Rigging:	Brigantine schooner
Sail area:	598 sq. yds.
Shipyard:	Majorca shipyards (Palma de Mallorca, Spain)
Designer:	The shipyard
Year of design:	1948
Launch:	1948
Restoration:	1977 Ibiza shipyards (Spain)
L.: 140 ft.	W.l.: 98 ft.
B.: 27 ft.	Df.: 11 ft.
Displ.: 188.5 tons	Engine: 200 Hp

Circe

This boat was designed as a Norwegian fishing cutter for the North Sea, but in 1947 it was completely refitted as a cargo boat for working around Bergen in Norway and the local fjords. At the beginning of 1979 the owners started work on converting this old fishing vessel into a cruiser. The work took three years and was supervised by the same people who had converted the famous triple-masted *Lindo*. The deck is in Scandinavian pine and pitch pine. A photo published in *Yachting World* in 1983 shows the boat already has a trysail rig with two gaff topsails. The interior is in pine, teak, and oak.

At Imperia in 1989 the boat won all the regattas it entered and was awarded the special Cape Horn medal. Sailing aboard *Circe* is a fantastic experience that I relive each time I re-read the article I wrote describing the second of *Circe*'s regattas:

"*Thursday September 21 – 08.45. For the first time in many years I went on board a boat flying the Austrian flag, colors that disappeared from the seas after 1918. Yesterday I followed its entrance into the port from the quayside – this timid, solemn boat with its black, Nordic hull, as fascinating and yet simple as ever. Its name is* Circe, *a mythical name that does not seem particularly suited to the cold, rocky waters of the Sognefiord or the old Norwegian landing-stages at Narvik, Tromso, or Hammerfest. This old 66.14-ton fishing schooner was launched in 1915; one look at it tells you that it belongs to a distant past. As I came on board I was met by that typical smell of tar and well-seasoned hemp impregnated with sea-salt. The deck seams appear to be original, as do the heavy blocks, the hand winch, the structures, the deckhouse, the skylights, the sail cloth, and the mast grommets. Each thing eloquently testifies to the passing of time. This is an emotional experience for me, being on this pleasantly simple boat, totally devoid of any ostentation, because its threadbare sheets and its booms worn and cracked by the wind, rain, and sun exude a sense of an old working-life amid the*

Rigging:	Trysail schooner
Sail area:	263 sq. yds.
Shipyard:	Ring Andersen (Svendborg, Denmark)
Designer:	The shipyard
Year of design:	1914
Launch:	1915
Restoration:	1947, 1979–81 (Denmark)
L.: 77 ft.	W.l.: 70 ft.
B.: 16 ft.	Df.: 9 ft.
Displ.: 66.14 tons	Engine: 120 Hp
Skipper:	Wolfgang Scholz (1989)

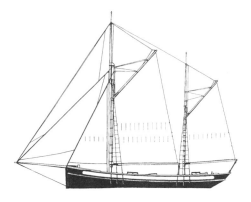

rough, unkind waves of the Atlantic Ocean and the North Sea. Remote thoughts and sensations come flooding back, as do memories of my late friend, Vittorio G. Rossi, who, were he on board right now, would be as happy as a lark. Circe, this passionate, elegant lady of the seas, has come through the test of time well. The hull is not too heavy, the sail plan and masting are well balanced. At the entrance to the port, right where the international monument to the Cape Horn Navigator stands, the customary two blasts on the ship's siren are sounded as a sign of respect, a ritual that is repeated several times a day.

Out to sea, with her spankers and jibs already trimmed, this schooner is truly in its element. A slight mist to the west and a tepid sun struggling to shine through the sails are the welcoming signs preceding a promising day's sailing. There's a good wind blowing from the south-east, perfect for this queen of the seas as she safely glides along, listing slightly, at seven knots. Aft, she leaves a barely perceptible wake on the crests of the waves; a docile, easily-handled vessel, she will win all of the regattas in her class. Each time she is put about with the sails balanced, her speed thrills; she glides across the short sea with a barely perceptible roll.

The boat's graceful lines, the low deckhouse, and the 263 square yards of canvas make her a true racer. I have rediscovered what I was looking for, the forgotten world of Jack London and his fishing schooners, which may have been slightly heavier but were similarly seaworthy. The skipper, a young Austrian, Wolfgang Scholz, is working with a makeshift crew – including an American lad who had dreamt of the 'dolce vita' and instead finds himself wearing away the palms of his hand handling these rough halyards – and is pleased to have me on board. I repay his hospitality by giving a hand with the maneuvers, although this hull, which responds brilliantly to every command, even the simplest one, seems to pay heed to its crew's every move.

The silence is broken only by the voices of the jury, which come in via radio and interrupt my journey into the distant past, contrasting clearly with that world of oil lamps with their gimbals still to be seen below deck. The buoys are far off, veiled by the mist: we move forward, checking the sails of the other yachts here and there on the horizon. We have been among the leaders virtually since the beginning of the regatta, if we can call this festive meeting of old boats a regatta. Between one tack and another, we get a glimpse of that 'dolce vita' sought by Bruce; Wolfgang emerges from the hatchway with some focaccia (flat Italian bread) and Vermentino wine, genuine local products from the harsh yet generous land of Liguria. They won't forget this experience! Imperia wins sailing's prize for its humanity and warmth, and these regular appointments are now a must for yachtsmen, welcomed as they are to a town where sea-faring history and tradition blend together into an irresistible attraction."

THIS PAGE: *Imperia 1989, two shots of* Circe. *Below deck you can still detect the smell of tar. The schooner is fitted out for charter hire (Photos: R. Minervini).*

Fleur de Lys

The "working" boat *Fleur de Lys* (the name is the same as that of the American schooner that used to race in the North Sea at the beginning of the 20th century), together with *Circe*, is a fine example of what sailing was once really all about. This former *langoustier* (lobster-fishing boat) launched in 1926 on behalf of a fisherman from Camoret, France, a certain Le Roy, continued to fish right up until the outbreak of World War II. It clearly had no engine at that time.

After the war it was recouped by the French Navy and transferred to Toulon, where it was transformed into a training yacht for navy cadets. In 1960 the boat took up fishing again, this time in the Mediterranean under the unusual name of *Miniguella*. The rigging was removed and the vivarium taken out, while a steering wheel was installed on the engine hatchway.

The years went by, and then in October 1981 José Masseda, founder of the Société Tropézienne des Voiliers de Tradition (Saint Tropez Society of Traditional Sailing Ships) and of the magazine *Capian*, noticed the boat, which by now resembled something of a wreck, and persuaded the owner to sell it. Restoration work designed to get the boat back to seaworthiness was overseen by the Maritime Cultural Committee. Subsequently, the hull was restored, the keel bolts were checked, and the mast was replaced. All work was carried out strictly according to the original designs of the traditional *langoustiers*.

In 1987 the boat was bought by Alain Fournier, who continued refitting operations. In 1989, after the gaff-topsail pole had fallen down, the boat was rigged without the fixed gaff-topsail, as it had originally been. Work continued in 1992, when the entire hull was re-riveted and the keel bolts replaced. Finally, the deck was recently rebuilt using $^3/_4$-inch iroko timbers glued onto $^1/_2$-inch marine plywood.

Fleur de Lys has an oak keel, framing and bottom, and a pitch pine topside. It is not an easy boat to maneuver, and the rudder is hard to control. The mast is 43 feet off the deck, while the boom and the spanker gaff are 28 feet and 25 feet respectively. The boat once again appears as a typical Breton boat, with its orange-colored hull and matching ocher jib. The shrouds (which the navigation lights rest on) are held taut by vintage dead-eyes.

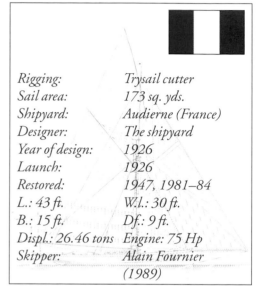

Rigging:	Trysail cutter
Sail area:	173 sq. yds.
Shipyard:	Audierne (France)
Designer:	The shipyard
Year of design:	1926
Launch:	1926
Restored:	1947, 1981–84
L.: 43 ft.	W.l.: 30 ft.
B.: 15 ft.	Df.: 9 ft.
Displ.: 26.46 tons	Engine: 75 Hp
Skipper:	Alain Fournier
	(1989)

THIS PAGE: *Imperia 1989,* Fleur de Lys, *a traditional* langoustier *launched in 1926 at Camaret (Photos: S. Pesato and R. Minervini).*

Francesco Petrarca

(sometime Gerlando)

Rigging:	Three-masted schooner
Sail area:	744 sq. yds.
Shipyard:	Benetti (Viareggio, Italy)
Designer:	The shipyard
Year of design:	1937
Launch:	1938
Restoration:	1960 Valdettaro shipyard (La Spezia, Italy)
L.: 124 ft.	W.l.: 112 ft.
B.: 27½ ft.	Df.: 13 ft.
Displ.: 460.8 tons	Engines (2): 450 Hp
Skipper:	Paul Simmonds (1987–91), Steve Ashford (1992–2000)

The Benetti shipyards were commissioned to build this schooner – designed to transport marble from the Apuan Alps – one of the last Italian cargo boats of its kind. It was launched with the name *Gerlando*, and it kept this name until the late 1950s. In 1960 it ran aground during a storm as a result of engine failure, and a British helicopter had to fly in supplies and parts in order that the boat be repaired so it could reach the nearest port.

It was bought in Alexandria (in Egypt) by a Panamanian company (shipping marble no longer being a profitable business). This company wanted to transform it into an auxiliary yacht given the good condition of the hull. Thus it was that on July 15, 1961 a newly transformed schooner called *Taitù* was launched at the Valdettaro yard in La Spezia, Italy.

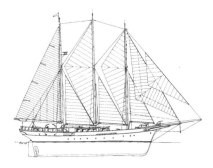

The transformation of the original hull had involved months of research, given the new standards of safety and comfort required of the restored boat. This research was carried out by the American Bureau of Shipping and was designed to ensure the boat the top class-rating for the hull and engine installation. Only the shell remained of the old *Gerlando* at this point. The masts, superstructure, engine equipment, hatchways, installations, and various fittings soon disappeared altogether, leaving just the sturdy hull with its oak framing, oak and pine planking, and iroko backing throughout the topside. The rigging was copied from the traditional three-masted, staysail-schooner design, not so much for the sake of performance but rather for that of appearance, given the specific nature of the hull. The masts were built from silver spruce and are partially hollow with a pear-drop section; the elliptical-section booms are also made from silver spruce. The rigging was made by Camper & Nicholson of England.

As *Taitù*, this three-masted schooner sailed the Mediterranean for a period of about 20 years, during which time – thankfully – it changed owners only once. In 1982 it was bought by an English yachtsman and its home port became Cannes in France. The boat's interior is truly sumptuous: the lounge extends the entire length of the main deckhouse and is the most fascinating part of the boat. During recent years, furniture, paintings, antiques, and carpets have been used to furnish the interior, while the operations rooms have the very latest equipment.

As a result of the considerable weight of the hull (the only completely original part of the boat), *Francesco Petrarca* is not fast, but it is certainly comfortable and relaxing. It needs a good wind of at least 20 knots in order to pick up a speed of 4 or 5 knots. Overall, the sail plan is extremely harmonious and is well distributed across this wonderfully evocative hull, a true testimony to the expertise of Viareggio's old boat-builders and carpenters.

BELOW: *Cannes 2000, the three-masted schooner* Francesco Petrarca, *formerly known as* Gerlando *and* Taitù *(Photo: J. Taylor).*

Intrepido

Launched as the cargo boat *Padre Pio* in Riccione, Italy, and subsequently transformed into a motor trawler, *Intrepido* was discovered at Porto Garibaldi in Italy in 1972 by the sports journalist Alfredo Pigna. The boat was in the water but was in a state of complete neglect. After four years' work at the Civitanova Marche boatyard in Italy, the old hull was finally transformed into a trysail schooner.

Intrepido has oak planking on the topside and larch planking on the bottom, steel ribs, and oak beams. The original larch deck was completely refitted using the same type of wood. The mizzenmast comes from an old Dutch sailing boat demolished in the 1940s at Civitanova Marche. The boat has no winches, so each maneuver has to be performed manually.

With a 10-ton keel, *Intrepido* can hug the wind to 40° and reach a speed of 10 knots, especially when sailed on a close reach. A fine figurehead, the work of Helmut Schmalz, can be seen beneath the boat's sturdy boom. The boat is currently used as a charter yacht.

Rigging:	Trysail schooner
Sail area:	478 sq. yds.
Shipyard:	Ponzoni (Riccione, Italy)
Designer:	Ponzoni
Year of design:	1945
Launch:	1945
Restoration:	1972
L.: 100 ft.	W.l.: 70 ft.
B.: 18 ft.	Df.: 12 ft.
Displ.: 49.6 tons	Engine: 200 Hp
Skipper:	Alfredo Pigna (1986–87)

BELOW: *The schooner* Intrepido, *a vintage Adriatic vessel (Photo courtesy of A. Pigna).*

Isla Ebusitana

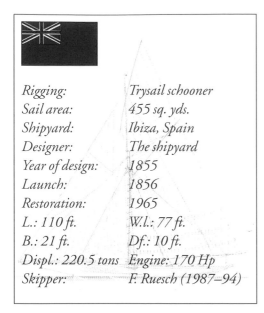

Rigging:	Trysail schooner
Sail area:	455 sq. yds.
Shipyard:	Ibiza, Spain
Designer:	The shipyard
Year of design:	1855
Launch:	1856
Restoration:	1965
L.: 110 ft.	W.l.: 77 ft.
B.: 21 ft.	Df.: 10 ft.
Displ.: 220.5 tons	Engine: 170 Hp
Skipper:	F. Ruesch (1987–94)

RIGHT: *Imperia 1994, the schooner* Isla Ebusitana, *once a cargo vessel, now a charter yacht (Photo: S. Pesato).*

*I*sla Ebusitana, launched in 1856 in Ibiza, is the oldest of all the boats that have taken part in the vintage yacht meetings held in Imperia. Originally it was fitted out to transport salt from the Balearic islands to the Spanish coast.

Despite the various modifications it has undergone over the years (an old photograph shows it with just one deckhouse at one time), the sail plan has not changed very much. The two Douglas fir masts were rebuilt in France, while general restoration and reconstruction work was carried out in Venezuela. A heavy boat with a double-planked hull, it has a 20-foot bowsprit topped by a figurehead of a dog's head.

Currently used for charter purposes, it still has a lot of its original fittings, blocks and belaying pins, and four-way fairleads, all of which testify to its distant past. It performs well under sail, and with a wind of 18 knots can reach a speed of 5 to 7 miles an hour. However, it clearly suffers a little when sailed close-hauled. It currently winters in the Caribbean – three months of splendid sailing away from Europe.

Madre Giulia

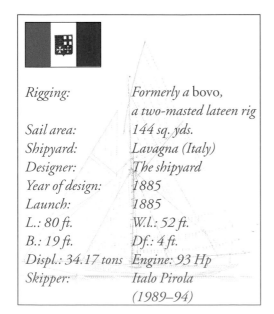

Rigging:	Formerly a bovo, a two-masted lateen rig
Sail area:	144 sq. yds.
Shipyard:	Lavagna (Italy)
Designer:	The shipyard
Year of design:	1885
Launch:	1885
L.: 80 ft.	W.l.: 52 ft.
B.: 19 ft.	Df.: 4 ft.
Displ.: 34.17 tons	Engine: 93 Hp
Skipper:	Italo Pirola (1989–94)

*M*adre Giulia, with its traditionally shaped hull, resembles the old Ligurian *bovo*, a two-masted lateen rig, and in fact that must be what it originally was when launched back in 1885 at the Lavagna shipyards in Italy. In 1916 it belonged to the Brusco brothers of Riva Trigoso, Italy, who rigged it for coastal trading in the northern Tyrrhenian Sea.

In 1936 it was bought by Attilio Bregante, nicknamed "Tilin," who continued to use it for trading in the company of the last remaining boats of its ilk along this part of the Ligurian coast. It was sunk during World War II, but "Tilin" managed to salvage and repair it and continued to use the boat until 1965 for transporting wine before beaching it forever at Sestri Levante in Italy, where it remained for years before being discovered by Italo Pirola.

The new owner attempted the rather difficult restoration operation needed if it were ever to sail again. The boat was completely dismantled and reassembled over a period of three years, with the owner spending every free weekend he had refitting the boat himself at a makeshift yard.

The boat's holds disappeared for good, the ultra-seasoned wood (mostly oak) was recouped, and a new bridge was built, which has made navigation and life on board much more comfortable. The present sail plan consists of a spanker and three jibs, and with the boat running on the quarter with a 25-knot wind, it can get up to a speed of 7 knots, a veritable sprint for such a fat-bellied vessel weighing in at 34.17 tons.

Marcantonio

This sturdy trysail schooner was launched at the SIPA yard in Porto Santa Stefano in Italy in 1947. This yard was specialized at the time in the construction of trawlers, and there were still numerous traditional carpenters working on such boats. Their skills are clearly evident from a glance at the interior and, above all, at the hull of this particular vessel. *Marcantonio* was fitted out as a cargo boat, but it would seem that immediately after World War II it was used to transport Jews towards Palestine, as were a number of similar Italian boats at that time.

During the 1960s it was used as a supply vessel for the oil rigs in the North Sea. It was then used simply as a cargo boat. Someone discovered it and decided to transform it into a yacht, but the costs involved and a series of legal problems led to the boat being abandoned in the port of Civitanova Marche in Italy. This seemed the end of the story, but a group of sailing enthusiasts managed to get it back in working shape again. While the framing and hull had survived the ravages of time, there was the problem of a new sail plan and the search for two new masts (for which two fir trees were ordered to be cut down in distant Czechoslovakia).

Today, with its 2½-inch oak planking and without any winches for hoisting the sails, the boat once again resembles the original drawings. It is currently crowned by a beautiful figurehead of Cleopatra (although we do not know whether this dates from the launching of the boat or was carved at a later time).

ABOVE AND BELOW LEFT: *Details of the boat's interior.*
BELOW: *A photograph of* Marcantonio, *an old auxiliary cargo boat from the late 1940s.*

Rigging:	Auxiliary sailing boat
Sail area:	837 sq. yds.
Shipyard:	SIPA (Porto Santa Stefano, Italy)
Designer:	The shipyard
Year of design:	1947
Launch:	1947
Restoration:	1991 Ascolani naval shipyard (Italy)
L.: 125 ft.	W.l.: 63 ft.
B.: 20 ft.	Df.: 12 ft.
Displ.: 141.1 tons	Engine: 320 Hp
Skipper:	Salvatore Pittorru (1990–91)

Oloferne

Rigging:	Trysail schooner
Sail area:	120 sq. yds.
Shipyard:	Nicola Russo (Palermo, Italy)
Designer:	Conti
Year of design:	1942
Launch:	1944
Restoration:	1967
L.: 73 ft.	W.l.: 60 ft.
B.: 17 ft.	Df.: 6 ft.
Displ.: 25.25 tons	Engine: 160 Hp
Skipper:	Giuseppe Mele (1986)

*A*t the Imperia meeting in 1986, the trysail schooner *Oloferne*, managed by the Oloferne Sailing Company, livened things up a little. This former working boat, used for years to transport foodstuffs (wine, oil, citrus fruit, cereals, and flour) from Palermo in Italy to the island of Ustica, was restored in 1958 and 1984. The boat's logbook mentions that it was used for a number of scenes in the film *The Count of Monte Cristo*. At present the boat is employed as a charter yacht.

THIS PAGE: Oloferne, *a schooner currently used as a charter yacht (Photos courtesy of O. Sguazzero).*

Thö Pa Ga

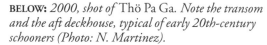

uilt in 1924 in Aguilas, at the Navarro Hermanos shipyard, this boat was originally named *Tres Hermanos* (*Three Brothers*). This traditional 230-ton schooner, with its 1,017 square yards of sails, was used to trade along the coasts of France, Spain, and North Africa at the beginning of the 20th century. The boat's first engine was installed in 1930. It is the only surviving schooner which still has its 120 square yards' hold with a hatchway of 22 square yards. It has seven cabins for charter cruises and was restored in 1978, 1985, and 1996.

Thö Pa Ga was a guest of honor at the vintage yacht regatta held in 1987, when it won first prize for the best-restored boat.

The schooner is currently managed by the Circum Navegaciones Hispania and is available for regattas and for private hire. In 1988 it flew the French flag when it took part in the bicentenary celebrations in Australia. On that occasion, it appeared on television and was chartered daily.

Rigging:	*Trysail schooner*
Sail area:	*1,017 sq. yds.*
Shipyard:	*Navarro Hermanos (Aguilas, Spain)*
Designer:	*The shipyard*
Year of design:	*1923*
Launch:	*1924*
Restoration:	*1978, 1985, 1996*
L.: 140 ft.	*W.l.: 93 ft.*
B.: 24 ft.	*Df.: 12 ft.*
Displ.: 165.3 tons	*Engine: 300 Hp*

BELOW: *2000, shot of* Thö Pa Ga. *Note the transom and the aft deckhouse, typical of early 20th-century schooners (Photo: N. Martinez).*

Wammsch

Rigging:	One-third cutter
Sail area:	57 sq. yds.
Launch:	1952
Restoration:	1987
L.: 42 ft.	W.l.: 35 ft.
B.: 6¾ ft.	Df.: 2¾ ft. (6 ft. with dagger board)
Displ.: 2.76 tons	
Skipper:	Raimund Deibele (1987)

This is one of the few surviving launches used by the German Navy as a training boat. It still has six rows of oars each side for 24 rowers. In the past it took part in 12 editions of Kiel Week in the Marine Cutter Class I. A relatively heavy boat with a one-third rig, it is extremely fast in trading winds and does not beat onto the waves. When sailing close-hauled the water reaches up almost to the stringer.

It was bought in 1985 in Hamburg and returned there after a few seasons spent in the port of Imperia. The boat has oak planking, pine masts, a heavy steel dagger board, and a bowsprit (not original) that fails to balance the boat and tends to make it bear away.

Wammsch is currently used in Germany by a private association for the benefit of young people.

RIGHT: *Imperia, 1987,* Wammsch, *a launch once used by the German Navy (Photo: Baldizzone).*

Classic Boats

This section of the book describes a collection of boats built after 1955, some of which may nevertheless be based on pre-1955 designs. These boats are characteristic of an era not only in terms of boat-building styles and techniques, but above all in the field of racing. Who does not remember the victories of *Levantades*, *Outlaw*, *Rocquette*, *Tarantella*, *Al Na' Ir IV*, *Artica II*, *La Meloria*, *Santander of Wight*, and *Susanna II*? A past era that seems like yesterday.

The racing spirit is more easily understood when it comes to boats of this kind: they resemble each other to a greater extent than the vintage yachts do, not only in terms of size but also in terms of their fittings and sail plans. The vivacity and, if you like, the occasional extreme competitiveness of the crews at regattas would seem to back up this theory. These classic boats are less noble or striking than their elder sisters and were nearly all deliberately designed for one particular type of regatta or other. They boast less brass; the first masts are made of alloy; they have a wider range of winches, a jib furler, or mainsail furler; and they have a clearer deck plan and a gradually increasing sailing area. The construction methods are still traditional ones, with frequent use of laminate materials, but the profiles have lost their rakes (especially astern) while the rigs are nearly always Bermudan.

The chief designers of such boats are Philip Rhodes, Olin Stephens, Robert Clark, Laurent Giles, Peter Nicholson, Eugène Cornu, John Illingworth, and Cesare Sangermani. Of these designers, Giles may be thought of as the true creator of the modern yacht, and Illingworth the inventor of "light displacement." While such boats are not as beautiful as the boats of old, they are perhaps more efficient, safer, and better designed for the purpose for which they were created.

Aigue Blu

Rigging:	Bermudan sloop
Sail area:	156 sq. yds.
Shipyard:	Eigger (Switzerland)
Designer:	André Mauric
Year of design:	1973
Launch:	1973
Restoration:	1988
L.: 43 ft.	W.l.: 37 ft.
B.: 12 ft.	Df.: 7 ft.
Displ.: 9.92 tons	Engine: 35 Hp
Skipper:	Trevor Evans and
	Eric Charpentier
	(1988)

A beautiful hull painted mahogany, the creation of French designer André Mauric, *Aigue Blu* is a very fast boat designed for racing and cruising. In 1974, shortly after its launch, it won the Marseilles Week and a multitude of regattas throughout the Mediterranean.

Its most important honors include second place in the Settimana delle Bocche regatta and victory at the International Mediterranean Championships, thanks to its first place in the Formentor regatta. In Class II of the Giraglia *Aigue Blu* came ninth in 1974, second in 1976, and fourth in 1977, all of this with its original owner, Mr. Fabre, at the helm (he also owned *Chin Blu III*).

In recent years the boat has completed two Atlantic crossings with its owner Eric Charpentier at the helm (he currently skippers *Karenita*). The boat has mahogany planking, a teak flush deck, a transom stern, and an aluminum mast. It was completely refitted in 1988.

Alba

Rigging:	Bermudan yawl
Sail area:	122 sq. yds.
Shipyard:	Abeking & Rasmussen
	(Bremen, Germany)
Designer:	Philip Rhodes
Year of design:	1955
Launch:	1956
Restoration:	1991
L.: 44 ft.	W.l.: 30 ft.
B.: 11 ft.	Df.: 4³⁄₄–8 ft.
Displ.: 14.33 tons	Engine: 28 Hp
Skipper:	Antonio Durante Silva
	(1991), Nello
	Saltalamacchia (1992)

Designed by Philip Rhodes, *Alba* was launched at the Abeking & Rasmussen yard in 1956, fourth in a series of 12 boats (sloops and yawls) of the same design with minimal differences between them. It had been commissioned by a North American owner and was eventually transferred to Europe, where it changed hands a number of times before being bought at Seville and transferred to Italy to be refitted. Due to a series of fortunate coincidences, 40 years later *Alba* is still in excellent condition after restoration work that has preserved the boat's original features. It has taken part in the vintage yacht regattas held in Minorca and Porto Cervo in Sardinia (where it came first in 1991).

Built of mahogany and teak, *Alba* has a light green-colored hull and a harmonious sail plan with raking, elegant lines. The boat was recently sold to a Spanish yachtsman who keeps the boat moored at Alicante. After a long period away, it has begun to take part in vintage yacht meetings once again.

RIGHT: *September 1991, the Bermudan yawl* Alba, *launched at the Abeking & Rasmussen yard in Germany (Photo: R. Villarosa).*

OPPOSITE PAGE: *Porto Cervo, 1991, a fine photograph of* Alba, *designed by Philip Rhodes (Photo: J. Taylor).*

Al Na' Ir

Rigging:	Bermudan sloop
Sail area:	74 sq. yds.
Shipyard:	Carlini (Rimini, Italy)
Designer:	J. Francis Jones
Year of design:	1956
Launch:	1957
Restoration:	1995–97
L.: 31 ft.	W.l.: 23 ft.
B.: 8 ft.	Df.: 5 ft.
Displ.: 7.72 tons	Engine: 28 Hp
Skipper:	Mario Sterzi

*A*l Na' Ir was the first of a series of boats all bearing the same name built by the Carlini shipyard in Rimini, Italy, on behalf of Toni Pierobon. The owner asked the architect, J. Francis Jones, to design this one, while all the subsequent boats of the same name were designed by Sparkman & Stephens.

The boat boasts mahogany planking, a teak deck, a spruce mast, and mahogany ribs. It has had only four owners so far and has taken part in numerous Italian regattas, including the Cannes–Ischia Race in 1960.

After years of cruising along the Lazio coastline of Italy it was purchased in 1995 by the present owner, who has had it completely refitted. This restoration project was completed only in 1997 by Marco Di Martino of Civitavecchia, Italy. The deck, deckhouse, and cockpit were all rebuilt. The boat, which has a rudder-tiller and relatively long keel, is well-balanced under sail and performs best in trading winds.

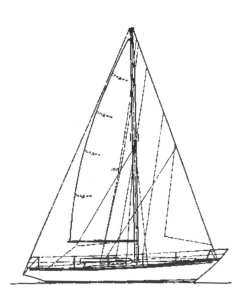

RIGHT: *Imperia, 2000: the sloop* Al Na' Ir *as it sails close-hauled towards the coast (Photo: J. Taylor).*

Al Na' Ir IV

One of Stephens' "22-footers," commissioned by Toni Pierobon and launched in 1967, *Al Na' Ir IV* got its racing career off to a great start with a brilliant performance in the One Ton Cup that very same year. At the start of the race the boat violated the rules when the current caused it to list, as a result of which it touched the starter buoy. It was automatically disqualified but started out just the same and crossed the finishing line a full 20 minutes ahead of the eventual winner! At the helm on that occasion was Beppe Croce, partnered by Stephens and Pierobon.

In 1968 *Al Na' Ir IV* righted the record books, however, when it came second in the One Ton Cup, won the Mediterranean Championships, came first overall in Class III of the Giraglia, and won the Settimana delle Bocche as well as the Montecarlo–Stintino regatta. It was the last boat that Stephens raced all year.

Al Na' Ir IV performs well in a strong breeze, and in a 40-knot headwind it is still unbeatable. Giorgio Falck bought the boat in 1969, and in 1981 the fourth owner, Ernesto Quaranta, put the rudder-tiller back and returned to the original sail plan and the original flat, flexible boom. The mast has always been of aluminum.

The rigging is held by trimmed shrouds. In order to reduce the wet surface Stephens had intended to eliminate that part of the keel plan lying between the ballast and the rudder. The latter, which had remained separate, was moved further astern and arranged in a vertical direction in order to achieve maximum efficiency with the smallest possible rudder-blade.

The boat has also been successful at the Imperia regattas, with Ernesto Quaranta at the helm, as always, and it is always easily identifiable with its blue hull up there among the leaders.

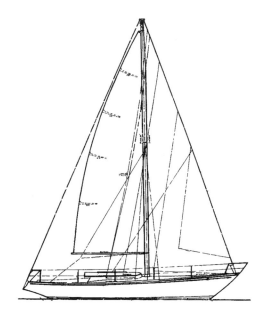

Rigging:	Bermudan sloop
Sail area:	65 sq. yds.
Shipyard:	Carlini (Rimini, Italy)
Designer:	Sparkman & Stephens
Year of design:	1966
Launch:	1967
Restoration:	1983
L.: 37 ft.	W.l.: 27 ft.
B.: 10 ft.	Df.: 6 ft.
Displ.: 7.22 tons	Engine: 18.5 Hp
Skipper:	Ernesto Quaranta
	(1987–92)

RIGHT: *Imperia, the sloop* Al Na' Ir IV *during a regatta (Photo courtesy of M. Quaranta).*

Amadeus Primus

Rigging:	Bermudan sloop
Sail area:	189 sq. yds.
Shipyard:	Vittorio Beltrami (Vernazzola, Genoa, Italy)
Designer:	Laurent Giles
Year of design:	1960
Launch:	1960
Restoration:	1967, 1971, 1989
L.: 57 ft.	W.l.: 47 ft.
B.: 12 ft.	Df.: 5 ft.
Displ.: 18.96 tons	Engine: 152 Hp
Skipper:	Giulio Frezza (1990), Vicenzo Quadrelli (1991, 1992)

BELOW AND OPPOSITE PAGE: *VBR 1999, Amadeus Primus, one of the last yachts launched at the Vernazzola shipyards (Photos: J. Taylor).*

This boat was constructed in 1960 on behalf of a Mr. Vaccari, who named it *Lola*. It was originally rigged as a cutter, with canvas sails, galvanized-iron rigging, no spanker trasto for the gaff sail, and the wheel in the cockpit situated to the left of the center of the boat.

In 1963 it was renamed *Bigrin*. From 1967 through 1976 it was owned by a Mr. Pozzi, who had some initial refitting work done to the boat. In 1969 the old rigging was replaced by stainless steel rigging, the boom was shortened by 6 feet in order to limit the boat's weather-helm tendencies, while the keel was lightened by about 1,780 pounds of lead so as to remedy the hull's excessive stern-heaviness. In 1971 the deck was rebuilt, the deckhouse restored, a "coffee grinder" installed, and the cockpit rebuilt.

The boat acquired fame for its worthy performances in the Santa Margherita–Capraia, Genoa–Alassio, and Giraglia Regattas (in the latter it came ninth in 1967, third in 1972 – Class 1B, and second in 1973) and during Genoa Sailing Week, where it raced against boats of the caliber of *Levantades*, *Tarantella*, *Mabelle*, and others.

In 1986 *Amadeus Primus* was bought by Franco Villani and was renamed *Vea*. Then in 1989 it was finally sold to the Amadeus Yacht Company, who had the boat thoroughly restored by the craftsmen of Santa Margherita in Italy. The winches were replaced, a new wooden boom was built, the spanker trasto was fitted, the sheet travelers of the genoa were replaced, and a jib furler was installed. The hull was carefully controlled by means of the West System.

During the winter of 1993, the boat was completely stripped down to the wood and the deck was rebuilt (including the deck-houses) by master-carpenter Giovanni Ambrosetti.

Ancilla II

A steel-hulled boat designed in 1958 by Angelo Penco and built by the Sturla naval shipyard in Genoa, Italy the same year, *Ancilla II* was commissioned by Ezio Cristiani and designed specifically for Mediterranean cruises. Its sail plan has been broken up to a considerable degree in order to sail safely in strong winds. To date, *Ancilla II* has never undergone any substantial refitting. However, in the late 1970s a flying bridge was adopted ahead of the rear cockpit so as to provide crew and passengers some protection from the spray and the rain.

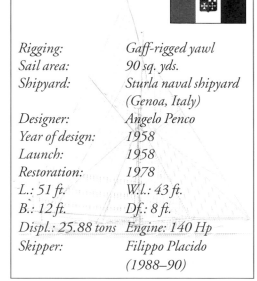

Rigging:	*Gaff-rigged yawl*
Sail area:	*90 sq. yds.*
Shipyard:	*Sturla naval shipyard (Genoa, Italy)*
Designer:	*Angelo Penco*
Year of design:	*1958*
Launch:	*1958*
Restoration:	*1978*
L.: 51 ft.	*W.l.: 43 ft.*
B.: 12 ft.	*Df.: 8 ft.*
Displ.: 25.88 tons	*Engine: 140 Hp*
Skipper:	*Filippo Placido (1988–90)*

THIS PAGE: *Photographs of the steel-hulled* Ancilla II, *designed by Angelo Penco, as it sails at a good speed (Photos: F. Taccola).*

OVERLEAF: *Porto Cervo 1991, a close-up of the boat's small transom (Photo: J. Taylor).*

Angélique

Angelique, designed by Charles Nicholson (design no. A 227), was launched in 1961 from the Clare Lallow shipyard in Cowes, England. Its first owner was Sir Kenneth Norman Rudd. Until 1969 the boat regularly took part in the Solent regattas off the south of England, including races that are part of yachting history, such as two editions of the Fastnet Race (1961 and 1963). In 1969 the boat was sold to Sir Peter Laurent Hunt, a member of the prestigious Royal Cruising Club. The new owner had a considerable impact on the life of *Angelique*: after two seasons preparing the boat, Sir Peter and a companion set sail on a round-the-world voyage that was completed in 1993.

In 23 years of sailing, *Angelique* has sailed all the world's oceans and throughout the entire Mediterranean, but it has never returned to the Solent. For reasons of age, Sir Peter decided to sell the boat to a new owner in 1993, but the boat continued to sail throughout the Aegean Sea and as far as the Red Sea, and it became the summer residence of a young Italian family. In 1998 it was transferred to the south of France, where it started to race once again, taking part in the circuit of vintage yacht regattas in the Mediterranean.

More than 40 years on from the day it was launched, *Angelique* continues to sail more than 2,000 miles a year. In 1995–96 it was refitted in Turkey. This included the replacement of 70 percent of the Honduran mahogany planking on the bottom of the hull, and the replacement of certain parts of the installations and the auxiliary engine. Apart from this, all the other components are original. During refitting the teak deck was strengthened.

The boat has a Honduran mahogany rudder and planking, and an aluminum mast. The sail plan is very similar to when it was launched: it has 11 sails, of which only the spanker and genoa were replaced in 1998. The other sails were all made by Ratsey & Lapthorn of Cowes in 1961 and, as the boat's results show, continue to perform superbly well to this day.

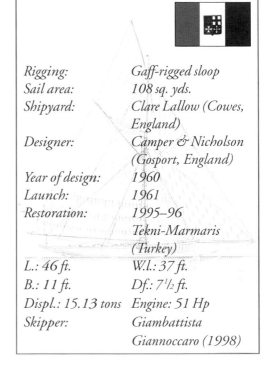

Rigging:	Gaff-rigged sloop
Sail area:	108 sq. yds.
Shipyard:	Clare Lallow (Cowes, England)
Designer:	Camper & Nicholson (Gosport, England)
Year of design:	1960
Launch:	1961
Restoration:	1995–96 Tekni-Marmaris (Turkey)
L.: 46 ft.	W.l.: 37 ft.
B.: 11 ft.	Df.: 7½ ft.
Displ.: 15.13 tons	Engine: 51 Hp
Skipper:	Giambattista Giannoccaro (1998)

BELOW: *Cannes 1999, a close-up of* Angelique *(Photo: J. Taylor).*

OVERLEAF: *Sailing with a trading wind (Photo: J. Taylor).*

THIS PAGE: *VBR 1999, two shots of* Angelique *(Photos: J. Taylor).*

Armelea

Rigging:	Bermudan ketch
Sail area:	355 sq. yds.
Shipyard:	Valdettaro (La Spezia, Italy)
Designer:	Franco Anselmi Boretti
Year of design:	1968
Launch:	1969
L.: 77 ft.	W.l.: 62 ft.
B.: 19 ft.	Df.: 8 ft.
Displ.: 61.73 tons	Engine: 180 Hp
Skipper:	Vito D'Antoni (1987)

Armelea is a large motorsailer launched at the Valdettaro yard in La Spezia, Italy, and designed by the architect Franco Anselmi Boretti. A sturdy, seaworthy boat with pitch pine planking, it has had only three owners and has not been substantially modified since it was launched, apart from the addition of a jib furler and mainsail furler in recent years. It has a teak deck, mixed framing, the original Douglas fir masts, and considerable space below deck, which makes it a comfortable boat for up to 14 people.

It has completed long cruises of the Mediterranean and the Red Sea, performing well in trading winds and when sailing at close-reach. The inside of the hull consists of 65 oak ribs, a galvanized steel frame-floor, and iroko beam shelf-pieces, planking, posts, and keel. The planking consists of $1^3/_4$-inch iroko timbers secured down with silicon bronze bolts.

The toerail, hatchways, and skylights are in teak, while the masts have a pear-drop section just like Camper & Nicholson's old boats had, each made up of ten splines with crossed scarves. The deck, which is clear and well protected by sturdy teak-top gallant boards, features a cockpit for guests flush with the deck with two steering positions, one of which is sheltered by a simple windshield designed for rough weather.

THIS PAGE: *Imperia, 1987, the debut of* Armelea, *designed by Franco Anselmi Boretti (Photos: M. Gentili and J. Taylor).*

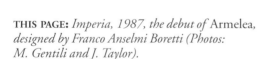

Artica II

Artica II is a myth in its own right within Italian sailing circles. It was initially designed as a racer and has remained so to this day, although from the point of view of age this boat deserves a place among the vintage boats described earlier. It is a true honor having this boat moored at the quayside!

In the summer of 1956, *Artica II*, which resembles the Duke of Abruzzi's boat of the same name, came to the attention of international yachting when it won a Sailing Training Association regatta, beating other boats representing sailing schools from all over the world. The efforts of this small Italian Navy yawl, in one of the first regattas beyond the Straits in which an Italian boat took part, successfully crowned the efforts of the Italian Navy's Yachting Club to create a first-class, open-sea crew capable of performing at an international level.

The boat was the end result of the passion and dynamism of the late Colonel Gianni Pera, an enthusiastic, famous yachtsman who decided to entrust the design of the boat to John Illingworth and its construction to the Sangermani yard in Lavagna, Italy. He wanted a boat capable of racing in all kinds of open-sea regattas regardless of weather conditions, and a fast boat at that, with a light displacement and thus with a clear edge when running free, with an average freeboard, and a raked sheerline.

The result was an extremely sturdy construction made of a mixture of materials: the skeg, rudder, and keel are mahogany; the simple planking is made of ³/₄-inch mahogany; the ribs, frame-floor, shelf-pieces, deck beams, and the intercostal ribbing between the frame-floor sections are all in corrosion-proof alloy ("peralluman" produced by the Montecatini Company).

It has a revolutionary design based on an extremely low displacement and raked sail-plan, and it underwent fine-tuning by Lieutenant-Commander Emanuele Junca, the boat's first skipper. The seven-person

Rigging:	Gaff-rigged yawl
Sail area:	97 sq. yds.
Shipyard:	Sangermani (Lavagna, Italy)
Designer:	John Illingworth
Year of design:	1954
Launch:	1956
Restoration:	1988–89 Beconcini shipyards (La Spezia, Italy)
L.: 43 ft.	W.l.: 33 ft.
B.: 10 ft.	Df.: 7³/₄ ft.
Displ.: 7.72 tons	Engine: 35 Hp
Skipper:	Admiral Mario Bini (1988–98), Piero Carpani (2000)

BELOW: *September 1994,* Artica II *with Admiral Giovanni Iannucci at the helm (Photo: S. Pesato).*

crew included midshipmen Giancarlo Basile and Giovanni Iannucci.

At the Torbay–Lisbon Race (in July 1956) *Artica II* was among 22 yachts from 11 different nations. The race was over a distance of 800 miles, and the boat's victory on that occasion was down to the professionalism of a carefully prepared and captained crew, the excellent quality of the boat, and its superb behavior during the entire course of the race. In 1958 it returned to top-level racing at the Brest–Las Palmas regatta, skippered by Commander Mario Bini. *Artica II* won another amazing victory, demonstrating great pace and strength especially under the spinnaker and mizzen staysail.

Beppe Croce, commenting on the former of these two victories, said at the time: "*…Risking such a small boat on such a long and difficult course, among so many boats specially trained and prepared for navy regattas, may have seemed a rather hazardous move, a romantic yet useless gesture. However, this proved not to be the case: it was, on the contrary, a carefully thought-out move, based on perfect preparations, which led to a triumphant performance thanks to a great skipper and a truly worthy crew…*"

In July 1960, still skippered by Mario Bini, *Artica II* won the Cannes–Ischia Regatta organized to celebrate the sailing Olympics held that year in the Gulf of Naples. In subsequent years, the boat won a long series of Mediterranean regattas which further strengthened its legendary fame. Given the considerable success of recent vintage yacht meetings, Admiral Iannucci, a veteran member of that first crew from 1956, proposed that the Italian Navy restore this glorious vessel, which it duly did at the Navy's Taranto yards.

This superb yawl is now as splendid as ever. It is always among the first places in any regatta it takes part in, nearly always manned by old members of those first two historic crews who now also come into the "vintage" category!

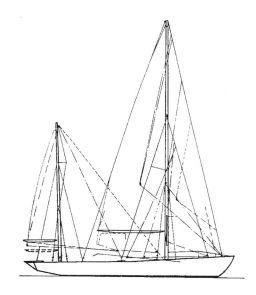

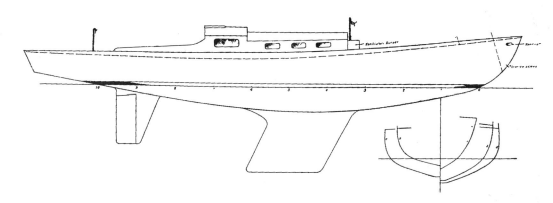

The principal victories of Artica II in the 1950s and 1960s			
Date	Skipper	Course	Classification
1956	Frigate Capt. Junca	Torbay–Lisbon	1st CT
Aug. 2/11, 1958	Frigate Capt. Bini	Brest–Las Palmas	1st CT 4th RT
Aug. 18, 1959	Frigate Capt. Bini	41st Parallel	1st CT
1960	Frigate Capt. Foschini	Cannes–Naples	1st CT
Jun. 16, 1963	Frigate Capt. Foschini	Anzio–T. Asturia–Anzio	2nd CT 1st RT
Jun. 29/30, 1963	Frigate Capt. Foschini	Giraglia (Toulon–San Remo)	2nd CT 2nd RT
Aug. 2/5, 1963	Frigate Capt. Foschini	Antibes–Ischia	1st CT 1st RT
Aug. 13, 1963	Frigate Capt. Foschini	Ischia–Anzio	1st CT 1st RT 2nd
Aug. 30/31, 1963	Frigate Capt. Foschini	Coppa–Monzino	1st CT 1st RT
Jun. 26/27, 1965	Frigate Capt. Foschini	Siracusa–Malta	1st CT 1st RT
Jul. 3/4, 1965	Frigate Capt. Foschini	Anzio–M. Cristo–P. Ercole	2nd CT 1st RT

OPPOSITE PAGE: *The boat with Admiral Mario Bini at the helm – a true kaleidoscope of colors (Photo: L. Fioroni).*

BELOW: *ASW 2001,* Artica II *sailing close-hauled (Photo: J. Taylor).*

ABOVE: *ASW 1989,* Artica II *sailing close-hauled (Photo: J. Taylor).*

RIGHT: *Imperia, 1994:* Artica II *in the middle of a regatta (Photo: L. Fioroni).*

Athena

Athena (originally called *Diana II*) was built and launched in Germany in 1955, at the Abeking & Rasmussen yard in Bremen, and was designed by Gil Rasmussen. It is a sturdy hull, initially rigged as a yawl but subsequently modified to a gaff-rigged cutter as a result of new international regulations. It was present at Cowes Week in England for a number of years and was usually well placed in the regattas. In later times it was purchased by a sailing club from northern Germany and sailed in the North Sea and the Atlantic.

The boat arrived in the Mediterranean in 1990, after having taken part in the Tall Ships Races held in 1986, 1987, and 1988. Bought first by Peter Harren, and then by Rudolf Geray in 1994, it subsequently underwent some provisional refitting that enabled it to take part in the Porto Cervo regattas off Sardinia, skippered by Mario Quaranta. It then returned to the Imperia shipyards to have 70 percent of the interior refitted, as well as the replacement of a number of frame-floor timbers and servicing of the aluminum mast (the first to be built in Germany back in 1958), which weighs some 2.2 tons. *Athena* has mahogany planking, an original 15-foot teak bridge, solid oak beams and ribs, and a mahogany interior.

It has once again returned to its original yawl rig and continues to race successfully, skippered by Aldo Sario who looks after it with loving care.

Rigging:	Bermudan yawl
Sail area:	239 sq. yds.
	(598 sq. yds.
	with spinnaker)
Shipyard:	Abeking & Rasmussen
	(Bremen, Germany)
Designer:	Gil Rasmussen
Year of design:	1955
Launch:	1955
Restoration:	1993–94 Imperia
	(Italy)
L.: 58½ ft.	W.l.: 49¼ ft.
B.: 10½ ft.	Df.: 9 ft.
Displ.: 38.58 tons	Engine: 80 Hp
Skipper:	Aldo Sario (1994–96)

BELOW: *Imperia 1994, a shot of* Athena *(Photo: S. Pesato).*

Aurora

Rigging:	Bermudan sloop
Sail area:	66 sq. yds.
Shipyard:	David Cheverton &
	Partners Ltd.
	(Cowes, England)
Designer:	David Cheverton
Year of design:	1958
Launch:	1960
Restoration:	1986
L.: 27 ft.	W.l.: 19½ ft.
B.: 13¾ ft.	Df.: 10 ft.
Displ.: 6.61 tons	Engine: 12 Hp
Skipper:	Peter H. Gleesmer
	(1990),
	Franco Lombardo
	(1994–2000)

This boat began life as *Calinda* in 1960, and it flew the English flag until 1986 when it was bought by Franco Lombardo, a resident of Barcelona in Spain. Thanks to the restoration work of two retired master carpenters from Palma de Mallorca, the new owner managed to save what was effectively an abandoned boat and could begin to race it at vintage yacht meetings.

Today the boat is called *Aurora*. It has a rudder with tiller and performs excellently under its spinnaker with a trading wind. A photograph taken of the boat at Palma de Mallorca would seem to suggest that it has no jib support.

ABOVE: *A photograph of* Aurora *under sail.*

Bagheera

Rigging:	Bermudan sloop
Sail area:	108 sq. yds.
Shipyard:	Mario Mostes
	(Genoa, Italy)
Designer:	Alex Robertson
Year of design:	1952
Launch:	1953
L.: 41¼ ft.	W.l.: 32¾ ft.
B.: 9 ft.	Df.: 7¾ ft.
Displ.: 9.92 tons	Engine: 40 Hp
Skipper:	Ezio Vannucci (1994)

Bagheera is a beautiful sloop launched at the Mostes shipyard at Genoa, Italy. It is one of the few boats with naturally varnished planking. Its first owner was Astor Williams Norrish, an Englishman residing in Genoa, who in the second half of the 1950s won a series of excellent placings at the Giraglia. A fast, seaworthy hull, it performs well when sailed close-hauled in a well-formed sea.

Around about the 1960s, *Bagheera* changed hands but remained in the regatta circuit in the northern Tyrrhenian Sea. Midway through the 1990s it underwent a complete refitting at the Tomei yard in Viareggio, Italy, when 40 percent of the planking was replaced. The boat features cedar planking, oak and acacia ribs, a teak deck, and a silver spruce mast. A number of its winches are still original.

RIGHT: *Imperia 1994,* Bagheera – *launched in Genoa in 1953 (Photo: S. Pesato).*

Balkis

*B*alkis was designed by Sparkman & Stephens in 1964 and launched in 1967. It has mahogany planking and acacia ribs and frame-floor timbers. In 1996, the deck was completely rebuilt by the Aldo Lario yard in Menton, France. The boat's original parts include the mast, the winches, the rudder wheel, and the small binnacle. It can hug the wind at 28° and is stable when running before the wind, but it gets "wet" when the wind exceeds 25 knots.

RIGHT: *A shot of* Balkis *(Photo: S. Pesato).*

Rigging:	Gaff-rigged sloop
Sail area:	63 sq. yds.
Shipyard:	Bertin Maurice & Son shipyards (Toulon, France)
Designer:	Sparkman & Stephens
Year of design:	1964
Launch:	1967
Restoration:	1996 Aldo Lario (Menton, France)
L.: 36 ft.	W.l.: 32³/₄ ft.
B.: 10 ft.	Df.: 6 ft.
Displ.: 10.47 tons	Engine: 25 Hp
Skipper:	Massimo Pagano (1998–2002)

Bonita

*T*his is a fast boat built at the Craglietto shipyard in Trieste, Italy, from a design by Olin Stephens. It belonged to Baron Chicco Aimerich, and in 1973 it took part in the One Ton Cup under the New Zealand flag. In 1976 it was bought by Giovanni Napoleone and Riccardo Cravero. The latter bought out his partner's share of the boat in 1989. The boat completed a number of summer cruises in the Mediterranean before going in for restoration work in 1989 at the Imperia shipyards.

It performs well when sailing close-hauled (or on a trading wind) and can surf with the spinnaker hoisted. It has solid mahogany planking and laminate mahogany ribs, ash beams and a teak deck (the original deck was in marine plywood). The mast is a "Proctor" alloy model. Its sailing area is subdivided as follows: genoa 65 square yards and spanker 32 square yards. If the spinnaker is hoisted this exposes a further 152 square yards of sail to the wind. Apart from the rebuilding of the deck, *Bonita* has not undergone any other significant modifications since it was launched except for the fitting of a jib furler.

Rigging:	Gaff-rigged sloop
Sail area:	97 sq. yds.
Shipyard:	Craglietto (Trieste, Italy)
Designer:	Olin Stephens
Year of design:	1972
Launch:	1973
Restoration:	1991–92 Imperia naval shipyards (Italy)
L.: 38¹/₄ ft.	W.l.: 27³/₄ ft.
B.: 11¹/₂ ft.	Df.: 6¹/₂ ft.
Displ.: 6.94 tons	Engine: 28 Hp
Skipper:	Luca Cravero (1992), Marcello Murzilli (1994, 1998)

LEFT: *Imperia 1992,* Bonita *under its spinnaker (Photo: F. Ramella).*

Bufeo Blanco

Rigging:	Gaff-rigged cutter
Sail area:	132 sq. yds.
Shipyard:	Sangermani (Lavagna, Italy)
Designer:	Cesare Sangermani
Year of design:	1962
Launch:	1963
Restoration:	1991
L.: 51 ft.	W.l.: 35 ft.
B.: 12¼ ft.	Df.: 6 ft.
Displ.: 16.53 tons	Engine: 68 Hp
Skipper:	Roberto Gandini (1992–94)

Designed by Cesare Sangermani, and launched in 1963 under the name *Luisma*, this gaff-rigged cutter is a First Class RORC (Royal Ocean Racing Club) boat that was originally rigged as a sloop. The boat has had three owners: Luigi Botto Steglia, Ido Minola, and Luigo Oneto. It is composed of mahogany planking, a teak deck, a mast with two spreaders and a spinnaker pole, and laminate framing reinforced with stainless steel ribs.

In 1991 *Bufeo Blanco* underwent refitting work, including the replacement of the deck and the addition of a baby stay, two loose shrouds, and two winches in order to transform the boat into a cutter. The original structural elements and interior furnishings have been preserved in perfect condition.

The boat has cruised throughout the Mediterranean and took part in the seventh Imperia vintage yacht regatta, where it came second to *Artica II* in its class.

RIGHT: *Imperia 1992,* Bufeo Blanco, *designed by Cesare Sangermani (Photo: A. Tringali).*

Calypso

alypso is one of four boats purchased by the Italian Navy's Sailing Club (Sport Velico) in the "Palinodie" Class. It was designed by Sparkman & Stephens and built by the Navy's shipyard at La Spezia. The other three boats in this series are *Penelope*, *Nausicaa*, and *Galatea*, launched in 1965, 1966, and 1969 respectively. The latter vessel incorporated a number of construction improvements.

The hull planking is in mahogany, while the mast is an alloy. All the Italian Navy's boats are registered with the Italian Association of Vintage Yachts.

Rigging:	*Bermudan sloop*
Sail area:	*194 sq. yds.*
Shipyard:	*Italian Navy shipyard (La Spezia, Italy)*
Designer:	*Sparkman & Stephens*
Year of design:	*1968*
Launch:	*1969*
L.: 40 ft.	*W.l.: 33¹/₂ ft.*
B.: 10 ft.	*Df.: 6³/₄ ft.*
Displ.: 8.82 tons	*Engine: 40 Hp*
Skipper:	*Domenico Scala (1998)*

BELOW: *Imperia 1998,* Calypso, *a member of the Italian Navy's Sailing Club (Photo courtesy of the Italian Navy).*

Calypso

Rigging:	Gaff-rigged yawl
Sail area:	132 sq. yds.
Shipyard:	Sangermani (Lavagna, Italy)
Designer:	Sparkman & Stephens
Year of design:	1954
Launch:	1958
Restoration:	1997, 1998 Porto Sole shipyard (San Remo, Italy)
L.: 47¹/₂ ft.	W.l.: 32¹/₂ ft.
B.: 12 ft.	Df.: 5¹/₂ ft.
Displ.: 12.93 tons	Engine: 50 Hp
Skipper:	Beppe Zaoli (1998)

Designed in 1954 by Sparkman & Stephens, *Calypso* was launched in 1958 at the Sangermani yard in Lavagna, Italy. This yacht boasts elegant overhangs and a dagger-board and reminds one of *Finisterre*, another Sparkman & Stephens creation. At the beginning of its life this boat raced fairly regularly, taking part in various editions of the Giraglia, where it came fourth in Class II in 1958, and tenth in Class I the following year. Other fine performances included its sixth place (out of 25) at the 1960 Cannes–Ischia Regatta, a regatta held to commemorate the sailing

RIGHT: *Cannes 1999: a close-up of* Calypso, *a Sparkman & Stephens creation (Photo: J. Taylor).*

Olympics that took place in Naples that year. Then the boat disappeared from the racing scene and was renamed *Vaivento*.

This was to mark the beginning of a period of decline during which the boat was half-abandoned on the Spanish coast, made an anonymous appearance in Sardinia, but was then fortunately saved by a boat-lover, and, after a period back in Lavagna, made its reappearance in 1997–98 at San Remo, Italy. Here a long, careful refitting operation was begun by the German architect Angelo Haasler. The deck was completely rebuilt,

and most of the mahogany beams were replaced, although the mahogany planking and the framing were still in good condition. The Douglas fir mast was kept but the sail plan was modified by Beppe Zaoli.

Calypso started to race once again, much to the satisfaction of its new owner who bought the boat in 1995. The boat came first at the 1998 and 1999 editions of Monaco Classic Week, at the 1999 Cannes Régates Royales, and at the 1998 Imperia Week, with Beppe Zaoli ever-present at the rudder (with tiller).

Capricia

This is the latest addition to the Italian Navy's fleet of training yachts, and the way it made its way into this fleet is of particular interest, as recorded in the *Official Gazette* of June 9, 1993: "*The donation of a yacht named* Capricia *to the Italian Navy by lawyer Gianni Agnelli, by public deed no.135.087 drawn up by Luigi Napoleone, notary in Rome, on January 11, 1993, has been accepted by the Ministerial Decree issued on May 24, 1993.*"

Capricia is more than 40 years old, a classic hull in the 1960s' style, designed by

Sparkman & Stephens of New York and rigged as a yawl.

It was originally commissioned by Einar Hansen in 1963, and the same Mr. Hansen led it immediately to victory in the 1963 Fastnet Race in what proved to be an unforgettable regatta. The boat crossed the finishing line ahead of other excellent yachts such as *Stormvogel*, *Bolero*, and *Corsaro II*.

It has a considerable freeboard and was originally designed more as a cruiser than a racer. In fact, it is extremely seaworthy,

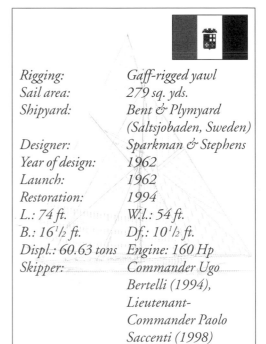

Rigging:	*Gaff-rigged yawl*
Sail area:	*279 sq. yds.*
Shipyard:	*Bent & Plymyard (Saltsjobaden, Sweden)*
Designer:	*Sparkman & Stephens*
Year of design:	*1962*
Launch:	*1962*
Restoration:	*1994*
L.: 74 ft.	*W.l.: 54 ft.*
B.: 16¹/₂ ft.	*Df.: 10¹/₂ ft.*
Displ.: 60.63 tons	*Engine: 160 Hp*
Skipper:	*Commander Ugo Bertelli (1994), Lieutenant-Commander Paolo Saccenti (1998)*

LEFT: *VBR 1999,* Capricia *donated by the lawyer Gianni Agnelli to the Italian Navy (Photo: J. Taylor).*

OVERLEAF: Capricia's *unmistakable hull and colors (Photo: J. Taylor).*

making it suitable for sailing on the open sea. However, its streamlined hull also makes it perfectly suited for regattas. The boat's interior underwent various modifications after Agnelli bought it in 1965.

The Italian Navy employ the boat as a training vessel for the cadets based at the Leghorn Naval Academy. It has a characteristic naturally colored hull, similar to that of *Agneta*; manual winches (the originals); wooden masts; and a teak deck, but it has no jib or mainsail furler. The interior furnishings are simple yet elegant; the owner's cabin was restored by Camper & Nicholson of England in 1971. The original layout of the boat envisaged nine berths. However, this was insufficient for the needs of a training crew (specifications similar to those of *Corsaro II* or *Stella Polare* are required), and so a study into eventual improvements in the capacity of the living quarters is currently being carried out, although this should not substantially alter the boat's basic characteristics.

Capricia quickly gained fame at the beginning of its military career when it took part, on June 11–12, 1994, in the open-sea regatta for vintage yachts named after the naval officer Luigi Durand de la Fenne. The race, on a course between Tino and Capraia in Italy, saw an excellent debut performance by the boat, which came first in its class, skippered by the evergreen, highly successful yachtsman, and my friend, Commander Giancarlo Basile.

BELOW: *Imperia 2000, a close-up of* Capricia *(Photo: J. Taylor).*

BOTTOM: *VBR 1999, the tricolored spinnaker bearing the coat of arms of the Maritime Republic (Photo: J. Taylor).*

Chaplin

Rigging:	Gaff-rigged cutter
Sail area:	138 sq. yds.
Shipyard:	Sangermani
	(Lavagna, Italy)
Designer:	Carlo Sciarelli
Year of design:	1973
Launch:	1974
L.: 55 ft.	W.l.: 47¹/₂ ft.
B.: 13³/₄ ft.	Df.: 7³/₄ ft.
Displ.: 16.53 tons	Engine: 75 Hp
Skipper:	Giovanni Novi
	(1994–2002)

s its designer Carlo Sciarelli wrote, Chaplin *"is a classy yacht designed for cruising and racing."* Built in 1974 by Sangermani, this is an elegant, well-balanced hull with a long waterline. It is extremely easy to handle thanks to its limited displacement.

Chaplin has always done extremely well in regattas: at the Giraglia it came 16th in 1975; it improved its position to come 4th in 1976 and 1977. In 1989 it won the Dipartimento Alto Tirreno Trophy in the Group B First Class reserved for vintage yachts.

The boat's interior displays considerable taste and loving care; all the paneling is in teak, as is the deck (1 inch), in keeping with the principle that the life of the boat is more important than are its fleeting regattas. *Chaplin* is one of Sangermani's most beautiful 1970s' creations.

RIGHT: Chaplin, *designed by Carlo Sciarelli (Photo: S. Pesato).*

BELOW: *A souvenir photo of Beppe Croce, Chairman of the Italian Yacht Club in the 1960s (Photo courtesy of G. Novi).*

Cin Cin

This boat started out life as *Shedir*, built by De Dood, the former yard manager at Abeking & Rasmussen, on behalf of an American boat-owner. Thirty years later, in 1993, the boat, which at that time belonged to a French owner, was bought by the doctor Raffaele Carlone, who transferred it from Nice in France to Imperia, where it underwent restoration work at Mario Quaranta's yard (including the rebuilding of the deckhouse and the painting of the interior).

The boat was then renamed *Carola*. It has solid mahogany planking, an alloy (proctor) mast, a teak deck, and wooden spreaders and boom (the original). In 1995 it was sold once again, this time to its present owner who decided to rename it *Cin Cin*.

The boat has since taken part in regattas at Santa Margherita in Italy and at Palma de Mallorca. *Cin Cin*, which among other things has a low deckhouse, performs well at all tacks.

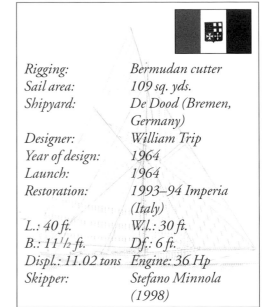

Rigging:	Bermudan cutter
Sail area:	109 sq. yds.
Shipyard:	De Dood (Bremen, Germany)
Designer:	William Trip
Year of design:	1964
Launch:	1964
Restoration:	1993–94 Imperia (Italy)
L.: 40 ft.	W.l.: 30 ft.
B.: 11½ ft.	Df.: 6 ft.
Displ.: 11.02 tons	Engine: 36 Hp
Skipper:	Stefano Minnola (1998)

Conchita III

Conchita III was the last boat in a series of such vessels designed by Antonio Ramognino, the famous protagonist of the Storm Troop Base of the 10th "Mas" Fleet at Algeciras against the Allied Fleet in Gibraltar. This eclectic character, a true lover of the sea (during the war he designed and tested a self-propelled system for "Gamma" raiders), created a boat that in

the past 30 years has often helped to salvage other boats in difficulty at sea (on nine separate occasions, in fact).

Conchita III has 1-inch mahogany planking, two silver spruce masts, acacia ribs, cabin planking in Oregon pine, and an iroko keel, rudder, and filling. The boat appears to be perfectly at ease in a lively sea and strong breeze.

Rigging:	Gaff-rigged ketch
Sail area:	156 sq. yds.
Shipyard:	Varazze (Italy)
Designer:	Antonio Ramognino
Year of design:	1961
Launch:	1962
Restoration:	1981–87
L.: 46 ft.	W.l.: 36 ft.
B.: 10¾ ft.	Df.: 6 ft.
Displ.: 12.68 tons	Engine: 50 Hp
Skipper:	Antonio Ramognino (1989)

LEFT: *A photograph of* Conchita III, *designed and built by Antonio Ramognino (Photo courtesy of A. Ramognino).*

Corsaro II

Rigging:	Gaff-rigged yawl
Sail area:	269 sq. yds.
Shipyard:	Costaguta (Voltri, Genoa, Italy)
Designer:	Sparkman & Stephens
Year of design:	1960
Launch:	1961
Restoration:	Various different occasions
L.: 68¹/₂ ft.	W.l.: 57³/₄ ft.
B.: 15¹/₄ ft.	Df.: 9¹/₂ ft.
Displ.: 46.3 tons	Engine: 130 Hp
Skipper:	Captain Luigi Diana (1996)

Corsaro II was designed by the famous naval architects Sparkman & Stephens and launched in 1960 at the Costaguta shipyard in Voltri, Genoa, Italy. It was originally designed to be crewed by 15 officer cadets at the Naval Academy, in training to accustom them to long-distance sailing in various conditions encountered when crossing oceans and being on the open sea. During the first six years this small yawl sailed all over the world and took part in numerous ocean regattas, honoring both the Italian flag and the Italian Navy with its successes.

Its first cruise began on February 20, 1961, when the boat was skippered by Commander Agostino Straulino, one of the greatest yachtsmen of all time. The boat crossed the Atlantic Ocean and then sailed through the Panama Canal before reaching Los Angeles, where it participated in the Transpac Race from Los Angeles to Honolulu. Before the regatta started, Beppe Croce, chairman of the Italian Yacht Club, came on board. There were many famous names among the 43 boats taking part in that regatta: *Escapade, Chubasco, Nam Sang, Sirius, Roland von Bremen, Odissey, Vixen, Ticonderoga, Queen Mab*, and *Ondine*, to name but a few. *Corsaro II* came a brilliant sixth in real time and was judged fourth overall (in compensated time). The boat also took part in the Honolulu–Kauai Island Regatta, coming first in real time and fourth overall.

In September of that year, *Corsaro II* finished off its first season at San Diego in the United States, after which it was laid up for some time. On his return to Italy, Commander Straulino was awarded the Albertis Plaque by the USVI, an annual award for the boat that had distinguished itself the most during the course of the year.

On its second cruise (March–August 1962), Commander Aldo Macchiavelli and Naval Lieutenant Giancarlo Basile joined the crew (they were to be Captain and Second-in-Command respectively). The boat and its new crew set sail for Newport in the United States in order to take part in the Newport–Bermuda Regatta, a really difficult test for yacht-builders, designers, and crews. It was the first time ever that this regatta had seen an Italian boat taking part.

Once again, Beppe Croce joined the crew that was to compete against the likes of *Stormvogel, Northern Light*, and *Highland Light* from the American Naval Academy; *Nina* and *Dyna* (the latter two had already won one edition of the regatta); *Royono*, again from the American Naval Academy and winner of the 1952 Bermuda Race; and

LEFT: *An historical photo of* Corsaro II *(Photo courtesy of the Italian Navy).*

OPPOSITE PAGE: *The boat with little wind in its sails (Photo courtesy of the Italian Navy).*

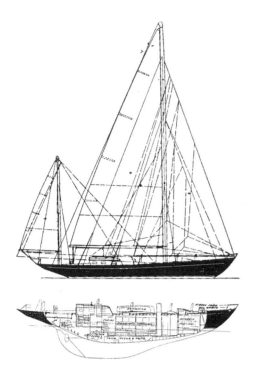

BELOW: *Imperia 1996,* Corsaro II *photographed abeam* Oneglia *(Photo: S. Pesato).*

Germania V, Giubilée, Argyll, Enchanta, and *Cotton Blossom.* In other words, the very best representatives of international yachting at that time. The regatta ended with *Corsaro II* winning a brilliant fifth place.

Immediately after the race, the boat moved on to Dartmouth in England to take part in the Torbay–Dieppe Race (34 yachts from six different nations entered), which it won both in real and compensated time. Afterwards it went on to Wilhelmshaven in Germany to be laid up for the winter.

Its third cruise (April–September 1963) saw the boat skippered by Commander Piero Bernotti and Lieutenant Giovanni Iannucci with a crew of seven midshipmen from the Samurai course. On April 13, *Corsaro II* left the German port to sail to Dartmouth, Puerto Rico, and Annapolis in the United States. It arrived in Annapolis on June 21, 1963 to take part in the Annapolis–Newport Regatta, in which it came ninth ahead of *Bolero* and *Royono.* Just three days later it took part in the Transatlantic Race, competing against boats such as *Bolero, Dyna, Carina, Figaro,* and *Windrose.* Once again it did remarkably well, coming second both in real and adjusted time, beaten only by *Ondine.* The young officers of the crew received enthusiastic praise for their fine performance against top international experts in the field of Atlantic crossings.

A few days later, the boat left Dartmouth for Cowes (on the Isle of Wight in England) to take part in Cowes Week, where it once again did really well. It then took part in the Fastnet Race, with the ubiquitous Beppe Croce aboard once again, against competitors such as *Capricia, Stormvogel, Bolero,* and *Outlaw.* Subsequently, *Corsaro II* returned to the Mediterranean after what had been three years away from its homeland.

The fourth ocean-racing season (May–September 1964) saw a new Commander, Ugo Foschini, on board, together with seven midshipmen from the Olympic course. The boat immediately took part in Operation Sail – a meeting of training yachts – with its entry to the Lisbon–Bermuda Race, where it won its class ahead of the English yacht *Tawau.* It then continued as far as Curaçao.

The fifth cruise (October 1964–February 1965) saw the transfer of the boat to Argentina for the Buenos Aires–Rio de Janeiro Regatta (preceded by the Buenos Aires–Porto Buceo Race where the boat came second). Many famous boats were present, such as *Ondine, Fearless* (from the American Naval Academy), *Germania VI,* and *Stormvogel.* On this occasion, the most prestigious regatta in the southern Altantic, *Corsaro II* came fifth in its class, skippered by Captain Emanuele Junca.

The sixth cruise (March–July 1965) saw a new commander, Lieutenant Giovanni Iannucci. After a new change of crew (in February 1965) the boat sailed around Cape Santa Rocco and entered the Pacific in order to reach Long Beach in California, in preparation for its second Transpacific Race (July 4–15). It won an honorable seventh place against the likes of *Kialoa II, Stormvogel,* and *Ticonderoga.*

On the seventh cruise, skippered by Captain Ugo Foscini, *Corsaro II* left Honolulu for Australian waters, where it took part in the Sydney–Hobart Regatta. During this period, the Italian Navy decided to replace the boat with *Stella Polare,* and so it had to return home. After being laid up for six months in Sydney, it thus set out on its eighth cruise, skippered by Lieutenant-Commander Mario Di Giovanni. The boat reached San Francisco, via Honolulu, sailing for the second time beneath the Golden Gate Bridge, and was subsequently laid up at San Diego. In March–August 1967, skippered by its new captain, Franco Faggioni, *Corsaro II* began its return journey to Italy after a further three years away from home.

The above is a summary of the boat's early life, which Captain Piero Bernotti describes more fully in his book *Corsaro II* (published by Mursia Editions), and it could have continued as such for many years to come in the company of the more modern vessel *Stella Polare.*

The boat started life with a seven-eighths rig on a wooden mast, and two loose shrouds had to be maneuvered on each side. Later, the wooden mast was replaced by an alloy one, fitted out at the masthead like *Stella Polare.* Moreover, *Corsaro II* had a rather low ballast–displacement ratio, and therefore the ballast had to be increased.

Despite its age, *Corsaro II* continues to be used as a training boat, one on which entire generations of Italian Navy officers have been schooled.

Crosswind

Crosswind is a sturdy, steel-hulled ketch with a teak deck, designed by Sparkman & Stephens and built by Abeking & Rasmussen (construction no. 5178) in Germany. Commissioned by Rockefeller, it was subsequently sold to a Canadian owner and was renamed *Wanderer* and then *Waifarer*.

It is fitted out as a charter yacht, with a comfortable, luminous interior. In terms of its hull lines and superstructures it resembles the ketch *Curlew III* designed by Philip Rhodes. It is a highly seaworthy vessel that performs well when sailed close-hauled.

The boat did not race at Imperia because it had been hired by the Carli Company for entertainment purposes. It was subsequently restored at the Marsic shipyard in Genoa, Italy, prior to being sold by its owner, the architect Ettore Agosti.

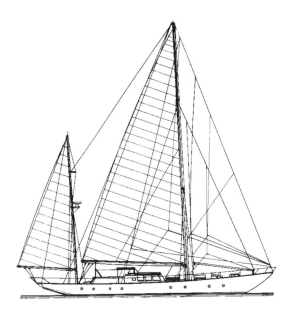

Rigging:	Bermudan ketch
Area of sails:	445 sq. yds.
Shipyard:	Abeking & Rasmussen (Bremen, Germany)
Designer:	Sparkman & Stephens
Year of design:	1950
Launch:	1957
Restoration:	1978, 1987, 1991
L.: 94 ft.	W.l.: 67½ ft.
B.: 20¾ ft.	Df.: 9¾ ft.
Displ.: 93.7 tons	Engine: 165 Hp
Skipper:	Piero Ciccolo (1988)

BELOW: *September 1988, Crosswind, a large, steel-hulled ketch designed by Sparkman & Stephens (Photo: C. Borlenghi).*

Crystal

Rigging:	Bermudan sloop
Sail area:	179 sq. yds.
Shipyard:	Beconcini shipyards (La Spezia, Italy)
Designer:	Alan H. Buchanan
Year of design:	1965
Launch:	1966
L.: 37 ft.	W.l.: 28 ft.
B.: 10 ft.	Df.: 6 ft.
Displ.: 13.23 tons	Engine: 25 Hp
Skipper:	Licio Comisso (1992–96)

Crystal is the result of a partnership between the Fratelli Beconcini shipyard in Italy and the architect Alan Buchanan. In 1966 the yard was situated some distance from the sea, and Buchanan lived in Trieste, where he designed for another shipyard. This typically British boat was supplied with deck-fittings from England (by Gibb & Lewmar) as well as English sails (by Ratsey & Lapthorn) specially imported for this project. The quantity of prize woods, together with its waterlines, make it a gem of a boat, a graceful and fast 13.23-ton cruising sloop. In Italy there are no other boats similar to *Crystal* still sailing and in good condition.

The boat has had four different owners and had been renamed *Albatros V* before the present owner changed its name back to *Crystal* in 1992. It takes part in the vintage yacht regattas, without any real competitive pretensions, crewed by a group of sailing enthusiasts for the pure pleasure of being in the company of like-minded yachtsmen.

RIGHT: *Imperia,* Crystal *under sail. The boat was designed by Alan Buchanan (Photo: A. Tringali).*

RIGHT: *Imperia 1996, a shot of* Crystal *(Photo: S. Pesato).*

Don Quijote

on Quijote was launched at the Arsenal naval shipyard in Buenos Aires in September 1953. At that time it was rigged as a yawl. Officially its first owner was Dr. Sigall, a close friend of President Peron, for whom the doctor probably acted as nominee.

Designed as a racer (its lines are similar to those of Sparkman & Stephens' boats), for a number of years it was considered to be one of the fastest boats in the whole of South America. In fact, it took part in certain editions of the Buenos Aires–Rio de Janeiro Race and always did very well.

In 1963 the boat was rigged as a ketch, while some years later (in 1979) its third owner, Felix Cordoba Moyano, replaced the rather bare interior furnishings and made it into a much more comfortable cruiser. It was at this time that the wooden masts were replaced by two Hood metal masts fitted with jib furlers.

In 1988 *Don Quijote* was bought by Pedro Serra, who virtually lived on board and sailed the boat along the Brazilian coast for six months non-stop. At that time it had already completed several transatlantic crossings via the Buenos Aires–Rio–Dakar–Canaries–Gibraltar route.

Finally, in 1963 the boat was sold to its present owner, Alcide Cerato, who had fallen in love with it minutes after he first set foot on it. It reached Italy via Antigua in order to be completely refitted at the Beconcini yard in La Spezia, in October 1993. Under the supervision of the architect Ugo Faggioni (who, among other things, designed the new interior), the job was completed in nine months.

The deck was restored (it was loose in a number of places), the beams and carlings were replaced, and the bottom was splintered. Argentinian timbers in keeping with the original design were bought: teak was used for the deck, American oak for the interior, and maple for some details. Finally, beams and booms were made using timbers that in Argentina are known as *vivaro*. The original frame-floor timbers were carefully preserved. The new-look *Don Quijote* made its first appearance at Imperia in 1994.

Rigging:	Bermudan ketch
Sail area:	257 sq. yds.
Shipyard:	Arsenal naval shipyard (Buenos Aires, Argentina)
Designer:	German Frers
Year of design:	1952
Launch:	1953
Restoration:	1993 Beconcini shipyards (La Spezia, Italy)
L.: 57¼ ft.	W.l.: 39 ft.
B.: 12¼ ft.	Df.: 8 ft.
Displ.: 20.5 tons	Engine: 106 Hp
Skipper:	Gustavo Bragagnolo (1994), Roberto Prussi (1996)

BELOW LEFT: *Imperia 2000,* Don Quijote *designed by German Frers (Photo: J. Taylor).*

BELOW AND BOTTOM: *Details of the interior (Photos courtesy of A. Cerato).*

OVERLEAF: *Running on the quarter with a customized spinnaker (Photo: J. Taylor).*

Eli

Eli is a Swedish "king's cruiser" with a light displacement and a ³/₄ inch-thick solid mahogany hull. The Göteborg shipyard that built this series of boats went on to update the rigging from one year to the next, and from one boat to the next, in an age when people began to think that yachting could finally be made widely available to all sailing enthusiasts, not just the very rich. *Eli* came to Italy after being commissioned by Ingo Galleani, who kept the boat until 1973 and then sold it to the engineer Bruno Pastore. The new owner cruised on the boat until the year 1986.

Eli possesses an appreciable sheerline and harmonious lines: even in a well-formed sea its overhangs mean that it does not beat against the waves but gently rises on the wave without luffing too much. The free-board is low, and the boat sails well close-hauled without sagging to leeward, although the cockpit gets fairly wet. The keel, posts, and cabin planking are made from selected white oak, the ribs are made from oak and maple, while the beams are in laminated mahogany and the mast and boom are made of Oregon pine. The deck has recently been rebuilt in teak; the original deck was made of marine plywood over masonite, with a cloth covering glued onto it and treated with linseed oil. In February and March 1994 the boat was completely stripped of its paint finish, down to the bare wood, as it had been in the past. In recent years it has changed hands a number of times and has won a series of regattas.

Rigging:	Bermudan sloop
Sail area:	41 sq. yds.
Shipyard:	A.B. Telfa (Göteborg, Sweden)
Year of design:	1955
Launch:	1962
Restoration:	1988, 1994
L.: 28¹/₂ ft.	W.l.: 23¹/₂ ft.
B.: 7 ft.	Df.: 4¹/₄ ft.
Displ.: 3.53 tons	Engine: 7 Hp
Skipper:	Nino Biagini (1990–98)

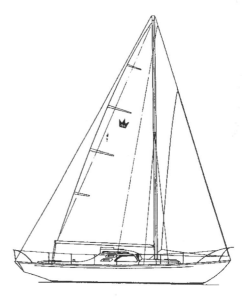

LEFT: *Imperia 2000, the small yacht* Eli, *originally launched in 1962 in Göteborg (Photo: J. Taylor).*

Ella

Rigging:	Gaff-rigged yawl
Sail area:	167 sq. yds.
Shipyard:	Sangermani (Lavagna, Italy)
Designer:	Sparkman & Stephens
Year of design:	1957
Launch:	1960
Restoration:	1976
L.: 48 1/2 ft.	W.l.: 34 3/4 ft.
B.: 12 1/4 ft.	Df.: 7 3/4 ft.
Displ.: 17.6 tons	Engine: 70 Hp
Skipper:	Pietro Pierini (1990–94), Urbano Pierini (1998)

BELOW: *September 1988, Ella has been the property of the Pierini family for many years (Photo: J. Taylor).*

OPPOSITE PAGE: *Under spinnaker (Photo: J. Taylor).*

Launched as *Oliana IV* and owned by Filippo Riva, this boat came seventh in the 1961 edition of the Giraglia with its new owner, Vittorio Zaffagni, who in the meantime had renamed it *Mabelle*, a name which was to feature in yachting news when the second *Mabelle*, a sloop, took part in the Fastnet Race and won the Middle Sea Race that year. In 1966 the boat was sold to the Pierini family, who renamed it *Ella*.

This is a boat designed for rough weather; fast when running free and before the wind, it finds it harder going when sailed close-hauled. It really comes into its own on long, triangular courses. It has mahogany planking, laminate maple ribs, and maple beams. The original spruce masts were replaced in 1972 by the present aluminum ones. The boom has been shortened. The interior was restored in 1976 and the deck in 1990. The boat was serviced during the period 1960 through 1990 by the master-carpenters Mino and Gaeta Viacava, two famous builders of Ligurian *gozzi* (small fishing boats).

From 1966 through 1969 *Ella* took part in three editions of the Alassio–Giraglia Race, and in the Cannes–Cagliari Race. On its first appearance at the Imperia meeting of vintage yachts in 1988, its skipper Pietro Pierini was awarded the prize as the oldest skipper present.

The boat is currently skippered by Urbano Pierini, who sailed it to victory in the Porto Cervo Regatta in Sardinia in 1989 and in the Nioulargue held in 1992. *Ella* boasts a longstanding boatswain, Arturo Calabrese, who has looked after the boat with loving care since 1980.

The boat is currently moored in the port of Lavagna, Italy, and is in generally good condition. A part of the planking was recently reconstructed by the master carpenter Giorgio Viacava.

Finisterre

Rigging:	Bermudan yawl
Sail area:	79 sq. yds.
Shipyard:	Seth Person (Saybrook, Connecticut, USA)
Designer:	Olin Stephens
Year of design:	1954
Launch:	1954
Restoration:	1997–98 Officine De Antoni (Povolaro, Italy)
L.: 38¼ ft.	W.l.: 27½ ft.
B.: 11¼ ft.	Df.: 3¾ ft.
Displ.: 11.2 tons	Engine: 32 Hp

BELOW: Finisterre, *Olin Stephens' winning masterpiece (Photo: M. Marzari).*

*F*inisterre was launched in 1954 by Seth Person, an expert boat-builder who followed Olin Stephens' design to the letter (design no. 1054). The boat's first owner was Carleton Mitchell, owner of *Malabar XII*. Mitchell, a keen yachtsman, journalist, and writer, was already well known for his highly individual ideas on boat design.

His articles in *Yachting World* underlined the three qualities he most admired in a boat: speed, comfort, and safety. In fact, *Finisterre* was designed in accordance with these ideas: a small, yet exceptional yawl with a dagger board. The boat at that time had a double-layered mahogany and cedar-planked hull and a keel reinforced with bronze beams in order to create as rigid a structure as possible. The framing was white oak (it was cut in winter), while the luxurious interior had African mahogany and teak paneling, together with the first electric icebox installed aboard a yacht. The deck was plywood covered with four layers of light cloth treated with resin, while the masting was Sitka spruce.

The boat's dimensions were unusual: very wide with considerable displacement, and very roomy on board. Bill Robinson, in his book *The Great American Designers*, wrote: "…Finisterre *was probably the most successful ocean racer of all time*" Juan Baader, in his *Lo Sport Della Vela* ("The Sport of Sailing"), described it as "…*one of the most interesting cruisers that won the greatest number of regattas…*"

As it was launched in the winter of 1954, it was unable to take part in that year's Bermuda Race, the toughest of American regattas. But it took part in other regattas, which it regularly won, while the owner prepared the crew for the tougher assignment ahead. Every single item of equipment on board was personally tested and prepared for the 1956 Bermuda Race, so that it was probably the one best prepared for victory: and so it proved to be. All its competitors, including *Bolero*, were beaten both in real time and compensated time. *Finisterre* went on to win the 1958 and

1960 editions of the same race, thus setting a record of three consecutive victories that no boat has equalled since.

The boat fully answered Mitchell's expectations: pronounced sagging, the main beam brought considerably forward, a significant freeboard, and a great ability to keep on course. "*A fast, ocean-going gunkholer*" were the words its owner used to describe it. Easy to maneuver and safe, *Finisterre* was simple to steer in any conditions. However, its successes were not to last long as the boat was sold in 1965 by its owner, who was tired of continuous penalizing of its rating, subject as it was to the pressing requirements of new technology and the very latest materials.

Destined for early retirement in a shipyard in sunny Florida in the United States, the boat was rediscovered in 1997 by an Italian yachtsman, an old admirer of *Finisterre*, who had read an advert announcing the sale of this famous racer. After a short telephone conversation, he concluded the purchase of the yacht and had it transferred to Italy, where a long and costly refitting operation was begun. Today, this completely rejuvenated yacht quietly sails the Adriatic.

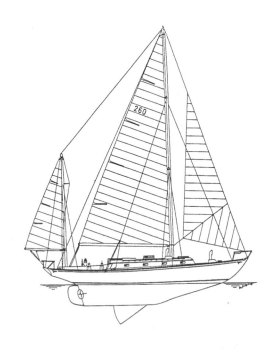

Folkboat

(sometime Monaco 1)

*F*olkboat is the popular one-off design created by Tord Sundén in the 1930s. This boat was built in 1958 for the Grimaldi family from Monaco. It was later acquired in Nice in France in a rather poor condition. In 1994 it was completely refitted (an operation that took 650 hours). It has Swedish pine clinker planking over acacia ribs and mahogany superstructures covered in cotton canvas. Restoration work involved the replacement of a dozen frame-floor timbers and the rebuilding of the deck (using ¹/₂-inch plywood). The boat also has a spruce mast.

At the end of the job, the boat had re-acquired its original splendor. The only modification made to the original design was the addition of a small outboard engine. The boat has taken part in various vintage yacht meetings in Imperia, where it has always done well in the regattas, performing well in strong winds and sailing close-hauled. It is still lovingly cared for at Imperia by its owner, Mario Quaranta.

Rigging:	*Bermudan sloop*
Sail area:	*33 sq. yds.*
Shipyard:	*Bowensen (Denmark)*
Designer:	*Tord Sundén*
Year of design:	*1955*
Launch:	*1956*
Restoration:	*1994–95*
L.: 24¹/₂ ft.	*W.l.: 19 ft.*
B.: 7 ft.	*Df.: 3¹/₄ ft.*
Displ.: 2.76 tons	*Engine: 7 Hp (inboard)*
Skipper:	*Mario Quaranta (1998)*

TOP LEFT: *Imperia 2000, a close-up of the crew (Photo: P. Maccione).*

LEFT: *Imperia 2000, details of* Folkboat, *a clinker-built hull lovingly cared for by its owner, Mario Quaranta (Photo: P. Maccione).*

Gael

Rigging:	Bermudan ketch
Sail area:	299 sq. yds.
Shipyard:	Abeking & Rasmussen (Bremen, Germany)
Designer:	Philip Rhodes
Year of design:	1962
Launch:	1962
Restoration:	1972, 1983
L.: 76 ft.	W.l.: 52 ft.
B.: 17 ft.	Df.: 10 ft.
Displ.: 57.3 tons	Engine: 216 Hp
Skipper:	Dzaja Josko (1990–91)

This fast ketch is one of Philip Rhodes' most important designs. It was launched in 1962 at the Abeking & Rasmussen yard in Bremen, Germany. It has double planking in Siamese teak, while the keel and the other principal parts are in iroko. Refitted in 1983, it is a very spacious, comfortable yacht.

RIGHT: *A shot of the powerful* Gael, *a beautiful Philip Rhodes creation built by Abeking & Rasmussen (Photo courtesy of N. Conzano Marone).*

Glad II

Glad II is the twin sister of J. Guzzwell's famous *Trekka*, with the difference that the latter was rigged as a yawl with a cross-jack, while *Glad II* has a shorter mast and a seven-eighths rig. The boat belonged to an English yachtsman who had completed a round-the-world voyage before sailing along the French inland waterways to reach Saint Tropez.

It has a mahogany hull, a teak plywood deck, a spruce mast that passes through the keel (the original mast), and ribs every half inch. The winches, rigging, and chain plates are also all original features. There is a 1,850-pound cast-iron bulb attached to the keel (a steel blade). The set of sails consists of two spankers, two genoas, a yankee, two fore-topmast staysails, a blooper, a jib, a spitfire, and a spinnaker.

When moored at the quayside, *Glad II* seems a little rounded due partly to its shortness, but under sail it becomes an elegant, stable, thoroughly seaworthy yacht.

Rigging:	Bermudan sloop
Sail area:	32 sq. yds.
Shipyard:	Gino D'Este (Fiumicino, Italy)
Designer:	J. Laurent Giles & Partners
Year of design:	1953
Launch:	1962
Restoration:	1984–86
L.: 20½ ft.	W.l.: 18½ ft.
B.: 6½ ft.	Df.: 4¼ ft.
Displ.: 1.65 tons	Engine: 6 Hp (outboard)
Skipper:	Enrico Caretti (1987–88), Giancarlo Montanari (1990)

Gloria

Designed by the Italian Technical Society of Naval Architecture and Equipment based in Santa Margherita, Italy, *Gloria* was built by the Beoro & Farina Company and launched at Genoa Prà in 1962. At that time it had pine planking; an iroko deck; acacia and ash steam-curved framing; mahogany superstructure; a marine plywood interior; top-quality spruce masts, boom, and gaffs; and a pitch pine bowsprit. The rivets and other connections are all in galvanized steel, the internal ballast is made of cement and steel, and the external ballast is cast iron. The master-carpenters Giacomo Delfino of Varazze and Gigi Sala of Camogli worked

on the boat. The standing rigging consists of Atlantic-type cabling, while the running rigging consists of hemp lines.

In the 1970s the boat was nearly destroyed by fire in uncertain circumstances. The wreck was subsequently sold and underwent a complete refitting using marine timber similar to the original wood.

Since 1982 the boat has been lovingly cared for by the present owners, who have undertaken to restore Arturo Lami's original sail plan using the canvas sails miraculously saved from the fire. In 1985 *Gloria* was able to set sail once again after what turned out to be an extended period of repair and restoration.

Rigging:	Trysail schooner
Sail area:	169 sq. yds.
Shipyard:	Boero & Farina (Genoa Prà, Italy)
Year of design:	1960
Launch:	1962
Restoration:	1974, 1983
L.: 48 ft.	W.l.: 34¼ ft.
B.: 12 ft.	Df.: 6 ft.
Displ.: 24.2 tons	Engine: 92 Hp
Skipper:	Antonio Pagano (1989–94)

Gustavia's Dream

Rigging:	Gaff-rigged cutter
Sail area:	144 sq. yds.
Shipyard:	Van Herek (Antwerp, Belgium)
Designer:	Oliver Van Herek
Year of design:	1958
Launch:	1958
L.: 42½ ft.	W.l.: 35 ft.
B.: 12½ ft.	Df.: 5½ ft.
Displ.: 16.5 tons	Engine: 30 Hp
Skipper:	Mario Bosio (2000–02)

This boat started out life as the *Oliver Van Moort* and was probably designed for a Dutch owner. In 1976 it became the property of Yves Becoquee. In 1982 it was renamed *Gustavia's Dream*. After a further two owners it was eventually acquired by the present skipper, Mario Bosio, at the Vitulano shipyard in San Remo, Italy, after being abandoned for a period of four years. It has a raked bow, a steel hull, a teak deck, the original halyard winches, a wide cockpit, wooden spreaders, a boom in Douglas fir, and an elegant mahogany interior. The wheel is also original. The deck is fairly clear and features a low, continuous deckhouse stretching as far as the foremast.

Gustavia's Dream is a very seaworthy boat well-suited to cruising, with its spacious, comfortable interior. It is, in fact, the residence of the present owner. The deck and deckhouse are soon to be refitted.

RIGHT: *Imperia 2000, a fine shot of the cutter* Gustavia's Dream, *a comfortable, seaworthy boat (Photo: J. Taylor).*

BELOW AND BOTTOM: *Details of the boat's interior (Photos: S. Pesato).*

Halifax III

This boat's design was the work of Stig Tiedeman from Saltsjobaden near Stockholm, Sweden. The boat was commissioned by Bengt Sodestrom and built by a certain Ericson.

In 1960 the boat was sold to Borje Nodstrom and took part in numerous regattas, including the Round Gotland Race, a famous Swedish open-sea regatta. *Halifax III* flew the Swedish flag until 1972, when it was sold to Captain K.M. Wollter who transferred it to the Mediterranean. It has elegant lines and features a raked bow, a transom stern, and a spruce mast. It has flown the Italian flag since 1984.

Rigging:	Gaff-rigged sloop
Sail area:	72 sq. yds.
Shipyard:	Graddo Batvaru (Stockholm, Sweden)
Designer:	Stig Tiedeman
Year of design:	1955
Launch:	1958
Restoration:	1985
L.: 34³⁄₄ ft.	W.l.: 25¹⁄₂ ft.
B.: 7¹⁄₄ ft.	Df.: 4¹⁄₂ ft.
Displ.: 7.72 tons	Engine: 24 Hp
Skipper:	Andrea Lusena (1990–92)

THIS PAGE: *The sloop* Halifax III, *launched in Sweden in 1958 (Photos courtesy of A. Lusena).*

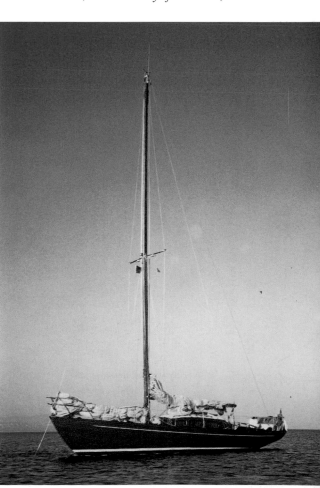

Harmonie in Blue

Rigging: *Gaff-rigged cutter*
Sail area: *110 sq. yds.*
Shipyard: *G.B. Hillyard*
                (Littlehampton,
                England)
Designer: *D. Hillyard*
Year of design: *1955*
Launch: *1956*
Restoration: *1989 (Cannes, France)*
L.: 43³/₄ ft.   W.l.: 40¹/₂ ft.
B.: 11¹/₂ ft.   Df.: 5¹/₄ ft.
Displ.: 19.3 tons Engine: 80 Hp
Skipper: *Michel Martini,*
                Jolande De Boreicha
                (1989–92)

This boat, designed by D. Hillyard, was launched as *Evening Breeze* under the British flag in 1956. A cutter with a typically "Norwegian" stern, *Harmonie in Blue* has mahogany planking, a 2 inch-thick deck in teak laid across pine timbers, and solid oak ribs and frame-floor timbers. Over the years the boat has undergone a number of modifications. In 1989 it was fitted with a sturdy 3-foot bowsprit and a series of modern winches and jib furlers. The Oregon pine mast was partially replaced, while the original deck has been completely preserved.

Harmonie in Blue has some uniquely attractive components, such as the beautiful steering wheel (present when the boat was launched), the galvanized iron pulpit, and its considerable freeboard. Based in Cannes, France, this is a seaworthy boat that performs well under sail but suffers a little when running before the wind.

Josephine of Hamble

Rigging: *Gaff-rigged sloop*
Sail area: *60 sq. yds.*
Shipyard: *A.H. Moody & Sons*
                (Hamble, England)
Designer: *Sparkman & Stephens*
Year of design: *1965*
Launch: *1965*
L.: 36 ft.   W.l.: 25¹/₂ ft.
B.: 9¹/₂ ft.   Df.: 6 ft.
Displ.: 11 tons Engine: 29 Hp
Skipper: *José M. Uriarte Centaño*

Designed by Sparkman & Stephens and launched in 1965 at A.H. Moody & Son's boatbuilding yard in England, *Josephine of Hamble* is a "one-tonner" that has taken part in the Fastnet Race. Under its original name of *Josephine VII* it took part in the Cowes Week regattas off the south coast of England from 1965 through 1986 and in the 1966 Island Race.

It flew the English flag up until 1986 and is currently owned and skippered by José M. Uriarte Centaño of Spain.

RIGHT: *2000, the Spanish sloop* Josephine of Hamble *(Photo: N. Martinez).*

Juana Argentina

This Bermudan sloop with a seven eighths rig was designed by German Frers. When it appeared for the first time in a regatta, in 1953, owned by Réne Salem, it highly impressed American yachtsmen, albeit used to seeing Argentinian yachts in the famous Buenos Aires–Rio de Janeiro Regatta or in the Bermuda Race. *Juana Argentina* won the Class A of that very first regatta, which was in fact the Buenos Aires–Rio de Janeiro Race.

It has a moderate displacement, is easily maneuvered, and is very fast. When designing the boat, German Frers bore in mind the English Royal Ocean Racing Club regulations and the American Cruising Club's Measurement Rules. The result was a hugely successful yacht.

South American woods were used for its construction – noted for their reliability and hardness – together with galvanized steel framing.

Rigging:	Bermudan sloop
Sail area:	245 sq. yds.
Shipyard:	Tandanor (Buenos Aires, Argentina)
Designer:	German Frers
Year of design:	1952
Launch:	1952
Restoration:	1993–94
L.: 62¼ ft.	W.l.: 42½ ft.
B.: 13 ft.	Df.: 10 ft.
Displ.: 38.6 tons	Engine: 180 Hp
Skipper:	José Garcia (1994)

BELOW: *Imperia 1994,* Juana Argentina, *a fast sloop designed by German Frers (Photo: S. Pesato).*

Kerilos

Rigging:	Bermudan yawl
Sail area:	279 sq. yds.
Shipyard:	Italian naval shipyard (Pisa, Italy)
Designer:	J. Laurent Giles & Partners
Year of design:	1961
Launch:	1961
Restoration:	1995–96 Beconcini shipyards (La Spezia, Italy)
L.: 78¼ ft.	W.l.: 54¾ ft.
B.: 17¾ ft.	Df.: 11¼ ft.
Displ.: 77.2 tons	Engine: 235 Hp
Skipper:	Enrico Pugliani (1991)

*K*erilos was launched in 1961 rigged as a ketch but was almost immediately turned into a yawl for reasons of rating. The boat has mahogany and iroko planking, acacia ribs, a teak deck, and a steel frame-floor. Initially, it regularly took part in regattas with excellent results. It won the Giraglia (in real time) on two occasions – 1965 and in 1967 (albeit coming only seventh and fifth, respectively, in compensated time). It came tenth in the 1962 edition of the same race, and sixth in the race held in 1968. It is mentioned in the 1961 *Yachting Annual* as a "first-class cruising yacht." On its launch it had wooden masts, but two months later these were replaced by similar masts in aluminum, while the rigging was replaced in 1991.

Kerilos, with its black hull, has been looked after for more than 20 years now by the Beconcini shipyard in Italy and by its loyal skipper Attilio Saccone. In 1994 and 1995 the deck was replaced at the Argentario yard, also in Italy, while in 1995–96 a number of frame-floor plates were replaced, together with parts of the bottom at the Beconcini yard.

The boat has only ever had two owners. It is a boat that performs well at all tacks, although it is at its best when sailed close-hauled. At present it is laid up at the Beconcini yard.

La Clé de Sol

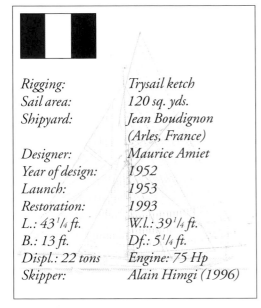

Rigging:	Trysail ketch
Sail area:	120 sq. yds.
Shipyard:	Jean Boudignon (Arles, France)
Designer:	Maurice Amiet
Year of design:	1952
Launch:	1953
Restoration:	1993
L.: 43¼ ft.	W.l.: 39¼ ft.
B.: 13 ft.	Df.: 5¼ ft.
Displ.: 22 tons	Engine: 75 Hp
Skipper:	Alain Himgi (1996)

OPPOSITE PAGE: *September 1996, the trysail ketch* La Clé de Sol, *designed by Maurice Amiet. It became famous for its round-the-world voyage begun in 1954 and completed in 1963 (Photo: J. Taylor).*

*O*n February 20, 1954, the French sailing magazine *Le Yacht* announced that the previous July a trysail ketch by the name of *La Clé de Sol*, designed by architect Maurice Amiet, had been launched. The interior furnishings of the boat had been designed by the owner. There was a whole series of modern comforts on board, including an icebox and even a grand piano.

The ketch, which had been designed for long cruises according to the wishes of Baron Jean de l'Espée, the boat's owner, gave the impression of an exceedingly seaworthy vessel with its "Norwegian" bow and its sturdy structure. With its rather limited sailing area (at the time it only had 90 square yards of canvas), it was rigged like the traditional Norwegian pilot vessels.

It completed its first transatlantic cruise in 1954 and returned to Marseilles in France aboard a cargo ship. It gained fame for a long round-the-world voyage it completed in various stages starting in the fall of 1954. In the spring of 1958 it crossed the Pacific to Tahiti, then in March 1959 it sailed from Tahiti to the Hawaiian Islands, followed by a crossing to Japan in April–May 1960. In March 1961 it reached Hong Kong. It then proceeded in stages, taking in Colombo, Port Sudan, and Suez, before reaching France in March 1963.

This extremely long cruise tested its seaworthiness to the full, and also gave it the chance to travel certain sections at a good speed. After the death of Jean de L'Espée, the boat changed hands three times, until Alain Himgi and Corinne Granéral decided to buy it and restore it to its original state (a job that took six months). Everything on board has been restored to, or left in, its original condition, with the exception of the grand piano, which has been removed. The interior is entirely in mahogany, and there is room for up to six passengers on board.

La Meloria

Rigging:	Bermudan sloop
Sail area:	103 sq. yds.
Shipyard:	Camper & Nicholson (Gosport, England)
Designer:	Camper & Nicholson
Year of design:	1967
Launch:	1967
Restoration:	1986
L.: 44¼ ft.	W.l.: 33¼ ft.
B.: 11¼ ft.	Df.: 6 ft.
Displ.: 11 tons	Engine: 35 Hp
Skipper:	Giorgio Aprà (1988)

BELOW: *The famous* La Meloria, *a boat that won numerous regattas skippered by Gianni Pera and Mary Blewitt (Photo courtesy of G. Aprà).*

Launched on July 13, 1967 at the famous Gosport yard of Camper & Nicholson in England, *La Meloria* has a pretty good track record in regattas. The day after its launch it took part in the Dinard Race (with skipper Peter Nicholson) and came a brilliant second behind *Firebrand*.

In September 1968, skippered by Gianni Pera, it won the Two Ton Cup ahead of Bertrand's *Arriana*, Coda-Nunziante's *Posillipo*, and Fabre's *Chin Blu*. In July 1968 it came fourth in its class in the Giraglia (skippered by Gianni Pera), only to better this two years later by winning the race outright. In the regattas held at the Lido di Albaro in Genoa in March 1969 it came second behind *Mirabelle*, while in the individual regattas held during Genoa Week it secured four second places and a third place.

Again, in 1969 the boat was a member of the Italian first team in the Admiral's Cup, together with *Mabelle* and *Levantades*. At the end of the 1960s, these three boats maintained the name of Italian yachting when they took part in the Channel Race, the Britannia Cup, the New York Yacht Club Challenge, and the Fastnet Race.

Meloria has a raked bow, a refined deckhouse coming just slightly above the level of the deck, a sunken elliptical stern, a keel with bulb, Lebanese cedar planking, and mahogany ribs. The history of the boat is closely interwoven with that of Mary Blewitt, an English aristocrat and keen yachtswoman, and that of *Santander of Wight*, another famous yacht. Blewitt, a descendant of a very old English family that included among its members Samuel Pepys, one of the major craftsmen in the British Navy (1633–1703), is a true sailor, both reserved and yet frank, who during the years from 1946 through 1955 took part in numerous

regattas, some with the great Illingworth on the *Myth of Malham*, others with Myles Wyatt, Commodore and then Admiral of the Royal Ocean Racing Club (RORC) and inaugurator of the Admiral's Cup.

During the course of her yachting career, Mary Blewitt took part in three editions of the Fastnet Race, one Bermuda Cup, one Cowes–La Coruña Race, two La Rochelle Races, one Dover–Kristiansund Race, two Giraglia, and many other regattas. She sailed thousands of miles in famous boats like *Santander* and *La Meloria*. In a small yachting manual that has become an international sailing bestseller, she writes: "*I love being aboard a boat. The boat becomes my home, just like a snail's shell. When I'm cruising I hardly ever go ashore but prefer eating, drinking, meeting my friends on board, as we English do.*" These words testify to the intense understanding between a person and her boat.

In 1955 Mary met Gianni Pera, an officer in the Italian Navy who did a great deal to get such beautiful RORC boats as *Orsa Minore*, *Chiar di Luna*, *Artica II*, *Corsaro II*, and *Stella Polare* built, and to get Navy officers to take part in open-sea regattas. Colonel Pera was the first Italian yachtsman to take part in the Fastnet Race (in 1955) aboard *Mouse of Malham*, a formidable, ultra-light 24-footer designed by John Illingworth. The boat romped to victory thanks to the skills of Pera and Illingworth, both members of that famous crew. Mary continued her extraordinary sailing career with Gianni Pera, first aboard *Santander*, and then on *La Meloria* – the former designed by Rhodes, the latter by Camper & Nicholson. Sadly, Gianni Pera died of a heart attack in 1969, bringing an abrupt end to the wonderful story of a happy couple at sea.

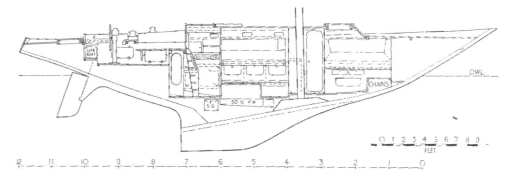

Levantades

Levantades, although not a vintage boat, is still a glorious, old boat dear to the Italian yachting community. Launched in 1967 (design no. 1885/66 by Sparkman & Stephens), the following year it won its first Giraglia, in 1972 it came second, and from 1969 through 1976 it gained a series of honorable placings in the same race. The passion and enthusiasm of its first owner, Beppe Diano, guaranteed that the boat was always highly competitive even when, some years later, it had to battle

Rigging:	Gaff-rigged sloop
Sail area:	124 sq. yds.
Shipyard:	Carlini naval shipyards (Rimini, Italy)
Designer:	Sparkman & Stephens
Year of design:	1966
Launch:	1967
Restoration:	1991 Carlini shipyards (Rimini, Italy)
L.: 50½ ft.	W.l.: 37 ft.
B.: 12 ft.	Df.: 7 ft.
Displ.: 7.72 tons	Engine: 24 Hp
Skipper:	Titti Carmagnani (1991), Cony Isemburg (1992–96)

LEFT: *Imperia 1991,* Levantades, *one of the most famous of all Italian yachts (Photo: S. Pesato).*

against extremely able crews and the most modern of creations.

No other Italian boat has ever had such an amazing series of successes as *Levantades*, with its relentless pace (especially when sailing close-hauled or running free). In fact, it is well worth listing the long series of honors that have gone to this incredible yacht:

- 1967 May: winner of the Airelia Cup, the Portoferraio Cup, and the Elba Cup.
- August: Cowes Week – second overall in the New York Yacht Club Challenge and in the Plymouth–La Rochelle Race.
- 1968 May: winner of the Mary Longary Cup, the Capraia Challenge Trophy, and the Airelia Cup (for the second consecutive year).
- July: winner of the XVI Giraglia and the First Mediterranean Championship.
- August: winner of the Antibes–Mahon Race and the Marcheville Trophy.
- September: winner of Genoa Week, the Gorgogna Race, and the YCT Championship.
- 1969 March: overall winner of the Monaco Cup and the Alassio–Giraglia–Alassio Race.
- April: winner of the Genoa–San Remo Race and the Islets' Race.
- May: final winner of the Airelia Cup for the third year running.
- July: selected for the Italian Admiral's Cup team (owner Beppe Diano, Team Captain).
- 1970 April: winner once again of the Genoa–San Remo Race, the Portoferraio Cup, the Islets' Race, and of the Alassio–Giraglia–Alassio for the second year running.
- 1971 June: overall winner of the Naples–Leghorn Race.
- July: selected once again for the Italian Admiral's Cup team (Beppe Diano again Team Captain).
- September: winner of the Gorgogna Race.
- 1972 July: winner of the Mary Longary Cup, and second in the XX Giraglia and in the V Mediterranean Championship.

- August: winner of the Genoa–Gallinara–Genoa Race.
- 1974 July: winner of the Aethelia Cup, the Costa Smeralda Cup, and the Mait II Cup.
- 1979 June: winner of the Croce del Sud Cup and the Gold Sail CITE Cup.
- 1980 June: winner of the Gold Sail CITE Cup for the second year running and of the Portovenere Cup.
- 1981 June: winner of the Mary Longary Cup.
- July: winner of the Rene Lainville Trophy and second place in the XXIX Giraglia.
- August: winner of the Portovenere Cup for the second consecutive year.
- 1982 May: winner of its class in the Middle Sea Race.
- June: winner once again of the Mary Longary Cup.
- 1984 July: third in its class in the XXXII Giraglia.
- 1991 September: second in the VI Italian Association of Vintage Yachts Regatta in Imperia.
- 1992 September: second in the VII Italian Association of Vintage Yachts Regatta in Imperia.

Of all these regattas, I would like to pick out the 1971 Admiral's Cup, when *Levantades*, *Tarantella*, and *Mabelle* formed the Italian Team that came an honorable seventh overall. Another impressive performance was the XV edition of the Martini Middle Sea Race, the longest of the Mediterranean classics (over 600 miles), when the old yet still aggressively competitive *Levantades* beat modern yachts such as *Orlanda* and *Nirvana*.

The boat has a mahogany keel and planking, white oak laminate-framing, a teak deck, and an aluminum mast. The changes made after its sale by Diano's heirs aimed to restore the boat to a rig more in keeping with a vessel built in 1967. They included the removal of a number of modern features and the refitting of the interior to make it more comfortable for long cruises, all without compromising the speed of this splendid sailing boat.

Lisa of la Tour

Launched as *Lisa*, this boat crossed the Atlantic towards Nice in France in about 1973, and after a few years it was sold to a Swiss–Mexican lady. Since 1985 it has belonged to Bernard Divorne, who renamed it *Lisa of la Tour* in 1988 after a place called La Tour-de-Peilz.

After having had it carefully refitted on Lake Leman (Lake Geneva), the new owner returned the boat to the sea where it has taken part in numerous vintage yacht regattas.

Lisa of la Tour has Brazilian mahogany (so-called "cedar") planking, a mahogany interior, pine masts (still original), and a teak deck. Despite not having a particularly long waterline this is a rather fast boat, as proven by its victories at the vintage yacht regatta held in La Spezia, Italy in 1989, in the Coppa Phocea Race, the Nioulargue, the Cannes Régates Royales, the Cannes–Saint Tropez Race of 1992, the Almirante Conde de Barcelona Trophy, and other subsequent races.

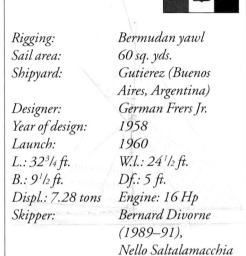

Rigging:	Bermudan yawl
Sail area:	60 sq. yds.
Shipyard:	Gutierez (Buenos Aires, Argentina)
Designer:	German Frers Jr.
Year of design:	1958
Launch:	1960
L.: 32³/₄ ft.	W.l.: 24¹/₂ ft.
B.: 9¹/₂ ft.	Df.: 5 ft.
Displ.: 7.28 tons	Engine: 16 Hp
Skipper:	Bernard Divorne (1989–91), Nello Saltalamacchia (1996–98)

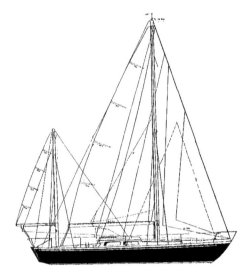

LEFT: *Cannes 1999,* Lisa of la Tour *during a regatta (Photo: J. Taylor).*

Mait II

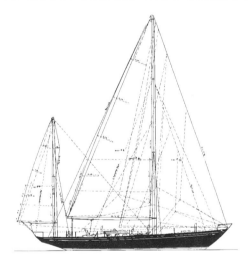

Rigging:	Bermudan yawl
Sail area:	311 sq. yds.
Shipyard:	Baglietto (Varazze, Italy)
Designer:	Sparkman & Stephens
Year of design:	1956
Launch:	1957
Restoration:	1987
L.: 62¼ ft.	W.l.: 49 ft.
B.: 14¼ ft.	Df.: 8¾ ft.
Displ.: 27.5 tons	Engine: 135 Hp
Skipper:	Fulvio Musumeci (1991–2000)

*M*ait II was designed in New York by the famous yacht designers Sparkman & Stephens and was built in 1956 using prized timbers by the famous Baglietto yard at Varazze in Italy. It has a cedar hull, teak deck, and mahogany superstructures and deckhouse.

This boat can be classified among the great ocean-racers. With its tapered, sea-worthy hull, classified as a I Class RORC (Royal Ocean Racing Club), it was designed to sail in the most important national and international regattas. A fast boat, *Mait II* is also well suited to ocean cruising. Its defining characteristics are its "long pitch" at all tacks and its gentle movement across the waves, be they short Mediterranean waves or longer ocean waves. "*One of our most satisfying designs was* Mait II, *completed for Commander Monzino,*" declared Olin Stephens and Alain Gil on September 18, 1990 when referring to their 40 years of experience in the field of boat design.

During its lifetime, *Mait II* has taken part in the most important Italian and inter-national regattas, including the Giraglia (it came fifth in 1958, eighth in 1959, second in 1960 and 1961, first in 1962, third in 1963, second in 1964, fifth in 1965 and

1966, third in 1967, eighth in 1968, 15th in 1970, first in 1971, and second in 1972). Given the boat's age, these later results attest to the boat's continuing ability to perform at the very highest levels. In the summer of 1959 it was the first Italian yacht to take part in the Fastnet Race, crewed by six Olympic yachtsmen: De Manincor, Canessa, Spigno, Reggio, Antonio, and Domenico Carattino. In this, the most difficult regatta in the world, *Mait II* performed very well, coming seventh out of 17.

It went on to win various regattas organized by the Royal Southampton Yacht Club and the Royal Thames Yacht Club, beating famous boats such as *Flica* and *Carina*. During those days, *Yachting World* magazine had the following to say about *Mait II*: "…*The striking* Mait II, *this large Italian yawl belonging to Commander Italo Monzino, a boat that performs almost like a 12-meter yacht, won the first regatta…*"

To wind up its tour of the northern seas, it came second in the Plymouth–La Rochelle Race. It then continued to win other regattas, such as the 1960 Malaga–Barcelona Race. A boat of considerable class! However, its most spectacular performance was in the 1962 Buenos Aires–Rio de Janeiro Race.

RIGHT: *ASW 2000, Monzino's famous* Mait II, *an unforgettable part of the history of Italian yachting (Photo: J. Taylor).*

Mait II was taken on board the cargo vessel *Augustus*, where a special launching cradle had been built to hold the yacht. It was greeted by thousands of Italian residents in Buenos Aires with the cry: "*Buena sorte, Italia!*" "Good luck Italy!"

As Captain De Manincor recollects: "*They were all unknown Italians, children of Italians who had never crossed the Atlantic and who even found it hard to speak our language, people from all walks of life. They all wanted to express their joy at seeing 'their flag' astern such an apparently fragile boat. I came on board with tears in my eyes and a lump in my throat...*" The skipper, De Manicor (a retired naval officer), was flanked by a young navigator, Lieutenant Giovanni Iannucci (the only representative of the Italian Navy on board). In the overall placings, *Mait II* was to finish second behind *Ondine* but ahead of several more famous boats, such as *Royono*, *Aldeberan*, *Stormvogel*, and *Germania V*.

Despite its age, the boat continued to perform well, taking part in a number of editions of the Middle Sea Race as well as one Capetown–Rio Race. This elegant, much-admired yacht is still sailing today.

ABOVE: *Detail of the interior (Photo: J. Taylor).*

LEFT: *ASW 1999,* Mait II, *designed by Sparkman & Stephens and launched by the Baglietto shipyard (Photo: J. Taylor).*

BELOW: *ASW 2000, the ever-youthful* Mait II *during a regatta (Photo: J. Taylor).*

Margareth II

Rigging: *Gaff-rigged sloop*
Sail area: *30 sq. yds.*
Shipyard: *Mostes Mario & Figli*
     (Genoa Prà, Italy)
Designer: *E.G. Van De Stadt*
Year of design: *1965*
Launch: *1966*
Restoration: *1991*
L.: 24 ^{1}/$_2$ ft.   *W.l.: 23 ft.*
B.: 7 ft.   *Df.: 3 ft.*
Displ.: 3.26 tons   *Engine: 5 Hp*
Skipper: *Emilio Maggi*
     (1991–92), Antonio
     Semeria (1998)

Margareth II is one of a series of seven hulls designed by the Dutch architect E.G. Van De Stadt. It was built at the Mostes shipyard in Genoa, Italy. The prototype boat, named *Bucaniere*, was exhibited at the Genoa Boat Show in 1996. This marked a return to wooden hulls, and in fact the hull of this particular boat is made from mahogany marine plywood coated in polyester. The boat, belonging to four residents of Alassio in Liguria, Italy, has an amusing nickname – "*Belurfa*" – a local dialect word for a small black fig. It enjoys racing and has reached a speed of 7 knots under sail, which is its maximum even with the aid of the auxiliary engine.

RIGHT: *Imperia 1991,* Margareth II, *launched at the Mostes yard in Genoa (Photo: L. Laura).*

Maria Galante

This is a motorsailer originally designed by Laurent Giles (in 1950) and subsequently modified, with the canoe stern being transformed into a transom stern, as on its twin sister *Pinna II*.

Maria Galante, with its green hull, appears in excellent condition after over 40 years of sailing, with no substantial modification having been made to its equipment.

Rigging:	*Gaff-rigged sloop*
Sail area:	*111 sq. yds.*
Shipyard:	*Navale di Sturla (Genoa, Italy)*
Designer:	*Laurent Giles*
Year of design:	*1950*
Launch:	*1962*
Restoration:	*1989, 1990*
L.: 38¹/₂ ft.	*W.l.: 34¹/₄ ft.*
B.: 10 ft.	*Df.: 3³/₄ ft.*
Displ.: 16.2 tons	*Engine: 93 Hp*
Skipper:	*Angelo Ferrari (1991–2000)*

LEFT: *September 1998, Maria Galante, designed by Laurent Giles in 1950 (Photo courtesy of A. Ferrari).*

BELOW: *Imperia 1966, the boat sailing at a good rate (Photo: P. Pittalunga).*

Mariangela

Rigging:	Bermudan ketch
Sail area:	102 sq. yds.
Shipyard:	Rino della Pietà
	(Chiavari, Italy)
Designer:	W. Gardner
Year of design:	1955
Launch:	1964
Restoration:	1989, 1993
L.: 39 ft.	W.l.: 27³/₄ ft.
B.: 10¹/₂ ft.	Df.: 6 ft.
Displ.: 13.2 tons	Engine: 14 Hp
Skipper:	Marco Tibiletti
	(1989–91)

RIGHT: *Imperia 1989, a shot of* Mariangela
(Photo: S. Pesato).

BELOW: *An old photograph of the boat*
(Photo courtesy of M. Tibiletti).

This boat was built together with two identical models on behalf of a broker who had bought the drawings from the naval architect W. Gardner. The boatbuilder was the master-carpenter Rino della Pietà from Chiavari in Italy.

In 1969 the boat was on sale at the quayside in Santa Margherita in Italy and was bought by Giacomo Togno, who sailed it until 1986. That summer, as a result of a crack caused by a collision, the boat was taken to the Porto Cervo shipyard in Sardinia and was subsequently left unused for a long time in Liguria, Italy. In 1989 it was purchased by Alberto Moricelli, who entrusted it to his friend Marco Tibiletti. In the haulage yard at Lavagna in Italy *Mariangela* was restored to seaworthiness within the space of two months.

During a later, more complete refitting, the boat's transom was rebuilt and three planking timbers were replaced. The boat has a mahogany keel and planking, a teak deck, and a Douglas fir mast.

Mio Mao

This gaff-rigged sloop was launched in 1961 at the Harry Hallberg (currently Hallberg Rassy) yard in Kungsviken, Sweden. Marketed as a P28, several boats of this type were built at that time and proved particularly popular in the United States.

Mio Mao, with its transom stern and raked bow, is in fact very similar to *Nina VII*; it can hug the wind to 40° and is very stable when running before trading winds. In 1992 the Beconcini shipyard in Italy carried out a number of refitting operations: the transom was rebuilt, the upper sections of a number of ribs were restored, and the first two topside planking timbers were replaced.

Mio Mao has cedar planking and a teak deck laid by the previous owner (the original deck had been of cloth-covered and painted marine plywood). The keel is made of oak, the cockpit and the interior are in iroko, and the mast and boom are made of spruce.

Rigging:	Gaff-rigged sloop
Sail area:	42 sq. yds.
Shipyard:	Harry Hallberg (Kungsviken, Sweden)
Designer:	Harry Hallberg
Year of design:	1960
Launch:	1961
Restoration:	1992–95 Beconcini shipyards (La Spezia, Italy)
L.: 28 ft.	W.l.: 22¼ ft.
B.: 6¾ ft.	Df.: 4¼ ft.
Displ.: 3.42 tons	Engine: 8 Hp
Skipper:	Carlo Musu (2000)

BELOW: *Imperia 2000, the sloop* Mio Mao *photographed at good speed (Photo: J. Taylor).*

Namar

Rigging:	Bermudan ketch
Sail area:	140 sq. yds.
Shipyard:	Beconcini shipyards (La Spezia, Italy)
Designer:	F. Anselmi Boretti
Year of design:	1962
Launch:	1964
Restoration:	1976
L.: 53 ft.	W.l.: 39 ft.
B.: 15 1/4 ft.	Df.: 8 ft.
Displ.: 27.3 tons	Engine: 90 Hp
Skipper:	Pietro Bonardi (1988–92)

RIGHT: *Imperia 1988,* Namar *sailing on the wind (Photo: S. Pesato).*

esigned by architect F. Anselmi Boretti, this boat was commissioned by Albino Buticchi and in 1964 was considered one of the best boats built by the Beconcini shipyard in Italy. Its speed running free and before trading winds was immediately apparent, whereas it struggled somewhat on a close reach (it drew 4 feet at the time). This was the reason why the second owner had the keel redesigned with the addition of an iroko appendix, while the lead ballast remained the same weight but reshaped.

The result was that the boat now drew 8 feet and sailed better close-hauled, its overall performance improved significantly. After changing hands a couple of times, and with the old masts replaced by new aluminum ones, *Namar* was bought by the present owner, who started to refit the boat: the deck was rebuilt, while the stringer, toerail, and bulb bolts were all replaced. The hull consists of mahogany planking, a teak deck, an iroko keel, and a lead bulb. Over the years the boat has clearly displayed its seaworthiness, even in rougher seas.

Nina VII

(sometime P28)

Rigging:	Gaff-rigged cutter
Sail area:	36 sq. yds.
Shipyard:	Harry Hallberg (Sweden)
Designer:	The shipyard
Year of design:	1960
Launch:	1960
L.: 28 ft.	W.l.: 20 1/4 ft.
B.: 7 1/2 ft.	Df.: 4 ft.
Displ.: 2.98 tons	Engine: 10 Hp
Skipper:	Silvano Barsiola (1991–98), C. Rossi (2000)

RIGHT: Nina VII, *a cutter built in Sweden in 1960 (Photo courtesy of S. Barsiola).*

ina VII, with its transom stern and raked bow, was launched as a P28 at the Island of Orust boatyard in Sweden. The yard was famous at the time for the construction of excellent seaworthy wooden boats with superb designs. This boat, in fact, has performed exceptionally well when both racing and cruising.

Its most noteworthy characteristics are its oak keel and posts, its fine cast-iron ballast, steam-curved ash ribs, African mahogany planking, the Swedish larch stempost and beams, special plywood and teak decking, and the spruce mast and boom. The 36 square yards of sails are made up of a 24 square yard spanker and a 12 square yard jib. The boat made its first appearance in Italian waters in 1977 when it was bought by Domenico Zino of Savona in Liguria.

ABOVE: *Imperia 2000, a shot of* Nina VII *(Photo: J. Taylor).*

Odin

Designed by Albert and Georges Schranz after years of experience in the field of yacht-racing and cruising, this boat has the light displacement characteristic of the RORC (Royal Ocean Racing Club) III Class. Its hull was built by the Bonnin shipyard in the Gironde in France, famous for the quality of its Dragons and its fixed-rating boats, as well as for its construction of the famous *Pourquoi Pas* of Captain Charcot. The boat has mahogany planking, which is still perfectly waterproof after more than 40 years of sailing, and all the rigging (personally constructed by the Schranz brothers) is still in good condition.

As soon as it had been fitted out, *Odin* displayed its excellent sailing qualities by winning a series of regattas, including the Monaco–Sète Race and the Sète–Ajaccio Race in 1961. It is also a familiar figure at the Giraglia and has always finished well in the various editions in which it has taken part – in 1963 it came first; then second in 1970; third in 1961, 1964, and 1967; and fourth in three further editions. In 1963, during the Sète–Port Vendres Regatta, held in really rough weather, *Odin* was the only boat that managed to cross the finishing line. That same year it was also Champion of the Mediterranean. With the coming to the fore of the IOR rating, *Odin* continued to race with the Schranz brothers. It was subject to a number of structural modifications including the fitting of a metal mast.

In 1986 it was bought by Olivier and Guillaume Wattinne, who the following year won the V Class in the Nioulargue and the first edition of the Coppa Phoecea. Today the boat continues to sail in the waters around the French port of Cannes.

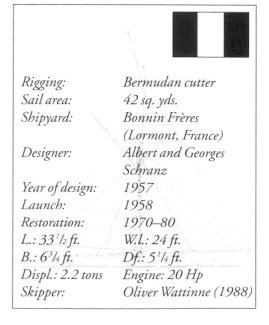

Rigging:	Bermudan cutter
Sail area:	42 sq. yds.
Shipyard:	Bonnin Frères (Lormont, France)
Designer:	Albert and Georges Schranz
Year of design:	1957
Launch:	1958
Restoration:	1970–80
L.: 33½ ft.	W.l.: 24 ft.
B.: 6¾ ft.	Df.: 5¼ ft.
Displ.: 2.2 tons	Engine: 20 Hp
Skipper:	Oliver Wattinne (1988)

Outlaw

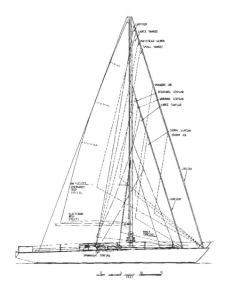

Rigging:	Gaff-rigged cutter
Sail area:	100 sq. yds.
Shipyard:	Souter (Cowes, England)
Designer:	J. Illingworth & A. Primrose
Year of design:	1962
Launch:	1963
Restoration:	1987
L.: 48 1/2 ft.	W.l.: 38 3/4 ft.
B.: 13 ft.	Df.: 8 ft.
Displ.: 16.3 tons	Engine: 36 Hp
Skipper:	Mike Horsley (1992–2001)

RIGHT: *Imperia 2000, the very fast* Outlaw, *a born racer. During its first regatta season it won the Myth of Malham, Colin Campbell, King Edward VII, and Trechemer Cups; moreover, it was a member of the winning Admiral's Cup team and winner of the Class I in the Royal Ocean Racing Club Championship (Photo: J. Taylor).*

Designed by John Illingworth and Angus Primrose, *Outlaw* (a Class I ocean racer) was launched in the spring of 1963 on behalf of Sir Max Aitken. Built of laminated wood, its main section is wide and deep. The planking consists of eight thin layers glued one on top of the other (cold-molded); the keel, posts, ribs, and deck beams are also made of laminated wood. When it was launched it was the largest boat the Souter yard had produced and had been constructed using avant-garde methods. Sir Max Aitken kept the boat from April 1963 until May 1964, when it was sold to the English Grains Company.

In the meantime the boat had been selected for the English team taking part in the 1963 Admiral's Cup. In this race it came sixth in its class. In 1964 it continued to race successfully in the English Channel before being bought by Roger Fuller from the company Deacon Boat Yard Ltd. near Southampton, England. 1964 proved to be one of the boat's finest years. The previous year it had already won the Royal Ocean Racing Club Championship; then in 1964 it came second in Class I in the Southsea–Harwich Race, third in both the North Sea Race and the Cannes–Dinard Race ahead of *Rocquette* (which came fifth skippered by Peter Nicholson), third in the Morgan Cup, and second in the Santander–La Trinité Race. Finally, it brilliantly finished the Plymouth–Santander Race ahead of the incredibly fast *Myth of Malham*. Outlaw then produced a stunning performance to win the Harwich–Copenhagen Race in 1966 (after 630 miles of the most important regatta of the year); it came first in its class and first in all the other categories, with a compensated time of just ten hours.

The year 1966 proved to be a year of grace for the boats designed by John Illingworth, which together won some 70 prizes in open-sea regattas, including: the Southsea–Harwich Race, the Falmouth–Douarnez Race, the Irish Sea Race, the Cherbourg–Eddystone Race, the Cowes–Dinard Race, the Channel Race, and the Cowes–St. Malo Race.

In 1969 *Outlaw* changed hands when it was bought by a Mr. Wakeham. Then in April 1972 it was sold to Bernard Bullough, who kept the boat until December 1975, the year in which it was purchased by Robert Fewtrell of the Isle of Wight, who sailed it for a period of five years, which included two transatlantic voyages. Then the boat went through a rough patch, being left half-abandoned in Cowes, England, until it was rediscovered by its present owner, Mike Horsley.

Despite the long period of inactivity, the boat had remained in excellent condition, so much so that, after some servicing, Horsley decided to take part in the 1990 Nioulargue and a number of other regattas. A light displacement hull (very much dear to the heart of its designer), *Outlaw* is a perfect racing machine and regularly takes part in the vintage yacht regattas.

Pacciora

*P*acciora means "quiet, peaceful." This gaff-rigged was launched in 1963 at the Mingo boatyard in Riva Tringoso, Italy. In 1982, having taken part in numerous regattas, it was sold by its original owner, Angelo Navone, to a certain Mr. Nucci, who in 1989 sold it again to Possa and Walter Tirrito. *Pacciara* has mahogany planking, an iroko keel, a teak deck, a cedar stringer, ash and mountain acacia ribs, and a spruce mast, boom, and spinnaker pole.

In 1982 the boat underwent a number of modifications: part of the cockpit was removed and a fore cabin with two berths was built. The planking is fastened down onto the 68 ribs (three screws every 4 inches) with copper screws covered with wooden belaying pins. The boat has been very carefully looked after by its present owners, who in recent years have entrusted servicing to the F. Della Pietà yard in Chiaravalle, Italy. In 1997 the boat changed owners once again.

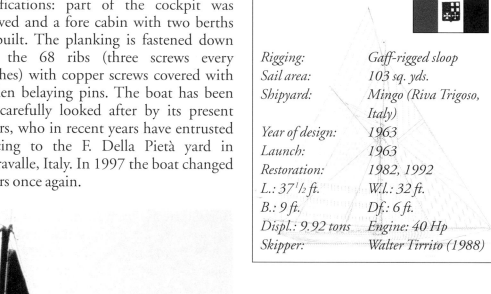

Rigging:	Gaff-rigged sloop
Sail area:	103 sq. yds.
Shipyard:	Mingo (Riva Trigoso, Italy)
Year of design:	1963
Launch:	1963
Restoration:	1982, 1992
L.: 37 1/2 ft.	W.l.: 32 ft.
B.: 9 ft.	Df.: 6 ft.
Displ.: 9.92 tons	Engine: 40 Hp
Skipper:	Walter Tirrito (1988)

LEFT: *September 1998, the sloop* Pacciora *during a regatta (Photo: A. Ansaldo).*

Paxos

Rigging:	Bermudan sloop
Sail area:	92 sq. yds.
Shipyard:	Graglietto (Trieste, Italy)
Designer:	Sparkman & Stephens
Year of design:	1972
Launch:	1972
Restoration:	1995, 1998 Beaulieu (France)
L.: 37 ft.	W.l.: 28¹/₂ ft.
B.: 12 ft.	Df.: 6 ft.
Displ.: 8.82 tons	Engine: 35 Hp
Skipper:	Andrea Campi (1998–2002)

RIGHT: *Imperia 2000, a shot of the sloop* Paxos *(Photo: S. Pesato).*

This boat was commissioned by Marina Spaccarelli Bulgari with the intention of entering it for the One Ton Cup (with Admiral Agostino Straulino, a mythical figure in Italian sailing, at the helm). *Paxos* is a fast, seaworthy hull that suffers when the wind drops below 5 knots. Its planking consists of three layers of laminate mahogany, and it has an alloy mast and boom and a varnished plywood rudder tiller and deck.

After a few years, Mrs. Bulgari sold the boat to two members of the crew, who initially used it for racing and later used it as a cruiser. In 1990 it was sold to the present skipper. The hull was in good condition, having been serviced regularly (the rigging was replaced). Recently it has undergone some "cosmetic" refitting at the Beaulieu shipyard in France, including repainting of the interior, while the sails have been completely renewed by the sailmakers Zaoli of San Remo in Italy. *Paxos* has taken part in numerous regattas, where it has often done well (such as at the Genoa and Marseilles Weeks).

Peer Gynt

Rigging:	Gaff-rigged sloop
Sail area:	48 sq. yds.
Shipyard:	Felix Silvestro (Marseilles, France)
Designer:	Maurice Amiet
Year of design:	1952
Launch:	1956
Restoration:	1989
L.: 27 ft.	W.l.: 23 ft.
B.: 7¹/₄ ft.	Df.: 4³/₄ ft.
Displ.: 3.21 tons	Engine: 11 Hp
Skipper:	Giovanni De Nigris (1990–92)

RIGHT: *Imperia 1990,* Peer Gynt *during a regatta (Photo: Tomatis).*

Felix Silvestro began his career as a boat builder in Nice, France, in 1951, when, at the age of 22, he met Maurice Amiet, designer-to-be of *Peer Gynt*, a Norwegian-style yacht. "*Thus started the beginning of a dazzling career which was consecrated by the unsolicited praise of Roderic Stephens, the brother and right arm of the famous person in the world of naval architecture, Olin Stephens.*" So wrote Amiet in the preface to his book *Le Sharpie*, which he dedicated to Felix Silvestro, builder of *Peer Gynt*.

Felix Silvestro wanted to keep the boat for himself, as his childhood friend the boat-builder Jean Louis Vivaldi had done after building the twin vessel *Solveig* (still

moored in the port of Nice). However, in 1956, the year in which *Peer Gynt* was launched, Felix Silvestro was given the opportunity to buy some land in Nice on which to build his own boatyard, and so he decided to sell *Peer Gynt*.

The new owner, Jean Cottalorda of Villefranche, kept the boat for a total of 34 years, during which he looked after and serviced it lovingly.

In December 1989 the boat was purchased by Paolo and Giovanni De Nigris. It was in perfect condition (mahogany hull, spruce mast and boom, mahogany interior, 2-inch acacia ribs, marine plywood deck, and so on).

In recognition of the attractive appearance of *Peer Gynt*, at the 1990 vintage yacht meeting in Imperia the boat was awarded the Città di Imperia Cup "for the originality and attractiveness of its design." *Peer Gynt* resembles the Australian cutter with the same name that came among the honors in various regattas in the late 1940s (including second place in the tough Auckland–Sydney Race in 1948).

BELOW: *Imperia 1990,* Peer Gynt *during a regatta (Photo: Tomatis).*

Peteteka of Ville

Rigging:	Bermudan sloop
Sail area:	72 sq. yds.
Shipyard:	Gino d'Este (Fiumicino, Italy)
Designer:	Camper & Nicholson (Gosport, England)
Year of design:	1959
Launch:	1961
L.: 38 ft.	W.l.: 29¹/₂ ft.
B.: 10 ft.	Df.: 6¹/₂ ft.
Displ.: 9.92 tons	Engine: 25 Hp
Skipper:	Gidon Graetz (1989–92)

This boat has taken part in numerous regattas during its lifetime, winning a number of races in the late 1960s. Rigged as a sloop, the *Peteteka of Ville* has a wooden mast and boom (with English stainless steel rail tracks and runners), mahogany planking, a teak deck, and laminate acacia ribs, as well as mahogany skylights, a cockpit, stringers, hatchways, a deckhouse, and a polished mahogany interior. At the Imperia regattas the *Peteteka of Ville* has always finished among the leading boats, proudly displaying its sound nautical and racing capabilities.

Pilon

Rigging:	Bermudan ketch
Sail area:	152 sq. yds.
Shipyard:	Sangermani (Lavagna, Italy)
Designer:	Cesare Sangermani
Year of design:	1962
Launch:	1963
L.: 52¹/₂ ft.	W.l.: 44¹/₂ ft.
B.: 13¹/₄ ft.	Df.: 5 ft.
Displ.: 9.92 tons	Engine: 25 Hp
Skipper:	Massimo Frigeri (1991), Enzo Bandinelli (1992–98)

The *Pilon* is a motorsailer that was launched in 1963 and has had just one owner. The boat appears today as it must have the day it was launched, not having undergone modifications of any kind apart from a refitting of the deck in 1983. It is suitably equipped for Mediterranean cruising. Apart from a little touching up of the teak planking and deck, the boat's parts have remained completely intact. It continues to be moored in the port of Fiumaretta in Italy.

RIGHT: *Imperia 1996, the motorsailer* Pilon, *one of the very few boats never to have changed hands* (Photo: S. Pesato).

Resaca of Kimberly

*R*esaca of Kimberly was built by the Carabela yard in Spain in 1967 after being commissioned by the famous yachtsman Mike Dacosta and designed by the British architect Angus Primrose.

The drawings of this unique prototype racer are currently conserved at the Greenwich National Maritime Museum in London. The boat has won a number of victories in Catalan and Mallorcan waters. Purchased by the present owner in 1999 in a rather poor state, it has since been restored to its original splendor.

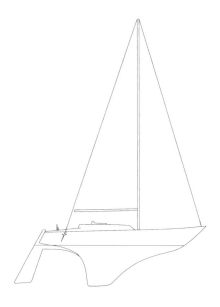

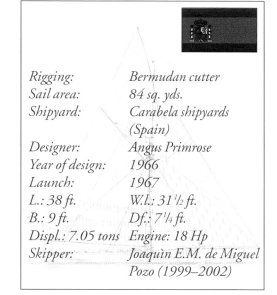

Rigging:	Bermudan cutter
Sail area:	84 sq. yds.
Shipyard:	Carabela shipyards (Spain)
Designer:	Angus Primrose
Year of design:	1966
Launch:	1967
L.: 38 ft.	W.l.: 31½ ft.
B.: 9 ft.	Df.: 7¼ ft.
Displ.: 7.05 tons	Engine: 18 Hp
Skipper:	Joaquìn E.M. de Miguel Pozo (1999–2002)

LEFT: *Detail of* Resaca*'s deck (Photo courtesy of J. Pozo).*

BELOW: Resaca *during a regatta (Photo courtesy of J. Pozo).*

Rocquette

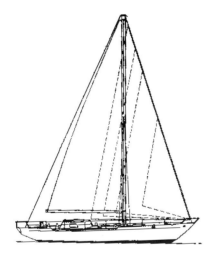

Rigging:	Bermudan sloop
Sail area:	128 sq. yds.
Shipyard:	Camper & Nicholson (Gosport, England)
Designer:	Peter Nicholson
Year of design:	1963
Launch:	1964
Restoration:	1984–85, 1987–88
L.: 41½ ft.	W.l.: 30½ ft.
B.: 11 ft.	Df.: 6¾ ft.
Displ.: 13 tons	Engine: 28 Hp
Skipper:	Andrea Rolli (1987–89), Giorgio Corte (1990), Ezio Robotti (1996–2002)

This was the personal yacht of its designer, Peter Nicholson. Peter is a member of the fourth generation of these famous boat-designers. It was specifically designed and built for the Admiral's Cup and was one of the leading boats in the 1964 regatta season. After winning the Gold Roman Challenge Cup ahead of some 325 other boats, it became part of yachting history with four successive wins at Cowes Week, skippered as always by Peter Nicholson.

The key to its success was the experimental move from a heavy draft to a lighter one, achieved as a result of the limited weight of the hull (10 percent lighter than the weight envisaged in the classification) obtained using laminate mahogany framing. Thus, *Rocquette* has a light displacement in relation to its ballast and stability, aided by a good freeboard and the conspicuous width of the main section of the boat. The hull was

built using various different materials and features laminate cedar and galvanized iron ribs, a mahogany plywood flush deck, cedar planking, a teak bottom, and a mahogany topside. Moreover, the superstructures are in mahogany (including the unmistakable low deckhouse standing out from a deck with a considerable beam), while the interior is in mahogany, cedar, and teak.

The boat has undergone a number of modifications during its lifetime, such as shortening of the aluminum mast and boom. This was probably the work of the boat's second owner, David Maw, an English yachtsman who single-handedly sailed some 35,000 miles. *Rocquette* changed hands again; the 1975 Register of Yachts records Martin Sharp as owner of *Vanity I*, formerly *Bluejacket III*, formerly *Rocquette*. Subsequently the boom has been lengthened to its original size, and the spanker sheet has also been repositioned where it had

RIGHT: *Imperia 1989, Rocquette, a Peter Nicholson design with fine racing credentials. Its victories include the Round the Island Race, the Britannia Cup, and the NYYC Cup (Photo: S. Pesato).*

PETER C. NICHOLSON

Telephone: Office (023) 80455019
Home (023) 80452172
Fax (023) 80455834

Mere House
Hamble
Southampton SO31 4JB
Hampshire

15th October, 1999.

Mr. & Mrs. Chelotti,
Via Brighinzio 7,
13100 Vercelli,
Italy.

Dear Mr. & Mrs. Chelotti,

Camper & Nicholson have asked me to write to you regarding *Rocquette*. I am very pleased to do so as this has proven one of the most successful boats I have ever owned. I am delighted to know that it is in safe hands because we lost trace of its whereabouts at the end of the 1960s, after I had sold it to a successful open-sea regatta yachtsman by the name of David Maw, who renamed it *Bluejacket III*. He raced very successfully with the boat for many years, and then I believe he sold it to a Frenchman; there can be no doubt that it left our country at the end of the 1960s and I had had no news of it since then. I would be very grateful if you could send me a photograph and news of the boat.

The following is the story of *Rocquette*.

In the 1950s and the early 1960s, Camper & Nicholson designed important sailing boats on the south coast of England and were very successful in British open-sea regattas at that time. At the beginning of the 1960s, Sparkman & Stephens began to create a number of boats for English boat-owners that challenged our supremacy at that time: in 1963 they designed a boat called *Clarion* for the British owner Derek Boyer. *Clarion* was different from the other yachts initially designed by Sparkman & Stephens in that it had a more streamlined shape, a smaller wet surface, and a more tapered stern, which made it better equipped for sailing into the wind than the majority of the American boats that had been designed up until then. *Clarion* was very successful, and in 1963 won the Fastnet Race.

I decided that we had to try and build a boat capable of beating *Clarion*, and in order to do so we had to follow their design lead. We wanted to produce a boat capable of sailing strongly into the wind, one that kept the wet surface to a minimum, but also one that would perform equally as well in light winds. In order to reduce the wet surface of the hull we had to design a hull with a low stability, and this required a high percentage of ballast, which in turn meant we needed a light hull. We managed to achieve this, as you know, by designing a construction featuring a triple layer of wood, the inside layer in spruce. I also wanted to design a flush deck, while at the same time ensuring a comfortable, sheltered cockpit for open-sea regattas. Moreover, at that time you could obtain a slight advantage by reducing the freeboard near the mast, because the highest point on the side was at right angles to the mast. As far as I know, *Rocquette* was the first boat of its kind to have a flush deck and a reasonable height below deck, without having the deckhouse extend beyond the mast. We wanted to install the engine as low as possible, and so at first we chose an Arona, an Italian diesel engine, but this gave a lot of problems and I was wondering whether you still have it on board.

I raced *Rocquette* successfully in the UK for the entire 1964 season. I think I am right in saying that we won all the main regattas in the Solent that year. We also won in our class at Cowes Week, and if I remember rightly we won all the races we took part in. I didn't take part in open-sea regattas with this boat because I was already taking part in these races with another Camper & Nicholson boat, but I did take part in the Cowes and the Dinard regatta, where we came second. Of the regattas we took part in, I think that this was the only one we did not win in 1964.

At the end of the season Mr. Maw made me an offer for the boat I really could not refuse, as our job was that of creating boats that our customers could win races with, rather than boats which I would have won lots of regattas with.

Camper & Nicholson tell me that you would like to ask me a number of questions about *Rocquette*, and if you would like to telephone me I would be more than happy to answer your queries. You are welcome to phone me either at my office or at home: both numbers are given at the top of the letter.

I would like to say once again that I am extremely pleased to hear that *Rocquette* is in good hands and clearly well looked-after, and I hope that it continues to give you great pleasure and satisfaction for years to come.

Yours sincerely,
Peter Nicholson

ABOVE: *Imperia 1996,* Rocquette *(formerly Peter Nicholson's own personal boat) during a regatta (Photo: S. Pesato).*

LEFT: *A letter sent by Peter Nicholson recounting the unique story of* Rocquette *(courtesy of E. Robotti).*

The Roquette *was designed by Peter Nicholson in 1964 and numbered among the most successful offshore racing yachts of the year. Her exceptional manoeuvrability was caused by the slim outline and a lighter body due to the skilful use of different layers of wood. The* Roquette *had a comfortable cockpit, a flush deck and was ideal for offshore races and on the high seas. In the season of 1964, Nicholson won nearly all Britain's important Cups of his class, among which Cowes Week.*

ABOVE: *1964, Rocquette in a splendid photo taken by Beken of Cowes, the best photographer of sailing boats (Photo: K. Beken, courtesy of E. Robotti).*

RIGHT: *A copy of a letter signed by Peter Nicholson (courtesy of E. Robotti).*

originally been. More recent work on the boat has included the restoration of the stempost at the Sangermani yards in Italy.

Rocquette, with its double-skinned hull, was based for years in the port of Gibraltar. It had been called *Vanity I* before two partners, Vittorio Stradella and Andra Rolli, bought it in 1983. At that time it took part in two editions of the Nioulargue and one Giraglia.

A boat that performs well when sailed close-hauled, *Rocquette* came fourth at Imperia in 1988 (behind *Al Na' Ir IV*, *Artica II*, and *La Meloria*) and fifth in the 1989 and 1990 editions of the same race. In 1990 it also won the Coupe Phocea, an international regatta held every two years in Marseilles in France. On that occasion the boat's crew (Andrea Rolli, Luvca Todros, Franco Orsini, and Mario Spinelli) had to battle it out with another 40 boats in a force-8 north-westerly. The overall winner of this really tough race was the ubiquitous old *Sif*.

As I write, the boat rocks gently back and forth at its mooring in the port of Imperia, with its unique, aristocratic lines that in 30 years of racing and cruising have contributed towards consolidating *Rocquette*'s fame.

PETER C. NICHOLSON

Telephone: Office (023) 80455019
Home (023) 80452172
Fax: (023) 80455834

Mere House
Hamble
Southampton SO31 4JB
Hampshire

15th February, 2000.

Mr. & Mrs. Chelotti,
Via Brighinzio 7,
13100 Vercelli,
Italy.

Dear Mr. & Mrs. Chelotti,

<u>ROCQUETTE</u>

    Further to my letter of January 17th, I now enclose the photograph of ROCQUETTE which I promised to send you.

    This was taken just after she was first launched in 1964 and she is racing in the famous annual race round the Isle of Wight in which she was the overall winner in a fleet of about one thousand five hundred yachts.

    With kind regards.

Yours Sincerely

Peter Nicholson.

Encl:

Rorqual

This boat was designed by the French architect Georges Auzepy Brenneur, and built at the Argo Capentieri shipyard in La Spezia, Italy, on behalf of the engineer Monaci. It was designed as a Mediterranean cruiser, and this is reflected in its comfortable, solid build. In fact, the boat spent the first few years of its life in the quiet ports of Le Grazie and Portovenere, and then found permanent moorings at Loano and San Remo, all in Italy.

During the 1970s and 1980s it took part in the occasional regatta, although it was mainly used for cruising once again. Then in the period from 1987 through 1989 the boat was rather neglected, until its new owners, Franco and Paolo Bistolfi decided to have it completely restored.

Rorqual has a limited number of winches, and compared with more modern boats it has a small sailing area given its displacement. A superbly well-balanced boat, it performs brilliantly on long tacks, responds well when sailed close-hauled, but is at its best when sailing on a beam reach or on a trading wind. It is an extremely stable, safe boat even in rougher seas, with its sheltered cockpit positioned to the center of the boat.

Recent restoration work included the reinforcement of the toerail, the replacement of some of the planking, and a new set of sails.

Rigging:	Bermudan ketch
Sail area:	114 sq. yds.
Shipyard:	Argo Carpentieri (La Spezia, Italy)
Designer:	Georges Auzepy Brenneur
Year of design:	1967
Launch:	1969
Restoration:	1990
L.: 41 ft.	W.l.: 32 ft.
B.: 11 ft.	Df.: 6 ft.
Displ.: 14 tons	Engine: 60 Hp
Skipper:	Alessandro and Federico Bistolfi (1992–2000)

LEFT: *Imperia 1992,* Rorqual *with its characteristic cockpit at the center of the boat (Photo: F. Ramella).*

BELOW: *Imperia 1998, a shot of the boat under sail (Photo: S. Pesato).*

Rubin III

Rigging:	*Bermudan sloop*
Sail area:	*165 sq. yds.*
Shipyard:	*Abeking & Rasmussen (Lemwerder, Germany)*
Designer:	*Sparkman & Stephens*
Year of design:	*1966*
Launch:	*1967*
Restoration:	*1990–91*
L.: *50¾ ft.*	W.l.: *37 ft.*
B.: *11¼ ft.*	Df.: *7¾ ft.*
Displ.: *19.3 tons*	Engine: *65 Hp*
Skipper:	*Andrea Rolli (1990), Antonio Chioatto (1991)*

BELOW: *September 1990,* Rubin III *during a regatta (Photo: S. Pesato).*

OPPOSITE PAGE: *Imperia 1991, another shot of the boat from a different angle (Photo: S. Pesato).*

Designed by Sparkman & Stephens when they were at their very peak, *Rubin III*, commissioned by Hans Otto Schumann (owner of all the German yachts named *Rubin*) was launched in 1967 at the Abeking & Rasmussen shipyard in Germany, which at that time was, together with Camper & Nicholson, the top European boat-builder.

A classic yacht with the purest of lines, *Rubin III* was designed and built using the very latest technology available at the time. It was immediately entered for the Admiral's Cup and led the German team in that race. It did well in a number of important races, including a second place in the Channel Race and a fifth place in the Fastnet Race of 1967. At that time, the RORC (Royal Ocean Racing Club) regulations were upheld for all yacht races. Subsequently, with the advent of the IOR, the boat suffered the only modification made during its lifetime: in order to enjoy the benefits of the new regulations for open-sea racing its sail plan had to be modified, leading to shortening of the boom and the fitting of large genoas and narrow spankers. However, despite these significant modifications, the boat continued to perform very well in regattas, given that its excellent response when sailed close-hauled was not affected at all by these changes.

After a number of editions of the Admiral's Cup the boat completed a series of ocean crossings, both racing and cruising, and won further honors in the Baltic and Irish Seas. It was eventually sold to the oldest sailing club in Hamburg, the Hamburgischer Verein Seefahrt, which renamed the boat *Störtbeker* and used it as a training vessel on the open sea. Thus it was that it sailed over the North Atlantic, from the Portuguese coast to the Caribbean and up to the deepest of the Canadian inlets.

In 1989 the boat was imported into Italy by a group of friends (Chioatto, Casaburi, Caffarena, Rolli, and Scarampi), who, after giving it back its original name, saw to restoring the boat in preparation for the classical yacht races held in the Mediterranean. *Rubin III* can be considered virtually the twin of *Levantades*. In fact, the designs submitted at the time by Stephens are identical, although during construction work, which was carried out at the same time on both boats but in different countries, the shipyards and owners made a number of modifications (to the deckhouse, steering gear, stern exits, etc.).

The boat's evergreen lines make it ideal for both racing and cruising. It boasts sizeable overhangs, double diagonal mahogany planking, laminate ribs and frame-floor timbers, a teak deck, and a mahogany deckhouse. The mast, boom, the two spinnaker poles, and the outriggers are all in silver-colored, anodized aluminum. The interior is particularly light thanks to the wood paneling used and to the two deckhouses, each with its own separate entrance. The deck plan and the cockpit were specifically designed for racing so as to make onboard maneuvers as easy and safe as possible.

Rubin III has a classical sloop rig, but if needs be it can be fitted out as a cutter using a loose staysail forestay. The position of the cockpit to the rear, together with the dome-shaped spray guards, protect the helmsman and crew as they sail the boat. The boat changed hands in 1993.

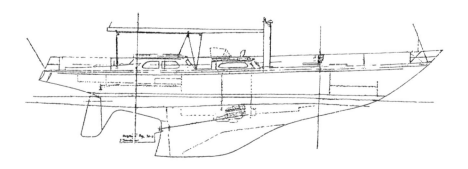

Sagittario

Rigging:	Bermudan cutter
Sail area:	132 sq. yds.
Shipyard:	Craglietto (Trieste, Italy)
Designer:	Carlo Sciarelli
Year of design:	1970
Launch:	1972
L.: 50½ ft.	W.l.: 45¾ ft.
B.: 12 ft.	Df.: 8 ft.
Displ.: 9.37 tons	Engine: 25 Hp
Skipper:	Lieutenant-Commander Riccardo Testa (1996)

*S*agittario, designed by Carlo Sciarelli, was built in just 78 days by the Craglietto shipyard in Italy in order for a naval officer to take part in the Ostar 1972 single-handed transatlantic regatta. Four Italian boats took part in that particular race, including *Sagittario*, the Italian Navy Yacht Club's cutter that was skippered by Franco Faggioni.

Sagittario was launched on April 11, 1972 but was not fitted out in time to take part in the 500-mile pre-race qualifying trial. In spite of this the organizers decided to allow the boat to take part in the race, but with an 18-hour penalty. In the end, *Sagittario* crossed the finishing line at Newport, Rhode Island, seventh of the fleet of 55 boats taking part, the first Italian boat home and the third of the single-hulled yachts. It was a great achievement for the designer, Carlo Sciarelli, who had created this light-displacement hull on orders from the Navy – a fast, stable boat with a limited sailing area.

The boat has ¾-inch spruce cross-planking laid over lengthways ribs. After testing, it was reinforced with intermediate laminate ribs at the bow end. The bottom has been coated with a triple layer of fiber-glass up to and beyond the waterline. It also has an iroko keel weighted with lead totaling nearly 4.41 tons. The mast is made of a light alloy.

After its intrepid entry to the world of racing, *Sagittario* continued to take part in and win regattas. For six consecutive years it took part in the Middle Sea Race, winning two years running (1980 and 1981 – skippered by Mario Di Giovanni). In 1998, with Agostino Straulino at the helm, the boat won a total of four honors and awards at the Barcolana regattas.

THIS PAGE: *Imperia 1996, two shots of the Italian Navy's cutter* Sagittario *(Photos: S. Pesato).*

San Marco

*S*an Marco was designed by Artù Chiggiato (1902–84), an architect who made a considerable contribution to modernizing boat design and yachting in Italy. A great friend of Laurent Giles, John Illingworth, and Uffa Fox, he was appointed technical adviser to the International Yacht Racing Union. "King Arthur," as he was affectionately called, not only raced but also designed yachts for his friends at the Venice Yacht Association (Compagnia della Vela di Venezia). Many of his designs were published in *Yachting World*, and one of these, the *Vento Perso*, became famous for its transatlantic crossing in 1947 from Venice to Rio de Janeiro.

San Marco left Venice for the Ligurian Sea and the port of Portofino in Italy in about 1955. A seven-eighths rigged sloop, up to now it has had five different owners. In the 1950s it had Zadro sails and was classified as a Class III RORC (Royal Ocean Racing Club). It has mahogany planking, bent acacia ribs, sawn oak ribs, reinforcing frame-floor plates in galvanized iron, a teak deck, and a mahogany deckhouse and cockpits. Between 1996 and 1998 it underwent some minor refitting and the replacement of five bolts fastening the bulb to the 2.31-ton cast-iron keel.

The boat is rigged at the masthead and performs well when sailing close-hauled.

Rigging:	Gaff-rigged sloop
Sail area:	72 sq. yds.
Shipyard:	Gino d'Este (Venice, Italy)
Designer:	Artù Chiggiato
Year of design:	1952
Launch:	1952
Restoration:	1996, 1998
L.: 31 ft.	W.l.: 25 1/2 ft.
B.: 8 1/4 ft.	Df.: 5 1/2 ft.
Displ.: 6.83 tons	Engine: 38 Hp
Skipper:	Pier Giovanni De Martini (1998)

LEFT: *Imperia 2000, the sloop* San Marco *designed by Artù Chiggiato (Photo: S. Pesato).*

BELOW: *Imperia 2000, the boat during a regatta (Photo: S. Pesato).*

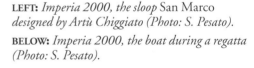

Santander of Wight

Rigging:	Gaff-rigged sloop
Sail area:	132 sq. yds.
Shipyard:	R.W. Clark (Cowes, England)
Designer:	P.L. Rhodes
Year of design:	1957
Launch:	1958
Restoration:	1982
L.: 47½ ft.	W.l.: 29½ ft.
B.: 11 ft.	Df.: 6 ft.
Displ.: 11.4 tons	Engine: 56 Hp
Skipper:	Andrea Boscu (1991–2000)

BELOW: *ASW 1999, Santander of Wight, winner of one Fastnet Race, sailing close-hauled (Photo: J. Taylor).*

Designed by the famous naval architect Philip Rhodes in 1957, *Santander of Wight* was launched the following year at the Clark boatyard in East Cowes (on the Isle of Wight in England), hence the name taken from the Santander–Cowes Regatta. As well as victory in the 1961 Fastnet Race, the boat has won a whole series of regattas during its lifetime.

The boat entered the Mediterranean in 1962 with its then owner Mary Blewitt, a famous yachtswoman and later the General Secretary of the Royal Ocean Racing Club. She had bought the boat from the actor Richard Greene. In 1963, the boat took part in Genoa Week in Italy and the Giraglia (where it came seventh in the II Class). Then, in 1964, it repeated its feat at the Giraglia (seventh place once again) and took part in the Antibes–Ischia Race.

In 1965 it was purchased by Ruggero Boscu, a retired Italian naval officer, and was immediately made a member of the Marivela (the Italian Navy's Yacht Club). At present the crew of the boat comprises Captain Boscu, his two sons, and his wife, who all regularly take part in the vintage yacht regattas. In the second regatta of the 1992 Nioulargue it came first ahead of *Ella*, *Phantom Light*, and *Outlaw*.

The construction specifications of this beautiful light-green hull give it as design no. C-632 by P.L. Rhodes. The following woods were used: African mahogany planking; Rangoon teak and English oak for the keel, stempost, and beams; and spruce for the mast and boom. The boat's lines reflect the highly personal style of its designer. In recent years the boat has been moored at the Cala Galera marina in Italy, where it is lovingly cared for by its owner.

THIS PAGE: *ASW 1999, close-ups of* Santander of Wight, *the boat that once belonged to Mary Blewitt (Photo: J. Taylor).*

Saorsain

Rigging:	Trysail schooner
Sail area:	141 sq. yds.
Shipyard:	Aberdeen (Scotland)
Year of design:	1976
Launch:	1989
Restoration:	1989
L.: 60 ft.	W.l.: 44¹⁄₂ ft.
B.: 13¹⁄₄ ft.	Df.: 6 ft.
Displ.: 27.6 tons	Engine: 95 Hp
Skipper:	Nicola Imola (1990)

S aorsain was discovered in July 1987 on the Greek island of Leskas, where it had been used for years as a charter yacht. It has pitch pine planking and a copal-finished wooden hull. It was noted at Imperia because of its two brick-red spankers.

RIGHT: *A shot of* Saorsain, *a trysail schooner launched in Scotland (Photo courtesy of L. Vannelli).*

Seilan

Rigging:	Gaff-rigged sloop
Sail area:	59 sq. yds.
Shipyard:	Ottonello naval shipyard (Varazze, Italy)
Designer:	Angelo Penco
Year of design:	1966
Launch:	1967
L.: 29¹⁄₂ ft.	W.l.: 24¹⁄₂ ft.
B.: 9¹⁄₄ ft.	Df.: 5¹⁄₂ ft.
Displ.: 8.82 tons	Engine: 24 Hp
Skipper:	Andrea Penco (1990–92)

T his boat was designed by its owner, Angelo Penco, who also designed *Ancilla II*. It was built by Baglietto's former boatyard manager, Ottonello, who had set up his own shipyard in Varazze opposite his former employer's yard. Thirty years on, *Seilan* (which in Scandinavian means "island of dreams") looks like it has only just been built.

It has mahogany planking (with the timber glued without joints), an iroko keel and posts, oak ribs, a silver spruce mast, ash beams, and a marine plywood deckhouse and deck (in one single piece). It was the first boat, still Royal Ocean Racing Club-rated at the time, to have a totally suspended, counterbalanced rudder, as a result of which it is a very gentle and responsive boat to maneuver. Another characteristic of the boat is the mast heel positioned on top of the deckhouse with mast partners on the reinforced bulkhead. No modifications have ever been made to the hull or deck, while the mast is still the original spruce model, and the sails, made by sail-makers Lami, are still the ones it had the day it was launched.

RIGHT: *1993, the sloop* Seilan *(Photo: A. Penco).*

Shelmalier of Anglesey

S *helmalier of Anglesey* is a traditional 18-meter English cutter with a displacement of 28.7 tons. Built by Berthon Boat Company at the company's Lymington yard, it was launched in 1965 on behalf of the Irish Team for the purposes of that year's Admiral's Cup. This ocean racer was designed by Jack Laurent Giles (design no. 505) and represents one of the last examples of technological design applied to the construction of a racer with caulked planking. For all of 17 years it remained the largest racer built in England.

Its profile is a clear example of the unique style of Giles, perhaps the only boat-designer capable not only of drawing those indispensable features that render a boat sailable but also of creating truly artistic designs. Initially the boat appears to resemble *Susanna II*, a highly successful Royal Ocean Racing Club (RORC) Mediterranean racer. This great English architect successfully designed a classic English cutter with a composite hull: the topside is in double mahogany planking, while the bottom is in single iroko planking, the ribs are in laminate oak, and the semi-flush deckhouse and doghouse are both in Siamese teak. The closely arranged double-thick ribs clearly represent a unique and brief period in the history of boat design and construction characterized by a splendid mix of modern technology, refined carpentry, and the ready availability of a considerable quantity of precious, well-seasoned woods. An innovative idea was used whereby a metal structure evenly distributed the weight of the mast and the lead keel onto the ribs and beams. Moreover, a lengthways aluminum stringer joined to large plates in the same material distributes the strain of the rigging across a large part of the hull, while its aeronautical-type construction makes the wooden framing both stronger and lighter. This is a solid boat with the purest of lines. Its raised bow is designed to plow through steep waves, while its sizeable sailing plan, supported by the very first light-alloy Proctor masts, guarantees speed in Mediterranean breezes.

Shelmalier of Anglesey was purchased by Sir Jan Lloyd in 1975, who exploited its qualities as a fast cruiser and a RORC Class I boat belonging to the exclusive Royal Yacht Squadron of Cowes, England (founded in 1815 and the longest-standing yacht club in the world). Since its launch in Lymington in 1965, very few modifications have been made to the boat, which has only really been subject to periodical routine servicing.

Upon the suggestion of Berthon International, managed by Bryan O. May, the boat was bought in France in June 1992 by a group of Italian yachtsmen, who immediately decided to have it refitted. The initial work was carried out by the Des Baux naval shipyard at Sanary sur Mer (Toulon). It is believed that between

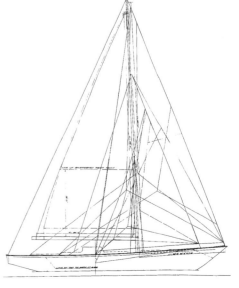

Rigging:	Bermudan cutter
Sail area:	251 sq. yds.
Shipyard:	Berthon Boat Company (Lymington, England)
Designer:	Laurent Giles
Year of design:	1965
Launch:	1965
Restoration:	1993 Des Baux naval shipyard (Sanary sur Mer, France), 1997–99 Imperia naval shipyards (Italy)
L.: 58¼ ft.	W.l.: 41¼ ft.
B.: 13½ ft.	Df.: 8½ ft.
Displ.: 28.7 tons	Engine: 125 Hp
Skipper:	Alfonso Crisci

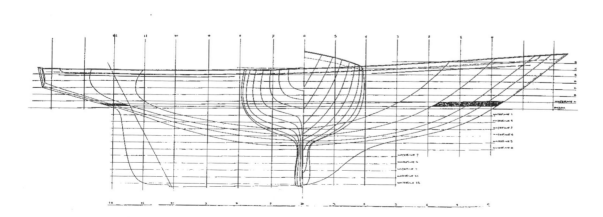

January and August 1993 the yard carried out initial refitting, including the installation of a new, powerful auxiliary engine and the repositioning of the propeller in the center with respect to the length of the boat. Moreover, the greater part of the original galvanized iron frame-floor plates and bolts were replaced by new ones in stainless steel.

This is a rare example of a balanced design, and this thoroughbred yacht, the wonderful creation of the late Jack Laurent Giles, currently sails the Mediterranean. A sturdy, comfortable boat with ample space, it is designed for ocean cruising as well as for racing. Between 1997 and 1999, *Shelmalier of Anglesey* was refitted at the Imperia shipyards. The director of works, the architect Mario Quaranta, had the boat stripped down to the wood (both inside and out), and the deck was rebuilt in teak. All of the rigging was chrome-plated, and the boat is currently in great shape once again.

RIGHT: Shelmalier of Anglesey *under sail (Photo courtesy of A. Crisci).*

OPPOSITE PAGE: *Details of the interior and a close-up of the deck (Photos: S. Pesato).*

Silver Cilly

Rigging:	*Bermudan sloop*
Sail area:	*61 sq. yds.*
Shipyard:	*Frederiksvaerk Badebjggri (V/Jorgen Basse, Copenhagen, Denmark)*
Designer:	*Olle Enderlein*
Year of design:	*1970*
Launch:	*1972*
Restoration:	*1996–2000*
L.: 35 ft.	*W.l.: 28½ ft.*
B.: 10 ft.	*Df.: 5½ ft.*
Displ.: 9.92 tons	*Engine: 17 Hp*
Skipper:	*Alberto Roberto (1998), C.H. Seidel (2000)*

This classic sloop, based on the design of *Hallberg-Rassy 33 Mistral* (another Enderlein design), with one or two variations, has very Scandinavian lines and is extremely well-built. It was ordered by a German, who subsequently used it for quiet cruises in the North Sea before taking it into the Mediterranean in the late 1980s.

After a change of ownership, it was registered at Leghorn in Italy under the name *Maco*. Then in 1995 it was purchased by its current owner, who is from Imperia. The boat is very seaworthy in high seas. It has mahogany planking; a teak deck; oak ribs and keel; a reinforced frame-floor with double stainless-steel plates; an aluminum mast and boom; and a teak, mahogany, and cedar interior. The hull was designed without heed to racing requirements as it was principally intended for cruising.

At the beginning of 2000 *Silver Cilly* changed hands once again.

BELOW: *Imperia 1998, the sloop* Silver Cilly *during a regatta (Photo: F. Ramella).*

Sparklet

This boat, which belongs to the South Coast One Design (SCOD) series designed by Charles Nicholson in 1955, won a series of regattas in the waters of Cowes, England, between 1958 and 1961 before being sold to a Californian student called Harold Weiss, who completed two transatlantic crossings in it.

After routine maintenance work carried out over the years, the boat currently consists of mahogany planking, oak ribs, a Douglas fir mast and boom (both original), a spruce deck, bronze winches (original), and a rudder-tiller.

A boat that enjoys being sailed close-hauled, *Sparklet* has had only four owners in its lifetime. In 1996 it was purchased by the present owner of *Gustavia's Dreams*, and it has taken part in the vintage yacht meeting held in Imperia in 1998 and the one held in Santa Margherita in Italy in 1989.

Put up for sale in San Remo's old port, the boat now has a new owner who is painstakingly restoring the boat. The deck has been relaid in decolay, and the rudder has been rebuilt from mahogany (based on the original model).

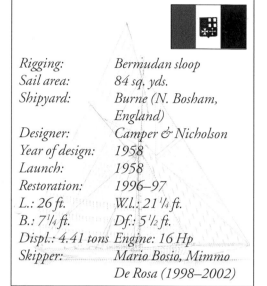

Rigging:	Bermudan sloop
Sail area:	84 sq. yds.
Shipyard:	Burne (N. Bosham, England)
Designer:	Camper & Nicholson
Year of design:	1958
Launch:	1958
Restoration:	1996–97
L.: 26 ft.	W.l.: 21 1/4 ft.
B.: 7 1/4 ft.	Df.: 5 1/2 ft.
Displ.: 4.41 tons	Engine: 16 Hp
Skipper:	Mario Bosio, Mimmo De Rosa (1998–2002)

BELOW: *A photograph of* Sparklet *(Photo courtesy of M. De Rosa).*

ABOVE: *Imperia 1998,* Sparklet *during a regatta (Photo: S. Pesato).*

RIGHT: *Close-ups of the interior and exterior (Photos: S. Pesato).*

BELOW: *A photograph of the boat sailing towards its mooring (Photo courtesy of M. De Rosa).*

Stella Polare

Commissioned by the Italian Navy following the success of *Corsaro II*, *Stella Polare* is another Sparkman & Stephens creation. It was launched on September 15, 1965 at the Sangermani yard in Lavagna, Italy, and was due to be deployed as a training vessel for naval personnel. It was designed to take over from *Corsaro II*, launched six years earlier at the Costaguta yard in Genoa Voltri, Italy. The boat's name evokes the ship that reached the Arctic Circle in 1899–1900 as part of the Duke of Abruzzi's expedition. On that occasion, Lieutenant-Commander Umberto Cagni got within 238 miles of the North Pole.

Stella Polare II was delivered to skipper Lieutenant Giancarlo Basile on October 8, 1965. Basile had been a familiar figure when skipper of *Artica II* (1956) and

Corsaro II (1962). This marked the beginning of a period of winter training prior to the boat's taking part in its first open-sea regatta – the 1966 Giraglia. With a crew of world-class yachtsmen (in the words of Franco Belloni), the boat beat the race's record time, finishing in 29 hours (over a course of 243 miles), an exceptional time that was to remain unbeaten for the following 18 years! This was an outstanding victory indeed, and *Stella Polare* made the headlines in the world's sailing press.

The following is Giovanni Garassino's account of the final stages of the race, printed in the pages of the *Navy News*: "*21.00 hours. After approximately 240 miles of navigation we are one of three boats separated by just 547 yards. We need to tack to get around the finish buoy in front of the Navy lighthouse. Hermitage with its little genoa,*

Rigging:	Gaff-rigged yawl
Sail area:	255 sq. yds.
Shipyard:	Sangermani (Lavagna, Italy)
Designer:	Sparkman & Stephens
Year of design:	1964
Launch:	1965
Restoration:	various and 1992
L.: 70¼ ft.	W.l.: 58 ft.
B.: 16 ft.	Df.: 10 ft.
Displ.: 49.5 tons	Engine: 120 Hp
Skipper:	Lieutenant-Commander Flavio Bugossi (1998)

BELOW: *Cannes 1998, a close-up of a glorious yacht (Photo: J. Taylor).*

has in the meantime overtaken us, as we point towards land before tacking to get round the buoy. At this point, Captain Basile, who hasn't stopped all day, displays his superb navigational skills by ordering that a small jib be raised. The crew, despite being soaked and tired, is still full of enthusiasm as it performs the maneuver with startling rapidity. We and Hermitage *turn while* Gitana, *which is further ahead (it turned first) is heading straight for the buoy. The additional jib enables us to hug the wind really tightly and over the final mile we catch up with and then overtake* Hermitage. *We are first over the line. Our cries of joy can be heard for miles around: we've beaten* Hermitage *and* Gitana, *who cross the line together, by 66 yards. The final classification sees us winners, with* Hermitage *1 minute 6 seconds behind, followed by* Gitana IV *1 minute 34 seconds behind. Almost a photo finish!"*

The brilliant victory in that edition of the Giraglia was to be repeated two years later in 1968 when the boat entered its first Atlantic race, the Bermuda–Travemunde Race organized by the North German Regatta Association to celebrate the 100th anniversary of the Club. Giancarlo Basile was once again at the helm (having since been promoted to Lieutenant Commander), and *Stella Polare* reached Port Hamilton on June 13. For the following three weeks it prepared for the race against the most powerful, most famous ocean-racers in the world: boats such as *Stormvogel, Ondine, Kialoa II,* and *Germania VI.* Once again we are going to leave it to a famous eye-witness, Beppe Croce, to tell the tale. Beppe had reached Travemunde in Germany to shake hands with Captain Basile and his brave crew, who had for the first time in history led an Italian boat in this transatlantic regatta.

" *Stella Polare, up against true giants of the open sea such as* Stormvogel, Ondine, Kialoa II, *and* Germania VI, *raced the regatta of a lifetime skippered by its wise captain Giancarlo Basile. Over the first thousand miles it lost touch with the leaders due to a persistent lull, and it did not appear to have much chance of catching up at that point. However, the technical expertise of its navigator came to the rescue when he decided to sail northwards and take better advantage of a north-westerly than his adversaries.*

In the end, the boat crossed the finish line just behind the race's 'thoroughbreds,' who had to concede a number of hours to Stella Polare in compensated time. This meant that the boat won hands down, approximately six hours ahead of Germania VI, *16 hours ahead of* Kialoa, *23 hours ahead of* Ondine *and 24 hours ahead of* Stormvogel.

I had the pleasure and honor of being the first Italian to be welcomed aboard Stella Polare *after its arrival at Travemunde. I had, and still have, fond memories of the company of Captain Basile, my fellow crew-member when we raced together on* Corsaro *in the 1962 Bermuda Race, and it was quite a moving moment for me, despite the fact that for years I had been used to this kind of thing, to see the only Italian boat ready for the victory celebrations, the focus of attention of hundreds of sailing enthusiasts, the number one attraction of a country that knows and understands the perils of the sea and knows how to appreciate such an important victory.*

These recollections mill around in my mind now, but one thing I can't forget is the modesty and simplicity of those 15 young Italians who, having just beaten the very cream of American, Dutch, and German sailing, in one of the most important races of the year, nevertheless refrained from any form of exhibitionism so fashionable these days. Stella Polare, *as we all know, was not designed as an ocean racer; it is basically a training boat, designed for the instruction of sailors rather than for beating race records or the 'race machines' that the abnormal interpretation of the regulations is producing*

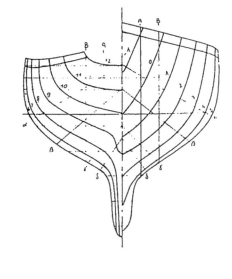

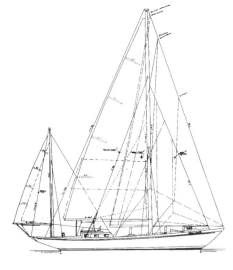

OPPOSITE PAGE: *Cannes 1998,* Stella Polare *with its unique, showy spinnaker (Photo: J. Taylor).*

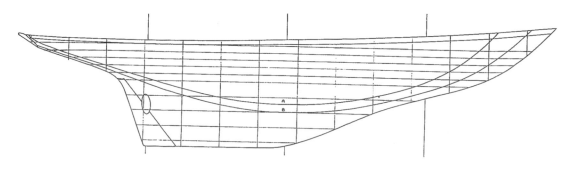

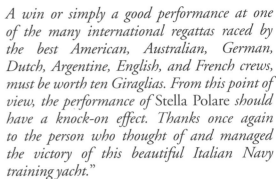

worldwide. Nonetheless, Stella Polare, *thanks to the professional expertise and thorough naval training of its crew, managed to get the most out of situations and to calculate probabilities as well as it could, thus giving Italy and all Italian sailing enthusiasts one of the greatest of all victories.*

In this Olympic year, this victory across the Atlantic augurs well and the example set by Giancarlo Basile and his crew, who the Italian Navy wanted at all costs at this important anniversary regatta of the oldest of German yacht clubs, should be followed in the near future by other Italian boats and crews, traditionally loath to leave their home waters to race in the important open-sea regattas held elsewhere. Yet the success of the Italian Navy, of Italo Monzino, Antonio Pietrobon, Beppe Diano, Gianni Pera, Aldo Macchiavelli, Agostino Straulino, and Marina Spaccarelli, should convince my fellow countrymen and women (who nowadays are the owners of high-quality international class yachts) to face up to the complicated, and at times unknown, nature of more difficult competitions.

The Mediterranean is too small: as Rascel would say, it has become 'tight around the shoulders.' The Fastnet Race, the Bermuda Race, the Transpacific, and – why not? – the Transatlantic, should stimulate the competitive yearnings of our more experienced yachtsmen.

ABOVE: *Imperia 1998, a shot of* Stella Polare *(Photo: F. Ramella).*

BELOW: *VBR 1999, a close-up of the crew (Photo: J. Taylor).*

A win or simply a good performance at one of the many international regattas raced by the best American, Australian, German, Dutch, Argentine, English, and French crews, must be worth ten Giraglias. From this point of view, the performance of Stella Polare *should have a knock-on effect. Thanks once again to the person who thought of and managed the victory of this beautiful Italian Navy training yacht."*

During the 1970 training campaign (skippered by Captain Bruno Petronio), during its transfer from La Spezia in Italy to Plymouth in England, the starting point for the Plymouth–Santa Cruz (in Tenerife) Race, *Stella Polare* took advantage of the opportunity to take part in the Palma de Mallorca–Cabrea–Palma de Mallorca classic race, which it won. This augured really well for the next race from Plymouth, organized by the Sail Training Association over a course of 1,450 miles and including such famous training boats as the Swedish *Falken* and *Urania*, and the French *Belle Poule* and *Étoile*; while in Class C its competitors included really strong vessels like *Zulu* and *Najade*. However, contrary to all expectations, the Italian boat won in both real and compensated time. It was a real triumph!

This was followed by victory in the 1976 Canaria–Bermuda Race, skippered by Lieutenant-Commander Franco Faggioni. At the starting line in Santa Cruz, during the second stage of Operation Sail (which was to see a fleet of 91 boats sail into New York Harbor), the attention of the crew of *Stella Polare* was focused on *Great Britain II* and *Störtebeker*, the race favorites. In a race that saw a constant changing of positions, *Stella Polare* once again came home the winner in compensated time.

In recent years, the boat has sailed thousands of miles in the name of the Italian Navy's Yacht Club, and it has taken part in numerous vintage yacht meetings. In 1992 it was selected to take part in the regatta organized to celebrate the 500th anniversary of the discovery of America, which started from Genoa in Italy on Easter Sunday.

Sunny Temper

*S*unny *Temper* was designed and built in 1974 by Mino Simeone at the Simeone boatyard, which has since closed down. The hull and deck are made from curved cedar staves glued down using red adhesive; this kind of wood is particularly light compared with the more traditional timbers used in boat-building. Designed exclusively for racing, *Sunny Temper* offers none of the usual comforts of a cruiser. The interior is very simple; there are no dividing walls, the cabin is low, and there is no toilet on board. However, this simplicity has a certain elegance about it, and the ribs, hull, and celino have been left bare with just a varnish finish.

The boat was bought by the present owner in 1978, and a few years later he was joined by a friend of his who became the joint owner. Together they have kept it in excellent condition (in fact it has never required any significant refitting as such). *Sunny Temper* was fairly successful during its first few years of racing: rated as a IOR Class VI, in 1981 it won the Ligurian Championship (it came third in 1983) and took part in Alessio Week and numerous other regattas.

Its vocation as a racer can be seen from its nine-elevenths rig and its structural steering wheels, as well as from the deck rigging (all original) characterized by an ergonomic design, and the spacious cockpit. However, over time it has lost its competitive edge with the advent of composite materials and revolutionary new hull designs, which meant the end of the IOR. *Sunny Temper* is now used as a daily cruiser, although it is not adverse to the occasional local regatta.

Rigging:	Bermudan sloop
Sail area:	32 sq. yds.
Shipyard:	Simeone (Naples, Italy)
Designer:	Mino Simeone
Year of design:	1974
Launch:	1974
Restoration:	1994
L.: 24 ft.	W.l.: 22½ ft.
B.: 9 ft.	Df.: 5½ ft.
Displ.: 1.43 tons	Engine: 8 Hp
Skipper:	Alessandro Gollin (1994), R. Cacciapuoti (2000)

Tarantella

*T*arantella is a dear friend indeed! The sight of the unique lines of its mahogany-colored hull in the waters of Imperia is a sharp reminder of a boat that in its time made Italian yachting history. The years have passed since then, and memories invariably fade.

Launched in August 1969, the *Tarantella* was immediately transferred to Genoa, Italy, and on September 20 that same year it won its first regatta, the Santa Margherita–Gorgogna Race (skippered by Vittorio Porta). From 1970 through 1976 it took part in all the regattas in the racing calendar and acquired a certain fame as a racer. In 1970 and in 1972 it won the Mediterranean Championships, and in 1975 it won the Giraglia (coming second in 1970 and 1973, and fourth in 1972).

In 1971 it was selected, together with *Mabelle* and *Levantades*, for the Italian Admiral's Cup team; at that time it was skippered by Pino Zucchinetti from Alassio. In the Fastnet Race the Italian boats finished with an honorable seventh place overall after having sailed all the way to the starting line.

In 1970 it won the Cannes–Port Mahon–Bonifacio Race; and in subsequent years it took part in numerous regattas and did rather well, although it was now employed less in competitive sailing. It won second place at the 1990 Giraglia and first place in the Coppa del Re at Palma de Mallorca in 1991. It has also taken part in numerous vintage and classic yacht regattas, winning honors at Imperia in 1989 and 1990. Its list of honors also includes the

Rigging:	Gaff-rigged sloop
Sail area:	156 sq. yds.
Shipyard:	Carlini shipyards (Rimini, Italy)
Designer:	Sparkman & Stephens
Year of design:	1968
Launch:	1969
Restoration:	1993
L.: 54½ ft.	W.l.: 39¼ ft.
B.: 14½ ft.	Df.: 9 ft.
Displ.: 26.5 tons	Engine: 85 Hp
Skipper:	Alberto Raffaelli (1988–89), Vincenzo Porta (1990), Peter Schmidt (1996)

Italian Yacht Club Open Championships, the Bocche regattas, the Genoa and Cannes winter regattas, and so on.

Over the years the sail plan has been somewhat modified, with shortening of the spanker and replacing of the original boom with a lighter, more modern model. In order to make maneuvering the boat easier, a "coffee grinder" has been installed in the center of the boat. Apart from partial rebuilding of the deck, *Tarantella* has always been regularly serviced and kept in perfect condition. The engine, winches, and standing rigging are all original still. As with all of Stephens' boats, this vessel is a good plyer in a medium or strong wind, and although it is not at its strongest at other tacks, at the end of a race it is always among the leading boats.

The boat, which since 1969 had only ever had one owner, was recently sold to a German skipper, Peter Schmidt, and we all hope to see it continue performing as brilliantly as always.

LEFT: *Imperia 1996,* Tarantella *with its unmistakable wooden-colored hull during a regatta. This boat needs no introduction and is still well preserved after almost a lifetime under its original owner, Alberto Raffaelli. Its successes include the 1971 Giraglia and a place in the Italian Admiral's Cup team that same year, together with* Mabelle *and* Levantades *(Photo: S. Pesato).*

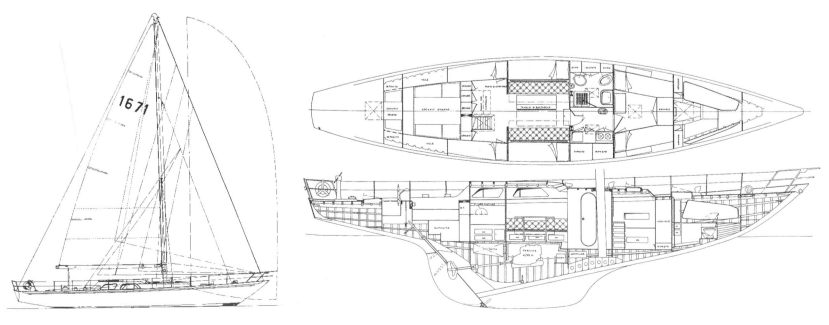

Tiziana

aunched as *Colibrì II*, this boat was rated as a RORC (Royal Ocean Racing Club) II Class (31-footer). During the period 1964–66 its owners, Gian Marco and Vincenzo Piaggio, entered it for various regattas organized by the Tigullio Yacht Club of Santa Margherita in Ligura, Italy. These included, among others, the Santa Margherita–Capraia Race, the Capraia–Portoferraio Race, and the Santa Margherita–Isola del Tino–Santa Margherita Race. In the last of the these races the boat came first, as it also did in the Santa Margherita–Portovenere Race. In 1968 it was sold and renamed *Tiziana*.

In the spring of 1987 the boat was partially refitted, with the restoration of the mahogany planking. It took part in the first edition of the Alto Tirreno Trophy and in the Obiectif Barcelona in 1992.

Below deck there are eight berths, a dining room, a kitchen, etc., and all has been preserved in excellent condition. The boat is manned by a pleasant, sociable crew, ever ready to invite friends aboard for a good meal.

BELOW: *Imperia 2000, a shot of* Tiziana (*Photo: J. Taylor*).

Rigging:	*Bermudan yawl*
Sail area:	*100 sq. yds.*
Shipyard:	*Mingo (Riva Trigoso, Italy)*
Designer:	*Gian Marco Piaggio*
Year of design:	*1964*
Launch:	*1964*
Restoration:	*1987*
L.: 43¼ ft.	*W.l.: 3¼ ft.*
B.: 9½ ft.	*Df.: 5½ ft.*
Displ.: 19.8 tons	*Engine: 80 Hp*
Skipper:	*Antonio Villa (1987–2000)*

Troll

Rigging:	*Gaff-rigged ketch*
Sail area:	*215 sq. yds.*
Shipyard:	*Evers*
Year of design:	*1953*
Launch:	*1955*
L.: 56 1/4 ft.	*W.l.: 41 1/2 ft.*
B.: 15 1/2 ft.	*Df.: 8 1/2 ft.*
Displ.: 39.7 tons	*Engine: 96 Hp*
Skipper:	*Jurgen Busse (1989)*

This is a light-green metal hull that has never undergone any substantial refitting: the sails and winches are still original. It is currently employed as a charter yacht.

RIGHT: *The ketch* Troll *(Photo courtesy of J. Busse).*

Vanille

(sometime Demua)

Rigging:	*Bermudan sloop*
Sail area:	*72 sq. yds.*
Shipyard:	*P. Jouet (Sartrouville, France)*
Designer:	*Eugène Cornu*
Year of design:	*1963*
Launch:	*1964*
Restoration:	*1995, 1998 Beconcini shipyards (La Spezia, Italy)*
L.: 31 1/4 ft.	*W.l.: 24 1/4 ft.*
B.: 9 ft. Df.: 5 1/4 ft.	
Displ.: 8.82 tons	*Engine: 28 Hp*
Skipper:	*Marino Gambaro (1994)*

This boat was designed by Eugène Cornu and was launched as *Vanille*. It was subsequently transferred to the Mediterranean by its second owner, where it was sold to its then skipper Marino Gambaro, who renamed it *Demua* and joined the fleet of the "Venturieri" ("Adventurers"). A good plyer, it has mahogany planking, a teak deck, a spruce mast, and very closely laid oak ribs.

In 1995 it underwent routine servicing, with the replacement of five planking timbers. *Vanille* still has its original rudder-tiller and winches. It was recently sold to a new owner who changed the mast (replacing it with another one in spruce) at the Beconcini shipyard in La Spezia, Italy, and then proceeded to give the boat back its original name, *Vanille*.

RIGHT: *Imperia 1994, a photo of* Vanille *when it was called* Demua *(Photo: S. Pesato).*

Wanderer

This boat was commissioned in the early 1950s and would seem to be the first built by the Gallinari yard in Italy. With its two Roman owners, *Wanderer* cruised the Tyrrhenian Sea and then the Aegean Sea, where it was dismasted during a storm. It remained a few years in a Greek port, and then, after a new aluminum mast had been fitted, it sailed back to Italy, where it was sold after some brief repair work had been completed in 1980.

It was completely refitted in 1988 by its third owner and restored to excellent condition. It has mahogany planking, a mahogany deckhouse, and a cast-iron bulb and is a fast boat that is easy to maneuver.

Rigging:	Gaff-rigged cutter
Sail area:	191 sq. yds.
Shipyard:	Gallinari (Anzio, Italy)
Designer:	Olin Stephens
Year of design:	1950
Launch:	1956
Restoration:	1988–89
L.: 47 ft.	W.l.: 33 1/2 ft.
B.: 10 1/4 ft.	Df.: 7 1/2 ft.
Displ.: 14.9 tons	Engine: 80 Hp
Skipper:	Giancarlo Rinaldi (1988–89)

Yhann

This sloop was designed by David Hillyard way back in 1935 but was not built and launched for another 20 years. It has mahogany planking: the timbers are 1-inch thick, caulked, and copper riveted. The ribs, frame-floor, and beams are all in oak. Under its three first owners it did not undergo any significant refitting work. The first of these owners, Étienne Du Fieff, Chairman of the Deauville Yacht Club, bought the boat directly from the yard.

It has a heavy hull with a considerable freeboard and a Norwegian-style stern. It moves gently across a high sea but suffers somewhat when sailed close-hauled. At Imperia, *Yhann* has competed against boats of a similar length (fewer than 40 feet), such as *Maria Galante*, *Crystal*, *Golondrina*, and *Eli*.

The current owner, Alberto Roberto, is replacing all the original keel bolts with new steel ones, and the deckhouse portholes with new ones in bronze. He also plans to rebuild the deck.

Rigging:	Bermudan sloop
Sail area:	84 sq. yds.
Shipyard:	The Shipyard (Littlehampton, Sussex, England)
Designer:	David Hillyard
Year of design:	1935
Launch:	1956
Restoration:	1989–90
L.: 37 1/2 ft.	W.l.: 31 3/4 ft.
B.: 10 ft.	Df.: 4 1/4 ft.
Displ.: 10.9 tons	Engine: 45 Hp
Skipper:	Gunnar Everhed (1998), Alberto Roberto (2000)

LEFT: *Close-up of* Yhann's *winch (Photo: S. Pesato).*

ABOVE: *Imperia 1998,* Yhann, *designed by David Hillyard, bears an uncanny likeness to* Umiak*. It still has the original spruce mast (Photo courtesy of A. Roberto).*

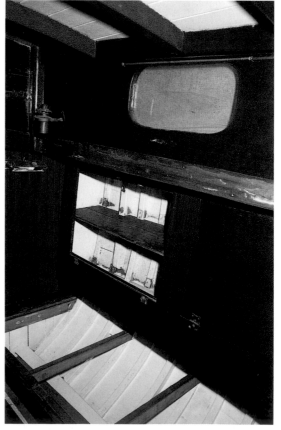

RIGHT: *Details of the interior of* Yhann *(Photos: S. Pesato).*

The Metric Classes

The Imperia Meetings have also seen the presence of a number of "International Tonnage" (SI) vessels – boats with pronounced overhangs, the "thoroughbreds of the yachting world" as they were called in the 1930s. They are less wedge-like than the previous generation of sailing boats and have a higher freeboard that is wider at the center. These 6-, 8-, 10-, and 12-meter SI yachts have come back into fashion after years of abandon in warehouses and boatyards. Apart from any interest they may have as a result of fleeting fashions that come and go over the years, they are of intrinsic interest because they were almost all designed as racers by the very best boat-designers, people such as Charles and Peter Nicholson, William Fife, Knud Reimers, and Olin Stephens.

The 6-meter boats that have been restored to their original splendor include *Twins V*, *Bau Bau* (the latter launched by Baglietto in 1939), and *Mizar III* (launched by Sangermani in 1946). The 8-meter yachts include the famous *Bona*, a Vittorio Baglietto design that in 1930 won the France Cup, and the equally famous *Italia*, a Costaguta creation and gold medalist at the 1936 Kiel Olympics. At Imperia, *Italia* and *Bona* reminded us all of such wonderful skippers as Giovanelli and Oberti.

Another 8-meter yacht with a wealth of successes to its name is *Stint*, designed by the talented young designer Max Oertz. At Imperia this boat was manned by an exclusively female crew. The 10-meter yachts include the famous *Vega I* (currently *Tonino*): while the 12-meter Class includes old acquaintances like *Tomahawk*, *Cintra*, *Flica*, and *Vim*, that nowadays all fly the Italian flag. *Cintra* is still a 19th-century yacht, with its boom and trysail rig, the result of an already successful design. *Vim*, on the other hand, was one of Stephens' first creations. Then there are the more modern French yachts *Ikra*, and *Sovereign*, which like the others is currently used as a cruiser, and whose most famous race ever was the extraordinary 1958 America's Cup.

Arcangelo

Rigging:	Bermudan cutter (6-meter SI)
Sail area:	67 sq. yds.
Shipyard:	Papst Werf (Copenick, Germany)
Designer:	G.A. Estlander
Year of design:	1923
Launch:	1923
Restoration:	1990 Beconcini shipyards (La Spezia, Italy)
L.: 37¼ ft.	W.l.: 25¼ ft.
B.: 6 ft.	Df.: 5½ ft.
Displ.: 4.96 tons	Engine: 10 Hp
Skipper:	Matteo Balestrero (1989–94)

BELOW: *The 6-meter SI* Arcangelo, *successful in numerous vintage yacht regattas (Photo: L. Fioroni).*

Formerly known as *Corona II*, *Bona*, and *Caramba* (its original name when it was launched back in 1923), this boat is classified as a 6-meter SI Class boat. From 1927 to 1931 it was based at Stockholm, Sweden, and belonged to a certain B. Linden (according to the entries in Lloyds Register). In 1936, still owned by Linden, it was moored in Naples, Italy. Then all trace was lost of the boat until 1958, when it reappeared in a book by Manlio Gusbetti Helfrich entitled *La Vela* (*The Ship*).

At that time an engine and deckhouse were fitted, and the boat reappeared on a Royal Ocean Racing Club tonnage certificate dated October 1965 as yacht no. 4530, the property of Alessandro Bacci of Milan and registered at the Leghorn Yacht Club. In 1955 the then *Caramba* belonged to a Dr. Carlo Schivardi and its home port was Santa Margherita in Liguria, Italy.

In 1971 the present owner, Giorgio Balestrero, discovered the boat at Portofino, Italy, beached at the wharf, and he immediately fell in love with it. The boat was renamed *Arcangelo* and from then on has always been moored at La Spezia, Italy, where it has successfully taken part in hundreds of regattas. In one of these regattas in 1982 it lost its mast, which was replaced by a white aluminum one. It was subsequently classified under IOR regulations and continued to win. In 1989 it took part in the Upper Tyrrhenian Vintage Yacht Regatta and won with ease.

In 1990 it was refitted: the deck was rebuilt and the deckhouse lowered by the Beconcini shipyard. In 1991 it was classified under IMS regulations and went on to win the IV Class of the Zegna Trophy held in Portofino. As the reporter Naldini said in 1983: "*Arcangelo has just celebrated its 60th year, but this uniquely elegant boat hardly shows its age. When it lays down and cuts into the waves it is like a swordsman's rapier in action…*"

Aria

The story of *Aria* and of its new start in life is undoubtedly one of the most wonderful of the stories told in the pages of this book. This boat, which is of considerable historical interest, was discovered at Favignana Island in April 1998, substantially modified from its original design. It was lying neglected in someone's garden, a wreck that failed to give any hint of its past. At that point, it was transported by the present owner, Serena Galvani, to the Argentario boatyards in Italy and was slowly and lovingly restored to its original splendid condition. The patience, passion and love for boats displayed by Serena should really be a lesson for all sailing enthusiasts.

This 8-meter SI was first owned by Benedetto Bruzzo, who raced it successfully for four seasons prior to the outbreak of World War II. Regattas at that time were won by the likes of *Germania III*, *Bona*, and *Italia*. *Aria* took part in its first regattas over the 12-mile Genoa course in 1934, and came second in the first race and third in the second race. During the course of 1935 it was always among the honors in races like the Mediterranean Cup, the Caterina Pozzani Cup, the Rylard Cup, and the Consiglio Provinciale Economia Corporativa Cup. It also took part that year in the Tigullio regattas (winning four of the

seven races) and the Naples regattas. In 1936 the tense political situation made it impossible to race against foreign yachts except for the German ones: in all three Rylard Cup regattas *Germania III* and *Aria* proved themselves too strong for the other competitors, with the Italian boat coming second each time behind the German yacht.

In 1936 it won the Pozzani Cup and came second in the Duca degli Abruzzi Race, the Duca d'Aosta Race, and the Rylard Cup. It was also selected for the Italian team taking part in the Kiel Olympics, won in the end by *Italia*. It was to get among the honors once again in 1937 and 1938, then in 1939 it won the Pozzani Cup for the second time.

During the war, *Aria* was laid up at the Delle Piane shipyard in Chiavari, and in 1939 it was sold to Marquis Francesco Spinola, the new Chairman (in 1945) of the Genoa Yachting Club. In 1950 it was donated for use to the Canottieri Savoia Club in Naples. Then, over a period of 11 years, it was subject to the first of a number of modifications that saw it change appearance radically.

In Naples, the boat was part of an exceptional fleet of boats that had survived the war: *Orietta*, *Miranda*, *Lycea*, *Italia*, *Bona*, *Elvi*, *Cheta*, and *Vica*. Its Naples period saw

Rigging:	Bermudan sloop (8-meter SI)
Sail area:	93 sq. yds.
Shipyard:	Ugo Costaguta
Designer:	Attilio Costaguta
Year of design:	1934
Launch:	1935
Restoration:	1998–99 Argentario naval shipyard (Italy)
L.: 46¼ ft.	W.l.: 30¼ ft.
B.: 8½ ft.	Df.: 6½ ft.
Displ.: 9.09 tons	
Skipper:	Dani De Grassi (1999), Roberto Ferrarese (1999), Alberto Leghissa (2000), Mauro Pelaschier (2001)

ABOVE: *Imperia 2000, a shot of* Aria *(Photo: S. Pesato).*

LEFT: *Porto Santo Stefano 2000, a shot of the recently restored* Aria *during the 8-meter SI World Championships (Photo: J. Taylor).*

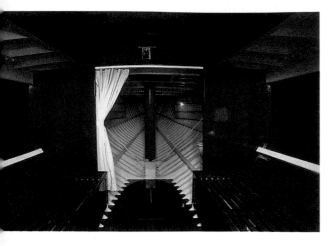

Aria take part in the Laura Cup, which was periodically held in the waters of Posillipo, as well as all the other regattas organized by the local sailing clubs. In 1954 it won the Keller Trophy, beating its old rivals, *Orietta* and *Italia*. In 1963 it changed hands once again, and ended up three years later stripped at Fiumicino. It was here that the boat was discovered by a doctor from Verona, Carlo Leone Mostacci, who was to be its owner for 31 years. The boat was still in good condition when it was transferred to Lake Garda, and for 13 years was the only 8-meter SI present on the Benaco.

The 1960s saw a decline in the boat's fortunes and radical modifications made to the hull, the rig, and the interior. The replacement of the broken mast with a similar one in aluminum was the last straw. In the summer of 1970, the boat's owner decided to transfer it to the island of Favignana where his family had their summer residence. It continued to race and was quite successful in the Settimana delle Egadi Race with the hull covered in a thin layer of fiberglass. After years of occasional use, the owner decided to ground the boat as there was increasingly little space in the small port of Favignana. So the boat ended up in a field above the village, positioned on a trailer and protected only by a dry-stone wall.

Fortunately, I did not see it in this terrible state, but the story is not dissimilar from that of the yacht *Samadhi*.

In April 1988, the boat's savior discovered *Aria* laid up in this rural retreat and, despite its precarious state, managed to make the necessary repairs to render it sufficiently seaworthy to be transferred back to the Tyrrhenian Sea, where it was to race in Prada Sailing Week at Porto Santo Stefano against the glorious old *Italia*. Then began a long, complicated historical restoration operation.

The hull's genetic imprint was closely analyzed, the shape of the ribs and its holes studied, in order to be able to reposition the set of spanker sheets, the hatchways, and the forestay attachment. In order not to lose the shape of the oak ribs, and given that the original drawings were not available, the decision was taken to replace alternate ribs with new, steam-curved ones without removing any of the existing planking. New mahogany timbers were mounted on the bottom, while the topside timbers were restored. New chains, floor timbers, and stays below-deck between the chains and the mast step were fitted, together with new silicon bronze bulb bolts.

The new sitka spruce deck was screwed directly onto the beams using silicon bronze screws, and was then caulked using cotton (the traditional oakum) in accordance with the time-honored method. The aluminum mast was of course removed, making way for a spruce mast with new fittings. Furthermore, as dictated by tradition, a 5-lire coin from 1935 (still legal tender in 1988) was placed at the foot of the mast by Serena Galvani. The original winches were recouped, as were some of the blocks and some of the original bronze parts.

Once again, a reading of the signs left on the boat enabled the owner to move the forestay attachment closer astern. The interior was restored to its original state, while a watertight bulkhead separated the cockpit from the main cabin. *Aria*'s new sails were made from horizontal Dacron panels.

On May 23, 1999, amid bunting and a fleet of other famous boats, *Aria* took to the sea once again. Dr. Pippo Della Vecchia, chairman of Naples' Canottieri Savoia Royal Yacht Club, had a hard time fighting back the tears. The boat had been born again.

In the fall of 2001 *Aria* took part in the most important meeting of the sailing calendar: the Jubileum America's Cup Regatta. It was the only boat designed, built, and restored in Italy with an Italian owner, crew, and flag, and it performed well for the Naples Yachting Club. Its skipper was the famous Mauro Pelaschier, skipper of *Azzurra*. *Aria* was among the smallest of the yachts in the Solent (one of five 8-meter SI boats) and literally flew around the course, coming second in Division 3 and seventh of the fleet of 48 vintage yachts present at Cowes on that occasion.

ABOVE: *Detail of the interior towards the stern (Photo: J. Taylor).*

OPPOSITE PAGE: *Porto Santo Stefano 2000,* Aria *running on the quarter (Photo: J. Taylor).*

BELOW: *Imperia 2000, the crew of the 8-meter SI* Aria *(Photo: P. Maccione).*

Bau Bau

Rigging:	Bermudan sloop (6-meter SI)
Sail area:	52 sq. yds.
Shipyard:	Baglietto (Varazze, Italy)
Designer:	G.A. Estlander
Year of design:	1937
Launch:	1939
Restoration:	1960, 1990 Sangermani (Lavagna, Italy)
L.: 35¼ ft.	W.l.: 24 ft.
B.: 6½ ft.	Df.: 4½ ft.
Displ.: 4.41 tons	Engine: 20 Hp
Skipper:	Angelo Traverso (1988–93)

BELOW: *September 1990, Bau Bau, a 6-meter SI launched in 1939 at the Baglietto yard (Photo: E. Taccola).*

au Bau may be considered a truly forgotten boat, and its return to the racing world can be put down to the efforts of Antonio Traverso, the former coxswain of *Artica II*, who in August 1988 came across the hull as it lay abandoned in a shed in the Tigullio yard in Santa Margherita, Italy. He was too young in 1939 when the boat was launched to recognize it for what it was – the glorious old *Bau Bau* (sailing no. I-58), launched by Baglietto shipyards on behalf of Count Mario Arlotta.

The boat had raced intensely, albeit briefly, and had shown what it was capable of in the Genoa Winter Regattas when it raced in the Matteo Lavarello Cup against *Twins V*, another brand-new 6-meter SI. It also raced against the Italian Naval Academy's *Vega III* (skippered by the already famous Straulino) at Leghorn. That same year it also took part in the National Regattas held in the Bay of Naples, when it raced against another 6-meter SI, *Bambetta*, over five days.

Bau Bau was subsequently sold to a Mr. Bruzzone of Genoa, who in 1959 sold it to Riccardo Giolli of Rapallo who had noticed it lying for years, half-abandoned, on the slipway at Portofino. At that time the boat was called *Grazia IV*, and as such had won a number of regattas. A tonnage certificate dated June 1960 gives the boat's new name as *Maria Galante*, and notes the installation of a 10 Hp engine and a deckhouse built by the Sangermani yard in 1949, at a time that the boat was fitted with a system of mechanical propulsion.

In fact, the engineer Giolli, who wanted to use the boat for short cruises, had a small toilet fitted, together with a rectangular deckhouse covering the central cockpit, and had the very light deck reinforced with layers of fiberglass. Furthermore, in 1966 he had the boat classified according to the new Royal Ocean Racing Club rules, modifying the sail plan by shortening the mast by about 4 feet, installing the jib at the masthead, lengthening the base of the stern triangle, and replacing the steering wheels with a stern forestay. The new hull raced in the Gulf of

Tigullio where it performed really well. The galvanized iron floor plates were replaced by stainless steel ones, and two fore spinnaker winches were fitted either side of the hatchway. However, the result was a boat that tended to bear away slightly. In 1974, the owner decided to haul the boat on to land, and for 14 years no more was heard of it.

It came to the attention of Antonio Traverso who, having decided to resuscitate the boat, gave it back its original name and transferred it to a boatyard in Chiavari, Italy, where work was started on a complete salvage and refitting. The planking was stripped to bare wood, the deck was rebuilt in teak, and the bolts of the original lead bulb were replaced with stainless steel ones.

Having found the original drawings of the waterline and the sail plan at the Baglietto shipyard, Traverso was thus able to replace the (shortened) alloy mast with a new spruce mast identical to the one the boat had when it was launched, and to rebuild the fixed shrouds and forestays and the loose shrouds.

Finally, in September 1990, completely restored, *Bau Bau* was able to take part in the Imperia and La Spezia vintage yacht meetings, where it met its old rival *Twins V*, won two regattas, and came second in another.

Bau Bau has mahogany planking, thin acacia ribs alternated with thicker oak ribs, oak beams, and a spruce boom and spinnaker pole. Apart from the keel, there are a number of other components that appear to be original, including the compass, the wheel plate bearing the boat's name, and the original set of cotton and linen sails dating from 1939.

In 1993 the boat was sold to Cesare Delogu. With the aid of the designer Massimo Gatti, owner of the Gatti boatyard in Genoa, Italy, *Bau Bau* underwent another series of refitting operations. The original winches were reinstalled and the deck was restored once again, as were the remaining items of the original fittings. In April 1995 this famous 6-meter SI made its comeback as the fast, competitive yacht it had once been.

Bona

This boat was launched in 1934 in the presence of the Duke of Ancona, Princess Bona of Savoia–Genoa, Prince Konrad of Bavaria, Dr. Guido Giovanelli, and the engineer Vincenzo Vittorio Baglietto. The boat was designed by the latter, son of Pietro Baglietto (founder of the Baglietto shipyard), on behalf of the Duke of Genoa.

Bona is built from mahogany planking laid over a mahogany keel to guarantee lightness and contains 5.29 tons of lead ballast. The hull has the traditional streamlined shape of a top-class racer, and during its lifetime it has left a permanent mark on Italian yachting history. The Duke of Ancona raced the boat for two years without much success. Then the boat underwent a series of small modifications.

Its first tonnage certificate dates from May 1934, when the boat had a displacement of 8.71 tons, a length of 30 feet at the waterline, an overall length of 46 feet, and a rated sailing area of 95 square yards. As we have said, the boat failed to win anything in the hands of its first owner, but the designer was so sure of the boat's potential that he offered to take it back, which he duly did at the end of 1935.

The boat underwent some slight modifications and was tested at sea, and then, in the summer of 1936, with its new owner, Harold Rosasco, it went on to win an incredible series of races. In 1936 it won 12 out of the 13 regattas it took part in, and came second in the 13th. During the winter of 1937, of the 12 regattas it took part in it won seven first places, two second places, two third places, and a fifth place, winning the Italian Cup, the Duca degli Abruzzi Cup, and the Duca d'Aosta Cup. In the summer of 1937 *Bona* entered 14 regattas, of which it came first ten times and second the remaining four times, its victories including, among others, the Re Imperatore Cup. In the winter of 1938, out of ten regattas it won six, came second three times, and fifth in the remaining race, winning among others the prestigious France Cup at Cannes. Never before had a boat won so many regattas, and important ones at that!

In the Italian Cup it repeated its lively battle with Baron Krupp's *Germania III*, *France*, and *Ilderim*. *Bona*'s magnificent capacity, together with the crew's great skill, saw it beat its traditional rivals at the end of a really tough race in a fresh breeze and on a slight sea. In the France Cup, traditionally dominated by French and English boats, only one other Italian yacht, *Artica* (1902) had won before *Bona*'s success.

In the tough Cannes regattas from April 24 through 28, 1938 the crew that won was as follows: Mordini, Poggi, Cosentini, Chiozza (helmsman), Caprile, and Carbone. The regatta consisted of five trials, and the winner needed to come first in at least three of them. *Bona* went one better, winning four out of five, and so could even afford to sit out the fifth. However, *France* (winner of the previous year's regatta), which had already been clearly beaten by *Bona* in other

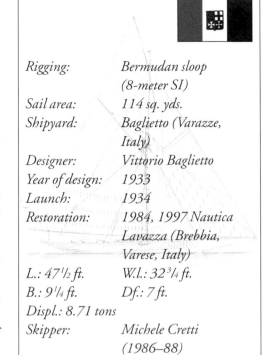

Rigging:	Bermudan sloop (8-meter SI)
Sail area:	114 sq. yds.
Shipyard:	Baglietto (Varazze, Italy)
Designer:	Vittorio Baglietto
Year of design:	1933
Launch:	1934
Restoration:	1984, 1997 Nautica Lavazza (Brebbia, Varese, Italy)
L.: 47½ ft.	W.l.: 32¾ ft.
B.: 9¼ ft.	Df.: 7 ft.
Displ.: 8.71 tons	
Skipper:	Michele Cretti (1986–88)

LEFT: *Porto Santo Stefano 2000, the 8-meter SI* Bona *has returned to the world of regattas* (Photo: J. Taylor)

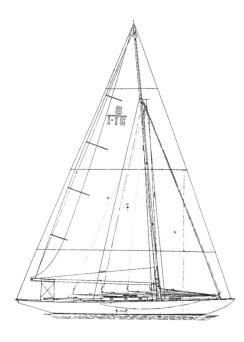

races, contested the latter's victory, entering into sophisticated discussions about the merits of this victory, and in the end *Bona* took part in the fifth and final race, which it duly won once again, thus completing an utter triumph over its rivals. A memorable performance which those who were lucky enough to see it will never ever forget. The boat then took part in the trials for the selection of the Italian team to go to the Kiel Olympics but, despite winning three out of five regattas, and being clearly the fastest of the 8-meter SI yachts, it was not chosen for the team. Its place went to the 8-meter SI *Italia*, which in any case won the gold medal.

Bona continued taking part in numerous regattas in its class, right through the period from 1936 to 1950. In 1937, equal on points with *Orietta*, it won the Covo di Nord Est Cup; in 1938 it took part in the Naples Regattas, and over the four days always finished first ahead of *Italia* and *Orietta*. In 1950 it won the regatta-cruise Naples–Ischia, the Circolo Forestieri Cup, and the CRV Italia Cup.

After 1950 *Bona* ended up left in a shed at the Canottieri Posillipo Yacht Club, where it remained, totally neglected, until the mid-1960s, when it was rediscovered by a Neapolitan architect who had it restored. The topside was modified to accommodate living quarters, and the deck and cockpit were raised in order to render it self-emptying to accord with RINA requirements. Moreover, a diesel engine and an aluminum mast were installed. The new sail plan was designed by Elvstrom France. Nowadays you can see a rectangular, Art Nouveau-style Italian flag flanked by two laurel branches on the side of the boat.

Bona has always been much-loved by boat-builders and yachtsmen. A few years ago, Alfredo Rebagliati (nicknamed "U Pria"), who worked all his life at the Baglietto yard (for 15 lire a day during the mid-1930s), had the following to say about the boat: "…*the* Azzurra *showed the Italians what we at Varazze had already discovered half a century ago; too late unfortunately for the revival of the fortunes of these yards.* Bona *was a triumph of our technical ability and skills: I remember that when it beat French or English boats, which at that time dominated*

the yachting scene, we always used to celebrate with a massive drinking session…"

Bona was sold in 1981 to Pietro Cretti. By then it had undergone a series of transformations and modifications to the original design, most of them performed in Neapolitan yards by expert craftsmen under the supervision of the architect Salvatore Nappi, a keen yachtsman himself. During the 1980s the boat had an aluminum mast and a jib running down from the masthead (it was originally a seven-eighths rig); the boom was shorter and the spanker smaller, while the jib was larger and the mast was set back further astern.

The deck had been rebuilt, losing some of its original character, while a toerail, stanchion, and pulpit had been added. A diesel engine had been installed beneath the cockpit with the propeller in a sloping position; the weight of the engine had been counterbalanced by removing some of the lead from the other side of the keel. The stern had also been modified and was now higher and longer than the original had been. Despite these radical changes, *Bona* (which had never changed its name) was still a very fast boat. In 1990 it was covered for protection and stored away while awaiting the right time to be put to sea once again, by someone capable of understanding and appreciating the historical worth of this magnificent yacht.

Between 1999 and 2000 the boat's new owner, Giovanni Mogna, had it completely refitted at the Lavazza di Brebbia boatyard. 11 inches of freeboard were eliminated, the frame-floor was rebuilt in stainless steel, and the deck was rebuilt using spruce staves screwed onto the beams with brass screws. Considerable work was done to get the boat back into the 8-meter Class. Around 85 percent of the frame was rebuilt, while the planking was completely overhauled. The unattractive metal mast was replaced by a wooden one, as were the boom and spinnaker pole (in spruce). New bronze and brass fittings were mounted, while the name of the boat was set into the transom. With its shiny blue hull, *Bona* was victorious once again in its class in the 8-meter SI World Championship held in June 2000 at Porto Santo Stefano. The inboard engine was finally removed, and now *Bona* has no engine at all.

OPPOSITE PAGE: *1994,* Bona *during a regatta (Photo: L. Fioroni).*

Cintra

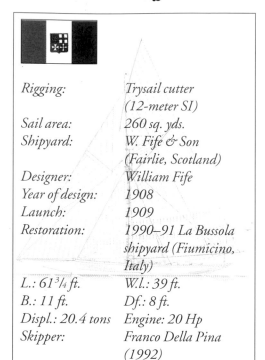

Rigging:	Trysail cutter (12-meter SI)
Sail area:	260 sq. yds.
Shipyard:	W. Fife & Son (Fairlie, Scotland)
Designer:	William Fife
Year of design:	1908
Launch:	1909
Restoration:	1990–91 La Bussola shipyard (Fiumicino, Italy)
L.: 61 3/4 ft.	W.l.: 39 ft.
B.: 11 ft.	Df.: 8 ft.
Displ.: 20.4 tons	Engine: 20 Hp
Skipper:	Franco Della Pina (1992)

BELOW: *1998,* Cintra *during a regatta (Photo: J. Taylor).*

OPPOSITE PAGE: *Imperia 1992,* Cintra *with all sails hoisted (Photo: F. Ramella).*

Launched in 1909, *Cintra* took part in all the regattas held on the River Clyde in Scotland up until the outbreak of World War I. It was an extremely competitive boat, and its rig was regularly updated and modernized from one year to the next. After the war, the boat changed hands and was transferred to the south coast of England where, fitted out with a Bermudan rig, it continued to race successfully. Its last recorded regatta dates back to 1956: the Round the Island Race. After that, the boat disappeared completely from the yachting news and was left, neglected, in a shed housing an old Thames barge. In 1955, the Register of Yachts lists the boat known as *Cintro* (formerly *Cintra*) as no. 1304, owned by an A.J. Walter.

In 1984 the boat was rediscovered by Camper & Nicholson in a very sorry state; a ghost of its former glorious self. The Giorgetti & Magrini Studio was informed of the boat's condition, and it was immediately drawn to the attention of the publisher Alberto Rusconi, a vintage yacht enthusiast who was particularly keen on 12-meter SI yachts (he owns *Tomahawk* and *Vim*). Rusconi decided to save the boat, which is now the oldest 12-meter SI left. So it was that in the autumn of 1990, *Cintra* was transferred to the La Bussola yard at Fiumicino in Italy and restoration work got underway.

The boat was in a terrible state on its arrival at the yard after a series of disastrous refitting operations in the past. This boat, which was designed for triangular regattas, had over the years been transformed into a cruiser, with a deckhouse of abnormal vertical proportions with respect to the freeboard on two floors, a large onboard engine, and a shortened overhang at the stern. Only the architect F. Giorgetti's intuition and his enthusiasm for challenges

BOTTOM RIGHT: *ASW 1998, a spectacular photo of the* Cintra *(Photo: J. Taylor).*

BELOW: *Two shots of the interior of the boat during refitting work (Photos: S. Navarrini).*

enabled him to perceive how the boat could be possibly restored. While the boatyard began the partial demolition of the deck and planking, Giorgetti & Magrini found some old photographs of the boat together with the original sail plan, the general design, and some drawings of the masting, which William Fife had designed for the construction of his boats in his Fairlie yard in Scotland.

Despite its age, 50 percent of the Honduran mahogany planking was in good condition, and it was deemed that this part at least could be salvaged. However, other parts of the boat, such as the ribs and the galvanized iron alternate structure frame-floor typical of hulls made at that time, were in a poor way. The acacia ribs were in excellent condition, making it possible to work on *Cintra*'s planking without compromising the shape of the boat. The elm deck beams, which had not been modified during previous refitting operations, were in good condition.

After the partial stripping of the planking, the deck was rebuilt from a sheet of ³/₄-inch marine plyboard covered with ¹/₂-inch yellow pine staves (the original deck had been made of this wood), and mahogany partners, stringers, and hatchways. In order to improve the quality of the surface of the planking, and ensure it lasted longer, nearly all the planking strakes were replaced while conserving the keel, the stempost, and the elm sternpost, which were all in excellent condition.

Another part of the boat that had been surprisingly well conserved, and thus entirely recouped, was the helmport and the top part of the helmport boom (probably in oak). Each restoration operation proved a perfect compromise between traditional methods and the latest technology. For example, the planking was laid and caulked as it would have been in 1900, but it was treated using products guaranteeing it a longer life (the "West System").

The lack of recoupable material meant that the restorers had to search high and low for photographs and books that might have given a clearer idea of the specifications of the masts, rigging, and deck, thus enabling them to restore it to its original splendor. The only concession to modernization was the installation of six small winches. In order to remain faithful to the

original design, the mast and boom were made from Douglas fir. Every single detail of the rigging was studied and designed separately, from the mast's steel collars to the wooden blocks, supplied by the Pichetto company of Genoa. The sails were made by Murphy & Nye who, in keeping with the original design, chose an ivory-colored Dacron that closely resembled the cotton first used. The spanker, gaff topsail, jib, staysail, yankee, and moonsail account for a total sailing area of 260 square yards. The rather small interior was redesigned in the original spirit of the boat.

All this considerable effort on the part of the boatyard, the designer, and the owner has meant that *Cintra* now looks 80 years younger than it did before and has started to sail again, showing off its aristocratic, elegant, agile lines. Today the boat resembles, once more, the vessel captured in a photograph taken by Beken in 1910, with just one or two slight differences: the length of the boom and the less pronounced sheerline.

Coppelia

Coppelia is an 8-meter SI designed by Johan Anker and launched in Norway in 1923 as *Enchantment IV*. A fast boat with heavy lines, in 1924 it won 19 out of 22 of its regattas. Between 1925 and 1950 it was seen in the port of Marseilles, France, with a new name, *Vert Galant*, and then at Saint Tropez with another name, *Volonté*.

In 1973 it was bought by Philippe Salvetat, and by that time it had changed its name yet again, this time to *Coppelia*. Its present owner had the boat refitted at the La Seyne sur Mer boatyard. It now has a new mast and a completely rebuilt deck, while the hull is made of pine and iroko. *Coppelia* took part in every single edition of the Nioulargue up until 1991.

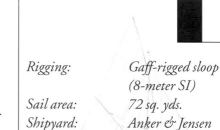

Rigging:	Gaff-rigged sloop (8-meter SI)
Sail area:	72 sq. yds.
Shipyard:	Anker & Jensen (Asker, Norway)
Designer:	Johan Anker
Year of design:	1923
Launch:	1923
Restoration:	1975
L.: 46 ft.	W.l.: 32³⁄₄ ft.
B.: 9 ft. Df.: 6¹⁄₂ ft.	
Displ.: 9.37 tons	Engine: 16 Hp
Skipper:	Philippe Salvetat (1990)

ABOVE: *A shot of* Coppelia *at the 1990 Nioulargue (Photo courtesy of M. Salvetat).*

LEFT: Coppelia, *an 8-meter SI designed by Johan Anker, was a highly successful racer during the 1930s (Photo courtesy of M. Salvetat).*

Dalgra III

Rigging:	*Bermudan sloop (5.5-meter SI)*
Sail area:	*72 sq. yds.*
Shipyard:	*Corsier-Port (Geneva, Switzerland)*
Designer:	*Henri Copponex*
Year of design:	*1957*
Launch:	*1957*
Restoration:	*1995 Caprera naval shipyard (Italy)*
L.: 31 ft.	W.l.: 23½ ft.
B.: 6 ft.	Df.: 4¼ ft.
Displ.: 2.05 tons	Engine: 12 Hp
Skipper:	*Marina Carpaneda (1996–2000)*

BELOW: *VBR 2001, a spectacular shot of* Dalgra III *during a regatta (Photo: J. Taylor).*

algra III is a 5.5-meter SI designed by the Genevan architect Henry Copponex and built at the Corsier-Port boatyard on Lake Geneva, Switzerland. Its first owner was Pierono Ferrara of Naples, who had the boat specially designed for the Italian Cup. As a result of trials, during which the boat proved to be the fastest in its field, it was entrusted to the famous, highly successful boat-owner Max Oberti. *Dalgra III* won the Cup and repeated this success in 1955.

In 1960 the boat was hired by the Spanish Olympic team to take part in the 1960 Naples Olympics. After being bought and sold a number of times, the boat was finally donated by Vittorio di Sambuj to the Caprera Sailing Club, but the fact that the Club was more interested in cruising than in racing meant the boat was abandoned for several years.

Its elegant hull was unfortunately coated in a layer of fiberglass. However, the hull was once again stripped down to the wood when it was later discovered by a group of sailing enthusiasts and entrusted to the Caprera boatyard in Italy for refitting. All of the screws were replaced, while the stempost and part of the bottom planking were rebuilt. Then the hull was clad in three layers of laminate wood using the "West System" gluing technique. Thus it was that the boat reacquired its original competitiveness, and went on to take part in the San Pellegrino Veteran Boat Rally in Porto Cervo, and the Régates Royales in Cannes in France in 1995. The following year *Dalgra III* took part in the ninth vintage yacht meeting held in Imperia, as well as in Classic Week in Monaco and, once again, the Régates Royales in Cannes.

From June 27 through July 3, 1998, the boat took part in the 5.5-meter Class World Championship held in Cowes, England. It was the only one of the 26 yachts present with a wooden mast, and it went on to win the 5.5-meter Vintage Yacht Class skippered by Marina Carpaneda.

Dan

an is a Swedish creation, designed and built by Bjarne Aas in 1931. In 1932 it was registered in the Lloyds Register of Yachts as the property of Copenhagen's Royal Yacht Club. It then became the property of the King of Denmark and it sailed for three seasons in the Mediterranean. It won a number of races in the Italia Cup, and in 1932 a team regatta, the Oro del Tirreno Cup (it came second in the same regatta in 1933 and 1934). It achieved the same result in the Genova Cup.

It was then sold to a French yachtsman, renamed *Davil*, and sailed another season in Italy before being transferred to Marseilles, France, where it was renamed first *Eole I* and then *Cabri III* (when it was the property of the Commodore of the Societé Nautique de Marseilles). All trace of the boat was lost from 1938 until 1985, the year in which it reappeared on Lake Como, where on one particularly windy day the boat unfortunately sank.

It was eventually salvaged and, thanks to the efforts and loving care afforded by a boatyard in Lezzeno, Italy, was gradually restored to its former self. The planking had to be removed completely, and the ribs were rebuilt before being clad in the original planking once again. The boat's original mast was discovered in a Genevan yard at Corsier-Port. The sails, which are no longer cotton, were made from Dacron cloth with traditional stitching and leather dressing.

Dan began the 1996 season at the ninth vintage yacht meeting in Imperia, followed by Monaco Classic Week and the 6-meter European Championship held during the Régates Royales in Cannes, France. The *Dan* raced under the YCCS burgee. Together with *Nyala*, it was voted the best restored boat in 1996.

Rigging:	*Bermudan sloop (6-meter SI)*
Shipyard:	*Bjarne (Trederikstad, Sweden)*
Designer:	*Bjarne Aas*
Year of design:	*1930*
Launch:	*1931*
Restoration:	*1996*
L.: 37½ ft.	*W.l.: 28 ft.*
B.: 6 ft.	*Df.: 5½ ft.*
Displ.: 4.41 tons	
Skipper:	*Luigi Carpaneda (1996–2000)*

THIS PAGE: *Cannes 2000, two shots of* Dan *during its regattas (Photos: J. Taylor).*

OVERLEAF: *Cannes 2000, a fine photograph of* Dan *(Photo: J. Taylor).*

Estérel

A splendid hull with elegant lines, *Estérel* has for the past two years been collecting honors at vintage yacht regattas: this 8-meter SI is designer Léon Sébille's masterpiece. Sébille had gained fame at the beginning of the 20th century with another hull, *Joliette III. Estérel* was launched in 1912 on behalf of brothers Michel and Jacques Henri. After a series of ups and downs and changes of ownership, the boat was purchased in 1990 by Patrick Williamson, owner of the Pointe-Rouge boatyard in France. This was to be the boat's saving grace, as at that time it clearly bore the marks of time, especially in the planking and the frame. Restoration work involved taking the boat apart, piece by piece, and restoring each section with great care (at that time – 1992 – Eric Tabarly suggested that the boat be considered a "historical monument").

Today the completely restored *Estérel* has reacquired its original splendor, thanks partly to the interest in the restoration project shown by the magazine *Yachting Classique*. The gracious shape of the hull, its long boom stretching beyond the stern, and the beauty of its sails make it a true gem. The rebuilt teak deck, the sails in champagne-colored Dacron, and the bronze belaying pins at the foot of the mast, together constitute proof of a truly exceptional piece of restoration.

Rigging:	Trysail cutter (8-meter SI)
Sail area:	132 sq. yds.
Shipyard:	Borelli & Sébille, Pharo shipyard (Marseilles, France)
Designer:	Léon Sébille
Year of design:	1912
Launch:	1912
Restoration:	1998 H2O Yachting naval shipyard (Pointe-Rouge, France)
L.: 39¼ ft.	W.l.: 25½ ft.
B.: 7 ft.	Df.: 5 ft.
Displ.: 6.06 tons	Engine: 60 Hp

LEFT: *Cannes 1999,* Estérel *during a regatta* (Photo: J. Taylor).

BELOW: *Cannes 2000, maneuvering the jibs* (Photo: J. Taylor).

Flica II

Rigging:	Bermudan sloop (12-meter SI)
Sail area:	213 sq. yds.
Shipyard:	W. Fife & Son (Fairlie, Scotland)
Designer:	Laurent Giles
Year of design:	1938
Launch:	1939
Restoration:	1991–92 Camper & Nicholson (Gosport, England)
L.: 67 ft.	W.l.: 46½ ft.
B.: 12 ft.	Df.: 12 ft.
Displ.: 30 tons	Engine: 80 Hp
Skipper:	Nicola Brissolese (1992–96)

BELOW: *Cannes 2000, a close-up of* Flica II *as it sails close-hauled (Photo: J. Taylor).*

OPPOSITE PAGE: *Cannes 2000, the crew on the stringer as the boat is put about (Photo: J. Taylor).*

Designed by Laurent Giles, this 12-meter SI was launched just before the outbreak of World War II. We do not have much information about the boat's early days, but we do know that it was used as a "hare" to *Sceptre*, the British challenger for the America's Cup, in 1958, at a time when the new sailing regulations envisaged regattas with 12-meter yachts.

After its period of fame, the boat was transformed into a ketch and chartered in the Mediterranean and the Caribbean before being abandoned at some point on a beach.

It was subsequently discovered by Renato Della Valle, owner of *Trivia*, another 12-meter SI. That was in 1991, and its new owner transferred the boat to England and convinced Stefano Tanzi to buy it. Tanzi fell in love with the boat and had it taken to the Camper & Nicholson shipyard to be restored. Restoration, which took a year to complete, involved consider-able work. Only a little of the original hull could be saved, together with a few ribs, the lead keel, and part of the rigging. The rest of the boat had to be rebuilt from the original drawings, which fortunately had been found in the meantime.

The new spruce mast was built by Spencer, a well-known craftsman on the Isle of Wight who had been the helmsman on *Flica II* when it competed against *Sceptre* in 1958. The planking was rebuilt in mahogany, while the deck, which had previously been in yellow pine, was rebuilt in pine. The interior is in cedar.

The rejuvenated boat made its second appearance on the racing scene in 1992, in the vintage yacht regattas, and won the Mediterranean Trophy that year. It won an impressive series of placings during the 2001 season: including first place in the Prada Trophy, third place in the Cannes regattas, fourth place in the Round the Island Race, and so on.

Folly

Rigging:	Trysail sloop (8-meter SI)
Sail area:	143 sq. yds.
Shipyard:	Camper & Nicholson (Gosport, England)
Designer:	Charles E. Nicholson
Year of design:	1909
Launch:	1909
Restoration:	1998 (Argentina), 2000 Argentario naval shipyard (Italy)
L.: 37³/₄ ft.	W.l.: 26¹/₂ ft.
B.: 7¹/₂ ft.	Df.: 5 ft.
Displ.: 8.82 tons	
Skipper:	Edgardo Cerezo, German Frers (1998)

The Argentario boatyards in Italy have completed a splendid job in restoring the 8-meter SI sloop *Folly*, the oldest boat of its class present at the recent World Championships. The first owner of this Charles Nicholson creation was one Don Celestro Fernandez Blanco, who saw this trysail rig with its large expanses of sail as a born winner. In fact, it raced in South America, winning the 100th Anniversary of Argentine Independence commemorative regatta under the colors of the Argentine Yachting Club.

The 1950 Register of Yachts gives the boat as being based in Buenos Aires in Argentina, the property of the engineer Ricardo Radaelli. The boat had definitely been transformed to a gaff-rigged sloop during that period. Its present owner,

German Frers, came across it among the boats at the Club Nautico San Isidro, and a few years later decided to buy it and have it completely restored. At that time *Folly* was in a rather precarious state, but with the aid of Beken's historical photographs and information supplied by the sail-makers Ratsey & Lapthorn of England, he managed to discover the original dimensions of both the hull and the rig.

Alberto Syzka's Argentine boatyard completed the essential refitting work, and further restoration was undertaken at the Argentario yard in Italy, including rebuilding of the gaff, renewal of the deck fittings, and fitting a new bowsprit. *Folly* has now reverted to its original trysail rig and once again boasts the gracious lines created by its famous designer.

BELOW: *ASW 2000, the 8-meter SI* Folly *rigged out by German Frers (Photo: J. Taylor).*

OPPOSITE PAGE: *A fine photo of the boat (Photo: J. Taylor).*

Fulmar

Rigging:	Gaff-rigged sloop (8-meter SI)
Sail area:	119 sq. yds.
Shipyard:	W. Fife & Son (Fairlie, Scotland)
Designer:	William Fife III
Year of design:	1930
Launch:	1930
Restoration:	1993 Fairlie Restorations
L.: 47½ ft.	W.l.: 27½ ft.
B.: 8¾ ft.	Df.: 6½ ft.
Displ.: 8.53 tons	Engine: 25 Hp
Skipper:	Doris Klaus (1998)

About *Fulmar*, a sloop designed by William Fife, the French journalist Jérôme Boyer has written: "… *Fifteen meters of simple, moving beauty, which defies time… it is such a beautiful boat it seems to have come straight out of a dream…*"

Fulmar has a very respectable past, especially as it was champion of the Clyde in Scotland in 1934, 1935, and 1936. The boat was found abandoned in 1991 in Canada. Today, thanks to Doris and Ernest Klaus, the new boat-owners and true sailing enthusiasts, the boat has rediscovered its long-lost youth through a complete refit at Fairlie Restorations in Scotland. This shipyard, set up by Walter Duncan, follows every detail of the craftsmanship of Fife, as is shown in the restorations of *Altair*, *Tuiga*, and *Kentra*.

The hull of Fulmar, which was launched in 1930 with the name of *Oonah*, has been to a large extent reconstructed, following the methods and using the materials of the period. The equipment, with its standing rigging, was created by Spencer of Cowes, England. There is no fixed motor on board, no winches, and nothing electronic to counteract the boat's harmony. As soon as its sails are unfurled, *Fulmar* glides over the water and every movement in its rigging confirms it as a fast and sensitive vessel.

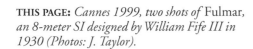

THIS PAGE: *Cannes 1999, two shots of* Fulmar, *an 8-meter SI designed by William Fife III in 1930 (Photos: J. Taylor).*

Ikra

The hull of this beautiful boat was designed by architect David Boyd; its forms are identical to those of *Sovereign* before its latest transformation. The names of the two boats recall the exciting days of the 1964 America's Cup, when two 12-meter SIs were to defend the British colors. That was the time when *Ikra* (then known as *Kurrewa*) used Hood sails and had better results than its twin *Sovereign*.

It was the latter, however, that won the British duel, but nevertheless lost the America's Cup. Both boats subsequently ended up in France, acquired by Baron Bich for practice by the French team, which was supposed to challenge the Americans. *Kurrewa* was then called *Lévrier des Mers*.

In 1972 it was acquired by another Frenchman, Jean Redele, creator of Alpine Renault cars, who transformed the boat for cruising and rechristened it *Ikra*. The new – and current – owner was very careful to respect the original lines, checking that the transformation work, at the Labbe shipyard in Saint Malo, France, under the direction of D. Presles, proceeded without significant alterations.

Today, the interior allows a comfortable cruise for 10–12 people while preserving the boat's appearance and sporting abilities, as well as the attractive lines of the flush deck. The sail arrangement of *Ikra* is no longer what it once was; it is partially reduced by a shorter boom and shorter mast than on the original vessel. Its hull, with high-quality mahogany planking, still remains the largest, in both length and width, of all the 12-meter SI series.

The design of the boat, the first with a truly modern form, offers much internal space, a characteristic that allowed the creation – according to Boyd – of a cruise yacht that is exceptionally comfortable and spacious, even for a boat born to take part in just one regatta. The transformations that were made to obtain improved comfort and living quarters, already surprisingly good for a 12-meter, are currently reconciled with the need to obtain excellent results and to respect the original aesthetics.

Rigged as a sloop and transformable into a cutter, *Ikra* has a 88½-foot mast, a sail surface of over 240 square yards, a set of 12 sails, 16 winches, and two "coffee-grinders." The boat has every kind of electronic equipment needed for navigation and general safety.

Since 1973 Ikra has sailed over 25,000 miles between cruises and races. It was the boat that led to the creation of the Nioulargue when it won a solitary challenge against the likeable United States boat *Fride*.

At vintage yacht regattas, *Ikra*, as well as re-encountering its old companion and adversary *Sovereign*, has raced with other boats from the same class, such as *Vim*, *Flica*, *Trivia*, and *Cintra*.

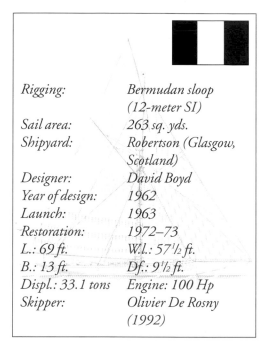

Rigging:	Bermudan sloop (12-meter SI)
Sail area:	263 sq. yds.
Shipyard:	Robertson (Glasgow, Scotland)
Designer:	David Boyd
Year of design:	1962
Launch:	1963
Restoration:	1972–73
L.: 69 ft.	W.l.: 57½ ft.
B.: 13 ft.	Df.: 9½ ft.
Displ.: 33.1 tons	Engine: 100 Hp
Skipper:	Olivier De Rosny (1992)

FOLLOWING PAGE: *Cannes 2000,* Ikra *during a regatta (Photo J. Taylor).*

BELOW: *Cannes 2000, close-up of the aft transom of Ikra (Photo J. Taylor).*

Italia

The gathering at Imperia has twice been honored by the presence of the glorious 8-meter SI *Italia*, which won the gold medal at the 1936 Olympics in Kiel, Germany. *Italia* (which replaced *Bona*) won the much sought-after title against nine determined nations crewed by Leone Reggio (the helmsman), Domenico Mordini, Massimo and Luigi Poggi, Gigi De Manicor, and Bruno Bianchi. After surviving the war (it seems it was hidden away), the boat was acquired in the late 1940s by the Nautical Club of Naples, who sold it to Eugenio di Leva of Sorrento, Italy. During this time it competed with YC Posillipo's *Bona* in the Coppa De Conciliis. Finally, *Italia* was bought by its current, highly scrupulous owner, Antonio Sisimbro of Naples, Italy.

The boat, which is maintained as though it were a monument, is original in all its rigging and its hull. The bronze winches and compass are from 1936; likewise, the teak deck has never been rebuilt. The planking is mahogany, the mast spruce. In recent years it has participated in all the regattas of its class in the Gulf of Naples. The harmonious lines of the vessel, adorned by the Olympic rings painted on the broadsides, arouse admiration and emotion. *Italia* arrives at the regatta venues in a truck, prompting general enthusiasm upon the quay on its arrival.

Rigging:	*Bermudan sloop (8-meter SI)*
Sail area:	*92 sq. yds.*
Shipyard:	*Costaguta (Genoa Voltri, Italy)*
Designer:	*Attilio Costaguta*
Year of design:	*1936*
Launch:	*1936*
L.: 45 ft.	*W.l.: 28½ ft.*
B.: 8 ft.	*Df.: 5½ ft.*
Displ.: 16.7 tons	*Engine: 24 Hp*
Skipper:	*Antonio Sisimbro, Luigi Reggio (1989–1992)*

THIS PAGE: *PSW 1998, two shots of* Italia, *gold-medalist at the Olympics in Kiel in 1936 (under helmsman Leone Reggio) (Photos: J. Taylor).*

Kukururu

Rigging:	*Bermudan sloop (5.5-meter SI)*
Sail area:	*36 sq. yds.*
Shipyard:	*Baglietto (Varazze, Italy)*
Designer:	*Arvid Laurin*
Year of design:	*1952*
Launch:	*1952*
L.: 31 ft.	*W.l.: 21¼ ft.*
B.: 6¼ ft.	*Df.: 4½ ft.*
Displ.: 33.1 tons	*Engine: 100 Hp*
Skipper:	*Gian Mario Bianchi (1994–96)*

*K*ukururu is one of the few vessels that have survived from the scant generation of 5.5-meter SIs that had their moment of glory after World War II. Who could forget names such as *Twins VIII*, *Mirtala*, *Volpina*, etc?

Kukururu was built in 1952 in the Baglietto shipyards in Varazze, Italy, from a design by the famous architect Arvid Laurin, who had adopted an innovative technique in the form of the bow, winning the Olympics in 1952. The boat had its debut under the colors of the Sailing Club of Rimini.

Sold and moved to Lake Como in Italy, *Kukururu* was acquired by the current owner, a collector of vintage boats, who undertook a complete restoration of the boat using the services of the Italian Nautical Club in Portoferraio. At Imperia, *Kukururu* competed with old fellow-voyagers such as *Dalgra III*, *Voloira III*, and *Dan D 43*. It is one of the oldest 5.5-meter vessels still sailing.

BELOW: *Imperia 1996, the 5.5-meter SI* Kukururu, *one of the few vessels of the class still active (Photo: G. Pittaluga).*

Magda XIII

At the Del Carlo shipyard in Viareggio, Italy, *Magda XIII* (at various times known as *Eolos*, *Rollo V*, and *Hermina III*) is currently undergoing major restoration work. It is the last boat of the famous Norwegian yachtsman Alfred Larsen, who has owned no fewer than 12 boats named *Magda*, almost all designed for regattas by Fife or Anker.

Magda VII was a 10-meter by Anker, *Magda VIII* was a 12-meter by Fife, *Magda IX* was a 12-meter by Anker, *Magda X* (formerly *Beduin* and *Sophie Elisabeth*) was a 15-meter by Fife, *Magda XI* was a 12-meter by Anker, and *Magda XII* (formerly *Halloween*) was a 15-meter cruise boat by Fife. *Magda XIII*, designed by Johan Anker and launched in 1938, was described as "*the best cruise boat ever built*." The planking was composed of Oregon pine and it has a 27.6-ton lead keel. In fall 1939, after winning everything that it was possible to win for half a century, Alfred Larsen sold the boat to Ingar Doublong, who, after the war, modified its sail plan into a yawl and installed a motor, keeping it until 1962.

Rollo V had two other owners, then ended up in Spain with a Greek buyer, who called it *Hermina III*.

Work on the boat, which was soon to have its original name, *Magda XIII*, restored, was supervised by an exceptional adviser who has spent his whole life on board yachts – Chicco Zaccagni, formerly the skipper-owner of *Alzavola*. Chicco found the boat's construction plans at the Norske Veritas and, amazingly, discovered the wording "15 MSI," and the signature of Johan Anker in 1937. The 15-meter SI Class had practically ceased to exist in that year. There being no more hulls available, the boat never engaged in official races, only in cruises.

Magda XIII has cedar planking and a teak deck (the original was pitch pine). It has an original spruce mast, composite frames (a steel one every two, the wood curved oak), and steel floor plates. To date, 1,300 feet of planking have been replaced, 80 percent of the beams and 20 percent of the floor timbers. The mast and boom will be lengthened, while the rig will return to being a three-quarters rig-cutter.

Rigging:	Gaff-rigged cutter (15-meter SI)
Shipyard:	Anker & Jensen (Norway)
Designer:	Johan Anker
Year of design:	1937
Launch:	1938
Restoration:	2001–02 Del Carlo shipyard (Viareggio, Italy)
L.: 74½ ft.	W.l.: 50 ft.
B.: 13¾ ft.	Df.: 10¼ ft.
Displ.: 52.9 tons	Engine: 150 Hp

Mizar III

This is the first 6-meter SI to be launched by Sangermani of Italy in the post-war period (in 1946) from a project by Olin Stephens. It was inspired by the famous United States 6-meter SI *Goose* (created by the same architect and one of the most famous boats in that class in the competitive seasons prior to the war).

Its first owner was Renato Marchese of Genoa, Italy: the sail number (which still exists) was I-63. The boat performed well competitively in the seasons 1948, 1949, and 1950, gaining the following placings, among others:

- International Regattas in Genoa, March 14–21, 1948: classified second in the

Tyrrhenian Cup, third position in the Tourism Cup, and first place in the C. Pozzani Cup.
- International Regattas in Genoa, March 6–18, 1949: fifth place in the Tourism Cup, fifth place in the Cosulich Brothers Cup, and third place in the Duke of Aremberg Cup.
- Regatta in Portofino, September 8–11, 1949: first place and winner for 1949 (best result achieved) in the Italian Yacht Club Cup (G. Canessa was the helmsman).
- International Regattas in Genoa, February 27–March 5, 1950: second place in the C. Pozzani Cup.

Rigging:	Bermudan sloop (8-meter SI)
Sail area:	78 sq. yds.
Shipyard:	Sangermani (Lavagna, Italy)
Designer:	Sparkman & Stephens
Year of design:	1946
Launch:	1946
Restoration:	1970, 1992
L.: 36¾ ft.	W.L.: 26¼ ft.
B.: 6 ft.	Df.: 6 ft.
Displ.: 4.02 tons	Engine: 6 Hp
Skipper:	Luigi Scardovi (1991–94)

- International Regattas in San Remo, March 31–April 2, 1950: second place in the City of San Remo Trophy.

Subsequently, in the 1950s and 1960s, due both to changes in ownership and to the presence of more competitive vessels and, later on, as a result of the decline of the class in international competitive circuits, *Mizar III* participated only occasionally in competitive activities. In 1955 it was owned by G.C. Longari, with Genoa, Italy, as its district of registration.

In the 1970s, as for many metric classes created for racing, the boat underwent work on the internal and deck structures,

acquiring its current appearance as a boat partially used for leisure.

Mizar III is built with double mahogany planking and, in contrast to the original design, has a rounded-duckbill stern, a very effective aesthetic detail typical of the 12-meter SI. Bought by the current owner in 1990 after a long period during which it was semi-abandoned, it now has a varnished hull; aluminum mast and boom instead of the original wood ones; and a small, harmonious deckhouse, fitted in the mid-1970s by a shipwright from the Sangermani shipyard. A small inboard motor is used for mooring maneuvers.

BELOW: *Imperia 1994, the 8-meter SI* Mizar III *(right), launched at the Sangermani shipyard in the immediate post-war period (Photo courtesy of L. Scardovi).*

Nereide II

Classed as a 5.5-meter SI, the hull of *Nereide II* was designed and built in 1963 by Captain Dario Salata at his own shipyard in Rapallo, Italy. The first owners were Dario Salata, Giorgio Cavallo, and Piero Sada. In 1964 the boat participated in Genoa Sailing Week and the A. Beniscelli Cup in Alassio, Italy. The most significant maintenance interventions took place in 1986, after around ten years of non-use of the boat, and in 1990, with the reconstruction of the deck using teak. In recent years it has participated in various classic and metric yacht regattas, achieving excellent results. Present for the first time at Imperia in 1996, it came second in its class.

Rigging:	Bermudan sloop (5.5-meter SI)
Sail area:	33 sq. yds.
Shipyard:	Salata (Rapallo, Italy)
Designer:	Dario Salata
Year of design:	1963
Launch:	1964
Restoration:	1986, 1988, 1990
L.: 29¼ ft.	W.l.: 23 ft.
B.: 6¼ ft.	Df.: 4¼ ft.
Displ.: 3.31 tons	
Skipper:	Paolo Alfonso Sada (1996)

BELOW: Nereide II, *a 5.5-meter SI designed by Captain Dario Salata (Photo courtesy of P.A. Sada).*

Nyala

Rigging:	Bermudan sloop (12-meter SI)
Sail area:	211 sq. yds.
Shipyard:	Nevins shipyard (City Island, New York, USA)
Designer:	Olin Stephens
Year of design:	1937
Launch:	1938
Restoration:	1995
L.: 68 ft.	W.l.: 45 ft.
B.: 12 ft.	Df.: 9 ft.
Displ.: 23.9 tons	Engine: 62 Hp
Skipper:	Patrizio Bertelli (1996–98)

THIS PAGE: *Cannes 2001,* Nyala, *a vessel with a glorious past (Photos: J. Taylor).*

On May 17, 1938, at the Nevins shipyard on City Island, New York, the 12-meter SI *Nyala*, designed by Olin Stephens, slipped into the sea. Its sail number was (and still is) US 12. *Nyala* was the third-last 12-meter to be launched before World War II: it was followed by *Northern Light* in the same year and *Vim* in 1939. Its first owner was Friederick T. Bedford, who wanted to offer it as a wedding gift to his daughter Lucie and son-in-law Briggs Cunningham, the famous skipper who was to be at the helm of *Columbia* in the America's Cup in 1968.

Nyala immediately proved to be a winning vessel, collecting victories in the 1939 and 1940 editions of the Yralis regattas. In 1942, while work was being done on *Nyala* to install a motor, generator, radio telephone, and a refrigerator cell, as Federico Nardi recalls, it was acquired by Bob Shelman, who later transferred it to the Great Lakes in North America, where it raced for some years. Here, in 1947, during a storm that broke over the Mackinac Race, *Nyala* lost its aluminum mast, which was considered highly futuristic when fitted in 1939 (as it was for *Vim*).

In 1950 the 12-meter was acquired by Gerald W. Ford, who, between 1950 and 1960, raced with many successes, including the Astor Cup, the Queen Cup, and the Vineyard Trophy. The vessel was also used as a "hare" in the selections of the defenders of the America's Cup in 1958, 1962, and 1964. But destiny had reserved a second dramatic event for *Nyala* when, in 1960, Hurricane Donna violently hit the Atlantic Coast, from the Caribbean to Boston, unmooring the 12-meter in City Island and dragging it onto the rocks.

Following this serious accident, it was necessary to repair the lead in the keel. Taking advantage of the opportunity, structural changes were also made to the boat: the stern was cut and "reversed," as was the trend at the time, and the mast was moved astern by three feet, with a consequent reduction in the sail plan. In 1961 *Nyala* miraculously escaped a fire.

In 1984 *Nyala* had a new owner and underwent further restoration work, remaining in a dusty shed in Newport in the United States where it was discovered by Federico Nardi, who could not help noticing the nobility of its lines and the skill of its creator. *Nyala* was therefore taken to Italy and the shipyards of the Argentario, which were available for a complete restoration. Apart from the changes to the aft transom the interior was still as originally laid out, sober and basic, with American cedar interior-planking. The frames were white oak from Connecticut, the beams sitka and white spruce.

Work began in September 1995 with partial replacement of the frames and reconstruction of the deck using 1¼-inch sitka spruce staves. The cockpit and mast step have returned to their original position. Fortunately all the original deck hardware has been saved, including the "coffee grinder" winches built in the Nevins shipyard. It must be noted that the same North American timber with which *Nyala* had been built was used in the restoration.

The boat has now returned to racing as it did in the past. In Prada Sailing Week in July 1998 at Porto Santo Stefano it beat *Tomahawk* and *Cintra*.

Osborne

Who could forget the beautiful images of *Hispania*, the superb 15-meter with which King Alfonso XIII raced before the Great War? The same sovereign rigged the 8-meter SI *Hispania II*, constructed by Johan Anker in 1923, and personally skippered it to various successes. This passion for 8-meter vessels also involved Queen Vittoria Eugenia, who, in 1928, commissioned *Osborne* from William Fife III. She sailed on board for many years.

Today, *Osborne*, now under private ownership, is still enrolled on the International Eight-Meter Register. Its hull is wood and today it has an aluminum mast. The boat was victorious in its class in the Nioulargue in 1994 and 1995.

During 1997, *Osborne* returned to Fairlie Restorations in Scotland, who restored it to its original splendor. The boat sails in the waters off Calpe in Spain, with Monaco as its port of registration.

Rigging:	Bermudan sloop (8-meter SI)
Sail area:	91 sq. yds.
Shipyard:	Sagredo Bros. (Santander, Spain)
Designer:	William Fife III
Year of design:	1928
Launch:	1929
Restoration:	1990, 1997
L.: 45¼ ft.	W.l.: 28½ ft.
B.: 8½ ft.	Df.: 6¼ ft.
Displ.: 9.37 tons	Engine: 18 Hp
Skipper:	Philippe Griset (1994)

Sovereign

Sovereign is associated with memories of the America's Cup of 1964, the 19th British challenge against boats from the United States. It was commissioned from the Alexander Robertson shipyard in Scotland in 1963 by J. Anthony Boyden, representing the Royal Thames Yacht Club of London. Its designer was David Boyd, who had already designed *Sceptre*, defeated in 1958.

The new 12-meter, on which all British hopes were pinned, was launched on June 6, 1963. With a very fine bow and slim hull, it immediately began trials with *Sceptre* as the boat it was compared against. At the conclusion of these, which had also included races with the old *Flica* by Laurent

Giles and the very new *Kurrewa V*, the challenger and champion were designated to be *Sovereign* and *Constellation*, designed by Olin Stephens. The four races resulted in another resounding defeat, however, due to the superiority of *Constellation* when close-hauled, the genius of Olin Stephens, the better quality of the Hard & Hood sails, the skills of the crew and the experience of Lieutenant-Commander Bob Bavier, skipper of the United States boat.

Sovereign was later acquired by Baron Marcel Bich on behalf of the French Association for the America's Cup. It remained in France, and today it is run by Claude Perdriel, president and general manager of Le Nouvel Observateur.

Rigging:	Bermudan sloop (12-meter SI)
Sail area:	287 sq. yds.
Shipyard:	Alexander Robertson & Sons Ltd. (Argyll, Scotland)
Designer:	David Boyd
Year of design:	1962
Launch:	1963
Restoration:	1985
L.: 69 ft.	W.l.: 46½ ft.
B.: 12½ ft.	Df.: 9 ft.
Displ.: 32.8 tons	Engine: 85 Hp
Skipper:	Jacques Fauroux (1992–94)

LEFT: *Imperia 1994,* Sovereign *during a phase of a regatta (Photo: A. Tringali).*

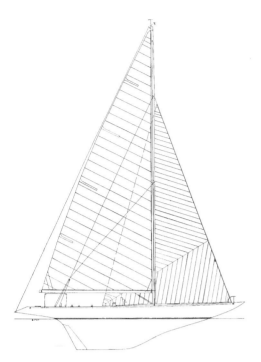

THIS PAGE: *Cannes 2000, the 12-meter SI Sovereign,* whose owner was Baron Marcel Bich *(Photos: J. Taylor).*

Stint

S tint, which is also the name of a small North Sea fish, was launched in 1911, designed by Max Oertz, one of the greatest German architects in the yachting field. Oertz had achieved considerable fame for having designed *Meteor IV* for Kaiser William II, a magnificent boat that competed with King George V's famous *Britannia* at the Cowes regatta in England, giving German yachting as promoted by the Kaiser, partly for political reasons, the highest levels of international prestige. In fact, at Court and in the German establishment, he encouraged the birth and development of prestigious yacht clubs and regattas at international level.

Stint, a 1906 8-meter SI, was built for Frederick Carl von Siemens, an advocate of the industrial and financial crème de la crème of Germany and of the court of the Kaiser and registered at no less than five prestigious yacht clubs around Cowes. In those years, *Stint* remained moored at the wharfs of the Club at Potsdam, Germany, where the imperial palace was based. Here it sailed on the Wannsee, demonstrating its exceptional greyhound-like speed. A boat conceived to race, it has never disappointed the expectations of its builder and its owners, winning many races in different periods and seas.

During World War I, legend has it that the Kaiser gave *Stint* to the now-legendary Red Baron, who on the day of his 25th birthday was invited to a birthday breakfast by the Kaiser, as a reward for the many planes he had knocked out of the sky. However, the event has never been borne out by historical documentation, and the legend probably came about from the fact that in 1922, on its arrival in Italy, the boat supposedly had a red-colored hull and also a pennant with a red background and a gold-colored fish in the middle. Traces of *Stint* are to be found, with the name of *Grete II*, on a certificate issued in 1921 by "Germanischer Lloyd" in Berlin [see overleaf], which indicates a certain Karl Karpzow as its new owner and the Wannsee as its place of mooring.

The tales of its 32 victories in just four years of racing evidently traveled far and wide. In Italy, Trieste's Royal Yacht Club Adriaco, looking for racing vessels for itself and its members, sent its very own Commodore Alberto Cosulich to Germany to acquire *Stint* and what was to become its antagonist in the regattas of the Upper Adriatic, *Giulia* (formerly known as *Munin V* and *Fee*), an 8-meter SI built in Bremen, Germany, by the Abeking & Rasmussen shipyards. During that period, diplomatic relations between Germany and Italy were still tense, and to avoid problems of importation the two boats went through the Consulate (the detached office of the Royal Yacht Club Adriaco of Fiume, then the "Libera Repubblica Dannunziana"), which provided the necessary certificates and warrants for them to be finally imported to Trieste.

From 1922 *Stint*, now named *Adriaco*, raced and won with the colors of the RYCA. In 1938, *Adriaco* was taken to the shipyard to be fitted with a deckhouse to make it more comfortable inside, the

Rigging:	Bermudan sloop (8-meter SI)
Sail area:	98 sq. yds.
Shipyard:	Max Oertz shipyard (Hamburg, Germany)
Designer:	Max Oertz
Year of design:	1908
Launch:	1911
Restoration:	1970, 1998
L.: 41 ft.	W.l.: 34¼ ft.
B.: 7¾ ft.	Df.: 5¼ ft.
Displ.: 10.8 tons	Engine: 18 Hp
Skipper:	Lucia Pozzo (1989–90)

BELOW: *La Spezia 1990, a spectacular tack from* Stint *with an all-female crew (Photo: L. Pozzo).*

bowsprit and gaff sail disappeared, the boom was shortened, while the mast was made taller. The sail arrangement was reduced from the 135 square yards of the trysail rig of sailmaker Mahlitz to the 86 square yards of the gaff rig of sailmaker Zadro. On July 23 of the same year, Captain Valdemaro Scala of the Royal Italian Sailing Federation signed the tonnage report, starting the long career of *Stint* as an association pleasure craft, first for the RYC, then for the owners who have loved and possessed it till today.

Thus began the Italian history of the vessel, well remembered by so many people of Trieste for having aroused long-lost sporting enthusiasms. Among the successes of the distant past were the 1922 victory at the international regattas in Venice (with the Silver Swan Trophy offered as a prize by the Italian Navy) and the 1929 victory in Genoa, at the celebrations of the 50th anniversary of the Italian Yacht Club. In 1963 the boat had its old name, *Stint*, restored and was bought by some associates of *Adriaco* (Lamioni & Co). In 1968 its sole proprietor was a certain Mr. S. Trois, who kept it for a few years. This was a period of considerably questionable rearrangement of the deck and the equipment to adapt *Stint* to fit the inconstant tonnage rules.

When in 1987 Lucia Pozzo acquired the boat, which she found abandoned in a garden in Venice, she found it had an aluminum deck and mast! During this period Lucia Pozzo formed a female crew, bringing together a keen group of sailing enthusiasts. And for *Stint*, rearranged, but always aggressive and lively, other victories presented themselves. At Imperia in 1989, and the following year, *Stint* provided further evidence of its eternal youth and the aesthetic purity of its lines.

In 1992 *Stint* came into the possession of the current owners, who moved it to a shipyard for a complete restoration. So *Stint* can return to racing and winning and will be used as a training and cruise boat, to be used by people with physical and psychological problems. In the Vibio Mestrom shipyard, the polyester covering was eliminated as this had encouraged decay of the underlying wood, and the planking was returned to mahogany. Today, *Stint* has a new Douglas fir mast, which is tougher than spruce and increasingly hard to find.

ABOVE AND BELOW: *The old and new sail plan of* Stint.

RIGHT: *A certificate issued in 1921 by Germanischer Lloyd of Berlin to* Grete II, *now* Stint.

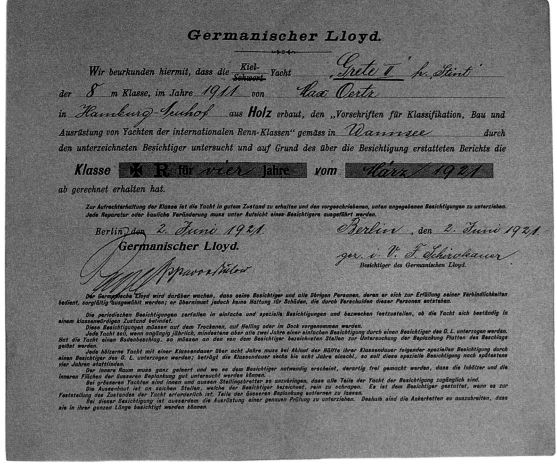

Sylphea III

*S*ylphea III has a beautiful history behind it. Its first owner, Mario Zerollo, a keen yachtsman and the former owner of the 6.5-meter SI *Sylphea I* and the 8-meter SI *Sylphea II*, participated in many regattas until 1934. All his boats were built at engineer Vittorio Beltrami's shipyard.

Sylphea III distinguished itself in 1929 in the Pozzani Cup, won by *Ramba*. On the Côte d'Azur in France it gained three victories, and a second and a third place, also beating *Aile VI* and *Catina V*. In 1930 the boat was present at all the regattas, winning the Macomber Cup in Monaco and the Cannes–San Remo cruise regatta. From 1935 to 1995, *Sylphea III* changed ownership five times (from 1946 to 1956 it belonged to the Italian Rowing and Sailing Club of Naples), until, with Dario Mezzano, it underwent a meticulous restoration in Monfalcone in Italy, supervised by the architect Franco Giorgetti. Some of the planking (the cladding) was replaced, as it was splintered. Some oak beams were also replaced in order to reconstruct the deckhouse with its original dimensions – it had been lengthened by the previous owners to increase its internal comfort. Finally, the original spruce mast was maintained.

With the return of its "Spartanness," *Sylphea III* reacquired its competitiveness of the 1930s. Its return to the sailing scene took place at Varazze in Italy when it was relaunched on April 25, 1996, and it was present at the vintage yacht regatta in Imperia the following September.

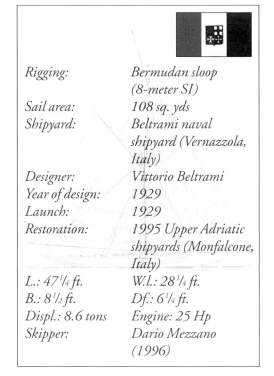

Rigging:	Bermudan sloop (8-meter SI)
Sail area:	108 sq. yds
Shipyard:	Beltrami naval shipyard (Vernazzola, Italy)
Designer:	Vittorio Beltrami
Year of design:	1929
Launch:	1929
Restoration:	1995 Upper Adriatic shipyards (Monfalcone, Italy)
L.: 47¼ ft.	W.l.: 28¼ ft.
B.: 8½ ft.	Df.: 6¼ ft.
Displ.: 8.6 tons	Engine: 25 Hp
Skipper:	Dario Mezzano (1996)

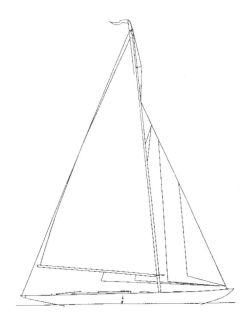

THIS PAGE: *Two shots of* Sylphea III *in the waters off Porto Santo Stefano (Photos: J. Taylor).*

Tamara IX

Rigging:	Gaff-rigged sloop (10-meter SI)
Sail area:	191 sq. yds.
Shipyard:	Soon Slip & Bath (Norway)
Designer:	Christian Jensen
Year of design:	1932
Launch:	1932
Restoration:	1999 Argentario naval shipyards (Italy)
L.: 51 ft.	W.l.: 38 ft.
B.: 9 ft.	Df.: 5 ft.
Displ.: 9.2 tons	
Skipper:	Doug Peterson (1998–2000)

Designed by Christian Jensen and launched in 1933, *Tamara IX* was commissioned by Halfdan Hansen, a very well-known yachtsman in the sailing world at the time. From 1936 through 1958 the boat had various owners, ending up at Newport Beach in the United States, where it remained until the late 1970s. In 1998 Doug Peterson, the yacht designer, discovered it in San Diego, California, in good condition. *Tamara IX* met the requirements of a professional such as Peterson, who did not hesitate to buy it.

The hull was sent to the Argentario shipyards in Italy, where Peterson supervised the refit: the replacement of all the frames (the new ones were steam-curved) and floor plates, replacement cladding, and rebuilding of the deck using teak. The deckhouse, skylights, and cockpit were adequately restored. *Tamara IX* was one of the most admired vessels during Sailing Week at Argentario.

THIS PAGE: *ASW 2001, two images of* Tamara IX*, recently restructured at the Argentario naval shipyards (Photos: J. Taylor).*

Tomahawk

Rigging:	Bermudan sloop
	(12-meter SI)
Sail area:	263 sq. yds.
Shipyard:	Camper & Nicholson
	(Gosport, England)
Designer:	Charles E. Nicholson
Year of design:	1938
Launch:	1939
Restoration:	1988 Beconcini
	naval shipyards
	(La Spezia, Italy)
L.: 69½ ft.	W.l.: 45½ ft.
B.: 12 ft.	Df.: 9 ft.
Displ.: 27 tons	Engine: 85 Hp
Skipper:	Bugliani and Della
	Pina (1988–2000)

Built by Camper & Nicholson, for many years *Tomahawk* was the protagonist of legendary challenges between the American Harold Vanderbilt and Sir Thomas Octave Murdoch Sopwith. *Tomahawk*, like *Vim*, entered the history of international yachting long ago. The early years of the rivalry are now but a distant memory, but the two boats continue to master the seas whenever they are involved in regattas.

The history of *Tomahawk* began in 1939 when, during the 12-meter SI regattas that were held in the Solent off the south of England, Vanderbilt commissioned a technically very advanced 12-meter (*Vim*) from two young naval designers, Olin and Rod Stephens. This boat, already avant-garde at the time, had a very light aluminum mast, better than wooden masts at conferring optimal tension on the forestay.

To meet the challenge, Sopwith ordered a new boat, *Tomahawk*, from the Camper & Nicholson shipyard. This boat had a huge impact on the world of competitive sailing on account of the extraordinary beauty of its lines and some significant innovations in its equipment. For instance, steel bars with aerodynamic sections were prefered to traditional rigging.

Tomahawk is a boat with generous and accentuated overhangs, particularly elegant lines, and an extremely streamlined hull. It has a maximum beam of 12 feet and a very reduced freeboard. It arrived in Italy in the early 1980s and, after almost 50 years of sailing, enjoyed further victories at the vintage yacht regatta in 1983 with Gianni Agnelli, its owner, at the helm and in 1985 under skipper Biandet. But the boat needed special restoration work. This took place in 1988, thanks to the new boat-owner, Alberto Rusconi.

The restructuring project was entrusted to the architects Giorgetti & Magrini, the work to the Beconcini shipyards in Italy. Almost all the light mahogany planking was replaced with fine Honduran mahogany, kept together by a transverse structure of galvanized steel frames. Some parts of the hull, keel, floor plates, ballast bolts, and shaft of the rudder, which were still in good condition, were maintained, while beams and structures were reconstructed using Columbian pine, with a deck made of plyboard and teak. The interior was rebuilt using marine mahogany plyboard and the cabin restored with cherry plyboard planking.

Furthermore, though the original proportions and the old Spartan identity has been preserved, a slight enlargement of the deckhouse has allowed better lighting for the "dinette." More could not be obtained from a boat entirely designed for regattas. The work was long and difficult: the original shipyard's plans had been destroyed during World War II, and recourse had to be made to documentation in the National Maritime Museum in Greenwich, London, and at Lloyds.

Tomahawk now lives again; a splendid marine vessel, it slides over the waves, solemn and almost always solitary because under a light breeze it is a very difficult boat to beat.

BELOW: *ASW 2000, an image of the ever-successful* Tomahawk *(Photo: J. Taylor).*

Tonino

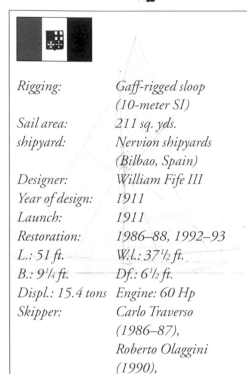

Rigging:	Gaff-rigged sloop (10-meter SI)
Sail area:	211 sq. yds.
shipyard:	Nervion shipyards (Bilbao, Spain)
Designer:	William Fife III
Year of design:	1911
Launch:	1911
Restoration:	1986–88, 1992–93
L.: 51 ft.	W.l.: 37½ ft.
B.: 9¼ ft.	Df.: 6½ ft.
Displ.: 15.4 tons	Engine: 60 Hp
Skipper:	Carlo Traverso (1986–87), Roberto Olaggini (1990), Aldo Manna (1996)

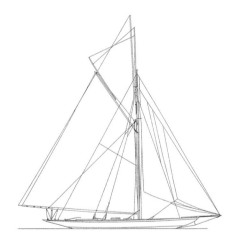

The history of this boat prior to 1986 is not very well-known. Launched back in 1912 as *Vega I*, a 10-meter SI, the boat had belonged to the Marquese Pallavicino of Genoa, Italy. This class was not numerous and it is likely that *Vega I* arrived in Italy's ports on the occasion of some regatta and was finally compared with the 10-meter Class. In fact, in the late 1930s, *Vega I* was rigged as a Bermudan sloop. In the 1950s it underwent significant restructuring, which involved the building of a deckhouse, necessary to allow standing below deck and for subsequent cruising (a destiny common to many boats of the period). The boat lost its identity: it was used for cruises of more or less short duration, according to the fashions of the time. In the 1950s *Vega I* was still sailing with sail number 709 RORC (Royal Ocean Racing Club): a competitive career lasting 40 years!

Its 1956 Tonnage Certificate (under the proprietor Corrado Vitali) describes the types of wood for the various components on board: main frames in oak, intermediary frames in ash, spruce beams, a cedar topside (a thickness of 1½ inch), and a spruce deck (a thickness of 1 inch). Another document, the Act of Nationality of September 1963, identifies the owners (having a 50:50 share) as Corrado Vitali and Gian Vittorio Vittadini, both resident in Milan, Italy.

Acquired by Sergio Parola and Marina Rapisarda in 1986, *Vega I* immediately underwent substantial restoration. Around 1,500 hours of specialist work were carried out on board, and around the same amount of time spent on research into materials, historical and technical studies, surveys, and drawings. Also involved in this work, which benefited from his suggestions, was the architect Sciarelli, while Bruno Veronese supervised.

After restoration the boat participated in the first vintage yacht regatta at Imperia (in 1986), obtaining good placings in the regattas and one "plate" for being the oldest vessel present in the port. The following year it was to win its class in the final classification. Again in that period (in 1987), *Vega I* won first place in the second regatta at the vintage yacht rally in Porto Cervo, Sardinia, coming fifth in the general classification out of 50 participants.

Close-hauled, the boat hugs the wind magnificently and is fast even with very weak winds; its movements are gentle. On the downside, it is very "wet," as is typical of its type. In 1990 Sergio Parola sold Fife's old boat to a new owner, Umberto Fabbiani, who was present at Imperia with the skipper Roberto Olaggini. There then followed a new period of restoration in the Canaletti shipyard in La Spezia, Italy, which in 1993 returned the boat (with the new name of *Tonino*) to its former design. With the elimination of the toerail, and the deckhouse with its large-chromed, brass portholes, the boat finally regains a charm that had seemed lost.

RIGHT: *Imperia 1996,* Tonino *in a regatta (Photo: S. Pesato).*

Trivia

*T*rivia was built by Charles Nicholson for V.W. MacAndrew in 1937 and began to compete with other 12-meter vessels at once, immediately obtaining exceptional results. With 13 firsts, 11 seconds, and six third places from 41 races, it took first place in its class. The two following seasons (1938 and 1939) also confirmed the success of *Trivia*, which measured itself against worthy adversaries such as the very new *Tomahawk* and *Vim*. However, the outbreak of World War II interrupted regattas for 12-meter vessels throughout Great Britain. After the war, *Trivia* once again showed its competi-tiveness as the training boat for *Sceptre*, the British contender for the America's Cup in 1968, winning all the regattas (three) of the Milkweel 12-Meter Series in the United States.

The boat has been recently restructured, from a project by Giorgetti & Magrini. *Trivia* combines high-level technical char-acteristics, which allow it to exploit even the slightest puff of wind, with an image of pure beauty. Its agile and light lines make it one of the most aristocratic vessels of its class. In May 2000 the boat changed ownership once again.

BELOW: *Cannes 2000, the 12-meter SI* Trivia *of Gosport, designed by Charles Nicholson (Photo: J. Taylor).*

Rigging:	*Bermudan sloop (12-meter SI)*
Sail area:	*263 sq. yds.*
Shipyard:	*Camper & Nicholson (Gosport, England)*
Designer:	*Charles E. Nicholson*
Year of design:	*1936*
Launch:	*1937*
Restoration:	*1991 Camper & Nicholson (Gosport, England)*
L.: 70 ft.	W.l.: 45½ ft.
B.: 11¾ ft.	Df.: 9 ft.
Displ.: 29.8 tons	Engine: 80 Hp
Skipper:	*Stefano Tanzi (1992–2000)*

Tuiga

Rigging:	*Trysail cutter (15-meter SI)*
Sail area:	*443 sq. yds.*
Shipyard:	*W. Fife & Son (Fairlie, Scotland)*
Designer:	*William Fife*
Year of design:	*1908*
Launch:	*1909*
Restoration:	*1989–93 Fairlie Restorations (Fairlie, Scotland)*
L.: 73³/₄ ft.	*W.l.: 48³/₄ ft.*
B.: 14 ft.	*Df.: 10 ft.*
Displ.: 55.1 tons	*Engine: 84 Hp*
Skipper:	*Olivier Campana (1996–2000)*

*T*uiga was launched in 1909 as a 15-meter SI from a design by William Fife. Fife made the boat in the image of *Hispania*, commissioned earlier by Alfonso XIII, King of Spain. Its first owner was the Duke of Medinaceli.

Tuiga collected a series of second places after the royal boat, perhaps because the duke would have felt rather embarrassed to have won against the king's boat. With the appearance of the huge, prestigious 19-meter boats, and consequent changes in the tonnage rules, *Tuiga* became too small to compete in the new regattas; its twilight years as a racer and a series of changes of name and owner therefore began.

In 1923 it was renamed *Dorina*. In 1935 it had a moment of glory with victory at the Fastnet Race under the new name of *Kismet III* and under the orders of one of the greatest helmsmen of the period, Colin Newman. His rival was the Stephens brothers' *Stormy Weather*, a fast boat that was subsequently to win the Transatlantic Race. From 1936, and for about 34 years, the boat became the property of the Douglas family, who transferred it to Scotland, almost always keeping it moored. In 1970 it came into the possession of a certain Mr. Rose of Glasgow, who named it *Nevada* and changed its rig, transforming it into a Bermudan cutter. Finally, in the late 1980s, a French couple acquired *Tuiga*, giving it back its original name.

Tuiga remained on sale in Cyprus following its owner's death and was found by Walter Duncan, whom Albert Obrist entrusted to acquire it, being an owner of old boats and particularly Fife's. *Tuiga* was taken back to Southampton in England, where restoration work began that was to take four years. The new Colombian pine mast was made by Harry Spencer of Cowes, England. Despite the excessive dimensions of the sail plan with respect to the original, and the considerable dimensions of the hull, *Tuiga* offers an impression of lightness and elegance that becomes all rake and speed with all its square yards of sail unfurled to the wind. Today, usually present in the most important regattas in the Mediterranean, *Tuiga* flies the flag of Monaco and is officially Prince Ranier's boat for entertaining.

RIGHT: *Cowes 2000, the harmony of lines and large rakes of* Tuiga *(Photo: J. Taylor).*

ABOVE AND LEFT: *Imperia 2000,* Tuiga *shot during the regatta (Photos: G. Pittaluga).*

BELOW: *A close-up of the boom head (Photo: F. Ramella).*

Twins V

Rigging:	Bermudan sloop (6-meter SI)
Sail area:	60 sq. yds.
Shipyard:	Baglietto (Varazze, Italy)
Designer:	Vincenzo Baglietto
Year of design:	1938
Launch:	1938
Restoration:	1985–86
L.: 57³/4 ft.	W.l.: 23¹/2 ft.
B.: 6 ft.	Df.: 6 ft.
Displ.: 33.1 tons	Engine: 100 Hp
Skipper:	Lamberto Pagnoni (1990–91)

*T*wins V, a 6-meter SI, is the only existing example of the series of *Twins* by brothers Max and Giuliano Oberti, who brought so much glory to Italian sailing before World War II. It was launched in 1938, the same year as *Bau Bau*, another splendid creation of the Baglietto shipyards. By 1939 it had participated in the Scandinavian Gold Cup at Helsingfors in Finland. World War II interrupted what would have become a magic time (perhaps equal to the Olympic successes of *Twins IV* in 1936 at Kiel in Germany) and forced the boat into a long period of dormancy, which at least served to enable it to be returned to excellent condition in the 1990s. With its cotton sails, *Twins V* carries with it the magnificence of the international regattas of the 6-meter SIs and the memory of Max and Giuliano Oberti.

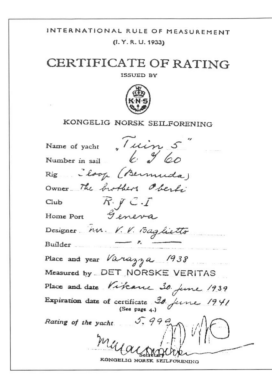

Vanity V

Rigging:	Gaff-rigged sloop (12-meter SI)
Shipyard:	W. Fife & Son (Fairlie, Scotland)
Designer:	William Fife III
Year of design:	1936
Launch:	1936
Restoration:	Guip shipyards (Brest, France)
L.: 70¹/2 ft.	W.l.: 46 ft.
B.: 12 ft.	Df.: 9 ft.
Displ.: 29.8 tons	Engine: 78 Hp

*V*anity V was the last 12-meter SI to be designed and built in Scotland by William Fife, in 1936. It is a true masterpiece, restored at the Guip shipyard in Brest, France, and returned to its original beauty in 2000. It made a roaring return in the various regattas at Cowes (England), Porto Cervo (Sardinia), and Cannes and Saint Tropez (France) where it ended up meeting with repeated success.

Restoration took place with the most profound respect for the original hull, even if today *Vanity V* is fitted with sails and rigging made of synthetics and a light motor that does not jeopardize its activity. The hull has teak and mahogany planking, steel frames, and an Oregon pine deck. The mast and boom are made of spruce. *Vanity V* sails between Newport in the United States and the Mediterranean (France and Italy).

RIGHT: *ACJ 2001, a close-up of* Vanity V, *taken during a tack (Photo: J. Taylor).*

Vega

Vega, designed by the engineer Vittorio Baglietto in August 1924 on the orders of Marquese Doria, Rodolfo Pallavicini, and Salvagno Raggi, was built and launched a year later, in 1925, at the shipyard of the same name in Italy. Since its debut in 1928, the year when it won the Corinthian–Caterina Pozzani Cup, *Vega* has proved to be a fast and highly competitive vessel. *Vega* is the fourth 8-meter SI to be built by Baglietto.

After a long period of anonymity (from 1937 through 1956), during which there is no certain information apart from its membership of the Royal Nautical Club of Naples until immediately after World War II, *Vega* was taken over by General Alessandro Santi. In 1959–60 he submitted it for restoration work. The most significant changes were the remaking of the teak deck, followed by partial replacement of the mast (remade from the mast-step to the first spreader). It was probably during this passage of ownership that *Vega* was rechristened *Beata III*, before returning to its original name in 1986, the year when it again changed hands.

It was precisely at the wishes of the new boat-owner that in 1986 significant restoration works began in order to return *Vega* to its original splendor. Thus the boat resumed competitive activity in 1998, participating in the tenth vintage yacht regatta in Imperia and taking first place among the vessels in its category. In the winter of 1999, under the supervision of skipper Luca Filippi, further interventions were carried out with the precise intention of restoring Vega's original appearance. Among its historic successes, besides that of 1928, we should mention third place in the Mediterranean Cup (1930), victory in the Prince of Piedmont Cup (1932), and first place in the Prince of Naples Cup (1936). It also gained various victories in regattas of lesser importance.

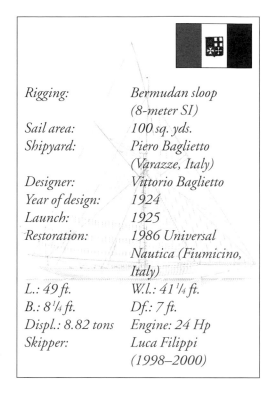

Rigging:	Bermudan sloop (8-meter SI)
Sail area:	100 sq. yds.
Shipyard:	Piero Baglietto (Varazze, Italy)
Designer:	Vittorio Baglietto
Year of design:	1924
Launch:	1925
Restoration:	1986 Universal Nautica (Fiumicino, Italy)
L.: 49 ft.	W.l.: 41¼ ft.
B.: 8¼ ft.	Df.: 7 ft.
Displ.: 8.82 tons	Engine: 24 Hp
Skipper:	Luca Filippi (1998–2000)

THIS PAGE: *Two photographs of* Vega, *an 8-meter designed by Vittorio Baglietto (Photos: J. Taylor).*

Vim

Rigging:	Bermudan sloop (12-meter SI)
Sail area:	288 sq. yds.
Shipyard:	Nevins shipyard (City Island, New York, USA)
Designer:	Olin Stephens
Year of design:	1938
Launch:	1939
Restoration:	1991 Beconcini shipyards (La Spezia, Italy)
L.: 72 ft.	W.l.: 46½ ft.
B.: 13 ft.	Df.: 10 ft.
Displ.: 30.9 tons	Engine: 85 Hp
Skipper:	Francesco Aiello, E. Giorguli (1991–2000)

BELOW: *Santa Margherita 1996, a tack towards the coast by* Vim, *designed by Olin Stephens in 1938 (Photo: P. Maccione).*

*V*im, a 12-meter SI, was launched in 1939 by the experienced Nevins shipyard of New York, from a project by Olin Stephens. It entered history as involved in the selection of the defenders of the America's Cup. When Sir Thomas Sopwith ordered the construction of *Tomahawk* in the same year, his rival, Harold Vanderbilt, had *Vim* transported by ship to England, to line it up in the regattas on the Solent off the south coast of England.

In 1939 *Vim*, a real wind machine, proved to be the best 12-meter of the year, with undisputed superiority, due to the creation of this project that was undoubtedly avant-garde for its time. The boat had a fantastic aluminum mast that allowed the forestay to be held under much more tension than with traditional wood masts.

That summer, *Vim* won no fewer than 19 regattas out of 27 contested. It was one of the first boats to be fitted with "coffee grinders," which regulated the genoa sail after tacking and during navigation. The interior of the boat was also studied in order to render it lighter. *Vim* therefore represented a new stage in yachting and a new way of looking at competitive sailing.

But the storm of war that was on the horizon cut short many of its triumphs; the boat was taken to the United States and kept on supports throughout World War II.

In 1951 it was bought by Captain John Matthews, who modified its deck plan and had a motor installed to enable him to use *Vim* as a cruise boat. The boat soon recovered from its long period of inactivity, winning the Larchmont Race Week. The American magazine *The Rudder* had this to say of *Vim* in January 1955: "…*one of the largest, most beautiful and certainly one of the most efficiently and aggressively sailed racing yachts on the East Coast today…*"

The boat, under the command of its owner, Captain Matthews, left evidence of its competitive presence everywhere. In 1958, in the selections for the America's Cup, *Vim* won various match-races with *Columbia* (a new project by Stephens) and *Easterner*, a fiery 12-meter designed for the challenge, but in the end the defender was actually *Columbia*, which proved faster when close-hauled with a strong wind.

Following the instructions of the architect Giorgetti, in fall 1990 *Vim* was acquired by Alberto Rusconi, formerly the owner of two 12-meter SIs (*Tomahawk* and *Cintra*), and transported to Italy by ship from Australia. In fact, in 1961 the boat had been used for training the Australian crew that was to participate in the America's Cup in 1962. The boat was then sent to the Beconcini shipyards in La Spezia, Italy, for a meticulous restoration to return it to its former glory.

Today, with its spacious and relatively empty interior to economize on weight, *Vim* has mahogany planking, steel floor plates, and a teak deck. Still fitted with "coffee grinders," it also possesses the original aluminum mast from 1939. In vintage yacht regattas (it has won regattas at Porto Cervo in Sardinia and the Régates Royales in Cannes, France), this splendid 12-meter sportingly renews its old challenges with classic boats such as *Tomahawk*, *Flica*, *Cintra*, *Ikra*, and others.

The "J Class"

The boats of the "J Class" represent a collection of inestimable value in the history of yachting and naval construction. They are a full-blown and spectacular technological revolution that embraces the past of the America's Cup.

Of the boats that participated in the cup between 1930 and 1940, only six survivors remain today, representing an indelible fragment of the America's Cup and the British attempt, which never succeeded, to recover the famous 100 Guineas Cup that was snatched from them by the Americans sailing the schooner *America* on August 22, 1851.

The "J Class" came about from the Universal Rule, the tonnage formula proposed by Herreshoff in 1903 with successive changes and limitations to the waterline with respect to the "rating," the minimum freeboard allowed in order to participate in the America's Cup. The absolute protagonists of the cup in 1930, 1934, and 1937 were sloops of about 131 feet in length, with over 837 square yards of sail on masts 164 feet high, with long, imposing, and very slender booms.

These extraordinary boats formed the "J Class," so-called from the letter of the American Universal Regulations that formulated their "rating." This was calculated as follows: 18 percent of the waterline multiplied by the square root of the sail surface, divided by the cube root of the displacement = waterline between 76 and 87 feet. In total, on both sides of the Atlantic, ten specimens were built (six in America and four in England). These met in thrilling challenges until prohibitive costs (even for multimillionaires) and the dark clouds of conflict caused a rapid decline in sailing. With the post-war period, the era of the 12-meter was born.

Taking part at Newport in the United States in the most famous and widely followed regatta in the world were *Shamrock IV*, the "J Class" commissioned to be built in 1930 by Sir Thomas Lipton for the challenge against *Enterprise*, and *Endeavour*, built for Sir Thomas Sopwith, the challenger of *Rainbow* in 1934. Added to these boats are *Cambria*, *Candida*, *Astra*, and *Velsheda*.

The boats still in existence had differing destinies. *Cambria*, now rigged as a ketch, is in the United States. *Candida*, later called *Norlanda*, had been rigged as a ketch and today has again returned with its old name and sail plan. *Astra*, after various adventures, has been restored and returned to its former splendor. *Velsheda* sails as a charter vessel. *Shamrock IV*, subsequently called *Quadrifoglio*, performed well at Portofino in Italy, rigged by the Crespi family, and was then acquired in 1986 by the Lipton Company to be given to the Yachting Museum in Newport. Finally, *Endeavour*, the challenger that came closest to regaining the Cup against Vanderbilt's *Rainbow*, tracked down in a wretched state by Elisabeth Meyer and taken to the Huisman shipyard in the Netherlands for a total refit, has returned to being a dream boat.

Today, with the vintage boat regattas, we are witnessing a major return of the "J"s. To favor the maintenance of these extraordinary boats, and to promote a series of gatherings and events to enable them to be made known to a wider public, the owners of these regenerated vessels have formed an association, the "J Class Society." Based in Rapallo, Italy, it has taken on the task, through its secretary Attilio Fantoni, of promoting rallies and regattas and a world championship for the class.

Astra

Rigging:	Bermudan sloop
Sail area:	795 sq. yds.
Shipyard:	Camper & Nicholson (Gosport, England)
Designer:	Charles E. Nicholson
Year of design:	1928
Launch:	1928
Restoration:	1987 Beconcini shipyards (La Spezia, Italy)

L.: 115 ft.	W.l.: 75 ft.
B.: 20 ft.	Df.: 14 ft.
Displ.: 154 tons	Engine: 500 Hp

BELOW: Astra *at full speed during a tack close to the wind (Photo: F. Taccola).*

A stra was built on behalf of Sir Mortimer Singer at the Gosport shipyard in England and was marked with sail number "K 2" (the number 1 belongs to the former royal yacht *Britannia*). As proof of its value, in 1929 it won four races out of five. As a "J Class" vessel, the boat participated in the elimination rounds, but never in the America's Cup proper.

After various adventures *Astra* arrived in Italy after the war, and was acquired in 1953 by Count Andrea Matarazzo, who kept it in the port of Naples until 1962, cruising the Mediterranean. The boat had already been subjected to a few modifications: the mast had been shortened by about 20 feet and the boom (which originally projected beyond the stern) by some 10–13 feet, while the bowsprit no longer existed.

In 1955 the boat flew the Panamanian flag under the ownership of the Atlas Shipping & Trading Company and President Paulo Matarazzo. In the period 1962–1973

it was based in the port of Salerno in Italy. In 1973 *Astra* was transformed into a ketch by the designer Guido Orsi, because the owner wanted a boat that was easier to handle and more suited to long cruises with smaller crews than in the past.

The transformation work was carried out at Monfalcone in Italy, including 2-inch thick Honduran mahogany planking on a steel structure, and five series of reinforcement crosspieces for its whole length. In 1984, only 11 years after this major restoration, *Astra*, moored at Castellamare in Italy, was in a state of complete abandonment. It was saved for a second time by Giancarlo Bussei, the cousin of Giovanni Agnelli. He wanted to return it to its former glory, and entrusted the work to the Beconcini yards in La Spezia under the technical guidance of Erik Pascoli, the project manager.

After four years of restoration and 35,000 hours of work, *Astra* has come back to life, and today it is the oldest among the

existing "J Class" boats. The Siamese teak deck has been completely reconstructed, the only difference being the application of impermeable adhesive between the staves. Part of the superstructure and the interior was rebuilt, and the old rigging was replaced. The new mast is aluminum (the old one was donated to the Emerald Coast Yacht Club, which uses it as a mast for signals); its base is 7 feet in circumference and it has a mainsail (as in the original project) measuring 598 square yards. The keel has a depth of 14 feet and, in order to counterbalance listing, 82.7 tons of ballast has been fitted.

At the headquarters of the Italian Yacht Club in 1988, *Astra* received the pennant of honor from the Italian Association of Vintage Yachts. The following year it crossed the Atlantic in search of its glorious past. At Newport in the United States it received the certificate for the best restoration from among the 100 boats present at the Yacht Classic Regatta. It was also able to measure itself once more against its sisters *Shamrock* and *Endeavour*, other survivors from the myth-making "J Class." Since 1993 the boat has been owned by Giuseppe Degennaro, already known as the owner of *Larouge*.

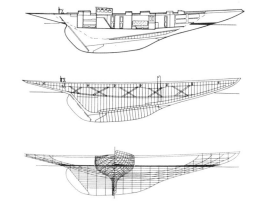

LEFT: *A spectacular aerial photo of* Astra *(Photo: F. Taccola).*

Candida

(sometime Norlanda)

Rigging:	*Bermudan sloop*
Sail area:	*828 sq. yds.*
Shipyard:	*Camper & Nicholson (Gosport, England)*
Designer:	*Charles E. Nicholson*
Year of design:	*1928*
Launch:	*1929*
Restoration:	*1991 Beconcini naval shipyards (La Spezia, Italy)*
L.: 118½ ft.	W.l.: 84½ ft.
B.: 20 ft.	Df.: 14 ft.
Displ.: 154 tons	Engine: 240 Hp
Skipper:	*Ottorino Palombo (1989), Ivo Marconi (1992)*

BELOW: *VBR 1991, a shot of* Candida *(Photo: J. Taylor).*

*C*andida, created as a 23-meter under International Regulations, was launched in 1929, commissioned by the banker Herman Andreae, former owner of the 19-meter *Corona*. At its launch, the boat unveiled a new, modern sail plan (the Bermudan), which contrasted with the trysail rig of *Cambria* and *Corona* of those years. During 1930 the boat participated successfully in numerous regattas, both as a 23-meter and as a "J Class." It was then transformed to come into line with the dictates of the new Universal Regulations that were to group together the great American and British boats.

Under the guidance of Herman Andreae (an excellent yachtsman) and skipper Jim Gilbey, *Candida* won three races and gained 13 second places in 1931. In 1932 it participated in 23 races, winning four of them, coming second seven times, and third seven times. It did not race in 1933, but the following year it gained a further five wins, two second places, and six thirds. *Candida* was then equipped with a metal mast and its draft was increased. Until 1938 it took part in various regattas, measuring itself

against the other "J Class" boats. In that year it was sold to Fred Milburn. *Candida* was rechristened *Norlanda* and transformed into a ketch, with the reduction of the lead ballast, increased freeboard, and the fitting of an auxiliary motor. The majestic and powerful cutter-masting disappeared, replaced by a 35-meter mainmast and a 15-meter mizzenmast. Thereafter came the dark years of World War II.

In 1946 *Norlanda* was rescued from the Gosport shipyard in England and changed hands twice; it was owned by a certain Mrs. Trenam in 1947, and by André Névi in 1952. The latter had a survey carried out in Genoa, Italy, from which it emerged that the hull was still in perfect condition. Photographs of the period showed that *Norlanda* had been fitted with two davits for boats. In 1956 the boat was acquired by Attilio Monti and sailed in the Mediterranean, always rigged as a ketch.

Sensitive to a return to the past, especially with the emerging of a new culture and the establishing of the vintage yacht circuits, in 1989 the Italian owner decided to return *Norlanda* to its original rig and

give it back the name of *Candida*. At the 1989 Imperia regatta, this lovely boat was still rigged as a ketch and was very attractive with its blue sails. Thanks to William Collier, manager of the Camper & Nicholson Vintage Yacht Division at Cannes, who miraculously found part of the original plans in the archives, and to the intervention of the Beconcini shipyard of La Spezia, Italy, it was possible to embark upon an extraordinary restoration project. The work involved the replacement of around 50 percent of the hull and the structures; the reconstruction of the deck; the construction and replacement of the 160-foot Douglas pine mast, rigging, and sail equipment; and the partial reconstruction of the interior (kitchen and crew quarters). For the shipyard, finding a 50–65-foot Douglas

pine mast was already difficult; finding a seasoned one of such dimensions was an almost impossible task.

With the exception of the shorter bowsprit and the taller freeboard, due to the removal of the ballast from 1938, today *Candida* is the cutter closest to the sail plan of the 1930s. The huge mast (only ten feet shorter than the original) is simply a masterpiece by La Spezia's shipwrights. The 22-foot bowsprit half protrudes over the end of the bow but can be adjusted and pushed outwards using a worm screw to stretch the stay of the "yankee" and move it away from that of the foresail.

With its new sail plan in place and old name of *Candida* restored, the boat appeared once more at Imperia in 1992, and had some splendid races with *Endeavour*.

ABOVE: *A spectacular shot of the deck seen from the bowsprit (Photo: G. Tagliafico).*

LEFT: *VBR 1991, good speed for the "J Class"* Candida *(Photo: J. Taylor).*

Endeavour

Rigging:	Bermudan sloop
Sail area:	960 sq. yds.
Shipyard:	Camper & Nicholson (Gosport, England)
Designer:	Charles E. Nicholson
Year of design:	1934
Launch:	1934
Restoration:	1989 Royal Huisman shipyard (The Netherlands)
L.: 129½ ft.	W.l.: 85¼ ft.
B.: 22 ft.	Df.: 16 ft.
Displ.: 179 tons	Engine: 400 Hp
Skipper:	Chick Moran (1992)

During the America's Cup 1934, *Endeavour* was the object of worldwide attention when it competed against Harold Vanderbilt's *Rainbow*, being badly beaten (four to two) even though it was the faster boat.

The boat had just been launched at Gosport, England, by the designer and builder Charles Nicholson on behalf of Sir Thomas Octave Murdoch Sopwith, the aeronautical industry magnate. Its rebirth after so many years is due to Elisabeth Meyer, the niece of Katherine Graham, owner of the *Washington Post*.

Endeavour, the fastest and most famous "J Class" ever built, lay neglected and abandoned in the mud under a hangar on the Isle of Wight off England. The boat was discovered in the late 1980s in a run-down condition by Elisabeth Meyer, who immediately took the riskiest decision of her life: to acquire *Endeavour*, restore it, and return it to its former splendor. A similar idea had already crossed the mind of the owner who had acquired it in 1978, but he had had to resist the temptation due to lack of funds.

For the reconstruction of *Endeavour* (the original plans of which had been destroyed in a fire at the shipyard during World War II),

Ms. Meyer chose three collaborators: Frank Murdoch, an engineer, aged 81, who had participated in the planning and construction phase of the boat; Gerry Dijkstra, the engineer, yachtsman, and designer of *Jessica*; and, finally, John Munford, who was given the task of designing the interior. While they were working fast to remake the hull (replacing at least two-thirds of the old plates) at Calshot Split (the shipyard put together from scratch by Ms. Meyer), she was resourcefully gathering funds from the sale of her book *Yachting*.

In August 1986 *Endeavour* was towed across the English Channel and then along inland waterways as far as Vellenhobe, in The Netherlands, where the internal restructuring work continued. Under the direction of Walter Huisman, the interior took shape. The furniture and furnishings were reconstructed in Edwardian style, all the benefits of high technology were used for the onboard instrumentation, while the sails were commissioned from Ted Hood in Marblehead in the United States. The original colors of the hull were respected: two tones of blue with a strip of pale grey along the waterline. The deck was planked with Siamese teak.

THIS PAGE: *Cowes 2001, two shots of* Endeavour, *perhaps the most famous "J Class" ever built (Photos: J. Taylor).*

The "Requin" Class

The "Requin" was highly significant in French yachting. When this vessel appeared on the scene of light yachting in 1934 it was the era of the 6- and 8-meter SIs. Until that time, nobody had thought of creating a series of cruise boats based on the same plan, destined to compete with absolute equality. In 1934 many yachtsmen in the Bay of Seine, including Jean Savoye and Alfred Farent, were in search of a single design that combined racing with accommodation for three people and enough seaworthiness to overcome the bad weather encountered on the English and French coasts.

The need was for a fast boat, cheap to build, sensitive at the helm, and easy to handle, even by people with little experience. In France no boat met these requirements, but in some Nordic countries boats existed that were built to these principles. The "Requin" class was introduced in France in 1933. Soon they were seen in Dieppe, Le Havre, and Fécamp, and they arrived in increasing numbers in English ports. The "Requins" sailed in a group, from port to port, sometimes in cruise-regattas for celebrations or local parties for the clubs to which they belonged.

On the eve of World War II, in 1939 alone, about 30 were built in France. In the post-war period, they increased visibly (justifying the birth of the "Requin" Owners' Association) and were built in yards at Fouvreau, Antibes, and Meulan.

From 1945 to 1949 French shipyards launched a hundred or so specimens, despite the appearance of a new racing boat, the "Dragon." Less aristocratic than the latter, the "Requin" has a nimble line and, without being truly habitable, is more comfortable than the "Dragon," which is more strictly suited to regattas. Its standard measurements are a length of 9.6 meters and a width of 1.89 meters. A "Requin" of the 1960s is almost identical to a 1934 example, apart from modernization of the equipment and synthetic sails.

The "Dragon" has evolved over time to meet the needs of competitive sailing, although today it is disappearing rather rapidly. The "Requin," on the other hand, has maintained its original line, perhaps because the two boats are no longer competitors or at least because today they appear to answer different requirements.

Constance

Rigging:	Bermudan sloop (Requin)
Sail area:	30 sq. yds.
Shipyard:	Pouvreau (Vix, France)
Designer:	Gunnar L. Stenback
Year of design:	1964
Launch:	1964
Restoration:	1986–88
L.: 32 ft.	W.l.: 22 ft.
B.: 6 ft.	Df.: 3¼ ft.
Displ.: 1.98 tons	Engine: 4 Hp (outboard)
Skipper:	Riccardo Trombetti (1990–97)

BELOW: *Imperia 1994, the "Requin" Constance with a good wind and little sail (Photo: S. Pesato).*

The "Requin" was designed in 1930 in Finland by Gunnar L. Stenback and became widely popular in France because of its speed and seaworthiness. *Constance* was launched in the Pouvreau shipyard in Vix, France (from which the highest number of boats of this kind has been released – 107 in total). "Requin" owners have formed an association that has almost 200 boats registered.

In 1964 *Constance* came to Italy on a train and was launched in Stresa, on Lake Maggiore, where its first owner used it for daily outings. In 1972 the boat was acquired by a determined sailing team, which used it in numerous regattas. It suffered some damage and questionable transformations (including the installation of a large outboard motor and the application of fiberglass-reinforced plastic to the deckhouse and deck) during this period. In 1981 the boat was acquired by two Lombard sailors with the intention of restoring it to a good condition, but "the best-laid plans…!" Subsequently, *Constance* lay abandoned and exposed for years in a shipyard in a village in the hills above Varese in Italy.

In 1986 the current owners, who became aware of the boat by chance, acquired it after mercifully brief negotiations and transported it to a shed in Milan, where they personally carried out the restoration work. After two years, the boat had been restored to its original condition. Anxiety and hopes intertwined in this long struggle: one day the sails were stolen and the mast disappeared into a fireplace somewhere. Finally, in 1988, *Constance* was returned to the water on Lake Maggiore, where it sailed happily for two years.

In 1990 the seas opened up for the boat. Imperia became its usual mooring place, where it was admired and appreciated at the first three vintage boat rallies, to the extent that in one of the "regatta dispatches," Ida Castiglioni recalls that passion and artisan methods can compete with the immense resources of multimillionaires' boats.

In 1997, during the transfer from Porto Venere to Santa Margherita Ligure, *Constance* was hit for a few seconds by a waterspout that quickly caused it to sink. The wreck is awaiting recovery.

ABOVE: *Imperia 1994, close-up of the deck of* Constance *(Photo: A. Tringali).*

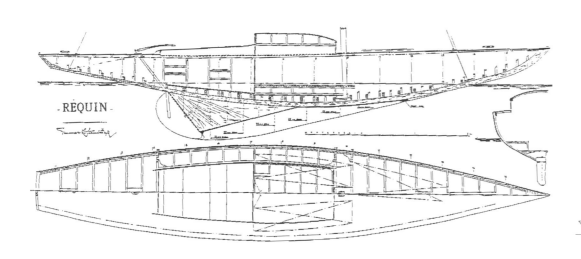

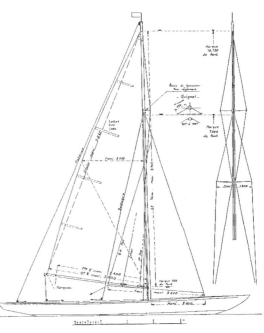

Shaula

Rigging:	Bermudan sloop (Requin)
Sail area:	30 sq. yds.
Shipyard:	Pouvreau (Vix, France)
Designer:	Gunnar L. Stenback
Year of design:	1930
Launch:	1971
Restoration:	1988
L.: 32 ft.	W.l.: 22 ft.
B.: 6 ft.	Df.: 3¼ ft.
Displ.: 7.75 tons	Engine: 10 Hp
Skipper:	Mario Sterzi (1990–94)

*S*haula is another "Requin," built with mahogany and teak at the Pouvreau shipyards in France in 1971. With its first owner, the boat raced on Lake Maggiore, then in 1988 it was restored by the Vidoli shipyard in Italy. In 1992 the current owner took *Shaula* to victory in its own category, against *Constance* (another "Requin"), a "Dragon," and a 6-meter SI.

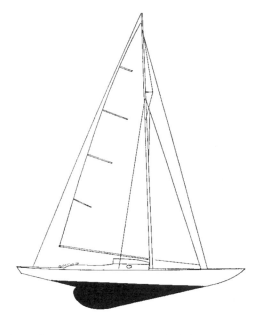

BELOW: *Imperia 1994, shot of* Shaula *(Photo: P. Maccione).*

The Sangermani Boats

*M*any of the boats that have taken part in the vintage yacht regattas were built at the Sangermani shipyards in Lavagna, Italy. Some, such as *Rondine II* and *Artica II*, are already to be rightfully considered "vintage" boats, while some of those launched subsequently may be described among the "classics" and include *Mizar III*, *Viola*, *Leticia do Sol*, *Oliana III* (now called *Voscià*), *Pilon*, *Susanna II*, *Mio Mao*, *Chin Blu*, *Giannella II*, *Huna II*, *Mabelle* (now called *Ella*), *Masa Yume*, *Ulisse*, *Valentina*, *Julie Mother*, and so on. For almost a century the yard, one of the most well-known in the Mediterranean, has been building regatta boats and yachts for a number of nations, from designs not only by Sangermani, but also by the world's most famous designers, such as Anselmi-Boretti, Brenta, Frers, Giles, Gurney, Mull, Olivari, Reiners, Rhodes, Stephens, Sciarelli, etc.

The history of the yard began in the early 20th century in Mulinetti, near Bogliasco, where Ettore Sangermano, known as "Dorin," wanted to build boats for his sons Cesare (1896–1976) and Piero (1909–86). The family became "Sangermani" because of an error in transcription; they were excellent sailors and collaborated with their father in the construction of yachts, the main speciality of the yard. In 1934 they found greater operational space at Rapallo, where, until the beginning of World War II, 40 or so splendid boats were built, among which was the 22-meter sloop *Samani II*, which is still sailing today.

In the period 1940–45, the Sangermanis moved to Riva Trigoso and became involved in war production. Only in 1946 did they find their definitive headquarters at the mouth of the River Entella, on the outskirts of Lavagna, in Via dei Devoto, a street that runs alongside the railway line. The first boat to be built in the post-war period was *Nibbio II*, designed by Cesare, who had become a naval engineer and builder while his brother Piero became head laborer and was better versed in the workshops and in the treatment of timber. I think it appropriate to reproduce a fond recollection of the Sangermanis from the memoirs

of Göran Schildt, taken from his famous book *Vent'anni di Mediterraneo* ("Twenty Years of the Mediterranean"): "*The two owners, the Sangermani brothers, who usually directed the evening conversations on the beach, are quite exceptional in Italy as employers. The older, Cesare, is an engineer and is a capable shipbuilder; the younger, Piero, is the head laborer and is well-versed in all the secrets and finishing touches of ship construction. Although the company has expanded, they have not become unscrupulous businessmen, big-time executives. Instead, they live in exemplary comradeship with their workers, dress the same way as they do (that is, atrociously), even lend a hand with the heavy work when necessary, and, like the workers, they don't – so to speak – have a private life. At six-thirty in the morning they are already on the beach, they rarely return home before ten in the evening, and on Sunday afternoon they hold court with friends, customers, and employees in the yard outside the office…*"

Nibbio was followed by many more small boats: stars, gozzos, dinghies, launches, and small tugs. But it was between 1950 and 1960 that the production of the yard began to be known universally, with the creation of various III Class RORCs (Royal Ocean Racing Club). In 1950, with the launching of *Chiar di Luna* and in 1956 with that of *Artica II*, both regatta boats for the Italian Navy, which immediately won prestigious victories, the yard began intense activity with orders from around the world.

Around 225 boats were launched up to 1993, including famous craft like *Stella Polare*, *Susanna II*, and *Mabelle*. The boats built in the Sangermani shipyard are distinguished by the purity of their lines, meticulous perfectionism and careful use of various woods. The shipyard has kept up with technological evolution in construction. In some sectors it has even been a trailblazer, with the construction of ultralight hulls with inverted structures and subsequent covering with layers of red cedar laminate. The yard nevertheless continues to maintain and restore vintage yachts.

Bateau Ivre
(sometime Aile Blanche)

Rigging:	Gaff-rigged cutter
Sail area:	275 sq. yds.
Shipyard:	Sangermani (Lavagna, Italy)
Designer:	Sparkman & Stephens
Year of design:	1962
Launch:	1963
Restoration:	1985, 1988–89 Sangermani (Lavagna, Italy)
L.: 67 ft.	W.l.: 49 ft.
B.: 15 ft.	Df.: 12 ft.
Displ.: 44.1 tons	Engine: 250 Hp
Skipper:	Ed Kasetelein (1986), Dieter Gulik (1987–89)

This boat was built with a yawl rig in 1962, from a project by Sparkman & Stephens. It was called *Tris* and was a sturdy and fast cruise vessel, winning second place at the Giraglia in 1965 (with its owner Sada). An Austrian owner renamed it *Comet V*; it was then renamed *Aile Blanche* by its Dutch owner Ed Kastelein in 1987. The boat has teak planking, a teak deck and deckhouse, a mahogany interior, and an iroko keel. The original mainmast, lost in a cruise to the Caribbean, has been replaced with a white aluminum mast.

With its owner Dieter Gulik, *Aile Blanche* underwent a total internal and external restoration during 1988–89 at the Sangermani shipyards in Italy. The work involved the motor, rudder system, electrical system, water and fuel tanks, and, above all, the sail plan, as today the boat is rigged as a sloop. It is therefore a less gentle, more competitive boat, with a 90-foot mast and the original wooden boom at the height of the cockpit.

The boat, which in the past has participated in rallies at Imperia, Porto Cervo in Sardinia, and Saint Tropez in France, has always gained top positions in the classifications and is a worthy representative of the style of Sangermani construction and the excellent lines of Sparkman & Stephens. It has recently taken the new name of *Bateau Ivre* and has been transformed into a cutter.

THIS PAGE: *Cannes 1999, Bateau Ivre, launched by Sangermani with the name of* Tris *(Photos: J. Taylor).*

Beatrice

*L*aunched as *Huna I*, this boat has had only two owners; the second took over in 1980. *Beatrice* has not undergone any particular restructuring apart from the shortening of the boom. It is used in cruises in the Mediterranean. Currently moored in the tourist port of Aregai (Imperia), the boat has recently undergone maintenance work, including the complete remaking of the deck.

Rigging:	Gaff-rigged yawl
Sail area:	117 sq. yds.
Shipyard:	Sangermani (Lavagna, Italy)
Designer:	Cesare Sangermani
Year of design:	1962
Launch:	1963
Restoration:	1999–2000
L.: 52 ft.	W.l.: 35 ft.
B.: 12½ ft.	Df.: 6 ft.
Engine: 69 Hp	
Skipper:	Fulvio Conti (1991), D. de Grassi (2000)

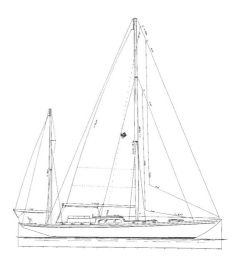

LEFT: *Imperia 2000, the yawl* Beatrice *photographed under full sail (Photo: J. Taylor).*

Caligo

Rigging:	Gaff-rigged yawl
Sail area:	237 sq. yds.
Shipyard:	Sangermani (Lavagna, Italy)
Designer:	Cesare Sangermani
Year of design:	1964
Launch:	1966
Restoration:	1990
L.: 75 ft.	W.l.: 51 ft.
B.: 18 ft.	Df.: 9 ft.
Displ.: 45.4 tons	Engine: 240 Hp
Skipper:	Alessandro Bucciarelli (1987), Sergio Fazzeri (1991)

RIGHT: *A detail of the interior (Photo courtesy of M. Dotti).*

BELOW: Caligo, *a gaff-rigged yawl (Photo: M Dotti).*

Caligo is construction no. 151 by the Sangermani shipyards in Italy. Launched with the name of *Paulena*, this "cruiser-racer" is the result of a project by Cesare Sangermani. It was inspired by similar great boats designed by Sparkman & Stephens, such as the famous *Corsaro II* and *Stella Polare*. On this model, the hull was conceived for the Transpacific Regatta that was in vogue in the 1960s – the "Transpac," a long race running from Los Angeles to Honolulu, won once by *Corsaro*. In *Caligo*'s design, provision was made for a mobile drift, which was not actually built.

Caligo is a boat that expresses itself best and with considerable speed under a strong breeze and in a high sea. Nevertheless, with its comfortable, elegant interior its main use is decidedly for cruising. The large cockpit, built on the deckhouse of the stern cabins, dominates the whole deck, offering an excellent view and shelter from spray and breakers.

In 1990 *Caligo* was acquired by a new owner, who has restructured it very well. Returned to wood, the perfect condition of the hull planking is a pleasant surprise, while the paintwork, which had previously been neglected, has been completely renewed.

Chin Blu III

Chin Blu III is a well-known frequenter of the Giraglia and a boat that the architects Illingworth and Primrose seem to have designed to go in all conditions. Launched in 1965 by the Sangermani shipyards in Italy, the boat appeared at the Giraglia in 1966 with its first owner, the Frenchman Fabre, who immediately won second place in Class II, preceded by *Karmatan II*. There followed, still with Fabre, sixth place in 1967, fifth place in 1968, and 13th place in 1969. In 1970 *Chin Blue III* grabbed tenth place, behind *Mabelle* and in front of *Mait II*. The following year it gained a fourth place behind *Mait II*, *Susanna II*, and *Benbow*, but it did not take long for it to establish itself. In 1972 *Chin Blu III* gained success in Class I-Division B, in front of *Mait II*, *Vagabonda*, and *Benbow*.

The boat's second owner was also French, Patrick Soudant, who, after a long period keeping it laid up, sold *Chin Blu III* to Nello Saltalamacchia, who immediately embarked on restoration work. For many months the boat occupied the slipway of the Massabò shipyard in Porto Maurizio, Italy. In 1989 Nello took the boat to the fourth vintage yacht regatta and again in 1990.

For two years it was the flag-bearing boat at the Imperia rally and was well handled by the very capable Saltalamacchia, who also distinguished himself in the seventh Almirante Conde de Barcelona Trophy in 1991, where he met with deserved success in Class IV, repeated in the editions that followed.

In 1992 *Chin Blu III* found an enthusiastic new owner, Riccardo Degiovanni, who did not need to be asked twice to participate in the seventh Imperia rally. Almost 40 years after its launch, the boat still appears in excellent condition. It has mahogany planking, a teak deck, and acacia frames.

Rigging:	Bermudan sloop
Sail area:	124 sq. yds.
Shipyard:	Sangermani (Lavagna, Italy)
Designer:	Illingworth & Primrose
Year of design:	1964
Launch:	1965
Restoration:	1989–90
L.: 41¼ ft.	W.l.: 31¼ ft.
B.: 11 ft.	Df.: 7 ft.
Displ.: 11.2 tons	Engine: 42 Hp
Skipper:	Nello Saltalamacchia (1990–91), Riccardo Degiovanni (1992–98)

BELOW: *Imperia 2000, good speed for* Chin Blu III *(Photo: J. Taylor).*

Cigno Nero

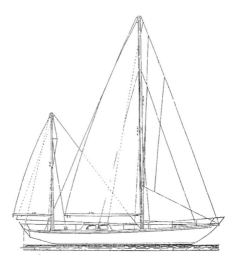

Rigging:	Bermudan yawl
Sail area:	152 sq. yds.
Shipyard:	Sangermani (Lavagna, Italy)
Designer:	Cesare Sangermani
Year of design:	1960
Launch:	1961
Restoration:	1989–91
L.: 56 ft.	W.l.: 37½ ft.
B.: 13 ft.	Df.: 8 ft.
Displ.: 19.4 tons	Engine: 75 Hp
Skipper:	Walter Lopez (1990–96)

Designed for a boat-owner from Trieste in Italy, *Cigno Nero* was launched in 1961. From 1962 to 1974 it participated in numerous regattas in the Adriatic and won conclusively, creating an aura of admiration and respect. It was subsequently sold and fell into a state of abandonment that lasted for a number of years.

In 1989 the current owner fell in love with it and began restoration work, respecting the original designs that were dusted off from the Sangermani archives in Italy. *Cigno Nero* returned to life and, as soon as it was launched, participated in rallies at Imperia, the Mariperman Trophy, and the Nioulargue, winning top positions.

RIGHT: *Imperia 1994,* Cigno Nero *sailing close-hauled (Photo: F. Ramella).*

BELOW: *Imperia 1990, a harmonious vessel (Photo: J. Taylor).*

Dragonera

Commissioned by Paolo Cravenna, this boat slipped into the sea in 1961 as *Cipi II* and immediately participated in the Giraglia, taking tenth place behind *Benbow*. It has mahogany planking, a teak deck, silver spruce masts, solid iroko frames, an iroko toerail and stringer, and mahogany superstructures. It has practically the same dimensions as *Cigno Nero*, also launched in 1961.

Dragonera has belonged to five owners and in 1989 underwent a complete and careful restoration by the current owner, who has returned the boat to the days of its launch, renovating the internal systems and rearranging the original winches. The boat was present at the first Sangermani Trophy at Portofino in Italy and performs well under all conditions.

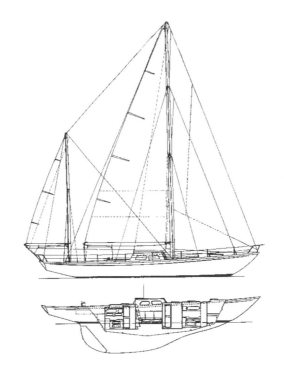

Rigging:	Bermudan yawl
Sail area:	152 sq. yds.
Shipyard:	Sangermani (Lavagna, Italy)
Designer:	Cesare Sangermani
Year of design:	1960
Launch:	1961
Restoration:	1989–90
L.: 56 ft.	W.l.: 38 ft.
B.: 13 ft.	Df.: 7 ft.
Displ.: 19.4 tons	Engine: 145 Hp
Skipper:	Claudio Dini (1990–91)

BELOW: Dragonera *(sometime* Cipi II*) designed by Cesare Sangermani (Photo: S. Pesato).*

Eos I

Rigging:	Gaff-rigged yawl
Sail area:	156 sq. yds.
Shipyard:	Sangermani (Lavagna, Italy)
Designer:	Laurent Giles
Year of design:	1960
Launch:	1962
Restoration:	1984 Argentario shipyards (Italy)
L.: 55 ft.	W.l.: 37 ft.
B.: 13 ft.	Df.: 7 ft.
Displ.: 27.2 tons	Engine: 132 Hp
Skipper:	Alfredo Delli (1990–2000)

RIGHT: *ASW 1998,* Eos I *in a regatta (Photo: J. Taylor).*

This boat was commissioned in 1960 from the architect Laurent Giles by Count Emanuele Pafundi di Zante. Its construction was entrusted to the Sangermani shipyard of Lavagna, Italy. Launched as *Giga* in 1962, the boat was used for a long time for cruises, though it participated in some editions of the Giraglia. After spending a few years laid up, *Giga* was acquired by a new owner, Santonocito of Rome, who sent it for a complete overhaul in 1984 at the Argentario shipyards in Italy. The boat was renamed *Eos I.* From 1988 it was owned by Alfredo Delli, with whom it participated in various yacht regattas at Imperia, La Spezia in Italy, and Porto Cervo in Sardinia.

In 1991 *Eos I* crossed the Atlantic, reaching the Antilles, the Virgin Islands, and finally Bermuda, where it remained throughout the winter of 1992.

In April 1993 the boat returned to Europe and underwent a complete overhaul in the port of Malaga, Spain. In August it participated in the Almirante Conde de Barcelona Trophy.

Eugenia V

Rigging:	Bermudan ketch
Sail area:	237 sq. yds.
Shipyard:	Sangermani (Lavagna, Italy)
Designer:	Philip Rhodes
Year of design:	1967
Launch:	1969
Restoration:	1985–86 Sangermani (Lavagna, Italy)
L.: 71½ ft.	W.l.: 57 ft.
B.: 18 ft.	Df.: 9 ft.
Displ.: 53.4 tons	Engine: 170 Hp
Skipper:	Terzilio Gazo (1986–98)

RIGHT: Eugenia V *in the waters of Imperia, 1986 (Photo courtesy of T. Gazo).*

This boat was commissioned from the Sangermani shipyard in Italy in 1967 by an officer in the French Naval Reserve, a true yachting enthusiast. He had observed *Tortuga III,* designed by Philip Rhodes, at sea and, immediately falling in love with it, he wanted an exact copy. With the exception of some very slight differences, the boats are twins.

Built using the most precious materials (it boasts a mahogany hull, iroko and oak internal structures, a teak deck and superstructure, and silver spruce masts), *Eugenia V* is still one of the masterpieces of the shipyard. With commendable seaworthiness, and performing well with average winds, it achieves fine speeds. Day-to-day maintenance has always been carried out at the shipyard where it was built, so the boat has remained faithful to its original plans and sound construction. *Eugenia V* has always belonged to the same family. During the last 25 years it has made long cruises in the Mediterranean and participated in numerous classic yacht regattas, winning in its class and winning three times at the Nioulargue in Saint Tropez in France, where it is usually moored.

Giadamar

Launched with the name *Sumbra II* from a design by Sparkman & Stephens, this sloop, with its light aluminum mast, has repeatedly produced evidence that it is a very fast boat. Among its famous results: 1966, second place at the Giraglia and first at the Ischia–Porto Cervo Race; 1967, victory at the Giraglia, in the Gorgona Trophy, and at the Genoa–Alassio Race; 1968, victory at the Genoa–Alassio Race, in the Montecristo Trophy, and in the Byron Cup; 1969, first place at the Livorno–Bastia Race, in the Montecristo Trophy, and in the Byron Cup, fourth place at the Giraglia; 1970, victory at the Giraglia and the Livorno–Bastia Race; 1971, sixth place at the Giraglia and placings in numerous Atlantic races; 1989, victory in the Tigullio Winter Championship and second place in the Christopher Columbus Trophy. The boat has a mahogany hull, a teak deck, and mahogany interiors.

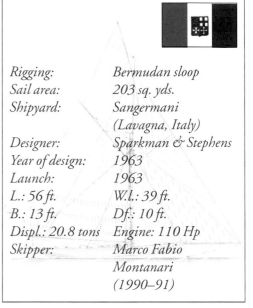

Rigging:	Bermudan sloop
Sail area:	203 sq. yds.
Shipyard:	Sangermani (Lavagna, Italy)
Designer:	Sparkman & Stephens
Year of design:	1963
Launch:	1963
L.: 56 ft.	W.l.: 39 ft.
B.: 13 ft.	Df.: 10 ft.
Displ.: 20.8 tons	Engine: 110 Hp
Skipper:	Marco Fabio Montanari (1990–91)

LEFT: *VBR 1991, the sloop* Giadamar, *a life full of successes (Photo: J. Taylor).*

Giannella II

The lines of this boat, the overhangs, and the marked sheerline reveal the signature of the famous French architect Eugène Cornu. *Giannella II*, which today is moored in the port of Antibes in France, has had just three owners.

It is a boat that under sail has speeds of over ten knots with a force 5–6 wind. It has mahogany planking, Burmese teak superstructure and deckhouse, and a teak and mahogany interior (saloon). The boat has two cockpits. The first, which is used for steering, sits forward of the mizzenmast. The second is raised and protected by a double balcony. The masts are spruce. Overall, *Giannella II* is one of the most interesting boats to have appeared from the Sangermani shipyards in Italy.

Rigging:	Bermudan yawl
Sail area:	207 sq. yds.
Shipyard:	Sangermani (Lavagna, Italy)
Designer:	Eugène Cornu
Year of design:	1966
Launch:	1966
Restoration:	1980
L.: 64 ft.	W.l.: 44½ ft.
B.: 15 ft.	Df.: 8 ft.
Displ.: 34.2 tons	Engine: 150 Hp
Skipper:	Jean Louis Scudo (1987)

Huna II

Rigging:	Bermudan cutter
Sail area:	287 sq. yds.
Shipyard:	Sangermani
	(Lavagna, Italy)
Designer:	Cesare Sangermani
Year of design:	1966
Launch:	1967
Restoration:	1986
L.: 64½ ft.	W.l.: 44 ft.
B.: 15 ft.	Df.: 9 ft.
Displ.: 25.6 tons	Engine: 140 Hp
Skipper:	Beppe Zaoli
	(1986–2000)

Huna II is one of the boats that have been most loyal to the Imperia regatta. Launched in 1967, it is one of the first vessels with a short keel and separate rudder to be made by the Sangermani shipyard. It has glued mahogany planking; a teak deck; a spruce mast, boom, and spinnaker pole; and, unlike other boats launched at the same shipyard, teak superstructures.

Huna II is a fast boat under all conditions and always has top-class sails, as it is the showpiece of the sailmaker Beppe Zaoli, its skipper. In 1986 it underwent a meticulous restoration and immediately appeared at Imperia, winning the first regatta in its class. It has also won vintage yacht regattas in Porto Cervo in Sardinia and the Nioulargue in Saint Tropez in France. Before the Imperia vintage yacht regatta in 1998, *Huna II* was sold, and the new owner, Sandro Cipollina, had the deck remade at the Aregai shipyard (at Imperia) using teak.

THIS PAGE: *Imperia 2000, images of* Huna II, *present for years in regattas with Beppe Zaoli (Photos: J. Taylor).*

Leticia do Sol

This boat was commissioned in 1957 by the Tiber Rome Oarsmen's Club and launched in 1958. In Anzio, Italy, its port of registration, it has participated in various regattas, Carlo Rubbiani Trophies, and Campilli Cups. In 1959 it came fourth at the Giraglia (Class II).

In 1988 the third owner carried out a lengthy restoration at a shipyard in Rapallo, Italy, completely rebuilding the deck and making changes to the rudder. The sail plan of the boat was redone based on its original design. Since 1989 *Leticia do Sol* has participated in vintage yacht regattas.

Rigging:	Gaff-rigged yawl
Sail area:	91 sq. yds.
Shipyard:	Sangermani (Lavagna, Italy)
Designer:	Sparkman & Stephens
Year of design:	1957
Launch:	1958
Restoration:	1988–89
L.: 44 ft.	W.l.: 31 ft.
B.: 11 ft.	Df.: 6 ft.
Displ.: 12.7 tons	Engine: 52 Hp
Skipper:	Marco Pomi (1989–90), Paolo Tomalillo (1991)

Mio Mao VII

Launched in 1964 and commissioned by Count Masazza of Turin, every part of this boat has remained faithful to the original plan.

Acquired in 1980 by its current owner, who manages it with great care and attention, *Mio Mao VII* currently cruises in the Mediterranean.

Rigging:	Bermudan yawl
Sail area:	116 sq. yds.
Shipyard:	Sangermani (Lavagna, Italy)
Designer:	Cesare Sangermani
Year of design:	1963
Launch:	1964
L.: 45½ ft.	W.l.: 32 ft.
B.: 11 ft.	Df.: 6 ft.
Displ.: 15.2 tons	Engine: 60 Hp
Skipper:	Giovanni Varia

LEFT: Mio Mao VII, *a Sangermani creation from 1963 (Photo courtesy of G. Varia).*

Samurai

Rigging:	*Gaff-rigged sloop*
Sail area:	*197 sq. yds.*
Shipyard:	*Sangermani (Lavagna, Italy)*
Designer:	*Cesare Sangermani*
Year of design:	*1962*
Launch:	*1962*
L.: 62 ft.	W.l.: 46 ft.
B.: 14 ft.	Df.: 9 ft.
Displ.: 28.3 tons	Engine: 100 Hp
Skipper:	*Luigi Pavese (1990–2000)*

BELOW AND BOTTOM: *Two images of* Samurai *in a regatta (Photos: J. Taylor).*

OPPOSITE PAGE: *Cannes 1999, shot of a willing boat (Photo: J. Taylor).*

In the early 1960s the Genoese entrepreneur Pavese ordered a racer from the Sangermani yard. It was to be fast, nimble, powerful, and light. The shipyard had a boat nearly completed that responded perfectly to the characteristics requested. It was love at first sight. The launch of *Samurai* took place in September 1962.

With a long keel, and rigged as a sloop, the boat was immediately on show at many regattas of the Tigullio Yacht Club and the Italian Yacht Club. It obtained respectable placings at the Giraglia, coming seventh in 1963, second in 1964, and third in 1965. In these regattas, *Samurai* took on board the correspondent of the *Corriere della Sera*, Giovanni Garassino, who for the first time in the history of open-sea regattas represented the editors of a newspaper dealing with sailing.

From 1970, with the introduction of the new tonnage method (from the Royal Ocean Racing Club to the IOR) that considerably penalized *Samurai* and all vessels with the pronounced rakes and classic keel of its generation, the boat began a tranquil phase of family cruises. In 1991 *Samurai* returned to regattas at the Nioulargue, and from then on it began an uninterrupted period of stirring successes and good placings that testify to the qualities of the boat and the crew, consisting of three brothers: Luigi, Filippo, and Edward Pavese, and some enthusiastic friends.

This is the list of *Samurai*'s triumphs: 1991, Nioulargue (Saint Tropez), first place in the Florida Cup, and second place in the Club 55 Cup; 1992, Nioulargue, third in the Club 55 Cup; 1995, Régates Royales (Cannes), second in Class B (from 16- through 25-meters); 1996, Régates Royales, first in Class B, second in real time at the Coupe d'Automne YC Monaco (Monaco–Cannes), and first in real time at the Coupe d'Automne YC France (Cannes–Saint Tropez); 1997, Régates Royales, third in

Class B and second in real time at the Coupe d'Automne YC Monaco.

Samurai has also participated in a number of regattas for modern IMS boats, such as the Croisière Bleue, an open-sea classic on the Côte d'Azur racing the Antibes–Calvi route and back. Of more than 200 participants, *Samurai* was the only classic boat. The result was amazing: third in real time, little more than an hour behind the racer *Gitana VIII*, and winner of its own class. The fact that this "old glory" could precede full-blown regatta monsters in real time was an exploit that surprised everyone, and the *Samurai* crew earned themselves a photograph on the front page of *Nice Matin*.

The list of successes continues: 1998, Les Voiles d'Antibes (Antibes), second place, Class B (fewer than 20 meters); Almirante Conde de Barcelona Trophy (Palma de Mallorca), first place, 1-mast Classic Boats; Coupe d'Automne YC Monaco, second place in real time; Régates Royales, first in Class B; ICYA European Grand Prix '98 Spirit of Pen Duick Trophy, second overall.

1999, Les Voiles d'Antibes, first place, Yacht Class; Almirante Conde de Barcelona Trophy; Copa SAR Don Juan de Borbon (Palma de Mallorca), first in Class 5 (Large Classic Boats), first overall Classic Yachts, winner Copa SAR Don Juan de Borbon; Monaco Classic Week, second place, Classic Yachts; Régates Royales, first in the Large Marconi Classic Class; Prada Cup, first overall Classic Yachts and winner. Coupe d'Automne YC France, first place Classic Yachts; Les Voiles de Saint Tropez, fourth in the Large Marconi Classic Class; Trophée Grimaldi '99, first place Classic Yachts; ICYA European Grand Prix '98 Spirit of Pen Duick Trophy, first overall; Prada Challenge Voiliers de Tradition, first place category E (Classic Yachts sloop-cutter rig), second overall. In 2000, Les Voiles d'Antibes, first place in the YC Class (Classic Yachts).

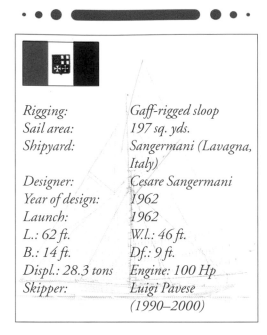

Susanna II

Rigging:	*Bermudan yawl*
Sail area:	*230 sq. yds.*
Shipyard:	*Sangermani (Lavagna, Italy)*
Designer:	*Laurent Giles*
Year of design:	*1962*
Launch:	*1964*
Restoration:	*1999*
L.: *64 ft.*	W.l.: *45 ft.*
B.: *15 ft.*	Df.: *9 ft.*
Displ.: *34.2 tons*	Engine: *110 Hp*
Skipper:	*Renato Cacciapuoti (1990–2000)*

S usanna II will always be remembered for its three consecutive victories in the Giraglia (1964, 1965, and 1966), a true record. A First Class RORC (Royal Ocean Racing Club) rigged as a yawl, *Susanna II* almost always led the field at its first Giraglia, although just launched. The boat's owner is Giuseppe Brainovich, who had already won a Giraglia (in 1961) with *Susanna I*. At the finishing line the new ocean-racer left behind it boats such as *Mait II*, *Benbow*, *Tarantella*, *Levantades*, and *Gitana IV*. In the 1966 race the architect who designed it, Jack Laurent Giles, was also in the crew. In the 1967 race *Susanna II* came fourth, behind *Mait II*. Its fourth success, in the 1968 race, was resounding but not ratified because it missed the "Cousteau" buoy (this was transcribed in the logbook).

In the years that followed *Susanna II* kept on winning regattas in the Tyrrhenian Sea. The 1990s saw its participation in numerous vintage yacht regattas under its new owner Renato Cacciapuoti. The boat has been maintained in good condition, and as recently as 1999 it had the cockpit rebuilt by the Argentario naval shipyard in Italy.

RIGHT: *VBR 1999, a shot of* Susanna II, *the winner of three consecutive editions of the Giraglia (in 1964, 1965, and 1966), one of the vessels that has gained the highest number of victories in regattas (Photo: J. Taylor).*

Swala

Swala, launched in 1969 on behalf of the notary Masini of Milan, is a Laurent Giles project. It is a very seaworthy vessel that combines the qualities of cruising comfort with safety and speed in regattas, as has been shown in recent years by its placings in the vintage sailing circuit.

The construction was carried out with the usual skill by the Sangermani shipyard in Italy, making the hull with juxtaposed 1-inch boards, mahogany for the topside and iroko for the cladding, on 3 × 2 inch laminated oak frames, alternated with smaller steam-curved acacia frames (2 × 1³/₄ inch). The planking is riveted to the frames with ³/₈-inch copper rivets. The mast, boom, and two spinnaker poles are original proctor aluminum. The deck is made of teak (replaced in 1993), while the superstructures are all mahogany heartwood.

Swala has never undergone any restoration or modification, apart from the sails. The satin-finish mahogany interior is very comfortable and pleasant, with a beautiful owner's cabin and spacious dinette. Over the years, Swala has confirmed its excellent nautical qualities. Close-hauled like the boats of its time, it is almost unbeatable, managing to maintain 20 knots with its sails completely raised by the wind. The long keel also ensures great course stability on a high sea. The boat's successes and its high standard of maintenance are due to its faithful skipper, Luciani Brovelli, who for 14 years has had a perfect relationship with Swala. It has gained significant successes: victories, second, and third places at Palma de Mallorca, Cannes and Saint Tropez in France, and Imperia. In 2000 and 2001, Swala excelled at Imperia and Cannes.

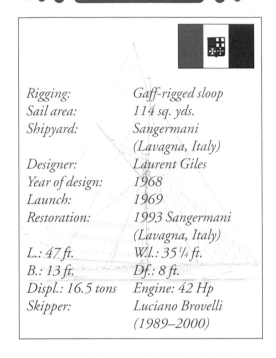

Rigging:	Gaff-rigged sloop
Sail area:	114 sq. yds.
Shipyard:	Sangermani (Lavagna, Italy)
Designer:	Laurent Giles
Year of design:	1968
Launch:	1969
Restoration:	1993 Sangermani (Lavagna, Italy)
L.: 47 ft.	W.l.: 35¹/₄ ft.
B.: 13 ft.	Df.: 8 ft.
Displ.: 16.5 tons	Engine: 42 Hp
Skipper:	Luciano Brovelli (1989–2000)

BELOW: Imperia 1996, Swala, well looked-after by its current owner (Photo: J. Taylor).

Valentina

Rigging:	Gaff-rigged sloop
Sail area:	328 sq. yds.
Shipyard:	Sangermani (Lavagna, Italy)
Designer:	Alan P. Gurney
Year of design:	1972
Launch:	1972
Restoration:	1987
L.: 55 ft.	W.l.: 44 ft.
B.: 15 ft.	Df.: 8 ft.
Displ.: 19.6 tons	Engine: 136 Hp
Skipper:	Luigi Alemagna (1989)

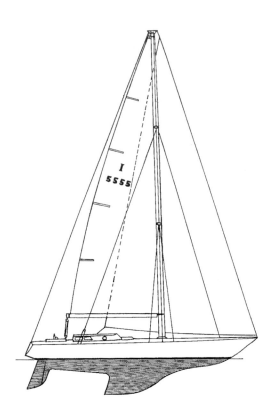

Launched in 1972 with the name *Valentina VI*, and owned by the Milanese notary Masini, this boat gained prominence in 1972 at the Giraglia (gaining seventh place) before going on to win the next edition and to gain good placings in 1974 and 1975. Among its successes was a Middle Sea Race.

With the name of *B&B Italia* the boat participated in the second Whitbread Round the World Race (with skipper Corrado di Majo), reaching the finish line in Portsmouth in England in ninth place after a good regatta performance, in which its nautical qualities and speed were emphasized during the hardest and longest test that a leisure boat can undergo. The boat has a teak deck and mahogany interior and planking. Its equipment has recently been modernized. Under the spinnaker, and with a wind of 30 knots, it can glide along at more than 16 knots; under normal conditions it can easily touch 12 knots.

Viola

Rigging:	Sloop
Sail area:	251 sq. yds.
Shipyard:	Sangermani (Lavagna, Italy)
Designer:	Jais
Year of design:	1957
Launch:	1958
Restoration:	1993 Sangermani (Lavagna, Italy)
L.: 70½ ft.	W.l.: 56½ ft.
B.: 16¼ ft.	Df.: 8 ft.
Displ.: 44.1 tons	Engines (2): 180 Hp
Skipper:	Andrea Bianchi (1988–2000)

Viola is a superb motorsailer, constructed entirely from mahogany and teak at the Sangermani shipyard in Lavagna, Italy. Maintained in perfect condition, it is used for charter activities in the Mediterranean. The boat has had only two owners (the first was Commander Gilera, the founder and proprietor of the motorcycle firm of the same name, who sold the boat in 1970).

The sail plan has recently been changed from the original one, with a new mast of around 10 feet. *Viola* has also undergone a meticulous internal restructuring, which has brought out the quality and inviting comfort of the boat when in use. *Viola*, which is now commanded by its owner and skipper Andrea Bianchi, is a vessel reserved for those who love traditional atmospheres yet do not want to give up comfort and a certain degree of luxury, even on the open sea. It currently cruises between Spain and the Balearics and between Sardinia and the Côte d'Azur.

Maintained in perfect condition, *Viola* is a top-class yacht that combines the romantic charm of sailing with comfort and modern needs.

THIS PAGE: *Images of* Viola, *used for charter. The interior is inviting and well arranged for guests (Photos courtesy of A. Bianchi).*

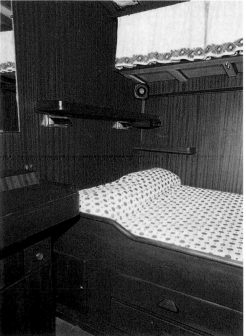

Voscià

Rigging:	Gaff-rigged yawl
Sail area:	180 sq. yds.
Shipyard:	Sangermani (Lavagna, Italy)
Designer:	Sparkman & Stephens
Year of design:	1957
Launch:	1959
Restoration:	1990
L.: 40 ft.	W.l.: 27 ft.
B.: 11¼ ft.	Df.: 5 ft. (with mobile centerboard)
Displ.: 9.37 tons	Engine: 35 Hp
Skipper:	Andrea Resnati (1990), Eugenio Bertuccelli (1992–98)

L aunched as *Oliana III* in 1959, this boat distinguished itself that year, gaining a brilliant second place at the Giraglia and then a victory in the Bermuda Race. Acquired by Admiral Luigi Durand de la Penne, it became *Givaré* (from the first letters of Gigi, Valeria, and Renzo), before again changing its name to *Voscià* ("your lordship") in 1971, the year it was acquired by its current owners.

Voscià has participated in the Imperia regattas in 1990, 1992, 1994, and 1998. It has mahogany planking, iroko structures with metal reinforcements, a teak deck, and a mahogany deckhouse. The deck was rebuilt in 1990 using teak heartwood and a plyboard base.

THIS PAGE: *Imperia 1998, two shots of* Voscià *(Photos courtesy of A. Resnati).*

Replicas and New Constructions

To tell the truth, replicas and new constructions do not appear in very large numbers at Imperia's regattas, alongside vintage, classic, and metric boats, but when they do, they arouse considerable curiosity and interest. Who could forget the schooner *Lady Ellen*, a huge, fiery Swedish vessel, the faithful reproduction of a "monster boat" of the North Sea? Used for entertaining and charter, *Lady Ellen* offers a high level of comfort in any season.

Another replica that has certainly not gone unnoticed is *Sant Troupes*, a faithful copy of a tartan from Saint Tropez. In its construction, timber that would have been in use in the 19th century was chosen. Gérard Bani, skipper of *Sant Troupes*, appeared in 1988 with the minuscule *Petit Julien*, a small tartan whose reconstruction is based on the type used in the French waters near Saint Tropez. Standing out among the new constructions are the ketch *Valentina*, the schooner *Delirio*, and the gaff-cutter *Winsome*, all projects by Carlo Sciarelli. The sail plan of *Delirio* is highly evocative. And, finally, what can we say of the fast gaff schooner *Borkumriff*, which, with a minimum of wind, boldly takes to racing on the sea?

The popularity of replicas is growing all over the world, especially in the United States, for those who yearn to rediscover the charm of boats of the past and to experience for real a way of life at sea that is now only a memory.

America

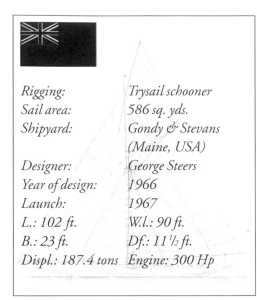

Rigging:	*Trysail schooner*
Sail area:	*586 sq. yds.*
Shipyard:	*Gondy & Stevans*
	(Maine, USA)
Designer:	*George Steers*
Year of design:	*1966*
Launch:	*1967*
L.: 102 ft.	*W.l.: 90 ft.*
B.: 23 ft.	*Df.: 11 1/2 ft.*
Displ.: 187.4 tons	*Engine: 300 Hp*

BELOW: America, *replica of an old classic (Photo: J. Taylor).*

The name of this boat evokes the legend of the schooner *America*, which, in August 1851, defeated a flotilla of English boats at Cowes on the south coast of England, then even more than now the center of yachting, thus winning the 100 Guinea Cup.

The New York Yacht Club had commissioned the schooner to be designed by architect George Steers for the famous challenge. *America* had a 102-foot hull and was 23 feet wide, with a sail surface of 586 square yards and a displacement of 187.4 tons. After its success at Cowes the schooner was sold on site and changed hands a number of times. In 1863 it was used as a training ship by the United States Naval Academy, until 1924, when it became a Museum Ship in Annapolis. In 1966 two American industrialists ordered the construction of an exact replica of *America*, which was built by the Gondy & Stevans shipyard in Maine.

Every part of the schooner was handcrafted, while the sails, once cotton, were ordered from Ratsey & Lapthorn in Cowes, the same sailmakers that had made them 116 years earlier. The new *America* slipped into the sea in May 1967. The current owner often lets the schooner attend vintage yacht regattas, and *America* continues to delight sailing enthusiasts, who are enchanted by its grace and slender, elegant lines.

Borkumriff

This is a faithful reconstruction of a trysail schooner of the North Sea. It has exceptional nautical qualities. Endowed with a considerable freeboard, *Borkumriff* is a boat that hugs the wind and reaches good speeds in trading winds. It has an iroko hull with oak frames, while the deck and superstructure are made of teak. The sail plan is harmonious. The interiors are teak, while the mast and boom are spruce.

RIGHT: *The trysail schooner* Borkumriff, *whose lines evoke the second half of the 19th century (Photo: R. Minervini).*

Rigging:	Trysail schooner
Sail area:	155½ sq. yds.
Shipyard:	Bueltjek Ditzen (Germany)
Designer:	Lunstroo
Year of design:	1930
Launch:	1981
L.: 59 ft.	W.l.: 47½ ft.
B.: 14¾ ft.	Df.: 7 ft.
Displ.: 47.4 tons	Engine: 130 Hp
Skipper:	Ed Kastelein (1987)

Delirio

This vessel, endowed with a harmonious trysail rig, appeared at the 1989 Imperia Regatta for its very first race. Its lines are inspired by the classic schooners of the turn of the last century.

Delirio has a hull made entirely of steel and a flush deck. Manual maneuvers are carried out using blocks, as there is no kind of winch on board. The deck is covered with teak plyboard and heartwood staves, and the deckhouses are made of the same wood. The ceilings of all the habitable rooms have fir staves arranged longitudinally and painted white. This is a very beautiful boat, with its interiors very well-organized and comfortable.

Rigging:	Trysail schooner
Sail area:	270 sq. yds.
Shipyard:	San Giorgio del Porto (Genoa, Italy)
Designer:	Carlo Sciarelli
Year of design:	1985
Launch:	1988
L.: 65½ ft.	W.l.: 55¾ ft.
B.: 14 ft.	Df.: 7 ft.
Displ.: 39.68 tons	Engine: 120 Hp
Skipper:	Rinaldo Corino (1989)

LEFT: *Imperia 1989,* Delirio, *a trysail schooner designed by Carlo Sciarelli (Photo courtesy of R. Corino).*

Fra Dolcino

Rigging:	Trysail schooner
Sail area:	203 sq. yds.
Shipyard:	Zennaro (Venice, Italy)
Designer:	Carlo Sciarelli
Year of design:	1986
Launch:	1986
L.: 53 ft.	W.l.: 48 ft.
B.: 13 1/4 ft.	Df.: 6 ft.
Displ.: 20.94 tons	Engine: 65 Hp
Skipper:	Bonni (1994)

RIGHT: *VBR 1991,* Fra Dolcino, *a schooner offering great satisfaction in return for hard work (Photo: J. Taylor).*

Fra Dolcino, a creation by Carlo Sciarelli, is inspired by the classic schooners that fished off the Banks of Newfoundland in North America, especially the *St. Ann,* built in 1786. When it appeared at the Boat Show in Genoa (in 1986), this boat was unanimously greeted with approval as quite the most interesting among those present.

Fra Dolcino has a classic line with masts tilted backwards and a trysail arrangement, which is typical of American schooners. I have personally found out how tiring every maneuver is without winches, working only with tackle. Yet the effort was worth the satisfaction of seeing this extraordinary steel vessel speed along. The boat has mahogany and teak finishes, fir masts, and, of course, a tiller. Close-hauled it can hug the wind up to 50 degrees: a modern vintage boat!

Lady Ellen

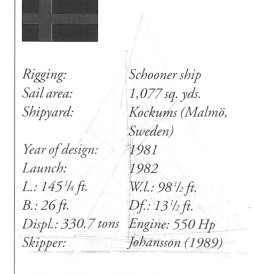

Rigging:	Schooner ship
Sail area:	1,077 sq. yds.
Shipyard:	Kockums (Malmö, Sweden)
Year of design:	1981
Launch:	1982
L.: 145 1/4 ft.	W.l.: 98 1/2 ft.
B.: 26 ft.	Df.: 13 1/2 ft.
Displ.: 330.7 tons	Engine: 550 Hp
Skipper:	Johansson (1989)

RIGHT: *Imperia 1989, light plays through the jibs (Photo: B. Re).*

Lady Ellen is a faithful reconstruction of a three-masted topsail schooner, used in the 19th century in the seas of the north. Its hull, deck, and deckhouses are made of steel covered with teak; the interior is paneled with precious mahogany. The masts and yards are built of Oregon pine, while all the crew's equipment is made of traditional wood. The boat has a spectacular sail plan, with a characteristic aft deckhouse. In a strong breeze it reaches high speeds thanks to the slender form of the hull. Besides the crew of eight people, its very spacious interior can also house 12 guests in six double cabins with air conditioning.

In 1989 *Lady Ellen* was hired by the Agnesi company during the fourth Imperia vintage yacht regatta. The guests on board were able to enjoy the highest levels of comfort and style. Unsurprisingly, it is also perfectly suited to ocean charter activities.

Pandora

*P*andora was built in 1994 by the Grumant shipyard in Petrozavodsk, 200 miles north-east of Saint Petersburg, in the Baltic zone of The Karelian Republic of Russia. It is a trysail topsail-schooner, a faithful replica of the fast vessels of the 18th century on the Baltic Sea, used for postal and customs services and for tender services for the great ships of the period.

After participating in the maritime festivals of Bristol and Brest, and visiting a number of ports in Portugal and Spain, *Pandora* arrived in Italy with the name of *Anna*. It was then abandoned by its captain and crew. In February 1999, after sinking for the second time in the port of Genoa, Italy, it was acquired by its current owner, Marco De Amici, with the collaboration of a true "band of brothers" of young volunteers and real professionals. *Pandora* returned to the sea in September 1999.

In April 2000 it completed its inaugural voyage, participating in the Tall Ships Race 2000 from Genoa to Cadiz in Spain. Pandora flies the pennant of the ARIE and is actively involved in all the Association's initiatives.

The planking, deck, and masts are made of Karelian pine, while the interior is oak. The hardware is bronze or galvanized iron. Its ballast consists of 16.53 tons of cast-iron ingots. To trim the sails, manual maneuvers are carried out using hoists and blocks, while the rudder blade is operated by a bar over ten feet long. At the bow is a bar capstan and, under the bowsprit, a beautiful carved figurehead has been affixed.

Rigging:	Trysail topsail-schooner
Sail area:	383 sq. yds.
Shipyard:	Grumant (Petrozavodsk, Russia)
Year of design:	1991
Launch:	1994
Restoration:	1998
L.: 65 ½ ft.	W.l.: 52 ½ ft.
B.: 16 ft.	D.f.: 7 ft.
Displ.: 72.75 tons	Engine: 150 Hp
Skipper:	Marco De Amici (2000)

LEFT: *Imperia 2000, the schooner* Pandora *(Photo: J. Taylor).*

BELOW: *Imperia 2000, the figurehead of* Pandora *(Photo: J. Taylor).*

Petit Julien

Rigging:	Tartan
Sail area:	36 sq. yds.
Year of design:	1887
Launch:	1988
L.: 12 ¼ ft.	W.l.: 12 ft.
B.: 7 ft.	Df.: 2 ft.
Displ.: 0.99 tons	
Skipper:	Gérard Bani

This faithful reproduction of a tartan (*Petit Jean*), the original now well over a century old, has attracted the attention and affection of a French couple, Gérard and Alix Bani. Gérard Bani is the President of the Saint Tropez Society of Traditional Sailing Ships.

Navigating with sails and oars, they took seven days to bring this tiny boat from Marseilles to Imperia, where it ran the risk of disappearing among so many imposing vessels such as *Puritan* and *Lelantina*. *Petit Julien* has cotton sails from the early 1950s and a mast from before 1930. In the last century, the fishermen of Saint Tropez would go out in these boats, called "*crabes*," in regattas on the first Sunday of each month, with the best fishing area as their prize. *Petit Julien* has obtained sixth place at the Coupe Phocea in Marseilles.

RIGHT: *Imperia 1988,* Petit Julien *is the reproduction of a tartan from over 100 years ago (Photo: C. Borlenghi).*

Petite Lande

On October 20, 1927 the great designer John G. Alden signed his project no. 366 with the wording "auxiliary schooner yacht." *Petite Lande* is a replica of that project, a beautiful schooner with generous overhangs that, seen from a distance, would deceive any vintage boat expert.

It has an aluminum hull and a teak deck, ending in a spacious cockpit. It has no winches for the halyards; instead, the helmsman has to steer a long bar in a standing position. The schooner slides gently over the water and recalls the reaches of boats such as *Malabar* and *Puritan*, also designed by John Alden. The long hull allows *Petite Lande* considerable course stability. The preferred sailing position for this classic schooner is obviously on a broad reach, when with a wind of around 25 knots it can manage a speed of almost 8 knots. There is an age-old elegance in the tapered profile of the deck, where only the deckhouse, of reduced dimensions, rises up. The interior, also reduced in size, is pleasant, thanks also to the quality of the oak and pine heartwoods.

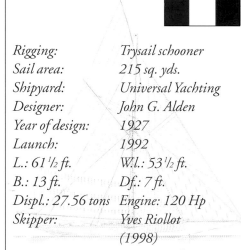

Rigging:	Trysail schooner
Sail area:	215 sq. yds.
Shipyard:	Universal Yachting
Designer:	John G. Alden
Year of design:	1927
Launch:	1992
L.: 61½ ft.	W.l.: 53½ ft.
B.: 13 ft.	Df.: 7 ft.
Displ.: 27.56 tons	Engine: 120 Hp
Skipper:	Yves Riollot
	(1998)

THIS PAGE: *Cannes 1998, images of the trysail schooner* Petite Lande *(Photos: J. Taylor).*

Presque Isle

Rigging:	Trysail schooner
Sail area:	178 sq. yds.
Shipyard:	Edinboro (USA)
Designer:	L.F. Herreshoff
Year of design:	1923
Launch:	1950–60
Restoration:	1990–95
L.: 50 ft.	W.l.: 43¼ ft.
B.: 13¼ ft.	Df.: 5 ft.
Displ.: 24.25 tons	Engine: 200 Hp
Skipper:	Michele Bojola
	(1998–2000)

Presque Isle is a trysail schooner built in the United States, probably after World War II. It is a replica of *Joann*, a schooner that L.F. Herreshoff designed in 1923, and has certainly been influenced by the traditional pilot boats of Massachusetts, and particularly by the pilot schooner *Clarence Barclay*.

Presque Isle is a very sturdy vessel with full lines and a wedge-like hull. With a modern draft, it has good course stability and is fast on a beam and a broad reach, managing an average of over 7 knots, almost without needing to steer. With strong breezes it easily reaches 10 knots. It has the typical "clipper-like" bow of hulls designed by Herreshoff; the trysail-schooner rig with hoists for the halyards, the elaborate lazy-jacks, and the boom foresail with brails all take us back in time. *Presque Isle* sails with the same rig and the same deck equipment envisaged by Herreshoff. There has been no skimping on the use of wood in the construction of the schooner: it has oak frames, white oak beams, pitch pine planking (cladding), a cedar topside, a teak deck, sitka spruce masts, mahogany deckhouses, and bulkheads and an interior prevalently made of Douglas pine and mahogany.

In 1986 it was completely restored to sail in the Caribbean. However, in September 1989 Hurricane Ugo surprised it in the Salt River Bay at Saint Croix in the United States, where it was damaged by a drifting dredger. In 1990 the hull was still afloat but practically abandoned, when the current owners decided to buy it. The restoration, carried out in the Salt River shipyard, was limited to the planking (cladding), the mechanics of the rudder, and the aft transom. Despite the abandonment and various acts of theft, the sturdy structure of the boat was intact.

In 1994, Florentine skipper Gianni Raddi was entrusted with the task of moving *Presque Isle* to the Mediterranean. Between the winter and spring of 1995, a limited amount of restoration work was carried out on the topside and the interior at the Argentario naval shipyard in Italy. The limited documentation available on *Presque Isle* suggests that we should cautiously include the schooner among the replicas, reserving the right to carry out further historical investigation to prove or disprove this choice.

From the Builder's Certification issued in June 1986 we can glean that *Presque Isle*'s previous name was *Tiab*.

THIS PAGE: *Imperia 2000, close-up of the stern and under sail (Photo: J. Taylor).*

OPPOSITE PAGE: *Argentario 1998,* Presque Isle *during a tack (Photo: J. Taylor).*

Sant Troupes

Rigging:	Tartan
Sail area:	203 sq. yds.
Shipyard:	Trapani Fils (Cassis, France)
Designer:	Court Picot
Year of design:	1989
Launch:	1989
L.: 46 ft.	W.l.: 42½ ft.
B.: 13½ ft.	Df.: 6 ft.
Displ.: 25.73 tons	Engine: 70 Hp
Skipper:	Gérard Bani (1990)

RIGHT: *Imperia 1990, Sant Troupes at Imperia, still incomplete (Photo: E. Perino).*

By 1925 the cargo tartans used for coastal transportation had almost disappeared. Common in the Ligurian area of Italy in the 17th and 18th centuries, and in the first half of the following century, they had a sail plan that remained unchanged over the years. They had a vertical mast that carried a large lateen sail and a jib boom.

When, in September 1990, *Sant Troupes* entered port, the old folk of the Borgo Marina in Imperia thought they had gone back in time to spring 1925, the period when they last remembered a similar ship moored there. *Sant Troupes*, launched at the Trapani Fils shipyard in Cassis, France, and belonging to the Companie Provençale des Gens de Mer, is a faithful and robust reconstruction of a tartan of Saint Tropez (especially as regards its topside), but with a hull whose waterline recalls the typical "bovo" of Cette.

It has iroko planking, a pine mast and spar, and oak frames. Not being used for trade and therefore having no cargo, it has a high freeboard with olive-green broadsides and yellow bands on the stringer and toerail. With strong crosswinds it provides a thrilling spectacle, reaching speeds of 8–9 knots, and even more on a broad reach.

Valentina

Rigging:	Gaff-rigged ketch
Sail area:	147 sq. yds.
Shipyard:	Crisman & Giraldi (Trieste, Italy)
Designer:	Carlo Sciarelli
Year of design:	1982
Launch:	1984
L.: 49 ft.	W.l.: 41¼ ft.
B.: 12 ft.	Df.: 6 ft.
Displ.: 15.98 tons	Engine: 100 Hp
Skipper:	Enrico Masini (1987–90)

Rigged as a ketch and designed by Carlo Sciarelli, *Valentina* has a traditional design and form. Very elegant and slender, with a tilted bowsprit and masts, the boat has a teak deck, spruce masts, steam-curved and riveted acacia frames, and steel floor plates.

Let us allow Carlo Sciarelli to describe "his" boat, as it appears in the book *Lo Yacht*: "…*The cut of the new boat was supposed to be traditional, with bulwark, skylights on deck, little cordage, fast with little effort, not big, but also a little bit shiplike…*"

And in fact, *Valentina* possesses all these qualities. Carlo goes on: "…*in 1987 I had the pleasure of seeing, from* Valentina, *the whole fleet, dozens and dozens of many-sailed boats, many double-length, and they seemed to be standing still compared with* Valentina, *which overtook them, both windward and leeward. That day we arrived before everyone: without ever changing a sail or leaving the cockpit. A classy boat.*"

Interestingly, at the Imperia Rally in 1990, *Valentina* measured itself against *Winsome*, another Sciarelli creation, and won again.

Winsome

uilt in the Cattaneo shipyards in Varazze, Italy, and commissioned by Lippo Riva, a well-known boat-owner, *Winsome*, with its graceful forms, drew the crowds at the third Imperia vintage yacht regatta. The boat has mahogany planking (from a consignment acquired directly from Thailand), a mahogany plywood deck, and oak beams and floor timbers. It behaves very well under sail, especially when sailed close-reached.

RIGHT: *Imperia 1998, a shot of* Winsome, *by Carlo Sciarelli (Photo courtesy of B. Zaoli).*

Rigging:	*Bermudan cutter*
Sail area:	*46 sq. yds.*
Shipyard:	*Cattaneo (Varazze, Italy)*
Designer:	*Carlo Sciarelli*
Year of design:	*1977*
Launch:	*1978*
L.: 24¼ ft.	*W.l.: 20 ft.*
B.: 9 ft.	*Df.: 5 ft.*
Displ.: 3.31 tons	*Engine: 16 Hp*
Skipper:	*Marco Colli (1988)*

Zaca a Te Moana

his splendid trysail schooner, launched in October 1992, recalls the pure lines of the American schooners of the Grand Banks of Newfoundland in Canada. Nothing has been forgotten in the interior and exterior fittings and furnishings of *Zaca a Te Moana*, which has a steel hull but splendid teak masting, deck, and interior. All the equipment has been built in the traditional manner, including the use of wood blocks and bronze hydraulic winches that are capable of lifting 3.31 tons and therefore avoid the need for a large crew. The interior is luxurious and spacious, elegantly furnished and endowed with every comfort for guests and well separated from the equally comfortable crew's quarters. All the radio, navigation, and safety equipment is state-of-the-art and meets the requirements of international regulations. Needless to say, *Zaca a Te Moana* is used for charter purposes.

Rigging:	*Trysail schooner*
Sail area:	*1,017 sq. yds.*
Shipyard:	*Amstel B.V. (The Netherlands)*
Designer:	*Olivier E. van Meer*
Year of design:	*1991*
Launch:	*1992*
L.: 143½ ft.	*W.l.: 88½ ft.*
B.: 24 ft.	*Df.: 14 ft.*
Displ.: 192.9 tons	*Engine: 300 Hp*
Skipper:	*Ed Kastelein (1994)*

LEFT: *The splendid lines of* Zaca a Te Moana *(Photo: J. Taylor).*

FOLLOWING PAGE: *The schooner tacking (Photo: J. Taylor).*

Other "Brothers" are discovered

Many other boats have appeared in various vintage yacht regattas at Imperia. They include: *Dalù, Icicle IV, Albebaran I, Julie Mother, La Romantica, Terza Santa Maria, Anni Venti, Phoenix, Santa Maria II, Volonté, Tyrsa, Nina VI, Swala, Mai Più, Benenel, Golondrina, Parsifal, Perla, Dida III, Ardi, Voloira III, Grifone, Giuvit III, Balkis, Ulisse, Emi, Whansheen, Sheherezade, Elefteria, Wayfarer Alpha, Gabrielle III, Marò II, and La Couronne de Marie.*

Argos - 1996 (Ph. N. Martinez)

Bloodhound - 1999
(Ph. J. Taylor)

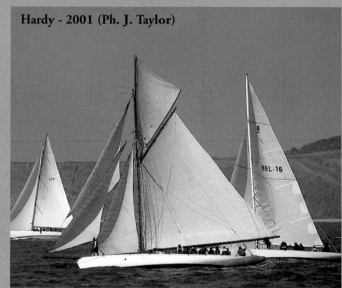

Hardy - 2001 (Ph. J. Taylor)

Arosa - 2000 (Ph. N. Martinez)

Owl - 2001 (Ph. J. Taylor)

Platero - 2000 (Ph. N. Martinez)

Nose - 1997 (Ph. N. Martinez)

Keep Trust - 2001 (Ph. J. Taylor)

Lutine - 2001 (Ph. J. Taylor)

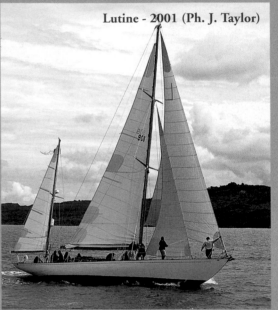

Meermint - 2000 (Ph. N. Martinez)

Rosen Gwen - 1999 (Ph. N. Martinez)

Rinamara - 2001 (Ph. J. Taylor)

Fortune - 2001 (Ph. J. Taylor)

Rosendo - 2000 (Ph. N. Martinez)

Windigo - 2001 (Ph. J. Taylor)

The most sacred

Cambria - 2001 (Ph. J. Taylor)

Velsheda - 2001 (Ph. J. Taylor)

Shamrock - 2001 (Ph. J. Taylor)

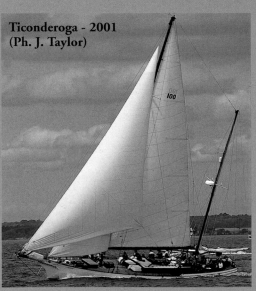
Ticonderoga - 2001
(Ph. J. Taylor)

Other vessels not present at muster:

Caribbee, Jane Dore IV, Corinthian, Jubilee, Niña, Taltohna, Vixen, Velsheda, Kong Bele, Gitana IV, Santana, Sincerity, Elise, Iolaire, Rona, Oyster River, Curlew, Veleda, Angela Aline, Margareita, Didone, Maid of Malin, Airy Mouse, Adela, Cora A, Kapocas, Keepsake, Strale, Roberta III, Sylvia, Calipso, Alì Babà, Esterel, Indigo, Rs1, Santa Maria Nicopeja, Flicka, Cariba, Vaar, Sirah, Landfall, Colen II, Maran, Maliki, Fedalah, Samphire, Marygold, Lona II, Etoile Molene, Skylark, Black Velvet, Heron, Arawak, Tahina, Tar Baby, Velsia, Leao Holandes, Wildfire, Polaris, Zomoura, Sea Gypsy, Pizzicotto, La Brillante, Amadour, Blue Clipper, Freda, Westword, Eye of the Wind, My Fida, Moonshine, Shiris, Ticonderoga, Vera, Wild Goose, Jolie Brise, Severn, Lady Belle, Isis, Evenlode, Primrose, Sazerac, Dreva, Clyde, Lotus, Magda IV, Starlight, Brigadoon of Boothbay, Baladin, Argyll, Sall, Carrina, Id, Matinicius, Lady Maud, Nancy Anne, Aurora von Altona, Freya, Valdivia, Lady May, Marling, Mingary, Taranto, Leala, La Goleta, Duenna, Mariquita, Merry Maid, Doris III, Enchanta, Tioga, Lumberjack, Highlander Sea, Eblis, Weatherbird, Staghound, Goodwill, East Wind, Stephen Taber, Mailiki, Wiki, Christina Grant, Chole May, Eleonora, Reineke, Nancy Backett, Paloma, Melisande, Wild Horses, Alla Blu, Halmo, Aile Blanche, Stavanger, Gury, Milena, Vera, Kokanee, Cesira, Ganimede, Lulworth, Melisarde, Clara, and Tern IV.

Notes on the most well-known naval architects

Nathaniel Herreshoff (1848–1938)

The career of Nathaniel Herreshoff was certainly one of the longest and most prolific in the field of cruise and regatta yacht design. Nicknamed "the magician of Bristol" (Rhode Island in the United States), he designed and built boats from 1864 through 1935, including no fewer than six America's Cup winners, a record only equaled by the Burgesses (father and son), each the creator of three vessels, while Charles Nicholson achieved only four.

"Captain Nat," as he was called, was an inflexible man with an extraordinary mathematical rigor, which did not leave room for compromise. Until 1915 he was assisted by his brother, John Brown, who generally dealt with customers and construction. On his death the decline of the shipyard began, and it officially closed down in 1924, even if "Nat" continued to design boats.

A man of extraordinary inventive skills (he designed the machines and tools necessary for construction), Herreshoff was also a skilled helmsman who steered boats such as *Defender*, *Reliance*, *Resolute*, *Vigilant*, and others to victory. He designed boats of various dimensions – steam yachts and cruise boats. Among his most memorable creations were the schooner *Wildfire* (built when Herreshoff was 75), *Westward*, his most famous schooner, and *Vagrant*.

His last project dates from 1935, three years before his death, which marked the end of a legendary career. Today his memory lives on in the Bristol Museum devoted to him, illustrated by over 2,000 boats and machinery of all types. He is universally considered to be the greatest American yacht designer ever.

William Fife III (1857–1944)

From the beginning of the 19th century until 1950, the Fife dynasty of Scottish designers and builders, all named William, created the most beautiful, the fastest, and the most prestigious boats in the history of yachting.

William I (1775–1865) began his career by designing fishing boats; he entered yachting with his cutter *Gleam*, which became champion of the Clyde.

Then came William II (1821–1902), who designed a fleet of successful boats, all rigged as cutters, deep and narrow-built. Among these are the famous *Bloodhound*, from 1874, which raced until 1922.

William Fife III (or Junior), however, was more prolific and active than either his father or his grandfather. His most famous boat was *Shamrock III*, which participated in the America's Cup for Sir Thomas Lipton. Then came the cutter *Clara*, a composite construction (17 victories in 20 races). William Fife Jr. was most active in the 1890s.

Still famous today is Fife's "dragon," the symbol with which the famous builder signed his boats, of which there were many: *Altair* (designed when Fife was 75 years old), the cutter *Moonbeam*, the sloop *Clio*, *Latifa*, and *Halloween*, one of the last boats to be designed before World War II. In 1938 came his final creation: *Solway Maid*, to the design of which his nephew, Robert B. Fife, also contributed.

Johan Anker (1871–1940)

Coming from a rich family of industrialists in Oslo, Norway, Johan Anker inherited a passion for sailing from his father, who had personally designed the family yacht. In 1905, after graduating in architecture and naval construction at the University of Charlottenburg, he founded a shipyard and a design studio with Christian Jensen. Anker was also known as an expert helmsman and had various boat-owner friends; among these, he found his first customers, to design regatta or cruise boats.

His first international success was *Fram*, a revolutionary 8-meter that, steered by him, gained gratifying successes in 1908. Most of his work was directed at the Metric Classes; the success of *Rollo* (1911) brought many orders to the shipyard.

In 1915 the association with Jensen was broken and Anker ran the shipyard alone. By now, hulls of every type were being built, from dinghies to large cruise yachts. The architect was also elected as president of the Scandinavian Yacht Racing Union, a position that he held until 1931.

Anker designed over 200 vessels, including *Desirée*, *Coppelia*, *Lasse*, *Eva Maria*, *Arabella V*, *Magnolia*, *Sirius*, *Neptune*, and *Solveig I*. In 1927 a project of his won a competition announced by the Royal Gothenburg Yacht Club. It was a small sloop of around 30 feet, fit to be inhabited by two persons, to be used for short cruises, and with speed enough for use in regattas. Anker called this vessel a "Dragone." In 1938 this new class, already very popular in Norway, arrived in Germany and England.

Anker continued to design boats until 1939. He died the following year, without being able to enjoy the great success of his beloved Dragone. At the end of the war, the Dragones were among the first boats to be built, and they became so numerous worldwide that the Olympic Class was created in 1948.

John G. Alden (1884–1962)

Among the many American designers that have characterized a whole era, we must remember John Alden, who was also a yachtsman and skipper in ocean races. In his native Rhode Island in the United States, the young Alden was influenced by the fishermen and sailors with whom he used to race.

In 1900 his family moved to Dorchester in Massachusetts. The new environment proved to be conclusive for his development: it was a world of fishing schooners that sailed the Grand Banks of Newfoundland. Alden managed to work for some time in the studio of the elderly architect Edward Burgess, who had designed the great cutters that defended the America's Cup in the 1880s. He also collaborated with Harling Burgess, Edward's son, who in 1930 was also to design other "defenders."

Burgess the Elder had drawn up the plans for the best fishing schooners for the fleet of the Grand Banks; his son transferred the experience to cruise and regatta boats. This considerably influenced young Alden, who worked for a while at the Crowningshield studio (in 1903 he had been taken on as a simple draftsman). After World War I, Alden set up by himself and took on other promising draftsmen and architects as partners, including Howard Chapelle. The schooners of both New England and Canada continued to influence his production: very sturdy boats coming out of the shipyards of the states of Massachusetts and Maine, with ample volume below deck.

The successes of the various *Malabar*s, sailed with experience and ability, increased his production output as did his victories in open-sea regattas (he won the Bermuda Race three times). His was a historic victory in the 1932 edition of the famous race: his boats occupied the first four places. Alden, with Herreshoff, Burgess, Olin Stephens, and Philip Rhodes, has rightfully entered the history of American yacht designers.

Charles E. Nicholson (1896–1954)

Nicholson was one of the greatest naval architects in the world. At just 15 he designed his first yacht, little imagining that he would take a highly significant place in the world of yachting, not only as an architect and builder, but also as a yachtsman and skipper. At the helm he was incomparable for his boldness and ability; he was never seen to abandon a regatta due to bad weather.

In 1914 he revolutionized naval construction with the use of steel and aluminum framing (we need only recall *Shamrock IV*). It was in fact the regatta boats for the America's Cup (*Shamrock IV* and *Endeavour*) that consolidated his success in yachting. Other famous "racing machines," always endowed with grace and harmony of lines, were *Bloodhound*, *Joyette*, and *Firebird*. Then came the time of the "J Class": *Astra*, *Candida*, and *Velsheda*, which consolidated his greatness.

Among his creations, we must also remember the 33-ton cutter *Flame*, launched in 1900, which gained third place at the Fastnet Race in 1933, and the schooner *Vira* (later known as *Creole*), which still sails the seas today.

Endowed with a tenacious will and a strong temperament, Charles Nicholson never surrendered, even when fate was against him. In 1910 a fire destroyed his studio, with the loss of all the construction plans; the same fate befell him again in 1941 when bombing reduced his shipyard in Gosport (in England) to ashes. However, he was able to draw new life from such events to return to work with furious determination. His comment to his shipyard foreman, on the occasion of bombing, has become famous: "*Never mind. Think how much rubbish was lost as well…*"

In cruise boats, Nicholson achieved a purity of lines that was most marked in the famous *Aile Blanche*. It can be said that Nicholson paved the way for Bermudan rigs in today's yachting; the class of boats such as *Foxhound* has entered the history of naval design. He was without doubt a highly talented man and artist, with a fierce will and unlimited sensitivity.

Jack Laurent Giles (1901–1968)

The wide-ranging production of cruise, regatta, and working boats tells of the aesthetic versatility and great technical capacity of this man, who is widely recognized as the greatest innovator among sailing-boat designers. From 1927 his studio was located in a street in Quay Hill in Lymington (England). His boats have the merit of reconciling exceptional seaworthiness with a lively esthetic equilibrium.

Giles worked with John Illingworth, the skipper and designer of highly successful boats such as *Dyarchy* and *Maid of Malham*. Then came the various *Wanderer*s. In the late 1930s, Giles devoted himself to designing cutters and sloops for Metric Class regattas, including the 12-meter *Flica*. He turned out more than 500 projects from the tiny *Vertue*. In Italy, many shipyards built from his plans.

John H. Illingworth

An officer of the Engineer Corps of the Royal Navy, Illingworth has been defined as the greatest English open-sea racing yachtsman, an undisputed authority who was also a draftsman and designer of yachts, a profession to which he devoted himself full-time after retiring from the Navy, having begun in China back in 1927. In that year he rerigged his first boat, the yawl *Queen Bee*, using a revolutionary concept at that time: putting the jib at the head of the mast.

In 1937 he created his first boat for open-sea racing, the cutter *Maid of Malham*, which immediately won various races and the 1938 RORC (Royal Ocean Racing Club) championship. Once World War II was over, Illingworth built his most famous yacht, the cutter *Myth of Malham*, with which he won the Fastnet Race in 1947, repeating the success in 1949. The hull of the boat was designed by Jack Laurent Giles, who then designed the rest together with Illingworth.

From 1952 Illingworth began to design boats himself. In 1957 he was joined by an assistant, Angus Primrose, who subsequently became a partner. Illingworth & Primrose produced many famous yachts, such as *Belmore*, *Brigantine*, *Outlaw*, and *Artica II*. After his collaboration with Giles for *Maid* and *Myth of Malham*, Illingworth specialized in the construction of light-displacement cutters, such as *Outlaw* and *Artica II*, which performed exceptionally and achieved noteworthy successes.

Olin Stephens (1908–)

The doyen of American naval designers (born in New York in 1908) is now retired, living in a village in Vermont. Towards the end of the 1920s, the young Olin (endowed with a talent for tracing the waterlines of boats) and who, together with his brother Rod, had sailed for a long time on the Long Island Sound, sent a drawing to *Yachting* magazine. The design, a "day sailer," was published and caught the attention and keen eye of Drake Sparkman, then known as one of the leading brokers of leisure boats. He called young Olin and not only offered him a job, but even made him an associate at his studio. So it was that Sparkman & Stephens came about.

During the Depression (in 1929), Olin's father commissioned a project (*Dorade*) from Sparkman & Stephens. From the moment of its launch, this boat was defined as the first modern "ocean racer." Everyone knows about the extraordinary success of *Dorade* at the Fastnet Race, when it crossed the finish line four days before the other competitors. Realising that, despite its many victories, *Dorade* had a tendency to roll a great deal, particularly in a high sea and stern winds, Olin Stephens studied its lines further to resolve the problem.

The opportunity arrived with the commissioning of *Stormy Weather*, to which Olin gave a different shape, especially in the submerged sections, slightly rounded-off compared with those of *Dorade* and with an increase in the main bay (the "rating" at the time penalized narrow hulls). *Stormy Weather* is probably the boat that has achieved the largest number of victories in the history of modern yachting. Olin Stephens has half a century of successes behind him, but the greatest was that of having contributed to no less than six victories for the "defenders" in the America's Cup.

He began in 1937 with the powerful "J Class" *Ranger*, then moved on to the 12-meter *Columbia* (1958), *Constellation* (1964), *Intrepid* (1967), *Courageous* (1974), and *Freedom* (1980). *Ranger*, the project for which he collaborated with Starling Burgess and on board which Olin was responsible for tactics, marked the official entry of the great architect in the history of the America's Cup.

Another great success for Olin was *Finisterre*, which won the Bermuda Race three times running (an unbeaten record) and either won or was placed second in all the regattas in which it took part, also thanks to its advantageous "rating."

The busiest period for Olin Stephens was between 1950 and 1980; he worked on more than 2,500 projects before retiring. Stephens conceived, rather than designed, boats. He provided the designer with the displacement, maximum width, and some of the lines of the stern and bow, a working method that his extraordinary, creative intuition and profound mastery of the profession made successful and decisive in every project.

The boats and their designers

John Alden (USA)
Karenita	1929
Puritan	1931
Royono	1936
Lord Jim	1936
Lelantina	1937
White Wings	1938
Nirvana	1950

Maurice Amiet (France)
La Clé de Sol	1954

Johan Anker (Denmark)
Desirée	1913
Coppelia	1923
Eva Maria	1931
Magda XIII	1938
Lasse	1940

Colin Archer (Scotland)
Aurora	1908
Gipsy	1927

Vittorio Baglietto (Italy)
Niña Luisita	1932
Bona	1934
Barbel	1937
Twins V	1938
Caroly	1948

Vittorio Beltrami (Italy)
Gabbiano	1934

Talma Bertrand (France)
Ellen	1931

Franco Anselmi Boretti (Italy)
Namar	1964
Armelea	1968

David Boyd (GB)
Ikra	1963
Sovereign	1963

Alan N. Buchanan (GB)
Crystal	1966

François Cansatte (France)
L'Iliade	1935
Nagaïna	1950

Artù Chiggiato (Italy)
San Marco	1952

Robert Clark (USA)
Cheone	1937
Phantom Light	1946

Robert Cole (GB)
Molly	1914

Eugène Cornu (France)
Jaline	1946
Ondine	1946
Janabel	1951
Yadic II	1950
Vanille	1964
Giannella II	1966

Attilio Costaguta (Italy)
Emilia	1930
Aria	1935
Italia	1936

William Crossfield (GB)
Moya	1910

P.C. Crossley (GB)
Elpis	1920

Henri Dervin (France)
Lily IV	1946
Croix des Gardes	1947
Saint Briac	1955

G.A. Estlander (Sweden)
Arcangelo	1923
Bau Bau	1939

William Fife III (GB)
Pen Duick	1898
Yvette	1899
Moonbeam	1903
Cintra	1909
Tonino	1912
The Lady Anne	1912
Sumurun	1914
Clio	1921
Kentra	1923
Halloween	1926
Osborne	1929

Belle Aventure	1929
Fulmar	1930
Altair	1931
Latifa	1936
Vanity V	1936
Merry Dancer	1938
Solvay Maid	1940
Navara	1956

German Frers (Argentina)
Juana Argentina	1952
Don Quijote	1953
Lisa of la Tour	1965

William Gardner (USA)
Mariangela	1964
Amore mio	1964

J. Laurent Giles (GB)
Dorade	1930
Helen	1935
Cerida	1938
Flica	1939
Dyarchy	1939
Iska	1948
Umiak	1955
Amadeus Primus	1960
Maria Galante	1962
Glad II	1962
Eos I	1962
Susanna II	1964
Swala	1969

Henry Gruber (Germany)
Nordwind	1939

Nathaniel Herreshoff (USA)
Linnet	1904
Vagrant	1910
Mariette	1915
Nirvana	1950

David Hillyard (GB)
Migrant	1934
Windswept	1936
Harmonie in Blue	1956
Yhann	1956

John Illingworth (GB)
Artica II	1956
Outlaw	1963
Chin Blu III	1965

Christian Jensen (Norway)
Tamara IX	1932
Eileen	1938
Kipawa	1938

Jarl Lindblom (Finland)
Daphne	1935
Marjatta	1945

A.R. Luke (GB)
Veronique	1907
Conti Bernardi	1928

Martinolich (Italy)
Croce del Sud	1933

André Mauric (France)
Kenavo II	1942
Sylphe IV	1946
Aigue Blu	1973

Alfred Mylne (USA)
Vadura	1926
The Blue Peter	1930
Galashiel	1934
Thendara	1937
Mariella	1938

C. and P. Nicholson (GB)
Partridge	1885
Avel	1896
Ilex	1899
Black Swan	1899
Joyette	1907
Folly	1909
Orion	1910
Shaula	1925
Creole	1927
Astra	1928
Candida	1929
Saharet of Tyre	1933
Endeavour	1934
Trivia	1937
Oiseau de Feu	1937
Tomahawk	1939

P. Nicholson (GB)
Peteteka of Ville	1961
Angelique	1961
Rocquette	1964
La Meloria	1967

Max Oertz (Germany)
Stint	1911
Romeo	1912
Aello	1921

Angelo Penco (Italy)
Ancilla II	1959
Seilan	1967

Murray Peterson (USA)
Fair Weather	1926
Coaster	1935

M. Rasmussen (Germany)
Aleph	1951
Athena	1955
Germania V	1955

Knud H. Reimers (Sweden)
Agneta	1951

A. Richardson (GB)
Varuna	1909

Paul Rodney (GB)
Coch y Bondhu	1936

Cesare Sangermani (Italy)
Gioanna	1948
Rondine II	1948
Samurai	1962
Bufeo Blanco	1963
Beatrice	1963
Caligo	1966
Cigno Nero	1966
Huna II	1967

Carlo Sciarelli (Italy)
Chaplin	1974
Winsome	1978
Valentina	1984
Fra Dolcino	1986
Delirio	1988

D. Severi (France)
Hygie	1930

Frederick Shepherd (GB)
Tirrenia	1914

Sparkman & Stephens (USA)
Stormy Weather	1934
Ice Fire	1936
So Fong	1937
Nyala	1938
Bolero	1939
Vim	1939
Mizar III	1946
Loki	1948
Santa Rosa	1949
Bolero	1949
Finisterre	1954
Mait II	1957
Crosswind	1957
Calypso	1958
Leticia do Sol	1958
Sparklet	1958
Voscià	1959
Ella	1960
Capricia	1963
Aile Blanche	1964
Giadamar	1965
Josephin of Humble	1965
Al Na' Ir IV	1966
Levantades	1967
Rubin III	1967
Balkis	1967
Tarantella	1969
Bonita	1973

Gunnar L. Stenback (Sweden)
Shaula	1930
Constance	1964

Bruno Veronese (Italy)
Nausicaa	1956

O. Watts (USA)
Old Fox	1938

Claude Worth (GB)
Alzavola	1924

Glossary

Aft transom: the flat face of the stern when this is not pointed (or "Norwegian").

Ballast: weight put on board to increase the stability of a boat or ship.

Beam: transverse structure that joins the opposing frames and supports the deck.

Belay pins: circular section pins, slightly conical, made of oak or acacia.

Bermuda: another name for the gaff sail (triangular).

Binnacle: a wooden column fixed on deck on which the compass bowl rests with cardanic suspension; the compensating magnets are housed there.

Block: seafaring name for pulley, composed of links, notches, bolt, pulley, strop.

Boom: a pole that supports the base of a sail (mainsail) and onto which the rope of the mainsail is hoisted.

Bottom: the part of the hull that is normally immersed in the water.

Bowsprit: pole or "mast" that sticks out from the bow to support the jibs.

Broad reach: a reach with the wind coming from a direction between 90° and 150–160° with respect to the bow of the vessel.

Bulb: enlarged part at the lower end of the centerboard, made of lead or cast iron and with a hydrodynamic profile.

Bulkhead: internal dividing wall.

Cabin planking: the interior floor, above the bottom.

Chain plates: metal clips fixed to the hull to attach the stays.

Cladding: the part of the hull that remains immersed.

Clinker (planking): a type of planking with the boards superimposed one over the other, which contributes to strengthening the structure of the hull.

Close-hauled (reach): to sail against the direction of the wind (to hug the wind).

Cockpit: the lowered part of the deck where the helmsman stands.

Coffee grinder: a type of vertical winch with two cranks for the sheets of the spinnakers.

Cutter: a sailing yacht with a mast positioned at around one-third of the length of the boat, supporting a mainsail and two jibs.

Deckhouse: superstructure on the deck.

Dismast: to lose the mast due to wrong maneuvers or due to the wind.

Displacement: the water moved by the hull: according to Archimedes' principle, the weight of the hull.

Draft: the immersion of the hull.

Figurehead: a sculpted ornament or figure fitted under the bowsprit.

Flush-deck: a deck free of any superstructure.

Flying jib: the third jib on cutters, fixed higher than the deck.

Forestay: fixed rigging that holds the mast.

Frame-floor: transverse beams on both sides of the keel.

Frames: also called "ribs."

Freeboard: height of the deck from the surface of the sea (waterline).

Gaff: the pole into which the upper part of a gaff sail is ridden.

Gaff sail: sail with a trapezoid shape (generally the mainsail).

Garboard: the first board of the planking along the keel.

Genoa: the large jib that covers part of the mainsail in modern boats.

Genoa staysail: an internal jib (stern).

Griping: tending to drift towards the wind.

Halyard: maneuvers the cable to hoist a sail.

Hardware: a general term indicating the metal parts of the equipment and the standing and running rigging.

Hatch: opening on deck for access to the spaces below.

Haul aft: to put under tension.

Hoist: system consisting of two blocks, one fixed, the other movable, and a cable that passes through the pulleys of both, used for reducing the force necessary to bear a weight or a resistance.

Jib: a triangular sail.

Keel: the lowest, most important structural part of a boat that connects the transverse frames and joins the planking of the two sides.

Ketch: a sailing yacht similar to the yawl, from which it differs because the mizzenmast is forward of the rudder.

Langoustier: a boat used for fishing lobsters.

Leeway: lateral movement of a sailing boat produced by the wind.

Lie-to: reduced speed to handle bad weather, with bow almost at sea level.

Lugsail (sail): a gaff sail inserted on a gaff with the halyard turned to a third of its length.

Mainsail: sail aft of the mast; it can be "trysail" or "gaff."

Mainsail furler: modern system for winding the mainsail around the boom.

Marconi: modern rigging with triangular or Bermuda sails.

Mast step: joint in the inner keel or on deck where the mast tenon enters.

Mizzen: stern sail or mast of yawl or ketch.

Mizzen-staysail: jib sail between foremast and main sail.

Partner: opening for the masts to pass through, reinforced around it and enclosed by a conical hood prevent the passage of water.

Peak: a room at the end of the hull, generally used for storage (sails, tools, ropes, etc.).

Pillar: internal height of a hull.

Planking: the covering above the ribs that covers the hull.

Pulpit: protective handrail at the bow.

Racer: term to indicate a regatta boat.

Rake: the part of the hull that continues beyond the waterline.

Ram: to collide with another boat.

Rating: a term indicating the tonnage with which the racing handicap is established.

Reaches: the directions that a boat follows with respect to the direction of the wind.

Reef: the portion of sail folded when its surface is reduced in the presence of strong wind (verb: "to reef").

Refitting: restoration or repair works on a boat.

Ribs: also called "frames." Transverse framing of the hull.

RINA: abbreviation of Italian Naval Register, the institute for the classification of ships and boats.

Roller furler: modern system for winding the roller around the stay.

Seam: the connections of the planking, which are filled by caulking.

Sheerline: the curvature of the deck in the direction of the length.

Sheerstrake: the highest line of planking on the bulwark.

Sheet: cable or hoist to put a sail under tension towards stern.

Skeg: the fixed part in front of the rudder in vessels with a separate rudder.

Skipper: the person that captains a boat.

Skylight: A "dormer" type hatch that provides light and air below deck.

Sloop: a yacht with a single mast, rigged with a mainsail and a jib.

Spar: long wooden pole (in one or two pieces) to which a lateen sail is hoisted.

Spinnaker: large triangular sail used instead of the jib with stern wind or with broad reach.

Spinnaker pole: pole inserted in the bow mast to keep the base of the spinnaker extended.

Spitfire: fore stay sail used in stormy weather.

Stanchion: metal pole that supports the handrail.

Standing rigging: the series of fixed cables that support the mast.

Stempost: the part of the structure that continues the keel at the bow.

Sternpost: the part of the structure that continues the keel at the stern.

Stern pulpit: stern protection handrail; the one at the bow is just called the "pulpit."

Stringers: rows of internal planking (from bow to stern) that rest on the ribs.

Tartan: a lateen-rigged, single-masted ship used in the Mediterranean.

Topside: the part of the hull above the waterline.

Trysail: a small, sturdy, fore-and-aft sail set on one mainmast; used in foul weather to keep the vessel's head to the wind.

Waterline: the line on the hull corresponding to the surface of the water.

Water lines: the traces of the waterline on the construction plan and on the hull.

Winch: device with a drum with a horizontal axis to raise the anchor.

Yankee: a type of jib.

Yawl: a boat with two masts, similar to the ketch, with the mizzen located astern of the wheel or tiller.

Addresses of vintage yacht restorers

ANTIGUA
Woodstock Boatbuilder – Antigua W.I.: *Nada*

FRANCE
Chantiers de Guip – Brest – Ile-aux-Moines (tel. 0033-97263710 fax 0033-97263731): *Piccanin, Diadem, Vanity V*

Saint-Malo Classic Boat – Saint-Malo (tel. 0033-99201117 fax 0033-99566700)

Les Ateliers de l'Enfer – Douarnenez (tel. 0033-98921420 fax 0033-98924507)

Charpentiers Réunis – Cancale (tel. 0033-99899999 fax 0033-99896669)

Chantier Hervé Fernand – La Rochelle (tel. 0033-46413236 fax 0033-46412176)

Chantier Naval Jézéquel – Carantec (tel. 0033-98670006 fax 0033-98672328)

Chantier Naval Olbia – Hyères (tel. 0033-94574934 fax 0033-94575643)

Chantier Pichavant – Pont-L'Abbé (tel. 0033-98823043 fax 0033-98823072)

Chantier Trapani – Cassis (tel. 0033-42017040 fax 0033-42010056)

Charpente de Marine Grall – Marseilles (tel. 0033-91601623 fax 0033-91603806)

GERMANY
Lürssen (tel. 0049-4216604166 fax 0049-4216604170)

The Wooden Boat Yard (tel. 0049-41437244 fax 0049-41437011)

GREAT BRITAIN
Fairlie Restorations (tel. 0044-1703-456336 0044-1703-456166): Many boats by Fife, including *Shamrock, Hispania, Hamble, Tuiga, Fulmar, Kentra, Madrigal, Osborne, Belle Aventure, Carron II, The Lady Anne, Angelique, Mariquita, Lucky Girl, Hispania*

Southampton Yacht Service: *Belle Aventure* (1987–89)

Camper & Nicholson: *Moonbeam* (1990), *Mariquita, Cintra, Lulworth, Endeavour, Flica II, Valsheda, Tuiga*

Pendennis Shipyard – Falmouth: *Shamrock V*

ITALY
Cantiere Nautico Sanremo Ship (Im) (tel. 0039-0184-505807): *Calypso, La Maia*

Cantiere Nautico Sanremo S.r.l. (Im) (tel. 0039-0184-505500 fax 0039-0184-505501)

Cantieri Navali di Imperia (tel. 0039-0183-274682 fax 0039-0183-297223): *Ohio* (1990), *Tirrenia, Croix des Gardes* (1993), *Swala, Umiak, Mai Più, Al Na' Ir IV, Bonita, Rondine II, Rocquette, Carola, Shelmalier* (2000), *Varuna* (2000)

Riparazioni Navali Giacomo Terrizzano (Im) (tel. 0039-0183-295544): *Al Na' Ir*

Centro Nautico Marina Uno S.n.c. (Im) (tel. and fax 0039-0183-650032): *Tirrenia, Silver Cilly, Halifax III, Gaudeamus*

Cantiere Navale Baglietto (Varazze – Sv) (tel. 0039-019-95901 fax 0039-019-96515): *Niña Luisita* (1987, 1988, 1990)

Cantieri Navali di Sestri Ponente (Ge) (tel. 0039-010-6512476 fax 0039-010-6512282): *Noroit, Pulcinella, Filkins*

Cantieri Navali Mostes (Genoa Prà) (tel. 0039-010-665292 fax 0039-010-6974079): *Amadeus*

Cantiere Amico & Co. (Ge) (tel. 0039-010-2470067): *Joyette, Crosswind, Gitana IV, Spagna, Zaca*

Cantiere Navale Sangermani (Lavagna – Ge) (tel. 0039-0185-307679): *Bau Bau* (1969, 1990), *Nordwind* (1983–84), *Aile Blanche* (1988–89), *Coch y Bondu* (1988), *Viola* (1993), *Janabel* (1993–94), *Valentina* (1995–2000), *Catina VI* (1996), *Bamba* (1997), *Parsifal, Cerida, Emi*

Antico Cantiere Topazio (Lavagna – Ge) (tel. 0039-0185-310041): *Valhalla*

Cantieri Navali Beconcini (Sp) (tel. 0039-0187-524127 fax 0039-0187-524136): *Candida* (1978–2000), *Mariette* (1979, 1980, 1983, 1985), *Croce del Sud* (1978, 2000), *Latifa* (1978–2000), *Kenavo II* (1982–85, 1990), *Skagerrak* (1983, 1993), *Astra* (1984, 87), *Altair* (1985–87, 1999), *Alzavola* (1986), *Adria* (1986–87), *Halloween* (1986–91, 1993), *Glad II* (1984–86), *Yali* (1986), *Amore Mio* (1986), *Sylvia* (1987–94), *Pen Duick* (1987), *Artica II* (1988–89), *Cariba* (1988), *Tomahawk* (1989), *Lulworth* (1990), *Caroly* (1990), *Emilia* (1990), *Arcangelo* (1990), *Vim* (1991), *Corsaro II* (1992), *Don Quijote* (1993–94),

Black Swan (1993–95), *Kerilos* (1995–96), *Demua* (1995–98), *Te Vega* (1997), *Orion* (1999), *La Maia* (1998), *Cariba* (1999), *Miranda III* (2000), *Aleph* (2000), *Capricia, Cintra, Moya, Sumurun, Latifa* (2002), *Black Swan* (2002)
Cantiere1 Navale Canaletti & Figli (Sp) (tel. 0039-0187-514000): *Tonino* (1993)
Cantiere Navale Valdettaro (Le Grazie – Sp) (now closed): *Raphaelo* (1960), *Orion* (1974, 1978, 1986), *Tonino* (1986–88, 1992–93), *Thendara* (1986, 1988), *Conti Bernardi* (1990), *Armelea, Galashiel, Joyette*
Cantiere Navale Tomei (Viareggio) (tel. 0039-0584-383905): *Tartuga* (1989), *Bagheera* (1994), *Nancy Anne* (2000)
Cantiere Navale Francesco Del Carlo (Viareggio) (tel. 0039-0584-309706 fax 0039-0584-940189): *Estella, Clever, Anni Venti, Magda XIII, Alzavola* (2002)
Cantiere Navale Gerolamo Ippolito (Li) (tel. 0039-0586-420147): *Four Winds* (1992)
Cantiere Navale dell'Argentario (Porto S. Stefano – Gr) (tel. 0039-0564-812975 fax 0039-0564-817202): *Puritan* (1981), *Maddalena II* (1983), *Clio* (1983–84), *Eos I* (1984), *Sheevra* (1985), *San Guido* (1986, 1994), *Cheone* (1989–90), *Old Fox* (1989–90), *Nyala* (1995), *Linnet* (1998), *Aria* (1998–99), *Dorade* (1998), *Cerida* (1999), *Stormy Weather* (1999–2000), *Weatherbird, Susanna II, Folly, Tamara IX, Akka, The Blue Peter*
Legno di Mare (inside Cantiere Esaom) (Porto Ferraio – Li) (tel. 0039-0338-2525441): *Alzavola, Islay, Solway Maid, Cheone, Gael*
Cantieri Navali di Porto Cervo (tel. 0039-0789-91444 fax 0039-0789-91423): *Mariella*
Cantieri Costa Smeralda (Porto Cervo) (tel. 0039-0789-91444): *Caroly*
Cantiere Navale Caprera S.n.c. (La Maddalena): (tel. and fax 0039-0789-722126): *Dalgra III* (1996), *Aquilone* (1995)
Cantieri Navali del Tevere La Bussola (Fiumicino – Rm) (tel. 0039-06-6880323): *Manihiki* (1980, 1990), *Cintra* (1991–92), *Yvette* (1992), *Eos I, La Romantica, Colomba, Ganimede*
Tecnomar Uno (Fiumicino) (tel. 0039-06-6580691): *Windswept* (2002)
Cantieri Carlini (Rimini) (tel. and fax 0039-0541-23919): *Desirée* (1984), *Agneta* (1989–90), *Levantades* (1991)
Cantiere Navale dell'Adriatico (Rimini) (tel. 0039-0541-52151): *Vistona, Chérie* (1989–90), *Al Na' Ir III*
Cantiere Navale Perinetti Casoni (Chioggia – Ve) (tel. 0039-041-5585000): *Ostro, Reineke, Four Winds*
Cantiere Alto Adriatico (Monfalcone – Ts) (tel. 0039-0481-43157): *Moya* (1993), *Sylphea IV* (1995), *Dyarchy*
Cantiere Pitacco Luxich e Ferluga (Muggia): *Tirrenia II*

MEXICO
Club de Yates – Acapulco: *Landfall*

THE NETHERLANDS
Royal Huisman (tel. 0031-52743131 fax 0031-52743800)

SPAIN
Astilleros Monty Nautic – Barcelona: *Rosalind*
Astilleros Palma de Mallorca: *Nordwind*
Astilleros de Tarragona: *Gipsy*
Astilleros del Nervion – Bilbao: *Tonino*

USA
International Yacht Restoration School – Newport R.I. (tel. 001-401-848-5777 fax 001-401-842-0669): *Coronet*
Classic Boatwork of Maine – Hancock: *Winona*
Brooklyn Boat Yard – Brooklyn N.Y.: *Misha, Enticer*
Wayfarer Marine Corporation – Camden (Maine)

Legend

NOTES FOR CAPTIONS
ACJ: America's Cup Jubilee (Cowes)
ASW: Argentario Sailing Week (Porto Santo Stefano)
Prada Week: Porto Santo Stefano
Vele d'Argento: Porto Santo Stefano
VBR: Veteran Boat Rally (Porto Cervo)

FLAGS

 Antilles

 Argentina

 Austria

 Belize

 Bermuda

 France

 Germany

 Great Britain

 Italy

 The Principality of Monaco

 Norway

 The Netherlands

 Peru

 Portugal

 Spain

 Sweden

 Switzerland

 USA

The main riggings of the lesser sailing boats

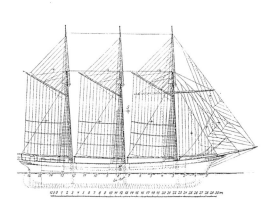

Three-masted schooner
(L. Middendorf)

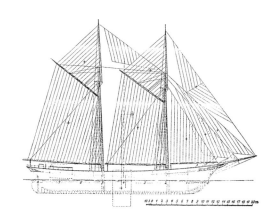

Gaff-sailed schooner
(L. Middendorf)

Schooner without gaff topsails
(G. Croppi)

Schooner with gaff topsails
(G. Croppi)

Schooner with gaff topsails with gaffs
(G. Croppi)

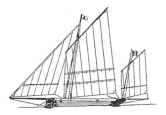

Yawl with mizzen-lugsail
(G. Croppi)

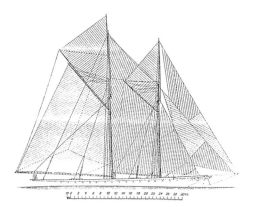

Modern schooner with gaff topsails
(L. Middendorf)

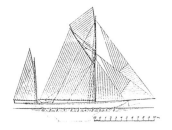

Trysail yawl with gaff
(L. Middendorf)

Yawl with mizzen-lugsail and gaff topsail
(G. Croppi)

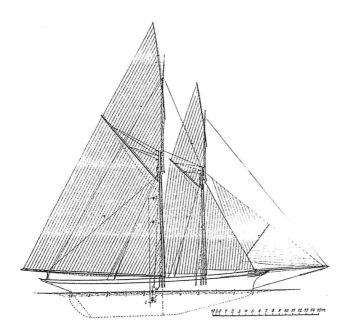

Gaff schooner with gaffs
(L. Middendorf)

Gaff schooner with gaffs
(L. Middendorf)

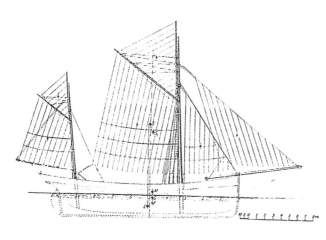

Logger
(L. Middendorf)

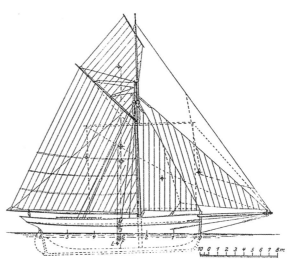

Trysail cutter with gaff
(L. Middendorf)

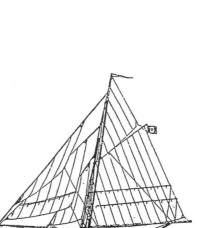

Trysail cutter with gaff topsail
(G. Croppi)

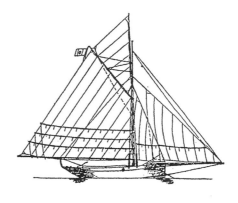

Trysail cutter with gaff
(G. Croppi)

Trysail cutter

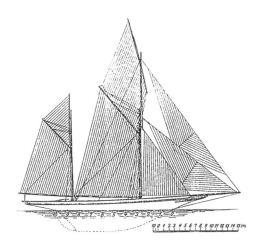

Trysail ketch with gaff
(L. Middendorf)

English pilot-cutter

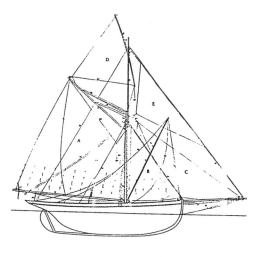

Cutter (1878)
(D. Kemp)

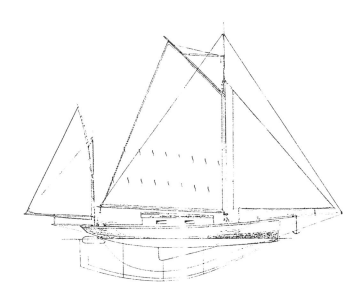

American skipjack rigged as a dandy (1890)
(Kunhardt)

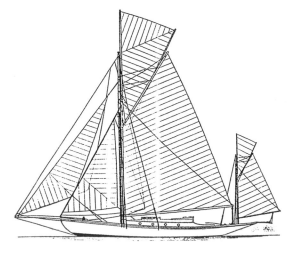

English yawl
(Cooke)

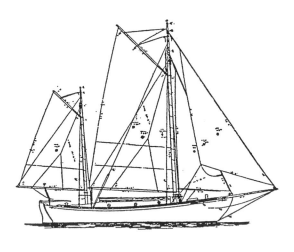

Colin Archer
(Archer-Atkin)

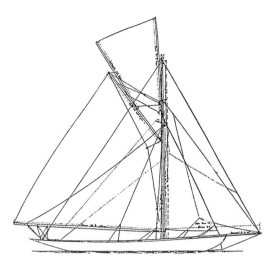

Trysail sloop
(A. Mylne)

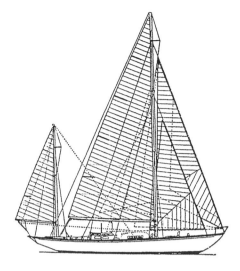

Modern Bermudan or gaff-rigged yawl
(Phil Rhodes)

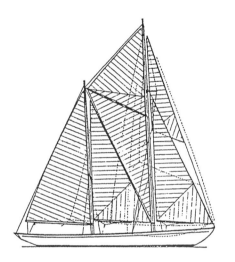

Wishbone Bermudan ketch

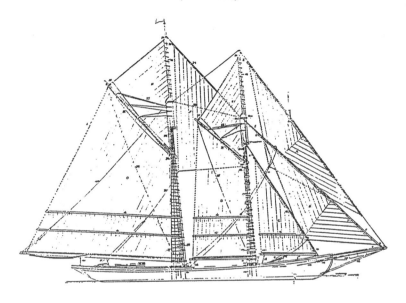

Fishing schooner from Gloucester
(E. J. March)

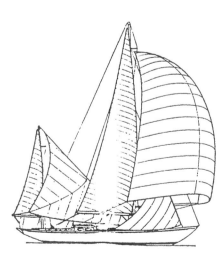

Modern Bermudan yawl
(C. Sciarelli)

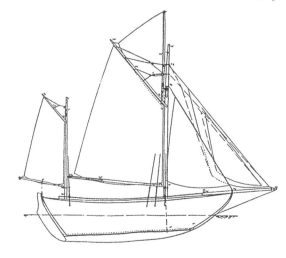

Redninskoite

Modern sloop or Bermudan cutter

Acknowledgments

The first edition of this book involved an unbelievable number of people, to whom I give my thanks and gratitude. Remembering them all is a truly arduous task, and I therefore apologize in advance if some names have slipped through the net of my memory. In order of chronological intervention in the long phase of drafting the text, I am duty-bound to mention Orazio Sappa, Director of the Chamber of Commerce of Imperia, and the officials and employees of that organization: Giorgio Marziano, Renzo De Giovanni, Roberto D'Amato, Silvano Drago. Also Fulvio Parodi of the Italian Naval League of Imperia, Cristina Tagliaferri of the boat *Niña Luisita* and Lucia Pozzo, skipper of *Tirrenia*. Particular thanks are due to Dr. Luigi Lang, Secretary of the AIVE (Italian Association of Vintage Yachts) for supporting me in the consultation of the association's archive, and to Assonautica of Imperia, who have allowed me to check and subsequently update the card files of the boats. Again in chronological order, I must mention the courteous and hard-working collaboration of Gian Marco and Battista Borea d'Olmo, Giuseppe Tomatis, Irene Cabiati, Gabriella Bossolo, Michele Amorosi, Gherardo Zaccagni, Franco and Titta Bosia. I have received significant collaboration from the Yacht Club of San Remo and Genoa, and from Pier Franco Gavagnin and Nello Saltalamacchia, always full of suggestions and precious information. Special thanks are due to Admirals Mario Bini and Giovanni Iannucci, veterans of *Artica II*, to Captains Giancarlo Basi and Piero Carpani, to Ernesto and Mario Quaranta of the Imperia shipyards, to Captain Eugenio Lanzardo of Murphy & Nye, to Captain Claudio Ressmann of the magazine *Lega Navale*, to Dr. Giorgio Casti of the magazine *Bolina*, to Dr. Marie-Claude Parpaglione of the Valdettaro shipyards, to Angelo Beconcini of the shipyard of the same name. I am grateful for the great help of the architect Ugo Faggioni, Gerard Bani of the French magazine *Capian*, the "Venturieri" Association of Chioggia, architect Mario Sculli of the Studio Giorgetti & Magrini of Milan, Francesca Della Vedova of the Compagnia della Vela of Venice, Petra Wolker of the boat *Jalina*, Eli Galleani, architect Ettore Agosti, Silvia Minas, Marianne Salvetat and Mauro Rovero. I must also mention Captains Sergio Guglielmone of *Croce del Sud* and Domenico Acquarone of the Imperia Mare Spa, Ugo Baravalle of *Nordwind*, Dr. Paolo Baldi of GBM Italia, Domenico Olivieri of Agnesi Spa, Commandante Piero Ranzini, former President of the Assonautica of Imperia, the famous photographer Keith Beken of Cowes and the skippers Michel Dejoie, Stephen Royce, Ignazio Torrente, Michel Roy, Beppe Zaoli, Jean Claude Lehöerff, Beppe Spreafico, Umberto Visconti, Franco Torrini, Giorgio Manfellotto, Leonardo Bagni, Michele and Piero Cretti, Antonio Traverso, Antonio Villa, Vincenzo Lamberti, Giovanni Aprea, Eric Tabarly, William McInnes, Michel Simon, Carlo Belenghi, Michele Sambonet, Giorgio Balestrero, Claudio Billi, Craig Hopkins, Alberto Raffaelli, Mario Dotti, Chicco Zaccagni, Luciano Locci, Riccardo Trombetti, Wolfang Scholz, Stephen Horner, Amedeo Ancarani Restelli, Renato Della Valle, Paul Simmons, Italo Viannelli, Enrico Casonato, Eric Charpentier, Jean Louis Scudo, Jan Staniland, Mario Sterzi, Silvano Barsiola, Lorenzo Orrù, Giovanni Broggi, Nick Douch, Eric Pascoli, Riccardo Degiovanni, Enrico Caretti, Jean-Marie Roux, Charles Nurit, Bertrand Danglade, Alain Fournier, James Gale, Salvatore Sgarellino, Lamberto Pagnoni, Sandro Placido, Emilio Maggi, Roberto Sartori, Jean Redele, Ernesto Paesani, Andrea Resnati, and Olivier Wattinne.

Further sincere thanks to the management of the Abeking & Rasmussen shipyards of Bremen, Jean-Marie Recamier of Camper & Nicholson, Federico Nardi of the Argentario shipyards, to the Sangermani shipyards, the Kieler Yacht Club, Simona Pierini, Aldo Codognato, Vibio Mestrom, Captain Ruggero Boscu, Attilio Fantoni of the "J Class" Society, Raffaella Stefani Andolina, Gabriel Fabre of the boat *Old Fox*, Mary Pera, Renzo Zanasi of the YCI, Francesco Boratto, Catherine Mattison, secretary of the RORC, Dr. Bruno Ziravello and his wife, Dr. Orietta Bernatzky; skipper Giancarlo Rinaldi, photographer Lino Pastorelli of Sanremo, Dr. Claudio Bondi, photographer Gerolamo Acquarone, Dieter Gulik of the boat *Aile Blanche*, to Walter Lopez, engineer Alfredo Martini of the boat *Samadhi*, Dr. Alfredo Bertollo, Adriano Frassinetti, Licio Comisso, Diego Munafò, Pierre Rouveret, Bernard Divorne, Italo Pirola, Marco Tibiletti, Dr. Pietro Bonardi, Walter Tirrito, Paolo De Nigris, Roger Castello, Cesare Logu, engineer Riccardo Giolli, Gidon Graetz, Raimund Deibele, skipper Andrea Rolli, Luca Alessandrini, Friedrich Goebel, Dr. Aldo Martinetto, Dr. Gianguido Bonatti, Dr. Claude Perdriel, architect Luigi Vietti, engineer Tiberio Gracco de Lay, Robert Simoni, Dr. Federica De Luca. Heartfelt thanks to Admiral Emanuele Junca, C.V. Virginio Pennino, C.V. Roberto Cesaretti, and Signora

Caramaschi of the "Notiziario della Marina," who assisted me in the research into the documentation for the boats of Marivela.

My gratitude for their kind collaboration to the architect Mario Fiori of the boat *The Blue Peter*, Renato Pirota of the boats *Moya* and *Sorella*, Dr. Paolo Noia of the prestigious *Joyette*, to engineer Angelo Penco, Serena Zaffagni, to architect Carlo Sciarelli, Dr. Gianni Loffredo, President of the AIVE, to the proprietors of Maritime Agencies Claude Smith, Rupert Nelson of Peter Insull Yacht Marketing, Mike Horsley, and Peter Wood. And finally, my thanks to Ludovico Sella of the Biella and Barbara Villani Foundation.

It is only right to mention all the friends who flooded me with photographic material, in chronological order: Antonio Tringali, Raffaele Minervini, Danilo Lanteri, Lauro Laura (of *La Stampa*), Giorgio Bracco, Gino Perotto and Lauro Menegatti, (of *Il Secolo XIX*), Giancarlo Terragno, Giuliano Gallo, Gianni Sbriscia, Gianni Boscolo, Enrico Viale, Federico Ramella, Marco Sassone, Giuseppe Tomatis, Simona Pierini, Natalino Famà, Giovanni De Nigris, Massimo Gentili, Giuseppe Caria, Sebastiano and Rino Guerriero, Carlo Falciola, Maurizia Siccardi, Alessandro Cirino, Corrado Cominetti, Bernardino Re, Giorgio Baldizzone, Gian Luigi Maretti, Giovanni Semeria, Luigi Romano, Antonello Ansaldo, and Federico Semeria. Sincere, warm thanks also go to the photographic agencies and/or professional photographers who have skillfully gathered together many of the most significant images of the Imperia vintage yacht regattas:

Alessandro Battini	Genoa
Keith Beken	Cowes
Carlo Borlenghi	Milan
Fotodomani	Trieste
Franco Pace	Trieste
Foto Perino	Imperia
Sandro Pesato	Imperia
Lino Pastorelli	San Remo
Bert Richner	Bodio Lamnago
Santo Piano	Genoa
Fabio Taccola	Livorno
Giorgio C. Tagliafico	Genoa
Vidigraf	Genoa
Carlo Vitello	Rozzano
Federico Ramella	Imperia

In particular, I am profoundly grateful to James Robinson Taylor and Federico Ramella, who have assisted and advised me in the choice of photographic documentation, together with the corresponding photographers of specialist magazines:

Livio Fioroni	Il Giornale della Vela
Franco Michienzi	Mondo Barca
Stefano Navarrini	Nautica
Daniele Pellegrini	Aqua
Luca Sonnino Sorrisio	Nautica
Paolo Venanzageli	Nautica
Riccardo Villarosa	Yacht Digest

In presenting this second edition, I am also duty-bound to remember Captain Schiavoni of Marivela, Dr. Lang, and architect Sciarelli for their collaboration. Particular thanks go to Massimo Roggero and Renzo De Giovanni, respectively President and Director of the Assonautica of Imperia, for their support and encouragement in this work, thanks which I also extend to Angelo and Andrea Beconcini, Federico Nardi, Giuseppe Tomei, Cesare and Andrea Sangermani for the updating of the information on the boats. Also Luigi Pavese, Matteo Salomon, and Federica Betti for their abundant advice and information, but, above all, photographers Federico Ramella, Antonio Tringali, Mario Marzari, and Sandro Pesato.

My thanks go to collaborators, skippers and boat-owners: Giulia Acherusio, Mike Horsley, Alessandro Degano, Mario and Ernesto Quaranta, Mario Sterzi, Serena Galvani, Marco De Amici, Alfonso Crisci, Maurizio Ficani, Luigi D'Angelo, Alberto Roberto, Andrea Capolei, Chicco Zaccagni, Ugo Faggioni, Erik Pascoli, Didier Mangin, Roger Quenet, Mario Bosio, Matteo Murzilli, Michele Sambonet, Giambattista Borea dell'Olmo, Angelo Hassler, Frederich Berthoz, Michel Martini, Alex Laird, Marino Gambaro, Luca Bojola, Duncan Walker, Giovanni Novi, Alessandro Gollin, Giambattista Giannoccaro, Pier Giovanni De Martini, Pierre Lembo, Alain Himgi, Walter Sobrero, Sante Panté, Francesco Giorgetti, Benoît Micollet, Albert Arrignon, Francesco Bistolfi, Paolo Alfonso Sada, and Luca Filippi. I also remember with gratitude the assistance of the Yacht Clubs of Monte Carlo and San Remo. And Liliana Lupi for the supervision of the texts.

I am grateful to Dr. Richard Ormond, former director of the National Maritime Museum in Greenwich, for his kind introduction to the volume.

I owe particular gratitude to the final team of collaborators: Stefano Faggioni, José Ramón Bono of the Fundación Hispania de Barcos de Epoca, Luigi Pavese, Federica Betti, José Albaladejo, Francisco Casariego, Grupo Godosa, Luis Olaso, Germán Ruiz, Ricardo Vilar, José Uriarte, Nicole Legler, Emilio Espinosa Marín, Jan T. Royse, Giammaria and Monica Della Porta, Luciano Brovelli, Giorgio Campanino, Mimmo De Rosa, Alberto Roberto (for the latest, very recent photographs), Paolo Maccione, Federico Ramella, Raffaele Minervini, Sandro Pesato, James Taylor, Angelo Gentile and, finally, a dear friend who shares my love for wooden boats: Enrico Zaccagni.

Bibliography

AIME, Historical Archive

AIVE, *1990 Yearbook*

AIVE, *1998 Yearbook*, Genoa 1998

AIVE, *Gli yacht di Fife con guidone*, AIVE, Genoa 1996

Accademia Navale, *Nave Caroly*, Livorno 1996

ARIE, *Bona – La rinascita di un mito*, Bologna 2000

ARIE, *Aria – La storia, il recupero, il restauro di un 8 Metri SI*, Bologna 1999

Assonautica Imperia, *Schedario delle barche* (1996–2000)

Juan Baader, *Lo sport della vela*, Mursia Editore, Milan 1968

Franco Belloni, *Giraglia*, Mursia Editori, Milan 1977

Franco Belloni, *Yacht Club Italiano 1879–1979*, Fabbri Editori, Milan 1979

Franco Belloni, *70 anni della Federazione Italiana Vela*, Genoa 1999

Piero Bernotti, *Il Corsaro II sui mari del mondo (1961–1967)*, Mursia Editore, Milan 1971

Piero Bernotti, *13,000 miglia a vela con il Corsaro*, Mursia Editore, Milan 1964

Robert W Carrick, *John G. Alden and his Yacht Designs*, International Marine, Maine

Howard I. Chapelle, *American Sailing Ships*, Bonanza Book, New York 1935

Howard I. Chapelle, *The History of American Sailing Ships*, Norton, New York 1946

Howard I. Chapelle, *Yacht Designing and Planning*, Norton, New York 1936

François Chevalier and Jacques Taglang, *J class Endeavour 1934*, Van de Velde, Fondette 2001

William Collier, *Classic Sails*, 1998

Mario Corsico, *Le barche d'Italia*, Briano Editore, Genoa 1948

Giorgio Croppi, *Sport Nautico*, Hoepli Editore, Milan 1925

E.A. D'Albertis, *Crociera del "Corsaro" a San Salvador*, Paravia, Turin 1920

Didier Depret, *Le tour du monde en 80 mois*, Calmann-Lévy, Paris 1968

Guido Fiorentino, *Tirrenia II – Una crociera alle Isole Baleari*, Vela e Motore, Trieste 1926

Uffa Fox, *Sailing Boats*, London

Uffa Fox, *Racing, Cruising and Design*, Davies, London 1937

John H. Illingworth, *Venti sfide per la Coppa America*, Mursia Editore, Milan 1968

John H. Illingworth, *The Malham Story*, Nautical Publishing Company, Lymington 1972

Francis S. Kinney and Russel Bourne, *The Best of the Best – The Yacht Designs of Sparkman & Stephens*, Norton Publisher

John Lammerts Van Bueren, *Otto Metri*, Yachting Library, Milan 2000

John Leather, *Colin Archer and the seaworthy double-ender*, Stanford Maritime, London 1979

Edward Lewis and Robert O'Brien, *Le Navi*, Mondadori Editore, Milan 1967

Lloyds Register of Shipping, *Register of Yachts*, (various yearbooks)

Mario Marzari, *Le barche di Sangermani*, De Agostini Editore, Novara 1993

Peter Heaton, *La grande avventura dello Yachting*, Mondadori Editore, Milan 1964

Gilles Martin-Raget, *Legendary Yachts*, Abbeville Press Publisher, NY – London 2000

John Nicholson, *Great Years in Yachting*, Nautical Publishing Company, Lymington, 1970

Franco Pace, *Vele d'epoca*, Mondadori Editore, Milan 1993

Franco Pace, *William Fife – Capolavori d'epoca*, Edizione Reporter, Trieste 1996

Franco Pace, *J Class – Le regine del mare*, Mondadori Editore, Milan 1994

Gilles Pernet, *Io Tabarly*, Mursia Editore, Milan 1977

RANC, *Barcos de Epoca*

Fabio Ratti and Margherita Bottini, *Admiral's Cup*, Overseas srl, Milan 1985

Bert Richner, *Mediterranean Yacht*, Industrie Grafiche Ripalta, Milan 1976

Wolfgang Rudolph, *Bateaux – Radeaux – Navires*, Editions Stauffacher SA, Zurich 1975

Carlo Sciarelli, *Lo Yacht*, Mursia Editore, Milan 1988

Göran Schildt, *Vent'anni di Mediterraneo*, Mursia Editore, Milan 1969

Flavio Serafini, *Vele nella leggenda*, Mursia Editore, Milan 1980

Flavio Serafini, *A Band of Brothers*, Edizioni Gribaudo, Cavallermaggiore 1994

Norman Lo Skene, *Elements of Yacht Design*, Yachting Inc., New York 1927

Nico Rode, *Barche a vela e la regata*, Istituto Geografico De Agostini, Novara 1968

Carlo Tagliafico and Tino Delfino, *Genoa Jib*, Marietti Editore, Genoa 1988

Eric Tabarly, *Pen Duick*, Editions Ouest, Versailles 1989

Eric Tabarly, *Da un Pen Duick all'altro*, Mursia Editore, Milan

Time-Life Books, *Racing*, New York 1976

A.B.C. Whipple, *Gli yachts da regata*, Italian Edition, Time-Life Books – CDE Mondadori, Milan 1989

YCI, *Yearbook* (annals 1930–1987)

Bruno Veronese, *Yacht – progetto e costruzione*, Editrice Incontri Nautici, Rome 1991

C. Worth, *Yachting Cruising*, I.D. Potter, London 1996

Foreign magazines:

Le Yacht (France)

Yacht Monthly (UK)

Yachting World (UK)

The Rudder (USA)

Ships and ship models

Chassemarée (France)

Classic Boat (UK)

Capian (France)

Mer & Bateaux (France)

Sails Fast International

Les Cahiers du Yachting

The Wooden Boat (USA)

Nautical Quarterly (USA)

Boat International (UK)

Navegar (Spain)

Skipper (Spain)

National magazines:

Vela e Motore, Lega Navale, Nautica, L'Italia Marinara, Yacht Digest, Bolina, Mare, Rivista Marittima, Yachting, Il Giornale della Vela, Yachting Italiano, Le Vie del Mare, Yachting Quarterly, Yacht Capital, Mondo Barca, Mare 2000, Arte Navale

Historical Photographic Archive of International Naval Museum (Imperia)

Editorials:

Bruno Veronese, Lino Pastorelli, Franco Anselmi Boretti, Gianni Botassis, Gian Marco Borea, Giancarlo Basile, Gabriella Bossolo, Carlo Sciarelli, Ugo Faggioni, Franco Michienzi, Riccardo Baffigo, Sergio Crepax, Paolo Maccione, Aldo Martinetto, Riccardo Villarosa, Clelia Pirazzini, Renato Polo, Stefano Navarrini, Walter Pagliero, Vincenzo Zaccagnino, Stanislao Soltan, Marco Adriani, Charles Serra I Nadol, Darwin Ziravello, Bruno Ziravello, G.B. Cattaneo, Paolo Bertoldi, Agostino Straulino, Barbara Villani, Mary Blewit, Gianni Pera, John Illingworth, Mario Marzari, Eric Tabarly, Franco Belloni, Flavio Serafini, Beppe Croce, Claudio Ressmann, Pier Franco Gavagnin, Aldo Macchiavelli, Aldo Bini, Alberto Coretti, Bianca Ascenti.

Index of Boats

Adria II	12	Cerida	39	Flica II	348
Aello	13	Chaplin	264	Folly	350
Agneta	15	Cheone	42	Folkboat	277
Aigue Blu	238	Chérie	43	Four Winds	65
Alba	238	Chin Blu III	389	Fra Dolcino	406
Aleph	17	Cigno Nero	390	Francesco Petrarca	230
Al Na' Ir	240	Cin Cin	265	Fulmar	352
Al Na' Ir IV	241	Cintra	340	Gabbiano	66
Altair	19	Circe	227	Gael	278
Alzavola	21	Clever	43	Galashiel	66
Amadeus Primus	242	Clio	45	Gaudeamus	68
America	404	Coaster	46	Germania V	69
Amore Mio	244	Coch y Bondhu	47	Giadamar	393
Ancilla II	245	Colomba	216	Giannella II	393
Angelique	247	Conchita III	265	Gioanna	70
Arcangelo	332	Constance	382	Gipsy	223
Aria	333	Conti Bernardi	48	Glad II	279
Armelea	250	Coppelia	343	Gloria	279
Artica II	251	Corsaro II	266	Gustavia's Dream	280
Astra	376	Creole	49	Halifax III	281
Athena	255	Croce del Sud	51	Halloween	71
Aurora (Colin Archer)	222	Croix des Gardes	52	Harmonie in Blue	282
Aurora	256	Crosswind	269	Helen	73
Avel	23	Crystal	270	Huna II	394
Bagheera	256	Dalgra III	344	Hygie	74
Balkis	257	Dan	345	Ice Fire	75
Barbel	26	Daphne	53	Ikra	353
Bateau Ivre	386	Delirio	405	Ilex	77
Bau Bau	336	Desirée	54	Intrepido	231
Beatrice	387	Don Quijote	271	Iska	78
Belle Aventure	27	Dorade	55	Isla Ebusitana	232
Belle Poule	29	Dragonera	391	Italia	355
Black Swan	29	Dyarchy	57	Ivanhoe	78
Bohème Deux	30	Eileen	59	Jalina	80
Bolero	32	Eli	273	Janabel	81
Bona	337	Ella	274	Jetta	82
Bonita	257	Ellen	60	Josephine of Hamble	282
Borkumriff	405	Elpis	217	Joyette	82
Bourru III	226	Emilia	60	Juana Argentina	283
Bruma	32	Endeavour	380	Karenita	87
Bufeo Blanco	258	Eos I	392	Kenavo II	89
By Albatros	34	Escapade	62	Kentra	90
Cala Millo	227	Estella	63	Kerilos	284
Caligo	388	Estérel	347	Kipawa	91
Calypso (SVMM)	259	Eugenia V	392	Kukururu	356
Calypso	260	Eva Maria	64	La Clé de Sol	284
Candida	378	Fair Weather	64	La Meloria	286
Capricia	261	Finisterre	276	Lady Ellen	406
Caroly	35	Fleur de Lys	229	Lasse	92

Latifa	93	Osborne	361	Sunny Temper	325
Laura III	96	Outlaw	298	Susanna II	398
Lelantina	97	Pacciora	299	Swala	399
Leticia do Sol	395	Palinuro	144	Sylphe IV	181
Levantades	287	Pandora	407	Sylphea III	365
L'Iliade	99	Partridge	146	Tamara IX	366
Lily IV	100	Paxos	300	Tamory	182
Limnoreia	100	Peer Gynt	300	Tapiner	183
Linnet	101	Pen Duick	147	Tarantella	325
Lisa of la Tour	289	Peteteka of Ville	302	Tartuga	224
Loki	103	Petit Julien	408	Te Vega	184
Lord Jim	104	Petite Lande	409	Thalatta	185
Lulù	106	Phantom Light	149	The Blue Peter	185
Maddalena II	106	Pilon	302	The Lady Anne	188
Madre Giulia	232	Piraña	150	Thendara	189
Magda III	357	Presque Isle	410	Thö Pa Ga	235
Mait II	290	Puritan	150	Tirrenia II	192
Manihiki	107	Resaca of Kimberly	303	Tiziana	327
Manta	108	Rocquette	304	Tomahawk	367
Marcantonio	233	Romeo	153	Tonino	368
Margareth II	292	Rondine II	154	Trivia	369
Maria Galante	293	Rorqual	307	Troll	328
Mariangela	294	Rosalind	157	Tuiga	370
Mariella	109	Royono	160	Twins V	372
Mariette	111	Rubin III	308	Umiak	196
Marjatta	115	Sagittario	310	Vadura	197
Mehalah	116	Saharet of Tyre	162	Vagrant	198
Membury	117	Saint Briac	163	Valentina (Replica)	412
Merry Dancer	118	Samadhi	164	Valentina (Sangermani)	400
Migrant	119	Samurai	396	Vanille	328
Mio Mao	295	San Guido	165	Vanity V	372
Mio Mao VII	395	San Marco	311	Varuna	199
Mizar III	357	Sant Troupes	412	Vega	373
Molly	120	Santa Maria II	166	Vera Mary	200
Moonbeam	121	Santa Rosa	167	Veronique	201
Moya	125	Santander of Wight	312	Vespucci	202
Nagaïna	127	Saorsain	314	Vim	374
Namar	296	Seilan	314	Viola	400
Nausicaa	128	Selamat	168	Vistona	219
Navara	129	Shaula (Requin)	384	Viveka	204
Nereide II	359	Shelmalier of Anglesey	315	Voscià	402
Nina VII	296	Shenandoah	168	Wammsch	236
Niña Luisita	129	Sif	171	Wanderer	329
Nirvana	131	Silver Cilly	318	West Wind II	205
Nocturne	133	Skagerrak	173	White Wings	205
Nordwind	134	So Fong	174	Windswept	207
Noroit	136	Solway Maid	175	Winsome	413
Nyala	360	Sorella	176	Yadic II	207
Odin	297	Sovereign	361	Yali	208
Ohio	137	Sparklet	319	Yhann	329
Oiseau de Feu	137	Spartivento	177	Yvette	211
Old Fox	139	St. Nicolas Saxo	177	Zaca	212
Oloferne	234	Stella Polare	321	Zaca a Te Moana	413
Ondine	140	Stint	363	Zephir	214
Orianda	141	Stormy Weather	178		
Orion	142	Sumurun	180		

General Index

PREFACE   7

INTRODUCTION   9

THE "BELLE ÉPOQUE" OF REGATTA SAILING   10

VINTAGE YACHTS   11

BOATS OF THE "VENTURIERI"   215

COLIN ARCHER   221

WORKING BOATS   225

CLASSIC BOATS   237

THE METRIC CLASSES   331

THE "J CLASS"   375

THE "REQUIN" CLASS   381

THE SANGERMANI BOATS   385

REPLICAS AND NEW CONSTRUCTIONS   403

OTHER "BROTHERS" ARE DISCOVERED   415

NOTES ON THE MOST WELL-KNOWN NAVAL ARCHITECTS   419
THE BOATS AND THEIR DESIGNERS   421
GLOSSARY   423
ADDRESSES OF VINTAGE YACHT RESTORERS   424
LEGEND   425
THE MAIN RIGGINGS OF THE LESSER SAILING BOATS   426
ACKNOWLEDGMENTS   430
BIBLIOGRAPHY   432
INDEX OF BOATS   433

Imperia, September 1992, Eric Tabarly (Photo: S. Pesato).

Eric Tabarly receives the Cape Horn Prize from the author (Photo: S. Pesato).

The World Monument to the Navigator of Cape Horn was officially inaugurated and donated to the city of Imperia on Tuesday May 24, 1983, on the occasion of the 39th International Congress of Cape Horn. Since that date it has become a point of reference and historical memory of which the city is rightfully proud.

Notice to Mariners

Si ricorda che entrando o uscendo dal porto, al traverso del Monumento internazionale dedicato al navigante di Capo Horn, tutte le navi a vela di qualsiasi tipo, per consuetudine effettuano due colpi lunghi di sirena o fischio in segno di deferente saluto.

All sailing ships entering or leaving the harbor, when abreast of the Cape Horn International Monument, should sound two long blasts of their siren in deference to the memory of sailors.

Tous les navires à voile en entrée ou sortie du port, au travers du Monument International dédié au Cap-Hornier, pour usage exécutent deux longs coups de sirène en témoignage de déférente salutation.